BYRON'S *DON JUAN*

A Variorum Edition

This work consists of four volumes

I. THE MAKING OF A MASTERPIECE

II. A VARIORUM EDITION: Cantos I–V

III. A VARIORUM EDITION: Cantos VI–XVII

IV. NOTES ON THE VARIORUM EDITION

BYRON'S *DON JUAN*

VOLUME III

A Variorum Edition

Cantos VI–XVII

Edited by TRUMAN GUY STEFFAN
and WILLIS W. PRATT

SECOND EDITION

UNIVERSITY OF TEXAS PRESS

AUSTIN AND LONDON

International Standard Book Number 0-292-70024-5
Library of Congress Catalog Card Number 70-126920
© 1957, 1971 by the University of Texas Press

Manufactured in the United States of America

Contents

[v]

Illustrations

BYRON'S *DON JUAN*

A Variorum Edition

"Dost thou think, because thou art virtuous,
there shall be no more Cakes and Ale?"—
"Yes, by St. Anne; and Ginger shall be hot
i' the mouth too!"

SHAKESPEARE *Twelfth Night,*
or What you Will

Preface to Cantos VI-VIII

THE DETAILS of the Siege of Ismail in two of the following Cantos (i.e. the 7th and 8th)[1] are taken from a French work entitled "Histoire de la Nouvelle Russie."* Some of the incidents attributed to Don Juan really occurred, particularly the circumstance of his saving the infant, which was the actual case of the late Duc de Richelieu,* then a young volunteer in the Russian service, and afterwards the founder and benefactor of Odessa, where his name and memory can never cease to be regarded with reverence. In the course of these cantos, a stanza or two will be found relative[2] to the late Marquis of Londonderry,* but written some time before his decease. Had that person's Oligarchy[3] died with him, they would have been suppressed; as it is, I am aware of nothing in the manner of his death or of his life to prevent the free expression of the opinions of all whom his whole existence was consumed in endeavouring to enslave. That he was an amiable man in *private* life, may or may not be true; but with

Cantos VI, VII, and VIII, together with the Preface, dated "1822," were published in one volume by John Hunt on July 15, 1823. For speculation about the dates of composition of Cantos VI and VII, see Appendix E, Volume I.

The manuscript pages of the Preface, written in Byron's hand, are prefixed to the M fair copy of Canto VI and dated "1822." In the variants below, cancellations are enclosed in brackets. Manuscript substitutions are designated by the abbreviation sub. and manuscript insertions by ins. Slight differences in ink and handwriting indicate that many changes and additions were made after this draft had been completed. If no comment is made on a manuscript reading that differs from the text, it is to be understood that the alteration or present text does not appear on this manuscript.

[1] in the following Cantos (i.e. the 7th & 8th . . .
[2] these cantos [some] a stanza or two will be found allusive to . . .
[3] Had that person's measures died . . . suppress . . .

this the Public have nothing to do; and as to lamenting his death, it will be time enough[4] when Ireland has ceased to mourn for his birth. As a Minister, I, for one of millions, looked upon him as the most despotic[5] in intention and the weakest in intellect that ever tyrannized over a country. It is the first time indeed since the Normans, that England has been insulted[6] by a *Minister* (at least) who could not speak English, and that Parliament permitted itself to be dictated to in the language of Mrs. Malaprop.

Of the manner of his death little need be said, except that if a poor radical,[7] such as Waddington or Watson,* had cut his throat, he would have been buried in a cross-road,[8] with the usual appurtenances of the stake and mallet. But the Minister was an elegant Lunatic—a sentimental Suicide—he merely cut the "carotid artery" (blessings on their learning) and lo! the Pageant, and the Abbey! and "the Syllables of Dolour yelled forth"* by the Newspapers—and the harangue of the Coroner* in an eulogy over the bleeding body of the deceased—(an Anthony worthy of such a Caesar)—and the nauseous and atrocious cant[9] of a degraded Crew of Conspirators against all that is sincere or honourable. In his death he was necessarily one of two things by the *law**—a felon or a[10] madman— and in either case no great subject for[11] panegyric. In his life he was—what all the world knows, and half of it will feel for years to come, unless his death prove a "moral lesson" to the surviving Sejani* of Europe. It may at least serve as some consolation to the Nations, that their Oppressors are not happy, and in some instances judge so justly of their own actions[12] as to anticipate the sentence of mankind.—Let us hear no more of this man; and let Ireland remove the Ashes of her Grattan* from the Sanctuary[13] of Westminster. Shall the Patriot of Humanity repose by the Werther of Politics!!![14]*

With regard to the objections which have been made on another score

---

[4] as to [weeping for] his death—it will be time enough [to do so] when Ireland . . . *Sub.* lamenting.

[5] the wickedest in intention . . .

[6] It is the first time too since . . . England has [gov] been misruled . . .

[7] a poor radical devil such as . . .

[8] crossroads

[9] [of] in eulogy [of] the deceased and [all] the nauseous [at] and atrocious cant . . . *Present text ins.*

[10] felon [and] or a madman . . .

[11] subject [of] panegyric . . . *Sub.* for.

[12] judge so justly of [themselves] as to anticipate . . . *Sub.* their own actions.

[13] from the [dishonoured] Sanctuary . . . *Sub.* once honourable.

[14] *This sentence does not appear on the manuscript.*

[4]

to the already published Cantos of this poem, I shall content myself with[15] two quotations from Voltaire:*—

"La pudeur s'est enfuite[16] des coeurs, et s'est refugiée sur les lèvres."

"Plus les moeurs sont dépravés, plus les expressions deviennent mesurées; on croit regagner en langage ce qu'on a perdu en vertu."

This is the real fact, as applicable to the degraded and hypocritical mass which leavens the present English generation,[17] and is the only answer they deserve. The hackneyed and lavished title of Blasphemer—which, with radical, liberal, jacobin, reformer, &c. are the changes which the hirelings are daily ringing in the ears of those who will listen—should be welcome to all who recollect on *whom* it was[18] originally bestowed. Socrates and Jesus Christ were put to death publicly as *Blasphemers,* and so have been and may be many who dare to oppose the most notorious abuses of the name of God and the mind of man. But Persecution is not refutation, nor even triumph: the "wretched Infidel,"[19] as he is called, is probably happier in his prison than the proudest of his Assailants. With his opinions I have nothing to do—they may be right or wrong—but he has suffered for them, and that very Suffering for conscience-sake[20] will make more proselytes to Deism than the example of heterodox Prelates* to Christianity, suicide Statesmen to oppression, or over-pensioned Homicides* to the impious Alliance which insults the world with the name of "Holy"![21]* I have no wish to trample on the dishonourèd[22] or the dead; but it would be well if the adherents to the Classes from whence those persons sprung should abate a little of the *Cant* which is the crying sin of this double-dealing and false-speaking time of selfish Spoilers, and[23]—but enough for the present.

[15] I shall content [with] myself with . . .
[16] enfuie
[17] the English [Nation] generation . . . . *Ins.* present.
[18] it has been . . .
[19] the "wretched Carlile"* . . .
[20] Suffering will make . . . *Ins.* for Conscience-sake.
[21] the example of [hedonistic] prelates to Christianity—[or of] Suicide Statesmen to Oppression *Sub.* heterodox. *The rest of this sentence* ("or over-pensioned . . . Alliance which [blasp] insults . . . 'Holy' ") *was inserted on the manuscript.*
[22] I have no wish to [triumph over the fallen disgraced] dishonoured—or the dead . . . *Sub.* trample on the.
[23] time of selfish [and] Spoilers—[and] [indignant] [their] [hungry and] and—but enough for the present.

Canto VI

1

"THERE is a tide* in the affairs of men
   Which taken at the flood"—you know the rest,
And most of us have found it, now and then;
   At least we think so, though but few have guess'd
The moment, till too late to come again.
   But no doubt every thing is for the best—
Of which the surest sign is in the end:
When things are at the worst they sometimes mend.

All manuscript readings are taken from BM (British Museum manuscript), Byron's original first draft, except those noted as M (Murray manuscript), which is Mary Shelley's fair copy. Wherever there are revisions for any one line on both manuscripts, each reading will be identified. For the treatment of Mary Shelley's copy changes, see section 20 in the introduction on editorial practice, pp. xxv–xxvi of Volume II.

   On the first page of the BM first draft above the first stanza Byron wrote the date but scratched it over so heavily that only the year "1822" is legible.

3*a* have proved it . . . BM
  b have found . . . M   *Mary Shelley's alteration.*

There is a tide in the affairs of women
    "Which taken at the flood leads"—God knows where:
Those navigators must be able seamen
    Whose charts lay down its currents to a hair;
Not all the reveries of Jacob Behmen*
    With its strange whirls and eddies can compare:—
Men with their heads reflect on this and that—
But women with their hearts or heaven knows what!

1*a* tide too in ... BM;   *b* tide in ... M   *Mary Shelley's alteration.*
7*a*–8*a* *In addition to the present text there are two alternative readings*
    on BM:
7*b*–8*b* [The] [Man's pensive part is mostly in the head]
    Man with his head reflects—(as Spurzheim tells)
    But Woman with the heart—or something else
7*c*–8*c* Man's pensive part is [mostly in] the head
                (now & then) ...
    [But] Woman's [in the] heart—or anything instead
    Woman's the heart ...
7*d*–8*d* *Mary Shelley copied only the present text on M.*
    e on heaven ... *In 1833 and in later editions.*

3

And yet a headlong, headstrong, downright she,
    Young, beautiful, and daring—who would risk
A throne, the world, the universe, to be
    Beloved in her own way, and rather whisk
The stars from out the sky, than not be free
    As are the billows when the breeze is brisk—
Though such a she's a devil (if that there be one)
Yet she would make full many a Manichean. *

5   [Like to a Comet's tail] *fragment*
7*a* Though—such [a woman is] a devil if that there be one
 b Though—such a [One is] a devil ...
 c *The 1823, 1833, and 1837 editions print* if that there be one.
 d *Modern editions print* if there be one.
8   Yet She would [form] [find] full ...

Thrones, worlds, et cetera, are so oft upset
　By commonest Ambition, that when Passion
O'erthrows the same, we readily forget,
　Or at the least forgive, the loving rash one.
If Anthony be well remembered yet,
　'Tis not his conquests keep his name in fashion,
But Actium lost, for Cleopatra's eyes *
Outbalance all the Caesar's victories.

2a　By commonest Ambition, that when [Love]　BM
　b　*Mary Shelley miscopied* cormorant *on M and Byron restored*
　　commonest.
　3　[Takes them] the same . . .
4a　Or at the least—forgive the [motive] *fragment*
　b　　　　　　　　　　　　　　　[young and] rash one
6–7　*Although the 1823 edition places a comma after* Actium, *Byron's*
　　manuscript clearly indicates a dash after lost. *The punctuation of*
　　lines 6–7 of the 1823 text has therefore been altered to follow
　　Byron's manuscript more closely.
8a　Oerbalance all the Caesar's Victories　BM
　b　[Oerbalance] Outbalance all the Caesar's . . .　M　*Byron's*
　　revision.
　c　Outbalance all the Caesar's . . .　*The 1823 edition.*
　d　Outbalances all Caesar's . . .　*In 1833 and in later editions.*
　　This change is unnecessary, if, as in the present text, eyes *and not*
　　Actium *is taken as the subject of the verb.*

He died at fifty for a queen of forty;
  I wish their years had been fifteen and twenty,
For then wealth, kingdoms, worlds are but a sport—I
  Remember when, though I had no great plenty
Of worlds to lose, yet still, to pay my court, I
  Gave what I had—a heart:*—as the world went, I
Gave what was worth a world; for worlds could never
Restore me those pure feelings, gone for ever.

2 I wish [that they] had been [eighteen] *fragment*
6 a [boy's] heart . . .
8 feelings [lost] forever

6

'Twas the boy's "mite," and like the "widow's"* may
  Perhaps be weighed hereafter, if not now;
But whether such things do or do not weigh,
  All who have loved, or love, will still allow
Life has nought like it. God is love, they say,
  And Love's a God, or was before the brow
Of Earth was wrinkled by the sins and tears
Of—but Chronology best knows the years.

No revisions.

We left our hero and third heroine in
   A kind of state more awkward than uncommon,
For gentlemen must sometimes risk their skin
   For that sad tempter, a forbidden woman:
Sultans too much abhor this sort of sin,
   And don't agree at all with the wise Roman,
Heroic, stoic Cato,.the sententious,
Who lent his lady to his friend Hortensius.*

4 For that [forbidden] sad tempter . . .
6a [Not being] *fragment* BM
 b And don't . . . that wise . . . BM
 c   the . . . M *Mary Shelley's alteration.*

8

I know Gulbeyaz was extremely wrong;
   I own it, I deplore it, I condemn it;
But I detest all fiction even in song,
   And so must tell the truth, howe'er you blame it.
Her reason being weak, her passions strong,
   She thought that her lord's heart (even could she
      claim it)
Was scarce enough; for he had fifty-nine
Years, and a fifteen-hundredth concubine.

2 I [kn] own . . . *Intended to write* know.

9

I am not, like Cassio, "an arithmetician,"
   But by "the bookish theoric"* it appears,
If 'tis summed up with feminine precision,
   That, adding to the account his Highness' years,
The fair Sultana erred from inanition;
   For were the Sultan just to all his dears,
She could but claim the fifteenth hundred part
Of what should be monopoly—the heart.

[10]

[CANTO VI]

1   [a great] "Arithmetician"
2   theorick" . . .   BM, M
3*a* If [calculated well with fit] precision
  b If [numb] tis [sum] summed . . .
4   That [taking into] account . . .
6   For, [was] the Sultan . . .
7*a* [All] She . . . fifteenth hundred part   BM, M
  b   fifteen   hundredth . . .   *In 1833 and in later editions.*

10

It is observed that ladies are litigious
    Upon all legal objects of possession,
And not the least so when they are religious,
    Which doubles what they think of the transgression.
With suits and prosecutions they besiege us,
    As the tribunals show through many a session,
When they suspect that any one goes shares
In that to which the law makes them sole heirs.

3 *Byron on BM wrote* less so, *which Mary Shelley on M changed to*
least so.

11

Now if this holds good in a Christian land,
    The heathen also, though with lesser latitude,
Are apt to carry things with a high hand,
    And take, what kings call "an imposing attitude";
And for their rights connubial make a stand,
    When their liege husbands treat them with
        ingratitude;
And as four wives must have quadruple claims,
The Tigris hath its jealousies like Thames.

2*a* with greater latitude   BM
  b with [greater] lesser . . .   M *Byron's revision.*
8*a* The Tigris has it's jealousies like Thames   BM
  b The Tigris [has] hath . . . like [the] . . .   M *Byron's revision.*

[11]

Gulbeyaz was the fourth, and (as I said)
  The favourite; but what's favour amongst four?
Polygamy may well be held in dread,
  Not only as a sin, but as a *bore:*—
Most wise men with *one* moderate woman wed,
  Will scarcely find philosophy for more;
And all (except Mahometans) forbear
To make the nuptial couch a "Bed of Ware."*

5*a* [All] wise men with one foolish woman wed   BM
  b Most wise . . . foolish woman wed   BM, M

13

His Highness, the sublimest of mankind,—
  So styled according to the usual forms
Of every monarch, till they are consigned
  To those sad hungry jacobins the worms,*
Who on the very loftiest kings have dined,—
  His Highness gazed upon Gulbeyaz' charms,
Expecting all the welcome of a lover,
(A "Highland welcome"* all the wide world over).

2–6 *Order of composition of Byron's first attempt:*
  [The greatest wisest bravest as was] [proved] [found] [best
  By all his edicts even to] [unto] [the blind]
  [Proved by] [By] [Tis] [By all his Sub] *fragments*
  [Who saw his Virtues as they saw the rest
  His Highness quite connubially inclined
  Had deigned that night to be Gulbeyaz' Guest]

Now here we should distinguish; for howe'er
    Kisses, sweet words, embraces, and all that,
May look like what is—neither here nor there,
    They are put on as easily as a hat,
Or rather bonnet, which the fair sex wear,
    Trimmed either heads or hearts to decorate,
Which form an ornament, but no more part
Of heads, than their caresses of the heart.

1   Now here [I mus] We should . . .
2a Kisses, embraces, sweet words . . .   BM
 b Kisses—sweet words, embraces . . .   M   *Mary Shelley's alteration.*
3a May look like what [I need not mention here]   BM
 b May look like what is neither here nor there   BM
 c   or there   M   *Mary Shelley's*
4   They are [easily got up] *fragment*   *alteration.*
6   Trimmed [as they please to] *fragment*
7   [But] which [are] an Ornament . . .
8   Of [them] than . . .

15

A slight blush, a soft tremor, a calm kind
    Of gentle feminine delight, and shown
More in the eyelids than the eyes, resigned
    Rather to hide what pleases most unknown,
Are the best tokens (to a modest mind)
    Of love, when seated on his loveliest throne,
A sincere woman's breast,—for over *warm*
Or over *cold* annihilates the charm.

2   delight [which shows]
5a Are [better signs, (if such things can be signed)]   BM
 b Are the best tokens [at least] (to a moderate Mind)   BM
 c   to a moderate mind   M

For over warmth, if false, is worse than truth;
   If true, 'tis no great lease* of its own fire;
For no one, save in very early youth,
   Would like (I think) to trust all to desire,
Which is but a precarious bond, in sooth,
   And apt to be transferred to the first buyer
At a sad discount: while your over chilly
Women, on t'other hand, seem somewhat silly.

3 For [Nobody except] very early youth
8a rather [chi] silly BM
 b somewhat silly M *Mary Shelley's alteration.*

17

That is, we cannot pardon their bad taste,
   For so it seems to lovers swift or slow,
Who fain would have a mutual flame confest,
   And see a sentimental passion glow,
Even were St. Francis' paramour their guest,
   In his Monastic Concubine of Snow;*—
In short, the maxim for the amorous tribe is
Horatian, "Medio tu tutissimus ibis."*

2 For so it seems [to "us youth"] *fragment*
3a confest BM, M; b confess'd *In 1833 and in later editions.*
4a And see [that fine etherial] passion glow
 b And see [a mighty mutual] . . .
5 Even [in] Saint Francis *fragment*
6. In [that] monastic . . .

18

The "tu" 's *too* much,—but let it stand—the verse
   Requires it, that's to say, the English rhyme,
And not the pink of old Hexameters;
   But, after all, there's neither tune nor time
In the last line, which cannot well be worse,
   And was thrust in to close the octave's chime:

> I own no prosody can ever rate it
> As a rule, but *Truth* may, if you translate it.

2*a* Requires it—that's [to be] the . . .
 b   that [is to] say . . .
 3 And not the [Latin] [Roman] *fragment*
 4 [A] But . . .
5–6 [In the damned line ('tis worth at least a curse)
      Which I have crammed] to close the Octave's chime
7–8*a* I own [there's neither time nor tune to make it
      Harmonious] *fragment*
 8*b* As a Rule, but Truth [will] if you translate it

19

> If fair Gulbeyaz overdid her part,
>   I know not—it succeeded, and success
> Is much in most things, not less in the heart
>   Than other articles of female dress.
> Self-love in man too beats all female art;
>   They lie, we lie, all lie, but love no less:
> And no one virtue yet, except Starvation,
> Could stop that worst of vices—Propagation.

 2 it succeeded, [that's enough]
3*a* [Self-Love, that Whetstone of Dan Cupid's dart]
 b less [of] the Heart
5*a* Self-Love, [that Whetstone of Dan Cupid's dart]   BM
 b Self-Love in Men, too . . .   BM, M
7*a* And [Nothing ever heard of but] starvation
8*a* Could [stop the progress yet] *fragment*
 b Could [stop the tendency to] propagation
7*b*–8*c* *After substituting the present text, Byron wrote an alternative
      couplet, which was almost the same as his previous cancellation:*
      And Nothing ever heard of save Starvation
      Could stop the tendency to Propagation
      Mary Shelley copied only the present text on M.

    We leave this royal couple to repose;
        A bed is not a throne, and they may sleep,
    Whate'er their dreams be, if of joys or woes;
        Yet disappointed joys are woes as deep
    As any man's clay mixture undergoes.
        Our least of sorrows are such as we weep;
    'Tis the vile daily drop on drop which wears
    The soul out (like the stone) with petty cares.

4 [And] disappointed . . .
5 As any, [our] Clay . . .
6 are [those] as . . .
8 Stone) with [lone despairs]

                          21

    A scolding wife, a sullen son, a bill
        To pay, unpaid, protested, or discounted
    At a per-centage; a child cross, dog ill,
        A favourite horse fallen lame just as he's mounted;
    A bad old woman making a worse will,*
        Which leaves you minus of the cash you counted
    As certain;—these are paltry things, and yet
    I've rarely seen the man they did not fret.

1 sullen [wife]—a bill
3 a [horse lame], dog ill,
4 A [horse] favourite fallen lame just as [one's] mounted
6 Which [diddles you] minus the cash you counted
7 paltry [ills] & yet

I'm a philosopher; confound them all!
    Bills, beasts, and men, and—no! *not* Womankind!
With one good hearty curse I vent my gall,
    And then my Stoicism leaves nought behind
Which it can either pain or evil call,
    And I can give my whole soul up to mind;
Though what *is* soul or mind, their birth or growth,
Is more than I know—the deuce take them both.

1   I'm a philosopher; G—d damn them all! BM, M
2*a* Bills—women—wives, [old women]—and mankind BM
 b   dogs, horses . . . BM
 c *Mary Shelley copied Byron's final BM version; Byron deleted it and*
    substituted the present text. M
3   I [pour *sic?*] my Gall
5   Which [she] can . . .
7*a* Though what [a Mind or Soul is] *fragment* BM
 b Though what is Mind or Soul . . . BM
 c   soul, or mind . . . M *Mary Shelley's alteration.*
8   Is more than I know, [and so damn] them both

23

So now all things are d – – n'd, one feels at ease,
    As after reading Athanasius' curse,*
Which doth your true believer so much please:
    I doubt if any now could make it worse
O'er his worst enemy when at his knees,
    'Tis so sententious, positive, and terse,
And decorates the book of Common Prayer,
As doth a Rainbow the just clearing air.

1   [my] one feels . . .
4*a* make a worse BM; *b* make it worse M *Mary Shelley's alteration*

Gulbeyaz and her lord were sleeping, or
At least one of them—Oh the heavy night!
When wicked wives who love some bachelor
Lie down in dudgeon to sigh for the light
Of the grey morning, and look vainly for
Its twinkle through the lattice dusky quite,
To toss, to tumble, doze, revive, and quake
Lest their too lawful bed-fellow should wake.

3–4 When [we lie down, wife, Spouse or Bachelor
By what] [we] [they love not—to sigh] for the light
[sighing] . . .
5 [looking] vainly for
8 Lest [our] their [infernal] bedfellow . . .

25

These are beneath the canopy of heaven,
Also beneath the canopy of beds
Four-posted and silk curtained, which are given
For rich men and their brides to lay their heads
Upon, in sheets white as what bards call "driven
Snow."*† Well! 'tis all hap-hazard when one weds.
Gulbeyaz was an empress, but had been
Perhaps as wretched if a *peasant's quean.*

5 sheets [as] white as bards . . .

Don Juan in his feminine disguise,
   With all the damsels in their long array,
Had bowed themselves before the imperial eyes,
   And at the usual signal ta'en their way
Back to their chambers, those long galleries
   In the Seraglio, where the ladies lay
Their delicate limbs; a thousand bosoms there
Beating for love as the caged birds for air.

4 taen their [eyes]

27

I love the sex, and sometimes would reverse
   The tyrant's wish,* "that mankind only had
One neck, which he with one fell stroke might pierce":
   My wish is quite as wide, but not so bad,
And much more tender on the whole than fierce;
   It being (not *now*, but only while a lad)
That Womankind had but one rosy mouth,
To kiss them all at once from North to South.

3 One Neck [that he might] *fragment*
4a My wish [were] quite as [general but no worse]   BM
 b My wish is quite as wide and not so bad   BM
 c   but . . .   M   *Mary Shelley's alteration.*
6 It being [only] . . .
7 8 That Womankind had [only one—say—heart]—mouth
   [That I might kiss them at] once [both] North [and] South

[19]

Oh enviable Briareus!* with thy hands
 And heads, if thou hadst all things multiplied
In such proportion!—But my Muse withstands
 The giant thought of being a Titan's bride,
Or travelling in Patagonian lands;*
 So let us back to Lilliput, and guide
Our hero through the labyrinth of love
In which we left him several lines above.

1–3 Oh enviable . . . with thy [heads]
  And [hands] if thou hadst all things [in proportion
  Thou wast indeed a Giant!] *fragment*
 4*a* The [thought Gigantic] *fragment*
  b The Giant thought [to be] a Titan's bride

29

He went forth with the lovely Odalisques,*
 At the given signal joined to their array;
And though he certainly ran many risks,
 Yet he could not at times keep, by the way,
(Although the consequences of such frisks
 Are worse than the worst damages men pay
In moral England, where the thing's a tax)
From ogling all their charms from breasts to backs.

2 signal [mixed with] their array
4*a* Yet he [contrived] *fragment* BM
 b Yet he at times could not [help] by the way BM
 c   keep . . . BM
 d Yet he could not at times . . . M *Mary Shelley's alteration.*
8 From [glancing] ogling . . . BM *Mary Shelley evidently refused to
copy this line, which had been legibly written on BM, for she left a
blank space on M, and Byron filled it in.*

Still he forgot not his disguise:—along
　The galleries from room to room they walked,
A virgin-like and edifying throng,
　By eunuchs flanked; while at their head there stalked
A dame who kept up discipline among
　The female ranks, so that none stirred or talked
Without her sanction on their she-parades:
Her title was "the Mother of the Maids."

5　A [Lady] who kept discipline among

31

Whether she was a "mother," I know not,
　Or whether they were "maids" who called her mother;
But this is her seraglio title, got
　I know not how, but good as any other;
So Cantemir can tell you, or De Tott:*
　Her office was, to keep aloof or smother
All bad propensities in fifteen hundred
Young women, and correct them when they blundered.

3　*Byron on BM wrote* Seraglio, *which Mary Shelley miscopied as*
　seraphic *on M; Byron corrected her mistake.*
4a　I know not where, [and quite as] good['s] *fragment*　BM
　b　I know not where but good as any other　BM, M
5a　[As] Cantamir can tell you—or {Rucant / De Tott}　BM
　b　　　Cantemir . . .　　　　　　De Tott　M

[21]

A goodly sinecure, no doubt! but made
  More easy by the absence of all men
Except his Majesty, who, with her aid,
  And guards, and bolts, and walls, and now and then
A slight example, just to cast a shade
  Along the rest, contrived to keep this den
Of beauties cool as an Italian convent,
Where all the passions have, alas! but one vent.

2 absence of all [males]
3 [by] her aid
7 Of beauties [chaste] as . . .

33

And what is that? Devotion, doubtless—how
  Could you ask such a question?—but we will
Continue. As I said, this goodly row
  Of ladies of all countries at the will
Of one good man, with stately march and slow,
  Like water-lilies floating down a rill
Or rather lake—for *rills* do *not* run *slowly*,—
Paced on most maiden-like and melancholy.

2   but [let us]
6a Like [the] Water lilies floating [down a rill]
 b   [past a Mill]
7   do not [flow] slowly

But when they reached their own apartments, there,
　　Like birds, or boys, or bedlamites broke loose,
Waves at spring-tide, or women any where
　　When freed from bonds (which are of no great use
After all) or like Irish at a fair,
　　Their guards being gone, and as it were a truce
Established between them and bondage, they
Began to sing, dance, chatter, smile and play.

1 *Byron on BM wrote* reached, *which Mary Shelley on M changed to*
entered. *Byron restored his original word.*
2 bedlam [all] broke loose
7–8 Established between them [and all Constraint
Began to sing, dance, play] *fragment*

35

Their talk of course ran most on the new comer,
　　Her shape, her hair, her air, her every thing:
Some thought her dress did not so much become her,
　　Or wondered at her ears without a ring;
Some said her years were getting nigh their summer,
　　Others contended they were but in spring;
Some thought her rather masculine in height,
While others wished that she had been so quite.

2 her [eyes] everything
4 [And others] *fragment*
5 Some [thought] her years were getting [night] their Summer
7 masculine [to sight]

But no one doubted on the whole, that she
   Was what her dress bespoke, a damsel fair,
And fresh, and "beautiful exceedingly,"*
   Who with the brightest Georgians might compare:*
They wondered how Gulbeyaz too could be
   So silly as to buy slaves who might share
(If that his Highness wearied of his bride)
Her throne and power and every thing beside.

5   wondered [that] Gulbeyaz . . .
6a to buy a Slave might share   BM
  b *Mary Shelley copied Byron's BM version on M; he deleted part of the
line and substituted the present text.*

37

But what was strangest in this virgin crew,
   Although her beauty was enough to vex,
After the first investigating view,
   They all found out as few, or fewer, specks
In the fair form of their companion new,
   Than is the custom of the gentle sex,
When they survey, with Christian eyes or Heathen,
In a new face "the ugliest creature breathing."

1 But what [is] strange [in all] this . . .
2-3 Though—[as I said none knew or guessed his Sex]
    After the first [astonishment and] view
5 In [their] *fragment*
7 survey [in] Christian [lands] or Heathen

And yet they had their little jealousies
　　Like all the rest; but upon this occasion,
Whether there are such things as sympathies
　　Without our knowledge or our approbation,
Although they could not see through his disguise,
　　All felt a soft kind of concatenation,
Like Magnetism, or Devilism, or what
You please—we will not quarrel about that:

7 [Which made them like their new Companion]

39

But certain 'tis they all felt for their new
　　Companion something newer still, as 'twere
A sentimental friendship through and through,
　　Extremely pure, which made them all concur
In wishing her their sister, save a few
　　Who wished they had a brother, just like her,
Whom, if they were at home in sweet Circassia,
They would prefer to Padisha or Pacha.*

2   newer still [than her]
4   [Exceeding] pure . . .
6a Who [thought] wished She had . . .   BM
 b Who wished she . . .   M
7   *Two fragments:*
 a [With] [Whom, were they on their Circassian]
 b   [Whom, were they once more at]
8   Padishah . . .   BM, M

Of those who had most genius for this sort
    Of sentimental friendship, there were three,
Lolah, Katinka, and Dudù;* in short,
    (To save description) fair as fair can be
Were they, according to the best report,
    Though differing in stature and degree,
And clime and time, and country and complexion;
They all alike admired their new connexion.

1–2 Of those . . . for this [kind/Of Sentimental] *fragment*
   4*a* fair as fair can be BM
    b [as] fair as fair . . . M   *Mary Shelley inserted* as, *which Byron deleted.*
   8*a* [They] [Alike] *fragments*
    b [Yet] they all [much] admired . . .

41

Lolah was dusk as India and as warm;
    Katinka was a Georgian, white and red,*
With great blue eyes, a lovely hand and arm,
    And feet so small they scarce seemed made to tread,
But rather skim the earth; while Dudù's form
    Looked more adapted to be put to bed,
Being somewhat large and languishing and lazy,
Yet of a beauty that would drive you crazy.

6 [Seemed] more adapted . . .
7 large and [indolent] and lazy
8 that would [quite amaze ye]

A kind of sleepy Venus seemed Dudù,
    Yet very fit to "murder sleep"* in those
Who gazed upon her cheek's transcendant hue,
    Her Attic forehead, and her Phidian nose:
Few angles were there in her form 'tis true,
    Thinner she might have been and yet scarce lose;
Yet, after all, 'twould puzzle to say where
It would not spoil some separate charm *to pare.*

1 sleep[ing] Venus . . .
2 in [others]
5 were [about] her form . . .
7 [And] Yet, . . .

43

She was not violently lively, but
    Stole on your spirit like a May-day breaking;
Her eyes were not too sparkling, yet, half-shut,
    They put beholders in a tender taking;*
She looked (this simile's quite new) just cut
    From marble, like Pygmalion's statue waking,
The Mortal and the Marble still at strife,
And timidly expanding into life.

1   violently [vivacious] lively . . .
2   a [Mild] Day breaking
4   They [soothed & won] in . . .
5a Similie's [part] new . . .;   b Similie's [half] new . . .
7a [Ere yet it knew exactly] [knew exactly] *fragment*
 b The [veins of blood] *fragment*

Lolah demanded the new damsel's name—
  "Juanna."—Well, a pretty name enough.
Katinka asked her also whence she came—
  "From Spain."—"But where *is* Spain?"—"Don't
    ask such stuff,
Nor show your Georgian ignorance—for shame!"
  Said Lolah, with an accent rather rough,
To poor Katinka: "Spain's an island near
Morocco, betwixt Egypt and Tangier."

5a [Said Lolah to the Georgian] *fragment*
  b [And] show your . . .
7 (To poor Katinka—) [don't you know that Spain]

45

Dudù said nothing, but sat down beside
  Juanna, playing with her veil or hair;
And looking at her steadfastly, she sighed,
  As if she pitied her for being there,
A pretty stranger without friend or guide,
  And all abashed too at the general stare
Which welcomes hapless strangers in all places,
With kind remarks upon their mien and faces.

3 And looking at her [now and then] she sighed
5 A [Stranger without friend or gentle] guide
7a Strangers [in all places]; b Strangers [everywhere]

But here the Mother of the Maids drew near,
      With, "Ladies, it is time to go to rest.
I'm puzzled what to do with you, my dear,"
      She added to Juanna, their new guest:
"Your coming has been unexpected here,
      And every couch is occupied; you had best
Partake of mine; but by to-morrow early
We will have all things settled for you fairly."

1 Mother of the Maids [approached]
4 [the] new Guest
7 [and] by . . .

47

Here Lolah interposed—"Mamma, you know
      You don't sleep soundly, and I cannot bear
That any body should disturb you so;
      I'll take Juanna; we're a slenderer pair
Than you would make the half of;—don't say no;
      And I of your young charge will take due care."
But here Katinka interfered and said,
"She also had compassion and a bed."

2 You don't sleep soundly—and [it were a pity]
6 *Byron wrote* due care *on BM; Mary Shelley altered it to* great care
on M, and Byron restored his original word.

"Besides, I hate to sleep alone," quoth she.
    The Matron frowned: "Why so?"—"For fear of
      ghosts,"
Replied Katinka; "I am sure I see
    A phantom upon each of the four posts;
And then I have the worst dreams that can be,
    Of Guebres, Giaours, and Ginns, and Gouls in hosts."*
The Dame replied, "Between your dreams and you,
    I fear Juanna's dreams would be but few.

1   to [lie] alone . . .
4a [One perched] *fragment*
  b A [Spectre] phantom . . .
5   And then I have [such horrid dreams] *fragment*
6   Of [flying Gouls, and Giaours, and Ginns, and Guebres' hosts]
7a [Between your Ghosts and dreams replied] *fragment*
  b The Dame replied "between your [Ghosts] and you

49

"You, Lolah, must continue still to lie
    Alone, for reasons which don't matter; you
The same, Katinka, until by and bye;
    And I shall place Juanna with Dudù,
Who's quiet, inoffensive, silent, shy,
    And will not toss and chatter the night through.
What say you, child?"—Dudù said nothing, as
Her talents were of the more silent class;

1   still to [sleep]
2   don't matter [much &]
7–8a What . . . Dudù said nothing, [twas for
      Her way to let most things in] *fragment*
8b Her talent [was for silence] *fragment*

But she rose up, and kissed the Matron's brow
   Between the eyes, and Lolah on both cheeks,
Katinka too; and with a gentle bow
   (Curtsies are neither used by Turks nor Greeks)
She took Juanna by the hand to show
   Their place of rest, and left to both their piques,
The others pouting at the Matron's preference
Of Dudù, though they held their tongues from deference.

4a [In Turkey no one Curtseys] *fragment* BM
 b Curtseys . . . BM, M
6a and [leaving to] their piques
 b and left [unto] to both . . .
7–8 The other [two still] pouting at the [preference
     The Matron showed] *fragment*

51

It was a spacious chamber (Oda is
   The Turkish title) and ranged round the wall
Were couches, toilets—and much more than this
   I might describe, as I have seen it all,*
But it suffices—little was amiss;
   'Twas on the whole a nobly furnished hall,
With all things ladies want, save one or two,
And even those were nearer than they knew.

5 [few things were] amiss
8 even [they] those . . .

Dudù, as has been said, was a sweet creature,
　　Not very dashing, but extremely winning,
With the most regulated charms of feature,
　　Which painters cannot catch like faces sinning
Against proportion—the wild strokes of nature
　　Which they hit off at once in the beginning,
Full of expression, right or wrong, that strike,
And pleasing or unpleasing, still are like.

1 Dudù, as [I] has been said, was a sweet [Soul]
5 the [bold] strokes . . .
6 Which they [strike] off . . .
7 [which] strike
8 unpleasing—[are made] like

53

But she was a soft Landscape of mild Earth,
　　Where all was harmony and calm and quiet,
Luxuriant, budding; cheerful without mirth,
　　Which if not happiness, is much more nigh it
Than are your mighty passions and so forth,
　　Which some call "the sublime":* I wish they'd try it:
I've seen your stormy seas and stormy women,
And pity lovers rather more than seamen.

1a landscape of [sweet flesh]
 b landscape of [kind Clay]
2   Where all [is] harmony . . .
3   Luxuriant, budding, [& beautiful and fresh]
　　　　　　　　　[happy] [lovely but not gay]
4-6 [Nor yet with aught that's] *fragment*
　　　[With nothing very grand to make a riot
　　　Of all the Elements which people say
　　　Is the Sublime—I wish that they would] try it
8   And pity [husbands,] lovers [not much less] than Seamen

But she was pensive more than melancholy,
   And serious more than pensive, and serene,
It may be, more than either—not unholy
   Her thoughts, at least till now, appear to have been.
The strangest thing was, beauteous, she was wholly
   Unconscious, albeit turned of quick seventeen,
That she was fair, or dark, or short, or tall;
She never thought about herself at all.

5–6a The strangest thing was; [beautiful and wholly
      Beautiful and] *fragment*
  6b Unconscious, although turned . . . BM
   c Unconscious, [although] albeit turned . . .   M   *Byron's revision.*
  7a That she was [beautiful] *fragment*
   b That she was fair or [plain] dark . . .

55

And therefore was she kind and gentle as
   The Age of Gold (when Gold was yet unknown,
By which its nomenclature came to pass;
   Thus most appropriately has been shown
"Lucus a *non* Lucendo,"* *not* what *was,*
   But what *was not;* a sort of style that's grown
Extremely common in this age, whose metal
The Devil may decompose but never settle;

2 Gold was [not] yet . . .
3 By which [no doubt] it's [Baptism] came to pass
4 [As] most appropriately [to be] shown
8 The Devil [in hell will melt] but never settle

I think it may be of "Corinthian Brass,"*
　Which was a Mixture of all Metals, but
The Brazen uppermost.)* Kind reader! pass
　This long parenthesis: I could not shut
It sooner for the soul of me, and class
　My faults even with your own! which meaneth, Put
A kind construction upon them and me:
But *that* you won't—then don't—I am not less free.

3 The [brass still] uppermost . . .
5 *Byron on BM wrote* Soul; *Mary Shelley on M substituted* life, *and
Byron restored his original word.*

57

'Tis time we should return to plain narration,
　And thus my narrative proceeds:—Dudù,
With every kindness short of ostentation,
　Shewed Juan, or Juanna, through and through
This labyrinth of females, and each station
　Described—what's strange—in words extremely few:
I have but one simile, and that's a blunder,
For wordless woman, which is *silent* Thunder.

1a should revert to . . . BM
 b should return to . . . M *Mary Shelley's alteration.*
4   Juan [and] or Juanna . . .
6   [And when described] in words [though rather] few
7a [Yet quite enough considering the extent]
 b [Which] [Which made him wonder more than any wonder]
8   [For Woman's Silence startles more than] Thunder

And next she gave her (I say *her*, because
  The Gender still was Epicene, at least
In outward show, which is a saving clause)
  An outline of the Customs of the East,
With all their chaste integrity of laws,
  By which the more a Harem is encreased,
The stricter doubtless grow the vestal duties
Of any supernumerary beauties.

1 And [then] She . . .
2 The Gender[s] still [were] Epicene . . .
4 [According to] the customs . . .
5 chaste [severity] of laws
6a Haram [was] increased BM; *b* encreased M *Mary Shelley con-*
   sistently altered Byron's spelling of this word, and the first edition
   followed her copy. Editions after 1833 generally used Byron's spelling.
   This variation will not be noted hereafter.
7 the [virgin]-duties

                              59

And then she gave Juanna a chaste kiss:
  Dudù was fond of kissing—which I'm sure
That nobody can ever take amiss,
  Because 'tis pleasant, so that it be pure,
And between females means no more than this—
  That they have nothing better near, or newer.
"Kiss" rhymes to "bliss" in fact as well as verse—
I wish it never led to something worse.

2–3 Dudù was [very] fond of kissing which
      [I am sure that nobody can] take amiss
4 Because 'tis [nothing] so that it be pure
6 That they hav[ing] nothing better [to] . . .
8a [But very often leads] to something worse
 b [But generally leads] to . . .

In perfect Innocence she then unmade
    Her toilet, which cost little, for she was
A Child of Nature, carelessly arrayed:
    If fond of a chance ogle at her glass,
'Twas like the Fawn which, in the lake displayed,
    Beholds her own shy, shadowy image pass,
When first she starts, and then returns to peep,
Admiring this new Native of the deep.

1-2 [And then] in perfect innocence [she made
    Or rather] *fragment*
  7 [And] first . . . returns—[and] peep[s]
  8 of the Deep[s]

61

And one by one her articles of dress
    Were laid aside; but not before she offered
Her aid to fair Juanna, whose excess
    Of Modesty declined the assistance proffered:
Which past well off—as she could do no less;
    Though by this politesse she rather suffered,
Pricking her fingers with those cursed pins,
Which surely were invented for our sins,—

6 [Although] Though . . .
7 Pricking [those] her . . .

Making a woman like a porcupine,
   Not to be rashly touched. But still more dread,
Oh ye! whose fate it is, as once 'twas mine,
   In early youth, to turn a lady's maid;*—
I did my very boyish best to shine
   In tricking her out for a masquerade:
The pins were placed sufficiently, but not
Stuck all exactly in the proper spot.

2   rashly [seized] but . . .
3   fate it [was—(it once was] mine)
4   to [be] a Lady's maid
5   I did my [best alas!—but did not] shine
6a In pricking her out . . . BM
  b In tricking . . . M *Mary Shelley's alteration.*
7–8 The pins were [stuck sufficiently] but not
      [Replaced exactly] [in the] [and] [in it's own spot]

63

But these are foolish things to all the wise,
   And I love wisdom more than she loves me;
My tendency is to philosophize
   On most things, from a tyrant to a tree;
But still the spouseless Virgin *Knowledge* flies.
   What are we? and whence came we? what shall be
Our *ultimate* existence? what's our present?
Are questions answerless, and yet incessant.

6 [and] what shall be
7 Our ultimate existence?—[or our present?]

There was deep silence in the chamber: dim
   And distant from each other burned the lights,
And Slumber hovered o'er each lovely limb
   Of the fair occupants: if there be sprites,
They should have walked there in their spriteliest trim,
   By way of change from their sepulchral sites,
And shown themselves as Ghosts of better taste
Than haunting some old Ruin or wild Waste.

2*a* burnt . . . BM; *b* burned . . . M
5*a* They [surely walked that Gallery] *fragment*
 b *Present text on BM. On M, Mary Shelley omitted* their, *which Byron inserted.*

65

Many and beautiful lay those around,
   Like flowers of different hue and clime and root,
In some exotic garden sometimes found,
   With cost and care and warmth induced to shoot.
One with her auburn tresses lightly bound,
   And fair brows gently drooping, as the fruit
Nods from the tree, was slumbering with soft breath
And lips apart, which showed the pearls beneath.

1 [were] those around
2 of different hue [and different clime]
4*a* [Reared by you] *fragment*
 b [Reared with much cost and care into their prime]
5 [Some] with [their] Auburn tresses . . .
6 And [white] brows . . .
7 [Bends] from the tree,—[were sleeping] with soft breath
8 And lips apart [with] which showed . . .

One with her flushed cheek laid on her white arm,
  And raven ringlets gathered in dark crowd
Above her brow, lay dreaming soft and warm;
  And smiling through her dream, as through a cloud
The Moon breaks, half unveiled each further charm,
  As, slightly stirring in her snowy shroud,
Her beauties seized the unconscious hour of night
All bashfully to struggle into light.

2*a* And [her dusky] ringlets gathered [like a cloud]
 b   in [a] crowd
7*a* Her beauties [struggling into light] *fragment*
 b Her beauties seized the [hour of rest & night]
8*a* All [timidly] to struggle . . .   BM
 b *Mary Shelley on M copied* timidly, *which Byron had deleted on BM;*
    he restored on M his BM substitution, bashfully.

This is no bull,* although it sounds so; for
　　'Twas night, but there were lamps, as hath been said.
A third's all pallid aspect offered more
　　The traits of sleeping Sorrow, and betrayed
Through the heaved breast the dream of some far shore
　　Beloved and deplored; while slowly strayed
(As Night Dew, on a Cypress glittering, tinges
　　The black bough) tear-drops through her eyes' dark
　　　　fringes.

3　A third's [more] pallid . . .
5　*Byron on BM wrote* breast, *which Mary Shelley on M changed to*
　　heart. *He restored his original word. Since Mary Shelley made this*
　　same mistake several times, it will not be noted hereafter. Byron
　　also corrected her reading of a far shore *to* some far shore.
6–8a　Beloved . . . while slowly [made
　　Their way through her sealed eyelids' glossy fringes
　　A tear or two] *fragment*
　　[A tear or two with their] *fragment*
　7b　[Like] Night-dew . . .
8b–d　*Three fragments:*
　　The [dark] bough) [tears through]
　　　　　　　　　　　　[tear drops through]
　　　　　　　　　　　　[stream *sic?*]

68

A fourth as marble, statue-like and still,
　　Lay in a breathless, hushed, and stony sleep;
White, cold and pure, as looks a frozen rill,
　　Or the snow minaret on an Alpine steep,
Or Lot's wife done in salt,*—or what you will;—
　　My similes are gathered in a heap,
So pick and chuse—perhaps you'll be content
With a carved lady on a monument.

3　as [lies] a frozen rill
4　of an Alpine . . .　BM, M
7a　chuse . . .　BM, M;　*b* choose . . .　*In 1833 and in later editions.*
8　carved [Beauty] on a Monument

And lo! a fifth appears;—and what is she?
　　A lady of "a certain age,"* which means
Certainly aged—what her years might be
　　I know not, never counting past their teens;
But there she slept, not quite so fair to see,
　　As ere that awful period intervenes
Which lays both men and women on the shelf,
To meditate upon their sins and self.

1a　what was She?　BM
　b　what is she?　M　*Mary Shelley's alteration.*
5　she [lay] . . .
6　As [in the] *fragment*
8　To [think about] To [moralize about] *fragments*

70

But all this time how slept, or dreamed, Dudù?
　　With strict enquiry I could ne'er discover,
And scorn to add a syllable untrue;
　　But ere the middle watch was hardly over,
Just when the fading lamps waned dim and blue,
　　And phantoms hovered, or might seem to hover
To those who like their company, about
The apartment, on a sudden she screamed out:

4　the [second] Middle Watch . . .

And that so loudly, that upstarted all
    The Oda, in a general commotion:
Matrons and maids, and those whom you may call
    Neither, came crowding like the waves of ocean,
One on the other, throughout the whole hall,
    All trembling, wondering, without the least notion,
More than I have myself, of what could make
The calm Dudù so turbulently wake.

No revisions.

72

But wide awake she was, and round her bed,
    With floating draperies and with flying hair,
With eager eyes, and light but hurried tread,
    And bosoms, arms, and ancles glancing bare,
And bright as any meteor ever bred
    By the North Pole,*—they sought her cause of care,
For she seemed agitated, flushed and frightened,
Her eye dilated and her colour heightened.

3   With [anxious] eyes . . .
6*a* they sought her [cause of dread]   BM
 b   cause of care BM
 c *Mary Shelley on M wrote* the cause, *and Byron restored* her cause.

73

But what is strange—and a strong proof how great
    A blessing is sound sleep—Juanna lay
As fast as ever husband by his mate
    In holy matrimony snores away.
Not all the clamour broke her happy state
    Of slumber, ere they shook her,—so they say
At least,—and then she too unclosed her eyes,
And yawned a good deal with discreet surprize.

6a till they shook . . . BM
 b ere they . . . M *Mary Shelley's alteration.*
8a [With no less true and feminine] surprize BM
 b And yawned a good deal of discreet : . . BM
 c   [of] with . . . M *Byron's revision.*

74

And now commenced a strict investigation,
    Which, as all spoke at once, and more than once
Conjecturing, wondering, asking a narration,
    Alike might puzzle either wit or dunce
To answer in a very clear oration.
    Dudù had never passed for wanting sense,
But being "no orator as Brutus is,"*
Could not at first expound what was amiss.

4 Might puzzle [Wits no less than] *fragment*
8 [At first] could not [declare] what was amiss

75

At length she said, that in a slumber sound,
    She dreamed a dream, of walking in a wood—
A "wood obscure" like that where Dante found
    Himself* in at the age when all grow good;
Life's half-way house, where dames with virtue crowned,
    Run much less risk of lovers turning rude;
And that this wood was full of pleasant fruits,
And trees of goodly growth and spreading roots;

1a At length she [stated] that [being fast asleep]
 b At length she said that [sleeping] *fragment*
2 [that] walking . . .
3 [An obscure] A "wood obscure" like [Dante's] *fragments*
4 when [men] grow good
5 [As Life's best half is over—and ladies] *fragment*
7 pleasant [trees] fruits

And in the midst a golden apple grew,—
   A most prodigious pippin—but it hung
Rather too high and distant; that she threw
   Her glances on it, and then, longing, flung
Stones and whatever she could pick up, to
   Bring down the fruit, which still perversely clung
To its own bough, and dangled yet in sight,
But always at a most provoking height;—

1   a Golden [pippin] grew
4   glances [at] it
6   Bring down the fruit, [perverse] *fragment*
7a dangled [still in sight]   BM
  b   [in its height]   BM
  c   still in sight   BM
  d   [still] yet . . .   M   *Byron's revision.*
8   But [out of reach—a most provoking sight]   *This version is to be
read with 7b.*

77

That on a sudden, when she least had hope,
   It fell down of its own accord, before
Her feet; that her first movement was to stoop
   And pick it up, and bite it to the core;
That just as her young lip began to ope
   Upon the golden fruit the vision bore,
A bee flew out and stung her to the heart,
And so—she woke with a great scream and start.

1a she least [expected];   b she least [could] hope
4a and [sev] it to the core   *Intended to write* sever.
  b and [cut] . . .
5   That [ere her unreluctant lips could] ope
6a [To eat] the Golden fruit the pippin bore   BM
  b Upon . . .   BM;   c [the pippin] . . .   M
  d   the Vision . . .   M   *Byron's revision.*
8a [Which] And . . . awoke . . .   BM
  b   awoke . . .   M, *1833, and most later editions.*

All this she told with some confusion and
   Dismay, the usual consequence of dreams
Of the unpleasant kind, with none at hand
   To expound their vain and visionary gleams.
I've known some odd ones which seemed really planned
   Prophetically, or that which one deems
"A strange coincidence,"* to use a phrase
By which such things are settled now-a-days.

2 Dismay, [no doubt] the consequence . . .
4 [false] vain & visionary gleams—
5 some [strange] ones . . .
8a [all] things . . . in these days BM
  b   [in these days] M
  c   now a days M *Byron's revision.*

79

The damsels, who had thoughts of some great harm,
   Began, as is the consequence of fear,
To scold a little at the false alarm
   That broke for nothing on their sleeping ear.
The matron too was wroth to leave her warm
   Bed for the dream she had been obliged to hear,
And chafed at poor Dudù, who only sighed,
And said, that she was sorry she had cried.

1 had thought . . . BM, M
3 To [wax] scold . . .
6 she [was] obliged . . .
7 And [xxxx] chafed—[&] at . . .
8 *Byron on BM wrote* sorry she had cried; *Mary Shelley on M wrote*
sorry that she cried, *and Byron restored his original version.*

"I've heard of stories of a cock and bull;
    But visions of an apple and a bee,
To take us from our natural rest, and pull
    The whole Oda from their beds at half-past three,
Would make us think the moon is at its full.*
    You surely are unwell, child! we must see,
To-morrow what his Highness's physician
Will say to this hysteric of a vision.

3 To [w]ake [one] us . . .
5a at the full BM; b at its full M *Mary Shelley's alteration.*
8 to [such] this hysteric . . .

81

"And poor Juanna too! the child's first night
    Within these walls, to be broke in upon
With such a clamour—I had thought it right
    That the young stranger should not lie alone,
And as the quietest of all, she might
    With you, Dudù, a good night's rest have known.
But now I must transfer her to the charge
Of Lolah—though her couch is not so large."

8a Of Lola—[and who no doubt is not] so large BM
  b   though her [bed is not] . . . BM
  c   [sofa's not] . . . BM
  d   couch is not . . . BM
  e Of Lolah . . . M *Mary Shelley's alteration.*

Lolah's eyes sparkled at the proposition;
　　But poor Dudù, with large drops in her own,
Resulting from the scolding or the vision,
　　Implored that present pardon might be shown
For this first fault, and that on no condition
　　(She added in a soft and piteous tone)
Juanna should be taken from her, and
Her future dreams should all be kept in hand.

1 Lola's . . . BM;   Lolah's . . . M   *Mary Shelley's alteration.*
2 in her [eyes]
4 [Beseeched the Governness] *fragment*
6 [Juanna should be taken from her] *fragment*
8a should be kept [under] hand   BM
 b should all be kept in hand   BM, M
 c should be all kept . . .   *In some modern editions.*

83

She promised never more to have a dream,
　　At least to dream so loudly as just now;
She wondered at herself how she could scream—
　　'Twas foolish, nervous, as she must allow,
A fond hallucination, and a theme
　　For laughter—but she felt her spirits low,
And begged they would excuse her; she'd get over
This weakness in a few hours, and recover.

3 *Byron on BM wrote* now herself, *which Mary Shelley on M changed
   to* at herself.
4 'Twas [very foolish, nervous she'de] allow
5 A [fond imagination], and a theme
7–8 And begged . . . she'de [recover]/In a few [hours] *fragment*

And here Juanna kindly interposed,
    And said she felt herself extremely well
Where she then was, as her sound sleep disclosed
    When all around rang like a tocsin bell:
She did not find herself the least disposed
    To quit her gentle partner, and to dwell
Apart from one who had no sin to show
Save that of dreaming once "mal-à-propos."

2   she [found] herself . . .
3–4 Where she then was, [that the disturbance caused
    Not the least inconvenience] *fragment*
    [No trouble to herself] *fragment*
5*a* She did not [feel] herself at all disposed BM
  b She did not find . . . BM; *c* [at all] disposed M
  d   the least . . . M *Byron's re-*
6 [nor] to dwell   *vision.*

85

As thus Juanna spoke, Dudù turned round
    And hid her face within Juanna's breast;
Her neck alone was seen, but that was found
    The colour of a budding rose's crest.
I can't tell why she blushed, nor can expound
    The mystery of this rupture of their rest;
All that I know is, that the facts I state
Are true as truth has ever been of late.

1 As [she sai] thus Juanna . . .
2 within [her partner's] breast
4 [At least·as red as the Flamingo's] Crest
8 Are true as [any Bu] [Metternich] *fragment*

And so good night to them,—or, if you will,
  Good morrow—for the cock had crown,† and light
Began to clothe each Asiatic hill,
  And the mosque crescent struggled into sight
Of the long caravan, which in the chill
  Of dewy dawn wound slowly round each height
That stretches to the stony belt, which girds
Asia, where Kaff looks down upon the Kurds.*

4 And the [pale minaret] struggled . . .
5 Of the [far] Caravan . . .
6 Of [the] dewy . . .
7–8 That stretches [far in]to the [Chain] which Girds
    [The heart of Asia] *fragment*

87

With the first ray, or rather grey of morn,
  Gulbeyaz rose from restlessness; and pale
As Passion rises, with its bosom worn,
  Arrayed herself with mantle, gem, and veil.
The nightingale that sings with the deep thorn,*†
  Which Fable places in her breast of Wail,
Is lighter far of heart and voice than those
Whose headlong passions form their proper woes.*

1 ray [of] or rather . . .
3 it's bosom [torn]
6 in her [bosom] of Wail
7 Is lighter far of heart [than those] *fragment*

[49]

And that's the moral of this composition,
   If people would but see its real drift;—
But *that* they will not do without suspicion,
   Because all gentle readers have the gift
Of closing 'gainst the light their orbs of vision;
   While gentle writers also love to lift
Their voices 'gainst each other, which is natural,
The numbers are too great for them to flatter all.

4   Because [they] all . . .
5   Of [hating those] *fragment*
7a [Their modest voices 'gainst the Bards who]
  b   [all . . .]

89

Rose the Sultana from a bed of splendour,
   Softer than the soft Sybarite's,* who cried
Aloud because his feelings were too tender
   To brook a ruffled rose-leaf by his side,—
So beautiful that art could little mend her,
   Though pale with conflicts between love and pride:—
So agitated was she with her error,
She did not even look into the mirror.

1   The [fair] Sultana from . . .
2   Softer than [even] the . . .
3   Aloud [with] because . . .
4a To brook too thick a rose-leaf [at] his side BM
  b   by . . . BM, M
5   [And] beautiful [she was,] Art could . . .

> Also arose about the self-same time,
>   Perhaps a little later, her great lord,
> Master of thirty kingdoms so sublime,
>   And of a wife by whom he was abhorred;
> A thing of much less import in that clime—
>   At least to those of incomes which afford
> The filling up their whole connubial cargo—
> Than where two wives are under an embargo.

1 Also arose [much] about . . .
3 [And] Master . . .
5 A thing of [no great] import . . .
6 [Where] At least to those of [rich] [who can] afford *Intended to write* riches.
7 The [maintenance of their] connubial cargo
8 Than [here where it is] under an embargo

91

> He did not think much on the matter, nor
>   Indeed on any other: as a man
> He liked to have a handsome paramour
>   At hand, as one may like to have a fan,
> And therefore of Circassians had good store,
>   As an amusement after the Divan;*
> Though an unusual fit of love, or duty,
> Had made him lately bask in his bride's beauty.

4 *Byron on BM wrote* as one may like; *Mary Shelley on M changed this to* as one likes, *and Byron restored his original phrase.*
5 [One two or three—or four or less or more;]
7*a* fit of [Constancy];   *b* fit of [love and beauty]
8 his bride's [eye]

And now he rose; and after due ablutions
    Exacted by the customs of the East,
And prayers and other pious evolutions,
    He drank six cups of coffee at the least,
And then withdrew to hear about the Russians,
    Whose victories had recently increased
In Catherine's reign, whom glory still adores
As greatest of all sovereigns and w—s.

2–3 [Of Oriental Scrupulosity
     He breakfasted and drank] *fragment*
     Byron had used in Canto V, stanza 148, the phrase he deleted here
     in line 2.
  7a [Beneath] Catherine's reign, whom Glory yet adores BM
   b *Mary Shelley on M left a blank space for the last two words of this*
     line and Byron wrote still adores.
  8a Whores BM; *b* w—res M *Mary Shelley again left a blank*
     space for this word, which Byron filled in.

93

But oh, thou grand legitimate Alexander!*
    Her son's son, let not this last phrase offend
Thine ear, if it should reach,—and now rhymes wander
    Almost as far as Petersburgh, and lend
A dreadful impulse to each loud meander
    Of murmuring Liberty's wide waves, which blend
Their roar even with the Baltic's—so you be
Your father's son, 'tis quite enough for me.

1–3 Oh thou [her lawful Grandson] Alexander!
    [Let not the latter quality] offend
    Thine ear [imperial, and just now] rhymes wander
6–7 Of murmuring . . . waves which [bend]
    Their [way even to the Nerea]—so you be

To call men love-begotten, or proclaim
    Their mothers as the antipodes of Timon,*
That hater of mankind, would be a shame,
    A libel, or whate'er you please to rhyme on:
But people's ancestors are history's game;
    And if one lady's slip could leave a crime on
All generations, I should like to know
What pedigree the best would have to show?*

1–2 To call [a man a whoreson]—or [to say
    His] mother [was of that] *fragment*
4 whateer [I] please . . .
5*a* But [a Man's <u>Grand</u>mother is deemed fair game]
 b   [may bear the blame]
6 [For] if one lady's [error cost a crime]
8 What pedigree [we all should] have to show

95

Had Catherine and the Sultan understood
    Their own true interests, which kings rarely know,
Until 'tis taught by lessons rather rude,
    There was a way to end their strife, although
Perhaps precarious, had they but thought good,
    Without the aid of Prince or Plenipo:
She to dismiss her guards and he his harem,
And for their other matters, meet and share 'em.

1 and the Sultan [but have known]
2 kings [neer] know
4*a* There was one way . . . BM
 b   a way . . . M *Mary Shelley's alteration.*
6 [He to dismiss his] *fragment*
7 She to dismiss her [army, and] . . .

But as it was, his Highness·had to hold
    His daily council upon ways and means,
How to encounter with this martial scold,
    This modern Amazon and Queen of Queans;
And the perplexity could not be told
    Of all the Pillars of the state, which leans
Sometimes a little heavy on the backs
Of those who cannot lay on a new tax.

6 Of [Vizier, Mufti]—of the State . . .

97

Meantime Gulbeyaz, when her king was gone,
    Retired into her boudoir, a sweet place*
For love or breakfast; private, pleasing, lone,
    And rich with all contrivances which grace
Those gay recesses:—many a precious stone
    Sparkled along its roof, and many a vase
Of porcelain held in the fettered flowers,
Those captive soothers of a captive's hours.

3 private [precious] lone
7 held in [it's captive] flowers

Mother of pearl, and porphyry, and marble,
  Vied with each other on this costly spot;
And singing birds without were heard to warble;
  And the stained glass which lighted this fair grot
Varied each ray;—but all descriptions garble
  The true effect, and so we had better not
Be too minute; an outline is the best,
A lively reader's fancy does the rest.

2a in this costly [cell] spot   BM;   b in this . . .   M
5a [Let in the Sun]—but all . . .
  b [Checquered] each ray . . .
8 [And] A . . .

99

And here she summoned Baba, and required
  Don Juan at his hands, and information
Of what had past since all the slaves retired,
  And whether he had occupied their station;
If matters had been managed as desired,
  And his disguise with due consideration
Kept up; and above all, the where and how
He had passed the night, was what she wished to know.

No revisions.

Baba, with some embarrassment, replied
  To this long catechism of questions asked
More easily than answered,—that he had tried
  His best to obey in what he had been tasked;
But there seemed something that he wished to hide,
  Which hesitation more betrayed than masqued;—
He scratched his ear, the infallible resource
To which embarrassed people have recourse.

6*a* [With] hesitation . . . masqued   BM
  b Which . . .   BM;   *c* masqued   M
  d mask'd   *In 1833 and in most modern editions.*
7*a* He scratched his ear [which is the great resource]
  b   [the great & true resource]
8   [Of all] embarrassed people *fragment*

101

Gulbeyaz was no model of true patience,
  Nor much disposed to wait in word or deed;
She liked quick answers in all conversations;
  And when she saw him stumbling like a steed
In his replies, she puzzled him for fresh ones;
  And as his speech grew still more broken-kneed,
Her cheek began to flush, her eyes to sparkle,
And her proud brow's blue veins to swell and darkle.

1*a* Gulbeyaz [as we have said was not too patient]
  b   [seen . . .]
6   And as [he floundered on without due speed]
8   And her [bright] brow's . . .

When Baba saw these symptoms, which he knew
   To bode him no great good, he deprecated
Her anger, and beseech'd she'd hear him through—
   He could not help the thing which he related:
Then out it came at length, that to Dudù
   Juan was given in charge, as hath been stated;
But not by Baba's fault, he said, and swore on
The holy camel's hump,* besides the Koran.

2 *Byron on BM wrote* great good; *Mary Shelley on M omitted* great,
   and Byron restored it.
5 that [with] Dudù
6 [Don] Juan . . .
8*a* [(If such should be required of him) the] Koran
 b [(If oaths . . .]
 c The holy Camel's hump [and by] the Koran

103

The chief dame of the Oda, upon whom
   The discipline of the whole harem bore,
As soon as they re-entered their own room,
   For Baba's function stopt short at the door,
Had settled all; nor could he then presume
   (The aforesaid Baba) just then to do more,
Without exciting such suspicion as
Might make the matter still worse than it was.

1 The [Matron] of the Oda [unto] whom
2 Haram [rested]
4*a* stopped BM; *b* stopt M *Mary Shelley's spelling.*
7 [some] suspicion as

He hoped, indeed he thought he could be sure
    Juan had not betrayed himself; in fact
'Twas certain that his conduct had been pure,
    Because a foolish or imprudent act
Would not alone have made him insecure,
    But ended in his being found out, and *sacked*,
And thrown into the sea.*—Thus Baba spoke
Of all save Dudù's dream, which was no joke.

3 his [had] conduct . . .
8 [Of all save Dudu's dream] *fragment*

105

This he discreetly kept in the back ground,
    And talked away, and might have talked till now,
For any further answer that he found,
    So deep an anguish wrung Gulbeyaz' brow;
Her cheek turned ashes, ears rung, brain whirled round
    As if she had received a sudden blow,
And the heart's dew of pain sprang fast and chilly
O'er her fair front, like Morning's on a lily.

4a [For such] an Anguish . . . BM
 b So deep . . . BM; c *Mary Shelley on M wrote* Too deep, *and Byron restored his original word.*
5 Her cheek [grew chill—her] ears rung . . .
7a And [the cold dew] of pain [rose] fast and chilly BM
 b And the heart's dew . . . sprung . . . BM, M
8 [Along her] front, [as Summer's] *fragment*

[58]

Although she was not of the fainting sort,
　　Baba thought she would faint, but there he erred;—
It was but a convulsion, which though short
　　Can never be described; we all have heard,
And some of us have felt thus *"all amort,"**
　　When things beyond the common have occurred;—
Gulbeyaz proved in that brief agony
What she could ne'er express—then how should I?

2　Baba thought She [had fainted,] but he erred
4–5　Can never be described; [though seen, not heard
　　For it is silent] *fragment*
7　Gulbeyaz [felt] in that . . .

　　　　　107

She stood a moment as a Pythoness
　　Stands on her tripod,* agonized, and full
Of Inspiration gathered from Distress,
　　When all the heart-strings like wild horses pull
The heart asunder;—then, as more or less
　　Their speed abated or their strength grew dull,
She sunk down on her seat by slow degrees,
And bowed her throbbing head o'er trembling knees.

1　[like] a Pythoness
2　[Upon] her tripod . . .
3　Of [dreadful *sic?*] inspiration . . .
6　their [wrath] grew dull
7a　She [paused *sic?*] [sank by slow degrees] *fragment*　BM
　b　She sank down . . .　BM
　c　She sunk . . .　M　*Mary Shelley's alteration.*
8a　And [bent] her [burning] head [on] trembling knees　BM
　b　And bowed her throbbing head toward . . .　BM
　c　　　　　　　　　　　　[toward] oer . . .　M　*Byron's re-*
　　　　　　　　　　　　　　　　　　　　　　　　vision.

Her face declined and was unseen; her hair
  Fell in long tresses like the weeping willow,
Sweeping the marble underneath her chair,
  Or rather sofa (for it was all pillow,
A low, soft Ottoman) and black Despair
  Stirred up and down her bosom like a billow,
Which rushes to some shore whose shingles check
Its farther course, but must receive its wreck.

3a [Strewing the marble] underneath . . .
 b [Reaching . . .]
5a–6a A [regular] Ottoman) [and like a billow
    Her bosom undulated] *fragment*
    [Rose and down] *fragment*
 5b A [soft low] Ottoman) [She was Despair]
 6b like a [bosom]
 7a Which [rises, foams, and breaks but not in vain]
  b Which rushes to [the] shore . . .

109

Her head hung down, and her long hair in stooping
  Concealed her features better than a veil;
And one hand o'er the Ottoman lay drooping,
  White, waxen, and as alabaster pale:
Would that I were a painter! to be grouping
  All that a poet drags into detail!
Oh that my words were colours!* but their tints
May serve perhaps as outlines or slight hints.

1–3 Her head hung down [her hair so beautiful
    And long concealed her features, and one hand/Drooped] *fragment*
 4 White, waxen, [stirless] *fragment*
 5a [Oh that] *fragment* BM
  b If I were but a painter, I'de be grouping   BM, M
 6 All that [as a] [b] [bard lengthens to] detail
 7 but [my hints]
 8 *Byron on BM wrote* slight hints; *Mary Shelley on M changed it
   to* faint hints, *and Byron restored his original word.*

Baba, who knew by experience when to talk
   And when to hold its tongue, now held it till
This passion might blow o'er, nor dared to balk
   Gulbeyaz' taciturn or speaking will.
At length she rose up, and began to walk
   Slowly along the room, but silent still,
And her brow cleared, but not her troubled eye;
The Wind was down, but still the Sea ran high.

1   when to [speak]
2a hold his tongue . . . BM, *1833, 1837, and later editions.*
 b hold [his] its tongue . . . M *Byron's revision.*
3   blow [over] . . .
4   Gulbeyaz' [silent or her] speaking will
7a And her brow [cleared so far as to] *fragment*
 b And her brow cleared [but if you read her eye]
8a The Winds were down . . . BM
 b The Wind was . . . M *Mary Shelley's alteration.*

111

She stopt, and raised her head to speak—but paused,
   And then moved on again with rapid pace;
Then slackened it, which is the march most caused
   By deep Emotion:—you may sometimes trace
A feeling in each footstep, as disclosed
   By Sallust in his Catiline,* who, chased
By all the Demons of all Passions, showed
Their work even by the way in which he trode.

1a She stopped and raised her head [as if to speak]
 b   to speak but paused
3   [And] [Then more slowly] *fragment*
5   [its] each footstep . . .
6   chaced BM, M *Since this is Byron's usual spelling, it will not be noted hereafter.*
8   [His] [Thus all] *fragments*

Gulbeyaz stopped and beckoned Baba:—"Slave!
　Bring the two slaves!" she said in a low tone,
But one which Baba did not like to brave,
　And yet he shuddered, and seemed rather prone
To prove reluctant, and begged leave to crave
　(Though he well knew the meaning) to be shown
What slaves her Highness wished to indicate,
For fear of any error, like the late.

6a　(Though he well knew [to whom]) *fragment*　BM
　b　　　　　　　　　her meaning) to be shown　BM, M
7　Highness [mea] wished . . .

113

"The Georgian and her paramour," replied
　The Imperial Bride—and added, "Let the boat
Be ready by the secret portal's side:
　You know the rest." The words stuck in her throat,
Despite her injured love and fiery pride;
　And of this Baba willingly took note,
And begged by every hair of Mahomet's beard
She would revoke the order he had heard.

5a　[And her large eyes] [As if her] *fragments*
　b　Despite her [angry] love . . .

114

"To hear is to obey," he said; "but still,
　Sultana, think upon the consequence:
It is not that I shall not all fulfil
　Your orders, even in their severest sense;
But such precipitation may end ill,
　Even at your own imperative expense:
I do not mean destruction and exposure
In case of any premature disclosure;

1   but [yet]
3   not [at] all fulfill   BM, M
4   *Byron on BM wrote* severest; *Mary Shelley on M wrote* secret, *and Byron restored his original word.*
6a [I do not] *fragment*   BM
 b Even at your own Imperial expence   BM
 c   [imperial] . . .   M
 d   imperative . . .   M   *Byron's revision.*
7   mean [from] destruction . . .

115

"But your own feelings. Even should all the rest
      Be hidden by the rolling waves, which hide
Already many a once love-beaten breast
      Deep in the caverns of the deadly tide—
You love this boyish, new, Seraglio guest,
      And if this violent remedy be tried—
Excuse my freedom, when I here assure you,
That killing him is not the way to cure you."

3 a [fair] love-beaten breast

116

"What dost thou know of love or feeling?—wretch!
      Begone!" she cried, with kindling eyes—"And do
My bidding!" Baba vanished, for to stretch
      His own remonstrance further he well knew
Might end in acting as his own "Jack Ketch";*
      And though he wished extremely to get through
This awkward business without harm to others,
He still preferred his own neck to another's.

1   [Slave!] Wretch!
4   [The Cons] *fragment   Intended to write* Consequence?
7   without [mischief] to others
8   [The parties] *fragment*

[63]

Away he went then upon his commission,
　Growling and grumbling in good Turkish phrase
Against all women of whate'er condition,
　Especially Sultanas and their ways;
Their obstinacy, pride, and indecision,
　Their never knowing their own mind two days,
The trouble that they gave, their Immorality,
Which made him daily bless his own Neutrality.

1 Away he went then [on his expedition]
2 Grumbling [to] in . . .
5 [He also blest his own] *fragment*

And then he called his Brethren to his aid,
　And sent one on a summons to the pair,
That they must instantly be well arrayed,
　And above all be combed even to a hair,
And brought before the Empress, who had made
　Enquiries after them with kindest care:
At which Dudù looked strange, and Juan silly;
But go they must at once, and Will I—Nill I.

1　[in] his aid
4a And above all [well] combed [out] to a hair　BM
　b 　　　　all combed even to . . .　BM
　c 　　　　all be combed [over] to . . .　M
　Mary Shelley's alterations. Byron restored even *and allowed* be to
　remain.
8　But [it was no use] *fragment*

And here I leave them at their preparation
　　For the Imperial presence, wherein whether
Gulbeyaz shewed them both commiseration,
　　Or got rid of the parties altogether,
Like other angry ladies of her nation,—
　　Are things the turning of a hair or feather
May settle; but far be't from me to anticipate
In what way feminine Caprice may dissipate.

2　[and] whether
6　Are [th] things . . .
7a　[Will] settle, [one way or the other] *fragment*
　b　May settle, [but not I] *fragment*

120

I leave them for the present with good wishes,
　　Though doubts of their well doing, to arrange
Another part of History, for the dishes
　　Of this our banquet we must sometimes change,
And trusting Juan may escape the fishes,
　　Although his situation now seems strange,
And scarce secure: as such digressions *are* fair,
The Muse will take a little touch at warfare.

*On the BM first draft below this stanza Byron wrote "End of Canto 6*th*"*
and a date. The month and day are illegible; the year is "1822." On the
M fair copy he wrote only "1822" with his usual signature-symbol.

2–3　Though doubts of their well doing, [and proceed
　　　Upon another potion] *fragment*　Byron's hasty writing of portion.
　6　[And meet us safely in] *fragment*
　7　And scarce secure;—[the Muse] *fragment*

Canto VII

1

OH Love! O Glory! what are ye? who fly
    Around us ever, rarely to alight;
There's not a meteor in the Polar sky*
    Of such transcendant and more fleeting flight.
Chill, and chained to cold earth, we lift on high
    Our eyes in search of either lovely light;
A thousand and a thousand colours they
Assume, then leave us on our freezing way.

For the date of publication see p. 3 of this volume.

All manuscript readings are taken from BM (British Museum manuscript), Byron's original first draft, except those noted as M (Murray manuscript), which is Mary Shelley's fair copy. Wherever there are revisions for any one line on both manuscripts, each reading will be identified. For the treatment of Mary Shelley's copy changes see section 20, in the introduction on editorial practice, pp. xxv–xxvi of Volume II.

1*a* Oh Love! Oh Glory! what are ye! who fly   BM
  b Oh Love! O Glory! what are ye? ...   M   *Mary Shelley's alterations.*
  c O Love! O Glory! what are ye ...   *In 1833 and 1837 editions.*
  d   what are you ...   *In some modern editions.*
4*a* transcendant [and such] fleeting ...   BM
  b   or more ...   BM
  c transcendant and ...   M   *Mary Shelley's alteration.*
5*a* Chill[ed] and chained to [the] earth ...   BM
  b   cold ...   BM
  c Chill[ed] ...   M
8   Assume, [and] leave us [to a frozen day]

[66]

And such as they are, such my present tale is,
   A non-descript and ever varying rhyme,
A versified Aurora Borealis,*
   Which flashes o'er a waste and icy clime.
When we know what all are, we must bewail us,
   But, ne'er the less, I hope it is no crime
To laugh at *all* things—for I wish to know
What after *all*, are *all* things—but a *Show?**

2*a* A nondescript and [ever changing] rhyme   BM
 b   often [changing] . . .   BM
 c   often varying . . .   BM
 d   ever varying . . .   M   *Mary Shelley's alteration.*
3   A [kind of] versified . . .
4   Which [dazzles] oer a waste and [sn] icy clime   *Intended to write*
5   [Now] When . . .   snowy?*

3

They accuse me—*Me*—the present writer of
   The present poem—of—I know not what,—
A tendency to under-rate and scoff
   At human power and virtue,* and all that;*
And this they say in language rather rough.
   Good God! I wonder what they would be at!
I say no more than has been said in Dante's
Verse,* and by Solomon and by Cervantes;

4*a* At human [Strength] and Virtue . . .
 b At human Power[s] . . .
7–8 *Order of composition:*
   I say no more than [what is said by] [in] [Dante's
   Poem—by Solomon and by Cervantes]
   [Also by] Solomon and [by] Cervantes
   I say no more than [many things of Dante's
   Also of] Solomon and [of] Cervantes
   I say no more than has been said in Dante's
                  hath . . .   *In 1833 and in later editions.*
   Verse; and by Solomon and by Cervantes

By Swift, by Machiavel, by Rochefoucault,
   By Fenelon, by Luther, and by Plato;
By Tillotson, and Wesley, and Rousseau,
   Who knew this life was not worth a potato.
'Tis not their fault, nor mine, if this be so—
   For my part, I pretend not to be Cato,
Nor even Diogenes*—We live and die,
But which is best, you know no more than I.

1a [By] Swift, [by] Machiavel, [by] Rochefoucault
  b [Of] ...   [of] ...   [of] ...
2a [By] Fenelon [by] Calvin and [of] Christ BM
  b [Of] ...   [of] ...   [of] ... BM
  c By Fenelon and Calvin and by Plato BM
  d By Fenelon [and] by Luther ... M
     Mary Shelley left a blank space, which Byron filled in with Luther.
3a [Of] Tillotson, [of] Wesley—[of] Rousseau BM
  b And Tillotson ... BM
  c [And] By Tillotson ... M *Byron's revision.*
4   *Mary Shelley on M changed* was *to* is, *and Byron restored his original word.*
5   Tis [their] not their ...
8   But which is [which] you know ...

Socrates said, our only knowledge was
  "To know that nothing could be known";* a pleasant
Science enough, which levels to an ass
  Each Man of Wisdom, future, past, or present.
Newton (that Proverb of the Mind) alas!
  Declared, with all his grand discoveries recent,
That he himself felt only "like a youth
Picking up shells by the great Ocean—Truth."*

4a All [future] Men of Wisdom [like the] present BM
 b All Men . . .   future—past or present BM
 c [All men] Each Man of . . . M *Byron's revision.*
5 Newton [said that] of the Mind . . .
6 his [disc] [great] discoveries . . .
8a "Picking [a pebble on the shore of Truth!"]
 b "Picking [a pebble by the great Ocean Truth!"]
 c   [near . . .]

6

Ecclesiastes said, that all is Vanity*†—
  Most modern preachers say the same, or show it
By their examples of true Christianity;
  In short, all know, or very soon may know it;
And in this scene of all-confessed inanity,
  By saint, by sage, by preacher, and by poet,
Must I restrain me, through the fear of strife,
From holding up the Nothingness of life?

1a [all] is Vanity;   b [everything] is Vanity
4a In [short we do]—or [have] *fragment*
 b In short all know or very soon [shall] know it
6 by Sage—by [Sophist,] Preacher . . .
7a Must I restrain [my vein?—No!—] *fragment* BM
 b *Present text on BM.*
 c *Mary Shelley on M began this line with* But, *which Byron deleted.*
8a [From fools who dread to know the truth] of Life
 b [With those who . . .]
 c [To meditate] the nothingness . . .

Dogs, or Men! (for I flatter you in saying
    That ye are dogs—your betters far)* ye may
Read, or read not, what I am now essaying
    To show ye what ye are in every way.
As little as the Moon stops for the baying
    Of Wolves, will the bright Muse withdraw one ray
From out her skies—then howl your idle wrath!
While she still silvers o'er your gloomy path.

5   *Mary Shelley on M wrote* a man *instead of* the Moon, *and Byron
    restored his original BM words.*
6a–7a Of Wolves, will [I withdraw a single] ray
      [To lighten you on to your tombs] *fragment*
  6b will the bright Muse withdraw [her] one ray
  7b Skies; [h and then] then howl . . .
  8   While [I] still silver oer . . .

8

"Fierce loves and faithless wars"*—I am not sure
    If this be the right reading—'tis no matter;
The fact's about the same, I am secure;
    I sing them both, and am about to batter
A town which did a famous siege endure,
    And was beleaguer'd both by land and water
By Suvaroff,* or anglicè Suwarrow,
Who loved blood as an Alderman loves marrow.*

6 And [perils *sic?* xxxx] beleaguered . . .
7a By [the inimitable *sic?* Suvaroff or] Suwarrow
 b By Suvaroff [alias by] Suwarrow

9

The Fortress is called Ismail,* and is placed
    Upon the Danube's left branch and left bank,*
With buildings in the Oriental taste,
    But still a fortress of the foremost rank,

> Or was at least, unless 'tis since defaced,
>> Which with your conquerors is a common prank:
>> It stands some eighty versts from the high sea,*
>> And measures round of toises thousands three.

2–4   [On the left bank of the left branch]
                         [on] [and upon . . .]
       [Of Danube—and built] *fragment*
       [Of Danube—with some strength but little taste
       Tis built, begirt with battery and trench] BM
  3*b* The buildings . . . BM; *c* [The] With . . . M   *Byron's re-*
  7 It stands [from] [about] some eighty . . .   *vision.*
  8 round in toises . . . BM, M

10

> Within the extent of this fortification*
>> A Borough is comprised along the height
>> Upon the left, which from its loftier station
>> Commands the city, and upon its site
> A Greek had raised around this elevation
>> A quantity of palisades *upright,*
>> So placed as to *impede* the fire of those
>> Who held the place, and to *assist* the foe's.

2   comprized [raised on] a height
4*a* Commands the City;—[as it] *fragment*
 b scite *In 1823 edition.*
5*a* [A] Greek [of great esteem amongst his Nation] BM
 b   [renown . . .] BM
 c A Greek had raised [along] *fragment* BM
 d   [about the] *fragment* BM
 e   around the elevation BM
 f   this . . . M *Mary Shelley's alteration.*
6 [For talent] [All] *fragment*
7*a* [Which circumstance as favouring the] *fragment*
 b   [to] *fragment*
 c [In such a way as to impede the fire]

This circumstance may serve to give a notion
   Of the high talents of this new Vauban:*
But the town ditch below was deep as ocean,
   The rampart higher than you'd wish to hang:
But then there was a great want of precaution,
   (Prithee, excuse this engineering slang)
Nor work advanced, nor covered way was there,*
To hint at least "Here is no thoroughfare."

3 But [neer the less the Ditch] was deep . . .
8 *Mary Shelley on M substituted* This *for* Here, *and Byron restored his
original word.*

12

But a stone bastion, with a narrow gorge,
   And walls as thick as most skulls born as yet;
Two batteries, cap-à-pie, as our St. George,
   Case-mated one, and t'other "a barbette,"*
Of Danube's bank took formidable charge;
   While two and twenty cannon duly set
Rose over the town's right side, in bristling tier,
Forty feet high, upon a cavaliere.*

2 sculls . . . *In 1823 edition.*
3 cap-a-pèe . . .   BM, M, *and 1823 edition.*
4 "a [barbottle] barbette"   M   *Byron corrected Mary Shelley's mistake.*

But from the river the town's open quite,
    Because the Turks could never be persuaded
A Russian vessel e'er would heave in sight;*
    And such their creed was, till they were invaded,
When it grew rather late to set things right.
    But as the Danube could not well be waded,
They looked upon the Muscovite flotilla,
And only shouted, "Alla!" and "Bis Millah!"*

1*a* [The] But from . . . BM
  b Mary Shelley on M wrote upon *instead of* from, *and Byron restored his original word.*
5   to [make] things right
7   [Nor their Flotilla disembark] *fragment*
8*a* "Alla" . . . BM, M;   *b* "Allah" . . . *In 1833 and in later editions. This common variation will not be noted hereafter.*

14

The Russians now were ready to attack;
    But oh, ye Goddesses of war and glory!
How shall I spell the name of each Cossacque
    Who were immortal, could one tell their story?
Alas! what to their memory can lack?
    Achilles' self was not more grim and gory
Than thousands of this new and polished nation,
Whose names want nothing but—pronunciation.

No revisions.

Still I'll record a few, if but to encrease
  Our euphony—there was Strongenoff, and Strokonoff,
Meknop, Serge Lwow, Arseniew of modern Greece;
  And Tschitsshakoff, and Roguenoff, and Chokenoff,*
And others of twelve consonants a-piece;
  And more might be found out, if I could poke enough
Into gazettes; but Fame (capricious strumpet)
It seems, has got an ear as well as trumpet,

1–3a Still I'll record a few—[if for the Sake
    Of] Euphony—there was [Tchitschagoff,] and [Stongenoff]
    [M] Meknop, Serge Lwow, [Arseniew] of modern Greece;
  3b   Lwdw . . . *Misprint in 1823 edition.*
   c   Low, Arsniew . . . *Misprint in 1833 and in*
  4 And Tschitssha[foff] . . .   *some later editions.*
7–8 [Into their Alphabet and persuade poor Fame]
    [Annals and . . .]
    [Who hath an ear—to chant] *fragment*

16

And cannot tune those discords of narration,
  Which may be names at Moscow, into rhyme;
Yet there were several worth commemoration,
  As ere was virgin of a nuptial chime;
Soft words too fitted for the peroration
  Of Londonderry, drawling against time,*
Ending in "ischskin," "ousckin," "iffskchy," "ouski,"
Of whom we can insert but Rousamouski.*

1a And [will not sing their damnable] *fragment*
 b And cannot tune those discords of [damnation]
7a "iffsky" [offsky] "ouski" BM
 b ["iffsky," "ouski"] iffskchy . . . M *Byron's revision.*
8 [Pomitouski] Rousamouski

Scherematoff and Chrematoff, Koklophti
   Koclobski, Kourakin, and Mouskin Pouskin,*
All proper men of weapons, as e'er scoffed high
   Against a foe, or ran a sabre through skin:
Little cared they for Mahomet or Mufti,
   Unless to make their kettle drums a new skin
Out of their hides, if parchment had grown dear,
And no more handy substitute been near.

1 Koklofty   BM, M
3 All [warlike] Men of weapons as eer [sal] *fragment   Intended to*
  write sallied?
5 *Mary Shelley on M substituted* they cared *for* cared they, *and Byron*
  restored his original order.
7 had [been] dear
8 *Mary Shelley on M substituted* was *for* been, *and Byron restored his*
  original word.

18

Then there were foreigners of much renown,
   Of various nations, and all volunteers;
Not fighting for their country or its crown,*
   But wishing to be one day brigadiers;
Also to have the sacking of a town;
   A pleasant thing to young men at their years.
'Mongst them were several Englishmen of pith,
Sixteen called Thomson, and nineteen named Smith.

3 Country [nor the] or it's Crown

Jack Thomson and Bill Thomson;—all the rest
　　Had been called "*Jemmy*," after the great bard;*
I don't know whether they had arms or crest,
　　But such a godfather's as good a card.
Three of the Smiths were Peters; but the best
　　Amongst them all, hard blows to inflict or ward,
Was *he*, since so renowned "in country quarters
At Halifax";* but now he served the Tartars.

3　I don't [exactly know their family] Crest
4　But such a Godfather's [no bad record]
5　[The] Three Smiths were [baptized] *fragment*

20

The rest were Jacks and Gills and Wills and Bills;
　　But when I've added that the elder Jack Smith
Was born in Cumberland among the hills,
　　And that his father was an honest blacksmith,
I've said all *I* know of a name that fills
　　Three lines of the dispatch in taking "Schmacksmith,"
A village of Moldavia's waste, wherein
He fell, immortal in a bulletin.

3a　amongst the hills BM;　b among the hills　M　*Mary Shelley's*
5a　all [that] I know of a name which fills　BM　　*alteration.*
　b　　　　　　　　　　　　that . . .　M　*Mary Shelley's alteration.*

I wonder (although Mars no doubt's a God I
   Praise) if a man's name in a *bulletin*
May make up for a *bullet in* his body?
   I hope this little question is no sin,
Because, though I am but a simple noddy,
   I think one Shakespear puts the same thought*† in
The mouth of some one in his plays so doating,
Which many people pass for wits by quoting.

1a [Now I should like to know being rather curious]
1b–2a [Now I should like to know although] [the] [a God, I
    Admire is Mars] *fragment*
  2b [Sing] if . . .
  7 in his [silly plays]

22

Then there were Frenchmen, gallant, young and gay:
   But I'm too great a patriot to record
Their Gallic names upon a glorious day;
   I'd rather tell ten lies than say a word
Of truth;—such truths are treason; they betray
   Their country; and as traitors are abhorred
Who name the French in English, save to shew
How Peace should make John Bull the Frenchman's foe.

1 Then [Russian] there were Frenchmen . . .
2a But I'me too good a patriot . . . BM
 b But I'm too great . . . M *Mary Shelley's alteration.*
5 Of truth; [which is for] *fragment*
7 Who name the French [except] *fragment*
8a [How H] *fragment*
 b [Peace still] should [find] John Bull a Frenchman's foe
 c *Mary Shelley on M changed* a Frenchman's foe, *which Byron had
  written on BM, to* the Frenchman's foe.

The Russians, having built two batteries on
    An Isle near Ismail, had two ends in view;*
The first was to bombard it, and knock down
    The public buildings, and the private too,
No matter what poor souls might be undone.
    The City's shape suggested this, 'tis true;
Formed like an amphitheatre, each dwelling
Presented a fine mark to throw a shell in.

1   The Russians, [who had] built . . .
5   No matter [how many] poor souls . . .
6   [The project seemed not difficult] tis true
7a   [Because] like an Amphiteatre; [the City]
 b   [Built] like . . .   each dwelling

24

The second object was to profit by
    The moment of the general consternation,*
To attack the Turk's flotilla, which lay nigh
    Extremely tranquil, anchored at its station:
But a third motive was as probably
    To frighten them into capitulation;
A phantasy which sometimes seizes warriors,
Unless they are game as Bull-dogs and Fox-terriers.

2   of the [Turkish] Consternation
4   tranquil [at it's usual] station
7–8 *Order of composition:*
     [A thing which sometimes happens to great warriors]
                         [hath occurred to . . .]
     [Unless they happened to be Game as tarriers]
     [Unless they xxxx are as bulldogs or even terriers]
     A Phantasy which sometimes seizes Warriors
     Unless they are Game as bulldogs or even tarriers BM
                    [as] Game as [Bulldogs or even terriers] M
                         Bulldogs [& Fox] M
                              and Fox-terriers M
                                   Byron's revision.

A habit rather blameable,* which is
   That of despising those we combat with,
Common in many cases, was in this
   The cause of killing Tchitchitzkoff and Smith;
One of the valourous "Smiths" whom we shall miss
   Out of those nineteen who late rhymed to "pith";
But 'tis a name so spread o'er "Sir" and "Madam,"
That one would think the FIRST who bore it "ADAM."

2   those we [fight withal]
3   cases [as] in this
4a The cause of killing [Chrenotoff]—and Smith   BM
 b   Schithenitzhoff . . .   BM
 c   Tchitchitzkoff . . .   M *Byron's revision.*
5a One of the [nineteen] Smiths whom . . .
 b One of the [numerous] . . .
7a But tis a name [so vulgar] [spread] oer "Sir" and "Madam"
 b But tis a name [so common] . . .

26

The Russian batteries were incomplete,*
   Because they were constructed in a hurry;
Thus the same cause which makes a verse want feet,
   And throws a cloud o'er Longman and John Murray,
When the sale of new books is not so fleet
   As they who print them think is necessary,
May likewise put off for a time what story
Sometimes calls "murder," and at others "glory."

3 [And] the . . .
7 May likewise [tend to] put off . . .

Whether it was their engineer's stupidity,
    Their haste, or waste, I neither know nor care,
Or some contractor's personal cupidity,
    Saving his soul by cheating in the ware
Of homicide, but there was no solidity
    In the new batteries erected there;
They either missed, or they were never missed,
And added greatly to the missing list.

3–4 Or [the] some [Contractor's] [miserly] cupidity
    [In] Saving his Soul, by [dealing at lead ware]
              [selling Murder's ware]
  5 Of [Murder] [certes] there was . . .
  6a [Within the] batteries [they] [const] erected [there] [there]
   b In the new batteries [then] erected there

28

A sad miscalculation about distance*
    Made all their naval matters incorrect;
Three fireships lost their amiable existence
    Before they reached a spot to take effect:
The match was lit too soon, and no assistance
    Could remedy this lubberly defect;
They blew up in the middle of the river,
While, though 'twas dawn, the Turks slept fast as ever.

1 A [like] miscalculation . . .
2 [Made] [In naval matters had the same effect]
4 Before they reached [where they] *fragment*
5a [And though as yet the Turks made no resistance]
 b [They lit the match] too soon . . .
6 Could [hinder] this . . .
7 middle of the [st] river. *Intended to write* stream?

At seven they rose,* however, and surveyed
    The Russ flotilla getting under way;
'Twas nine, when still advancing undismayed,
    Within a cable's length their vessels lay
Off Ismail, and commenced a cannonade,
    Which was returned with interest, I may say,
And by a fire of musquetry and grape
And shells and shot of every size and shape.

1a And seven . . . and [behel] surveyed   BM
  b At seven . . .   M   *Mary Shelley's alteration.*
5a [Of the to] *fragment   Probably intended to write* town.
  b Off [the town] and [begun a cannonade]
7a Musquetry . . .   BM, M;   b musketry . . .   *In 1833 and in later editions. In other cantos Byron uses both spellings. This variation will not be noted hereafter.*
8a [And Cannister of] [Cannister] *fragments*
  b And [Round] and Shot . . .

30

For six hours bore they without intermission*
    The Turkish fire, and aided by their own
Land batteries, worked their guns with great precision;
    At length they found mere cannonade alone
By no means would produce the town's submission,
    And made a signal to retreat at one.
One bark blew up, a second near the works
Running aground, was taken by the Turks.

2 and [seconded] by their own
3 with great [decision]
4 [But then] they found [that] Cannonade alone
6 [They sounded the] retreat at One *fragment*
7a One bark blew up, [in action,] a second [ran ashore]
7b–8   [aground/The] *fragment*

The Moslem too had lost both ships and men;
 But when they saw the enemy retire,
Their Delhis* manned some boats, and sailed again
 And galled the Russians with a heavy fire,
And tried to make a landing on the main;
 But here the effect fell short of their desire:
Count Damas drove them back into the water*
Pell mell, and with a whole gazette of slaughter.

1 lost both [men and barks]
3a Their bravest manned . . . BM
 b Their [bravest] Delhis manned . . . M *Byron's revision.*

32

"If" (says the historian here) "I could report*
 All that the Russians did upon this day,
I think that several volumes would fall short,
 And I should still have many things to say";
And so he says no more—but pays his court
 To some distinguished strangers in that fray;
The Prince de Ligne, and Langeron, and Damas,*
Names great as any that the roll of Fame has.

5 [He then] *fragment*

33

This being the case, may show us what fame *is:*
 For out of these three *"preux Chevaliers,"* how
Many of common readers give a guess
 That such existed? (and they may live now
For aught we know). Renown's all hit or miss;
 There's Fortune even in Fame, we must allow.
'Tis true, the Memoirs of the Prince de Ligne*
Have half withdrawn from *him* oblivion's screen.

2 [who] how
3 Many [out of the] readers . . .
5–6 For . . . Renown [is] hit or miss
[And there's a fate] in fame [as all below]

34

But here are men who fought in gallant actions
    As gallantly as ever heroes fought,
But buried in the heap of such transactions
    Their names are rarely found, nor often sought.
Thus even good Fame may suffer sad contractions,
    And is extinguished sooner than she ought:
Of all our modern battles, I will bet
You can't repeat nine names from each Gazette.

5–6 Thus [even the best names] suffer sad contractions
    Thus [even good names] may suffer . . .
    And [are forgotten sooner] than [they] ought
7 Of all our modern [I will not] *fragment*

35

In short, this last attack, though rich in glory,
    Shewed that *somewhere, somehow,* there was a fault,
And Admiral Ribas (known in Russian story)
    Most strongly recommended an assault;
In which he was opposed by young and hoary,
    Which made a long debate; but I must halt,
For if I wrote down every warrior's speech,
I doubt few readers e'er would mount the breach.

No revisions.

There was a man,* if that he was a man,
    Not that his manhood could be called in question,
For had he not been Hercules, his span
    Had been as short in youth as indigestion
Made his last illness, when, all worn and wan,
    He died beneath a tree, as much unblest on
The soil of the green province he had wasted,
As e'er was locust on the land it blasted.

5–7 [The] Made his last illness, when [with scarcely one
    To witness his last hour—a most unblest one]
    He [lay] beneath a tree as much unblest on
    The [grass] of the Green . . .

This was Potemkin—a great thing in days
    When homicide and harlotry made great;
If stars and titles could entail long praise,
    His glory might half equal his estate.
This fellow, being six foot high, could raise
    A kind of phantasy proportionate
In the then Sovereign of the Russian people,
Who measured men as you would do a steeple.

2a When [Stars and Whores and Despots could make] great
  b When Homicide and [Whoredom] made great
3a titles could [inherit] praise BM
  b   entail long praise BM
  c *Mary Shelley on M wrote* can *instead of* could, *and Byron restored his
    original word.*
4 might [be] half . . .
7a [In his immortal Sovereign's] *fragment*
  b [Unto his inches in his Sovereign's eye]
  c In [that] the [great] Sovereign . . .
8 as [if] you . . .

While things were in abeyance, Ribas sent
　　A courier to the Prince,* and he succeeded
In ordering matters after his own bent;
　　I cannot tell the way in which he pleaded,
But shortly he had cause to be content.
　　In the mean time, the batteries proceeded,
And fourscore cannon on the Danube's border
Were briskly fired and answered in due order.

4 in which he [plotted]

39

But on the thirteenth,* when already part
　　Of the troops were embarked, the siege to raise,
A courier on the spur inspired new heart
　　Into all panters for newspaper praise,
As well as dilettanti in war's art,
　　By his dispatches couched in pithy phrase;
Announcing the appointment of that lover of
Battles, to the command, Field Marshal Souvaroff.

2　Of the troops [reimbarked to raise] the siege
4a Into all [aspirants for martial] praise　BM
　b　　　　[lovers of] Newspaper . . .　BM
　c　　　　panters for . . .　BM
　d　　　　[partners of one] newspaper['s] praise　M　*Mary Shelley's*
　e　　　　panters for . . .　M　*Byron's correction.*　*copy change.*
6　*The 1823 edition misprints* praise *for* phrase, *which Byron had on his manuscripts.*
7　Announcing [that without] *fragment*

The letter of the Prince* to the same Marshal
   Was worthy of a Spartan, had the cause
Been one to which a good heart could be partial,
   Defence of freedom, country, or of laws;
But as it was mere lust of power to o'er-arch all
   With its proud brow, it merits slight applause,
Save for its style, which said, all in a trice,
"You will take Ismail at whatever price."

3*a* heart [to] be partial   BM
  b heart could be . . .   BM
  c *Mary Shelley on M substituted* had been *for* could be, *and Byron restored his original words.*

41

"Let there be light! said God, and there was light!"
   "Let there be blood!" says man, and there's a sea!
The fiat of this spoiled child of the Night
   (For Day ne'er saw his merits) could decree
More evil in an hour, than thirty bright
   Summers could renovate, though they should be
Lovely as those which ripened Eden's fruit,
For war cuts up not only branch, but root.

3*a* spoilt . . .   BM;   *b* spoiled . . .   M   *Mary Shelley's spelling.*
6–8 Summers could [re-instate] though they should be
   Lovely as those [that kindled *sic?*] Eden's fruit[s]
   For War not only [levels] branch but root   BM
              cuts up . . . . . BM
   For War cuts up not only branch . . .   M   *Mary Shelley's alteration.*

Our friends the Turks, who with loud "Alla's"* now
  Began to signalize the Russ retreat,
Were damnably mistaken; few are slow
  In thinking that their enemy is beat,
(Or *beaten* if *you* insist on grammar,* though
  I never think about it in a heat)
But here I say the Turks were much mistaken,
Who hating hogs, yet wished to save their bacon.

1*a* with loud "Allahs" [had] now   BM
  b *Mary Shelley on M inserted* their *before* loud, *and Byron deleted it.*
2   [their] the Russ retreat
6   I never think [upon] it [in] a heat
7   But here I say [our friends] were much mistaken

43

For, on the sixteenth, at full gallop, drew
  In sight two horsemen, who were deemed cossacques
For some time, till they came in nearer view.
  They had but little baggage at their backs,
For there were but *three* shirts between the two;
  But on they rode upon two Ukraine hacks,
Till, in approaching, were at length descried
In this plain pair, Suwarrow and his guide.*

2   horsemen [whom they thought] Cossacques
5   [I doubt if] three shirts [were] between the two
6   [And] But . . .
7*a* [But as] [On their approach] *fragments*
  b Till [with their] approaching; were . . .
8   In [these two men] Souwarrow . . .

"Great joy to London now!" says some great fool,
　　When London had a grand illumination,*
Which to that bottle-conjurer, John Bull,
　　Is of all dreams the first hallucination;
So that the streets of coloured lamps are full,
　　That Sage (*said* John) surrenders at discretion
His purse, his soul, his sense, and even his nonsense,
To gratify, like a huge moth, this *one* sense.

1　[in] London . . .
6a　That [fool] John Bull . . .　BM
 b　That Sage John Bull . . .　BM, M
7　his sense[s] . . .

45

'Tis strange that he should further "damn his eyes,"
　　For they are damned; that once all famous oath
Is to the devil now no further prize,
　　Since John has lately lost the use of both.
Debt he calls wealth,* and taxes, Paradise;
　　And Famine, with her gaunt and bony growth,
Which stare him in the face, he won't examine,
Or swears that Ceres hath begotten famine.

1a　[No wonder] that he [often] damn[s] his eyes
 b　'Tis strange that he should further . . .
 c　　　　　　　　　farther . . .　*In 1833 and in later editions.*
3a　Even to the Devil is now no further prize　BM
 b　Is to the Devil now no further prize　M
　　Here Mary Shelley substituted Is *for* Even; *Byron inserted* to.
 c　farther . . .　*In 1833 and in later editions.*
6　boney . .,　BM, M
7a　[Which] [Who] Which . . .
 b　*The 1823 edition misprints* wont. *Both BM and M have* won't.
8　[But] Or . . .

But to the tale;—great joy unto the camp!
  To Russian, Tartar, English, French, Cossacque,
O'er whom Suwarrow shone like a gas lamp,
  Presaging a most luminous attack,
Or like a wisp along the marsh* so damp,
  Which leads beholders on a boggy walk,
He flitted to and fro a dancing Light,
Which all who saw it followed, wrong or right.

2a [Of] To Russian, Tartar[s] . . . Cossacque[s] BM
 b [Of] To Russian[s], Tartar[s], English, French, [Cossacques]
                                      Cossacque[s] M
*The four changes in 2b are Byron's corrections of Mary Shelley's
alterations.*
4 Presaging [an immediate] attack
6 [When all was vapourish in his] boggy walk

                47

But certes matters took a different face;
  There was enthusiasm and much applause,*
The fleet and camp saluted with great grace,
  And all presaged Good Fortune to their cause.
Within a cannon-shot length of the place
  They drew, constructed ladders, repaired flaws
In former works, made new, prepared fascines,
And all kinds of benevolent machines.

3a with [good] grace BM;   b with much . . . BM
 c with [much] great . . . M *Byron's revision.*
4 [The] And . . .
5 [He approached within] *fragment*

'Tis thus the spirit of a single mind
    Makes that of multitudes take one direction,*
As roll the waters to the breathing wind,
    Or roams the herd beneath the bull's protection;
Or as a little dog will lead the blind,
    Or a bell-wether form the flock's connection
By tinkling sounds, when they go forth to victual;
Such is the sway of your great men o'er little.

1 a single [Man]
3 As roll[s] the Water . . .
4 Or [the] roams . . .
7 By tinkling sounds [such is] *fragment*
8 Such is [your] the [sway] of your Great Men [and] little

49

The whole camp rung with joy; you would have thought
    That they were going to a marriage feast:
(This metaphor, I think, holds good as aught,
    Since there is discord after both at least.)
There was not now a luggage boy but sought
    Danger and spoil with ardour much encreased;*
And why? because a little—odd—old man,
Stript to his shirt, was come to lead the van.

4 Since there is [fighting] after . . .
6 Danger [as if a bride, ardour] much increased
7 And [all for why?] *fragment*
8 Cloathed in his shirt . . . BM, M

But so it was; and every preparation
  Was made with all alacrity: the first
Detachment of three columns* took its station,
  And waited but the signal's voice to burst
Upon the foe: the second's ordination
  Was also in three columns, with a thirst
For Glory gaping o'er a sea of slaughter:
The third, in columns two, attacked by water.

1–3 *Order of composition:*
     But so it was—and [all the dispositions] BM
                     [every] BM
                     [preparation solemn] BM
                     every preparation BM
     Were made with [such] alacrity; the first BM
                     all . . . BM
     Was made . . . M *Mary Shelley's correction.*
     [Attack was in three Columns] *fragment* BM
              [was of the three Columns] *fragment* BM
              [composed . . .] *fragment* BM
              [formed . . .] *fragment* BM
  4a And waited but the signal [but] to burst
   b   [given] . . .
   6 Was also in three columns [as was] *fragment*
 7–8 *Order of composition:*
     [For Glory equal to the other two] [three]
                     [to the first, the third
     Was in two columns] *fragment*
     [The third was in two columns] *fragment*
     For Glory [framing a deal of] Slaughter

New batteries were erected,* and was held
 A general council, in which Unanimity,
That stranger to most councils, here prevailed,
 As sometimes happens in a great extremity;
And every difficulty being dispelled,
 Glory began to dawn with due Sublimity,
While Souvaroff, determined to obtain it,
Was teaching his recruits to use the bayonet.*

1*a* New batteries were constructed and [they were held] BM
 b   [then] was [called] held BM
 c   erected ... M *Mary Shelley's alteration.*
2*a* A general Council, [which] in ... BM
 b *Mary Shelley on M wrote* great *instead of* general, *and Byron restored his original word.*
4 [For once by some odd sort of Magnanimity]
5 *Byron had written* dispelled *on BM; Mary Shelley substituted* expelled *on M, and Byron restored his original word.*
6*a* [Things] [qui] [speedily were waxing *sic?* to extremity]
 b [Bellona shook her spear with such Sublimity]
 c [Victory] began to [approach] with due Sublimity
7 [While her beloved Souvaroff] *fragment*
8*a* Was [showing] his recruits to [use] the bay[o]net
 b   bay'net

It is an actual fact, that he, Commander
    In chief, in proper person deigned to drill
The awkward squad, and could afford to squander
    His time, a corporal's duty to fulfil;
Just as you'd break a sucking salamander*
    ·To swallow flame, and never take it ill;
He showed them how to mount a ladder (which
Was not like Jacob's) or to cross a ditch.

1*a*–2 [This] is an actual fact [that He the Chief/In his own] *fragment*
1*b*–2   [that He the Marshal . . .] *fragment*
  3 The awkward Squad, and [deign] *fragment*
  5 Just as [you b] break [in a young] Salamander
  6 To swallow flame, and [neither swerve nor spill]
  8 [Led not to heaven] *fragment*

53

Also he dressed up, for the nonce, fascines
    Like men with turbans, scymitars and dirks,
And made them charge with bayonet these machines
    By way of lesson against actual Turks;*
And when well practised in these mimic scenes,
    He judged them proper to assail the works;
At which your wise men sneered in phrases witty:
He made no answer; but he took the city.

2*a* Like [Turks, and took the bayonet in hand]
  b Scimitars . . . *BM, M, 1833, and later editions. This variant will not be noted hereafter.*
7–8 [For] which your wise men [laughed, but all their Wit is Lost, for his Repartee[s] was taking Cities]

Most things were in this posture on the eve
   Of the assault, and all the camp was in
A stern repose; which you would scarce conceive;
   Yet men, resolved to dash through thick and thin,
Are very silent when they once believe
   That all is settled:—there was little din,
For some were thinking of their home and friends,
And others of themselves and latter ends.

1   [While] things . . .
2   [while all] the Camp was in
3a A [Still] repose which you could . . .   BM
  b A stern . . .   BM
  c A stern repose which you would . . .   M   *Mary Shelley's alteration.*
4   Yet [people ready to] dash . . .
5   they [can] believe
7-8 *First alternative:*
       For some were thinking of their wives and families
       And others of themselves (as [my friend] Samuel is)*
               (as poet Samuel is)
      *The second alternative (same as present text) was selected by Mary
      Shelley as she copied Byron's first draft.*

Suwarrow chiefly was on the alert,
    Surveying, drilling, ordering, jesting, pondering;
For the man was, we safely may assert,
    A thing to wonder at beyond most wondering;
Hero, buffoon, half-demon and half-dirt,*
    Praying, instructing, desolating, plundering;
Now Mars, now Momus;* and when bent to storm
A fortress, Harlequin in uniform.

1 Suwarrow [only] was . . .
4 beyond [all] wondering
5 half [deity and] half dirt
6 Praying, [destroying] desolating . . .
7a [In mind a Mars, a Momus in his] *fragment*
  b Now Mars, now Momus, and [about] *fragment*
  c   when bent [at] to storm

56

The day before the assault, while upon drill,
    For this great Conqueror played the corporal,
Some Cossacques hovering like hawks round a hill,
    Had met a party towards the twilight's fall,
One of whom spoke their tongue or well or ill,
    'Twas much that he was understood at all;
But, whether from his voice, or speech, or manner,
They found that he had fought beneath their banner.

2 Conqueror [was a] Corporal
3 Some Cossacques [soaring] like hawks . . .
5 spoke their [language] . . .
6 [But still enough] [But quite enough] *fragments*

Whereon immediately at his request
    They brought him and his comrades to head quarters;
Their dress was Moslem, but you might have guessed
    That these were merely masquerading Tartars,
And that beneath each Turkish-fashioned vest
    Lurked Christianity; which sometimes barters
Her inward grace for outward show, and makes
It difficult to shun some strange mistakes.

1   at his [desire]
2*a* comrades to [their Chief]
 b   [Hero]
3*a* guest BM; *b* guessed M *Mary Shelley's spelling.*
4*a* [Their Islamism] *fragment*
 b [That but Christianity beneath th] *fragment*
 c That [they] were merely . . .
7   [It's] inward . . .

58

Suwarrow, who was standing in his shirt
    Before a company of Calmucks, drilling,
Exclaiming, fooling, swearing at the inert,
    And lecturing on the noble art of killing,—
For deeming human clay but common dirt,
    This great philosopher was thus instilling
His maxims,* which to martial comprehension
Proved death in battle equal to a pension,—

7 His [military] maxims—[which] to [every] Comprehension

Suwarrow, when he saw this company
  Of Cossacques and their prey, turned round and cast
Upon them his slow brow and piercing eye:—
  "Whence come ye?"—"From Constantinople last,
Captives just now escaped," was the reply.
  "What are ye?"—"What you see us." Briefly past
This dialogue; for he who answered knew
To whom he spoke, and made his words but few.

2   turned round and [bent]
3   his stern brow . . .   BM, M   *The manuscript version seems preferable to the text here.*
5   [Escaped] Captives [escaped was] . . .
8a [To whom he spoke, who] [and] *fragment*
  b [Suwarrow] *fragment*

60

"Your names?"—"Mine's Johnson, and my comrade's
     Juan,
  The other two are women, and the third
Is neither man nor woman." The Chief threw on
  The party a slight glance, then said: "I have heard
Your name before, the second is a new one;
  To bring the other three here was absurd;
But let that pass;—I think I have heard your name
In the Nikolaiew regiment?"—"The same."

All manuscript variants for this stanza are fragments:
4a [The Orator a glance]
  b [A Glance upon the party]
7   But let that pass—I [have heard]
8   [Did]

"You served at Widin?"—"Yes."—"You led the attack?"
   "I did."—"What next?"—"I really hardly know."
"You were the first i' the breach?"—"I was not slack
   At least to follow those who might be so."
"What followed?"—"A shot laid me on my back,
   And I became a prisoner to the foe."—
"You shall have vengeance, for the town surrounded
   Is twice as strong as that where you were wounded.

3*a* first in the . . . BM
  b first [in] i' the . . . M   *Byron's revision?*
7–8 [Well! you shall have revenge and that unbounded
   This town] *fragment*

62

"Where will you serve?"—"Where'er you please."—
   "I know
You like to be the hope of the forlorn,
   And doubtless would be foremost on the foe
After the hardships you've already borne.
   And this young fellow? say what can he do?
He with. the beardless chin and garments torn?"
   "Why, General, if he hath no greater fault
In war than love, he had better lead the assault."

7 [I really do not] *fragment*

"He shall if that he dare." Here Juan bowed
   Low as the compliment deserved. Suwarrow
Continued: "Your old regiment's allowed,
   By special providence, to lead to-morrow,
Or it may be, to-night, the assault; I have vowed
   To several saints, that shortly plough or harrow
Shall pass o'er what was Ismail, and its tusk*
Be unimpeded by the proudest Mosque.

1 [Is it so? and these two women, and the]
2 [As such] Compliment . . .

64

"So now, my lads, for Glory!"—Here he turned
   And drilled away in the most classic Russian,
Until each high, heroic bosom burned
   For cash and conquest, as if from a cushion
A preacher had held forth (who nobly spurned
   All earthly goods save tithes) and bade them push on
To slay the Pagans, who resisted battering
The armies of the Christian Empress Catherine.*

4 For cash and conquest, [beyond all] *fragment*
6 [had] bade them . . .
7 [The Pagan people] who [dared] *fragment*

Johnson, who knew by this long colloquy
    Himself a favourite, ventured to address
Suwarrow, though engaged with accents high
    In his resumed amusement. "I confess
My debt in being thus allowed to die
    Among the foremost; but if you'd express
Explicitly our several posts, my friend
And self would know what duty to attend."

3 [in] accents high

66

"Right! I was busy, and forgot. Why, you
    Will join your former regiment, which should be
Now under arms. Ho! Katskoff, take him to—"
    (Here he called up a Polish orderly)
"His post I mean, the regiment Nikolaiew.
    The stranger stripling may remain with me;
He's a fine boy. The women may be sent
To the other baggage, or to the sick tent."

1–5 Right—I was busy—and forgot, [you'll go
      And] join your regiment, which [is now]
                          [ere this] should be
      [Just] under arms;—[Kerllahousky *sic?* show] *fragment*
      [(Here he called up an orderly)] *fragment*
      [Johnson his post]—the regiment Nikolaiew BM
  3b [ho!] ho! Katskoff—take him to BM
   c [ho!] ho! ... M *Byron's revision.*
   7 He's a fine boy; [and shall be under] *fragment*
   8 [Back] *fragment*

But here a sort of scene began to ensue;
  The ladies,—who by no means had been bred
To be disposed of in a way so new,
  Although their haram education led
Doubtless to that of doctrines the most true,
  Passive obedience,—now raised up the head,
With flashing eyes and starting tears, and flung
Their arms, as hens their wings about their young,

4 *The 1823 edition misprints* haream. *Both BM and M have* haram, *which is also Byron's consistent spelling on the manuscripts of other cantos. The first edition, however, usually prints* harem, *except in Canto I, stanza 87. The spelling of this word throughout the poem varies in later editions.*
5 Doubtless to that [great] doctrine [ever true]   BM
7 and [falling] tears . . .
8 *Byron on BM wrote* athwart their young; *Mary Shelley on M changed this to* about their young.

68

O'er the promoted couple of brave men
  Who were thus honoured by the greatest Chief
That ever peopled hell with heroes slain,
  Or plunged a province or a realm in grief.
Oh, foolish mortals! Always taught in vain!
  Oh, glorious laurel! since for one sole leaf*
Of thine imaginary deathless tree,
Of blood and tears must flow the unebbing sea.

1*a* cuple . . .   BM;   *b* couple . . .   M   *Mary Shelley's spelling.*
7-8   Of . . . deathless [bough
      The unebbing Sea of blood and tears must flow]

Suwarrow, who had small regard for tears,
And not much sympathy for blood, surveyed
The women with their hair about their ears
And natural agonies, with a slight shade
Of feeling; for however habit sears
Men's hearts against whole millions, when their trade
Is butchery, sometimes a single sorrow
Will touch even Heroes,* and such was Suwarrow.

The manuscript variants for the last three lines of the stanza are all fragments.

1 small respect for tears   BM, M
2 for blood, [beheld]
3a These women . . .   BM;   *b* The women . . .   M   *Mary Shelley's*
6 [Our] Men's hearts [for Masses]   *alteration.*
7 Is butchery; [a single Groupe]
8 Will [pierce a heart]

70

He said,—and in the kindest Calmuck tone,*—
"Why, Johnson, what the devil do you mean
By bringing women here? They shall be shown
All the attention possible, and seen
In safety to the waggons, where alone
In fact they can be safe. You should have been
Aware this kind of baggage never thrives;
Save wed a year, I hate recruits with wives."

7 [Aware—that] this . . .
8a [I always hate recruits] *fragment*
 b [Unless] [(Save Wed a year)] *fragments*

"May it please your Excellency," thus replied
   Our British friend, "these are the wives of others,
And not our own. I am too qualified
   By service with my military brothers,
To break the rules by bringing one's own bride
   Into a camp: I know that nought so bothers
The hearts of the heroic on a charge,
As leaving a small family at large.

1 [said] thus replied
3 not [of] our . . .
5 bringing [our] own bride

72

"But these are but two Turkish ladies, who
   With their attendant aided our escape,
And afterwards accompanied us through
   A thousand perils in this dubious shape.
To me this kind of life is not so new;
   To them, poor things, it is an awkward step:
I therefore, if you wish me to fight freely,
Request that they may both be used genteelly."

6a awkward step   BM, M;   b awkward scrape   *In 1833 and in later*
                                                         editions.

Meantime these two poor girls, with swimming eyes,
    Looked on as if in doubt if they could trust
Their own protectors;—nor was their surprise
    Less than their grief (and truly not less just)
To see an old man, rather wild than wise
    In aspect, plainly clad, besmeared with dust,
Stript to his waistcoat, and *that not* too clean,
More feared than all the Sultans ever seen.

2   Looked [as] if . . .
4   (and truly [it was] just)
6*a* In aspect, [plainly covered oer with] *fragment*
 b In aspect, [hardly] clad, besmeared . . .
7   [Without his Coat] *fragment*
8   [As much obeyed] *fragment*

74

For every thing seemed resting on his nod,
    As they could read in all eyes. Now to them
Who were accustomed, as a sort of God,
    To see the Sultan, rich in many a gem,
Like an Imperial Peacock stalk abroad,
    (That royal bird, whose tail's a diadem)
With all the Pomp of Power, it was a doubt
How Power could condescend to do without.

4 rich with many . . .   BM, M
5 [With full] [Conducted] *fragments*
6 [Save that his] *fragment*
7 With all the Pomp of Power, [could not make out]

John Johnson, seeing their extreme dismay,
  Though little versed in feelings Oriental,
Suggested some slight comfort in his way:
  Don Juan, who was much more sentimental,
Swore they should see him by the dawn of day,
  Or that the Russian army should repent all:
And, strange to say, they found some consolation
In this, for females like exaggeration.

2 [Administered] *fragment*

75

And then with tears, and sighs, and some slight kisses,
  They parted for the present, these to await,
According to the artillery's hits or misses,
  What Sages call Chance, Providence, or Fate—
Uncertainty is one of many blisses,
  A mortgage on Humanity's estate—
While their beloved friends began to arm,
To burn a town which never did them harm.

4 What [some] Sages . . .
6 [Entailed up]on Humanity's estate

77

Suwarrow,—who but saw things in the gross,
  Being much too gross to see them in detail,
Who calculated life as so much dross,
  And as the wind a widowed nation's wail,
And cared as little for his army's loss
  (So that their efforts should at length prevail)
As wife and friends did for the boils of Job,*—
What was't to him, to hear two women sob?

4 [So that] as the wind . . .
7 [As did] [did his dear friends for the] *fragment*

Nothing.—The work of Glory still went on
    In preparations for a cannonade
As terrible as that of Ilion,
    If Homer had found mortars ready made;
But now, instead of slaying Priam's son,
    We only can but talk of escalade,
Bombs, drums, guns, bastions, batteries, bayonets, bullets;
Hard words, which stick in the soft Muses' gullets.

7*a* [And bombs and drums, guns guns b] *fragment*
 b   [bastions] *fragment*
 c Bombs, drums, guns, bastions, batteries [bullets] bay'nets, bullets

79

Oh, thou eternal Homer! who couldst charm
    All ears, though long; all ages, though so short,
By merely wielding with poetic arm,
    Arms to which men will never more resort,
Unless gun-powder should be found to harm
    Much less than is the hope of every Court,
Which now is leagued young Freedom to annoy;
But they will not find Liberty a Troy:—

7*a* Which now is [leg] leagued [against Mankind] *fragment*
 b   ['gainst Freedom] *fragment*
 c   young Freedom to [destroy]

80

Oh, thou eternal Homer! I have now
    To paint a siege, wherein more men were slain,
With deadlier engines and a speedier blow,
    Than in thy Greek gazette of that campaign;
And yet, like all men else, I must allow,
    To vie with thee would be about as vain
As for a brook to cope with Ocean's flood;
But still we Moderns equal you in blood;

1   I [am] now
2   To [show] paint a Siege . . .
3*a* With deadlier engines [and as angry brow]   BM
  b   and a [mode less]   BM
  c   quicker blow   BM
  d   [quicker] . . .   M
  e   speedier . . .   M   *Byron's revision.*
4*a* Than [all] thy Greek Gazette [could eer contain]
  b Than in . . .   [may long . . .]
  c   of [the] [each one]
  d   that Campaign
7   As [a brook's stream] to cope with Ocean's flood [shed]
8   in blood [shed]

81

If not in poetry, at least in fact,
    And fact is truth, the grand desideratum!
Of which, howe'er the Muse describes each act,
    There should be ne'ertheless a slight substratum.
But now the town is going to be attacked,
    Great deeds are doing—how shall I relate 'em;
Souls of immortal generals! Phoebus watches
To colour up his rays from your despatches.

  3*a* the Muse [exalts] each act   BM
    b the Muse describes . . .   BM
    c Mary Shelley on M wrote the instead of each, and Byron restored his
      original word.
  5–8*a* [As in a General's letter when well whacked,
      Whatever deeds be done—I will relate 'em
      With some small variations in the list
      Of killed and wounded, who will not be misst] [missed]
    8*b* To [pass *sic?*] his rays . . .

Oh! ye great bulletins of Bonaparte!
  Oh! ye less grand long lists of killed and wounded!
Shade of Leonidas,* who fought so hearty,
  When my poor Greece was once, as now, surrounded!
Oh, Caesar's Commentaries! now impart ye,
  Shadows of glory! (lest I be confounded)
A portion of your fading twilight hues,
So beautiful, so fleeting, to the Muse.

1a Oh! ye grand bulletins of Buonaparte! BM
 b Oh! ye great bulletins of Bonaparte M *Mary Shelley's alteration.*
4 When [Greece] *fragment*

83

When I call "fading" martial immortality,
  I mean, that every age and every year,
And almost every day, in sad reality,
  Some sucking hero is compelled to rear,
Who, when we come to sum up the totality
  Of deeds to human happiness most dear,
Turns out to be a butcher in great business,
Afflicting young folks with a sort of dizziness.

4 hero is [oblige] compelled . . .

84

Medals, ranks, ribbons, lace, embroidery, scarlet,
  Are things immortal to immortal man,
As purple to the Babylonian harlot:*
  An uniform to boys, is like a fan
To women; there is scarce a crimson varlet
  But deems himself the first in Glory's van.
But Glory's Glory; and if you would find
What that is—ask the pig who sees the wind!*

1a Ribbons, [and] Lace . . . BM; *b* ribbons . . . M; *c* ribands *In*

1833 and in later editions. In other cantos Byron uses both spellings. Since the editions are also inconsistent, this variation will not be noted hereafter.

2 [And] Are things [to] immortal . . .
3 [Whose leisure hours are wasted on a harlot]
5 To women; [who] there is . . .
8 *Mary Shelley on M wrote* saw *instead of* sees, *and Byron restored his original word.*

85

At least *he feels it,* and some say he *sees,*
    Because he runs before it like a pig;
Or, if that simple sentence should displease,
    Say that he scuds before it like a brig,
A schooner, or—but it is time to ease
    This Canto, ere my Muse perceives fatigue.
The next shall ring a peal to shake all people,
Like a bob-major from a village steeple.*

1*a* and [you] say he say he sees [it]   BM
 b and some say he say he sees [it]   BM
 c and some say he sees   M   *Mary Shelley on M corrected Byron's mistake on BM.*
3 that [true] simple . . .
4 he [runs] before . . .
5*a* A Schooner—[Cutter or what not] *fragment*
 b A Schooner—or—[but] it is . . .
6 [My] This Canto, eer my Muse [may] *fragment*
8*a* Like a Bob Major [from] from a Steeple
 b   [triple,] . . .

Hark! through the silence of the cold, dull night,
   The hum of armies gathering rank on rank!
Lo! dusky masses steal in dubious sight
   Along the leaguered wall and bristling bank
Of the armed river, while with straggling light
   The stars peep through the vapours dim and dank,
Which curl in curious wreaths—How soon the smoke
Of Hell shall pall them in a deeper cloak!

1   of the [clear] cold . . .
2   gathering [in their] rank[s]
3a And dusky . . . BM; b [And] Lo! . . . M *Byron's revision.*
4   bank[s]
5   while with [quiet] light
6   The Stars peep[ed] through . . . BM, M
7–8a Which curl in curious wreaths;—[the Smoke of Hell
    Shall soon] *fragment*
8b Of Hell shall [wrap] them . . .

Here pause we for the present—as even then
    That awful pause, dividing life from death,
Struck for an instant on the hearts of men,
    Thousands of whom were drawing their last breath!
A moment! and all will be life again!
    The march! the charge! the shouts of either faith!
Hurra! and Allah! and, one moment more,
The Death-cry drowning in the battle's roar.

)n the last page of the BM first draft below this stanza, Byron wrote "End of Canto 7^(th)" and a date, which he deleted. The month seems to be "June." The year, which he rewrote, is "1822"; the signature "NB." On M, the fair copy, only the year "1822" appears, with the usual signature-symbol.

2a The awful pause [which] dividing life from death BM
 b *Mary Shelley on M wrote* and *instead of* from, *and Byron rest℮
     original word.*
3   Struck for a [moment] on . . .
4   were [breathing] their last breath

Canto VIII

1

OH blood and thunder! and oh blood and wounds!
  These are but vulgar oaths, as you may deem,
Too gentle reader! and most shocking sounds:
  And so they are; yet thus is Glory's dream
Unriddled, and as my true Muse expounds
  At present such things, since they are her theme,
So be they her inspirers! Call them Mars,
Bellona, what you will—they mean but wars.

For the date of publication see p. 3 of this volume.

*All manuscript readings are taken from Tx (Texas manuscript),
Byron's original first draft, except those noted as M (Murray manuscript),
which is Mary Shelley's fair copy. Wherever there are revisions for any one
line on both manuscripts, each reading will be identified.*

*On the first page of the Tx first draft above the first stanza is the date
"1822."*

  2   oaths—[no doubt you] deem
  3   Too [vulga] gentle . . .
4a–5 and yet they are Glory's dream/[Expounded] and . . .   TX
  4b yet [they are] thus is . . .   M   *Mary Shelley omitted* and;
      Byron substituted thus is.
  6   [as] they . . .
 8a you please—they mean . . .   TX
  b *Mary Shelley on* M *changed* you please *to* you will *and* mean *to*
     are. *Byron restored only* mean.

All was prepared—the fire, the sword, the men
   To wield them in their terrible array.
The army, like a lion from his den,
   Marched forth with nerve and sinews bent to slay,—
A human Hydra, issuing from its fen
   To breathe destruction on its winding way,
Whose heads were heroes, which cut off in vain
Immediately in others grew again.

3*a* [Each Soldier] like the Lion . . .   TX
  b The Army like the . . .   TX
  c The Army like a . . .   M   *Mary Shelley's alteration.*
4   [Came] forth with nerve and [mind] bent [up] to slay
7   cut off [or slain]

3

History can only take things in the gross;
   But could we know them in detail, perchance
In balancing the profit and the loss,
   War's merit it by no means might enhance,
To waste so much gold for a little dross,
   As hath been done, mere conquest to advance.
The drying up a single tear has more
Of honest fame, than shedding seas of gore.*

1   [Save *sic?*] *fragment*
4*a* War's merit [it could] by no means it might [advance]   TX
  b   Enhance   TX
  c   it by no means might . . .   M   *Mary Shelley's alteration.*
7   up [of] a . . .

And why? because it brings self-approbation;
   Whereas the other, after all its glare,
Shouts, bridges, arches, pensions from a nation,
   Which (it may be) has not much left to spare,
A higher title, or a loftier station,
   Though they may make Corruption gape or stare,
Yet, in the end, except in freedom's battles,
Are nothing but a child of Murder's rattles.

6a Though they make [the whole Earth] gape . . .
  b   may make [the] Corruption gape . . .
7 Yet [it] in the end—[they will not much avail]
8 [They] are . . .

5

And such they are—and such they will be found.
   Not so Leonidas and Washington,*
Whose every battle-field is holy ground,
   Which breathes of nations saved, not worlds undone.
How sweetly on the ear such echoes sound!
   While the mere victor's may appal or stun
The servile and the vain, such names will be
A watchword till the future shall be free.

5a How [different] on the ear [these] such [names will] sound TX
 b *In his revision Byron wrote* echos *on* Tx *, which Mary Shelley on* M
  spelled echoes.
7 names [shall] be
8 [The] Watchword . . .

The night was dark, and the thick mist allowed
  Nought to be seen save the artillery's flame,
Which arched the horizon like a fiery cloud,
  And in the Danube's waters shone the same—
A mirrored Hell! The volleying roar, and loud
  Long booming of each peal on peal, o'ercame
The ear far more than thunder; for Heaven's flashes
Spare, or smite rarely—Man's make millions ashes!

3 Which [girt] the . . .
5 the [Mighty] Roar . . .
7 Heaven's [lightning]
8 Spare[s] or smite[s] rarely,—Man's, make [th] Millions˙Ashes
Intended to write thousands?

        7

The column ordered on the assault* scarce passed
  Beyond the Russian batteries a few toises,
When up the bristling Moslem rose at last,
  Answering the Christian thunders with like voices;
Then one vast fire, air, earth and stream embraced,
  Which rocked as 'twere beneath the mighty noises;
While the whole rampart blazed like Etna, when
The restless Titan hiccups in his den.*

1 the Assault [had now]
2a [Their] Beyond their . . . few [paces] toises   TX
 b   Beyond the . . .   M   *Mary Shelley's alteration.*
3 [Than] [When the Turks] *fragment*
4 [And answered back the] *fragment*
5 Then one vast fire [the] [all heaven as] *fragment*
8 The restless Titan[s struggle] in [their] den

And one enormous shout of "Allah!" rose*
   In the same moment, loud as even the roar
Of War's most mortal engines, to their foes
   Hurling defiance: city, stream, and shore,
Resounded "Allah!" and the clouds which close
   With thick'ning canopy the conflict o'er,
Vibrate to the Eternal name. Hark! through
All sounds it pierceth, "Allah! Allah! Hu!"*

2   loud [as was] the roar
3a [Which the] *fragment*; *b* Of War's [im]mortal Engines . . .
6a [Over the Conflict] *fragment* TX; *b* thickening . . . TX
  c thickning . . . BM *Mary Shelley's alteration.*
7–8 Vibrate [with] the Eternal name!—Hark! [How
    It rolleth—Allah—Allah] *fragment*

9

The columns were in movement* one and all,
   But of the portion which attacked by water,
Thicker than leaves the lives began to fall,
   Though led by Arseniew, that great son of Slaughter,*
As brave as ever faced both bomb and ball.
   "Carnage" (so Wordsworth tells you) "is God's
      daughter":*
If *he* speak truth, she is Christ's sister, and
Just now behaved as in the Holy Land.

1   movement [all and] all—
7a [And here] *fragment*
  b She['s] Christ's [Sister] and

10

The Prince de Ligne was wounded in the knee:*
   Count Chapeau-Bras too had a ball between
His cap and head, which proves the head to be
   Aristocratic as was ever seen,

Because it then received no injury
More than the cap; in fact the ball could mean
No harm unto a right legitimate head:
"Ashes to ashes"—why not lead to lead?

2–3 [The Duke of Richelieu] had a ball between
      [de . . .]
  His [bonnet] and head . . .
  7 harm [to] a . . .

11

Also the General Markow, Brigadier,*
    Insisting on removal of *the Prince*
Amidst some groaning thousands dying near,—
    All common fellows, who might writhe, and wince,
And shriek for water into a deaf ear,—
    The General Markow, who could thus evince
His sympathy for rank, by the same token,
To teach him greater, had his own leg broken.

2 on [the carriage] of the Prince
3 some [thou] groaning . . .
5 [Any call] for water . . .
7 His [pity for] sympathy . . .

12

Three hundred cannon threw up their emetic,*
    And thirty thousand musquets flung their pills
Like hail, to make a bloody diuretic.
    Mortality! thou hast thy monthly bills;
Thy Plagues, thy Famines, thy Physicians, yet tick,
    Like the death-watch,* within our ears the ills
Past, present, and to come;—but all may yield
To the true portrait of one battle-field.

1 Cannon [gave] up . . .
3 Like Hail [by way of causing a slight] *fragment*

There the still varying pangs, which multiply
    Until their very number makes men hard
By the infinities of agony,
    Which meet the gaze, whate'er it may regard—
The groan, the roll in dust, the all-white eye
    Turned back within its socket,—these reward
Your rank and file by thousands, while the rest
May win perhaps a ribbon at the breast!

4a [Until] *fragment*;   b Which [th] meet[s] the Gaze whateer . . .
5   The shriek—the roll in dust . . .   TX, M
6   Turned back [und] within . . .

14

Yet I love Glory;—glory's a great thing;—
    Think what it is to be in your old age
Maintained at the expense of your good king:
    A moderate pension shakes full many a sage,
And heroes are but made for bards to sing,
    Which is still better; thus in verse to wage
Your wars eternally, besides enjoying
Half-pay for life, make mankind worth destroying.

5   [As] And heroes [are expressly made to] *fragment*
8a Half-pay for life—[Ennobles] *fragment*
 b   Makes [the World worth] destroying
 c   Makes Mankind worth . . .

The troops, already disembarked, pushed on
    To take a battery on the right; the others,
Who landed lower down, their landing done,
    Had set to work as briskly as their brothers:
Being grenadiers they mounted one by one,
    Cheerful as children climb the breasts of mothers,
O'er the entrenchment and the palisade,*
Quite orderly, as if upon parade.

2   To [make] a . . .
7a [To make full many Mothers sonless] *fragment*
 b [To make too many Mothers Childless] *fragment*

16

And this was admirable; for so hot
    The fire was, that were red Vesuvius loaded,
Besides its lava, with all sorts of shot
    And shells or hells, it could not more have goaded.
Of officers a third fell on the spot,
    A thing which victory by no means boded
To gentlemen engaged in the assault:
Hounds, when the huntsman tumbles, are at fault.

1a–2a And this was admirable, for [the fire
    Was damnable, Conceive] Vesuvius loaded
1b–2b And this was admirable for so hot
    The fire was that [if you'd] were red Vesuvius loaded
    5 [One third of Officers] fell on the Spot
7a-8 [For when the Huntsman breaks his neck, at fault
    The Hounds stand] *fragment*
   7b To . . . an Assault TX; c the assault M *Mary Shelley's*
                                               alteration.

But here I leave the general concern,
   To track our hero on his path of fame:
He must his laurels separately earn;
   For fifty thousand heroes, name by name,
Though all deserving equally to turn
   A couplet, or an elegy to claim,
Would form a lengthy lexicon of glory,
And what is worse still, a much longer story:

2 To trac[e] our . . .
3 [Men] must [their] laurels . . .
4 For [if] fifty . . .
7 Would form a [long Vocabulary]

18

And therefore we must give the greater number
   To the Gazette—which doubtless fairly dealt
By the deceased, who lie in famous slumber
   In ditches, fields, or wheresoe'er they felt
Their clay for the last time their souls encumber;—
   Thrice happy he whose name has been well spelt
In the despatch: I knew a man whose loss
Was printed *Grove*, although his name was Grose.*

6 *Mary Shelley on M substituted* rightly spelt *for* well spelt, *and Byron restored his original word.*
7 In the [report] I knew . . .
8a <u>Grosse</u> TX; b Grose M *Mary Shelley's alteration.*

19

Juan and Johnson joined a certain corps,
   And fought away with might and main, not knowing
The way which they had never trod before,
   And still less guessing where they might be going;
But on they marched, dead bodies trampling o'er,
   Firing, and thrusting, slashing, sweating, glowing,

But fighting thoughtlessly enough to win,
To their *two* selves, *one* whole bright bulletin.

5 marched, [dead dying] trampling oer
6 Firing, and [hacking,] slashing . . .

20

Thus on they wallowed in the bloody mire
    Of dead and dying thousands,—sometimes gaining
A yard or two of ground, which brought them nigher
    To some odd angle for which all were straining;
At other times, repulsed by the close fire,
    Which really poured as if all Hell were raining,
Instead of Heaven, they stumbled backwards o' er
A wounded comrade, sprawling in his gore.

2 Of [dying thousands] *fragment*
8 [Some] wounded Comrade [swimming] in his gore

21

Though 'twas Don Juan's first of fields, and though
    The nightly muster and the silent march
In the chill dark, when courage does not glow
    So much as under a triumphal arch,
Perhaps might make him shiver, yawn, or throw
    A glance on the dull clouds (as thick as starch,
Which stiffened Heaven) as if he wished for day;—
Yet for all this he did not run away.

2 The [silent] nightly . . .
3a doth not glow TX; b does not glow M *Mary Shelley's alteration.*

Indeed he could not. But what if he had?
There *have been* and *are* heroes who begun
With something not much better or as bad:
Frederick the Great from Molwitz deigned to run,*
For the first and last time; for, like a pad,*
Or hawk, or bride, most mortals after one
Warm bout are broken into their new tricks,
And fight like fiends for pay or politics.

5–7a For the first . . . for [after <u>One</u>
      Warm action, mortals like a dog, or pad,]
      [Are] [br] [Or new bride] are broken in to . . .
  6b Or [dog] or bride; most mortals after one
  7b Warm [field] bout are . . .

23

He was what Erin calls, in her sublime
  Old Erse or Irish, or it may be *Punic*;—
(The Antiquarians who can settle Time,*
  Which settles all things, Roman, Greek or Runic,
Swear that Pat's language sprung from the same clime
  With Hannibal, and wears the Tyrian tunic
Of Dido's alphabet; and this is rational
As any other notion, and not national);—

3   For Antiquarians [whole] who . . .
4   Wh[o settle] all . . .
5a [That] [Insist that Irish] sprang . . .   TX
 b Swear that Pat's language sprang . . .   TX
 c   sprung . . .   M   *Mary Shelley's alteration.*
6a With Hannibal, & [wore the self same]
 b   & wears the [Babel tunic]
7   [With Afric's] Alphabet, [and this can not]
8a and [as] national
 b and [quite] . . .

But Juan was quite "a broth of a boy,"*
   A thing of impulse and a child of song;
Now swimming in the sentiment of joy,
   Or the *sensation** (if that phrase seem wrong)
And afterwards, if he must needs destroy,
   In such good company as always throng
To battles, sieges, and that kind of pleasure,
No less delighted to employ his leisure.

5*a* afterwards . . . TX, M
  b afterward . . . *In 1833 and in later editions.*

25

But always without malice; if he warr'd
   Or loved, it was with what we call "the best
Intentions," which form all mankind's *trump card,*
   To be produced when brought up to the test.
The statesman, hero, harlot, lawyer—ward
   Off each attack, when people are in quest
Of their designs, by saying they *meant well;*
'Tis pity "that such meaning should pave Hell."*

3*a* Intentions" which [are Mankind's] *fragment* TX
  b Intentions" which form all Mankind's . . . TX
  c Mary Shelley on M substituted men's *for* Mankind's, *and Byron restored his original word.*
4*a* [Which] they produce when brought [unto] the test TX
  b That . . .   up to . . . TX
  c Mary Shelley copied the final Tx version on M, and Byron substituted the present text.
6 Off [all] attack[s with] *fragment*
7*a* Mean[t] Well TX; *b* Mean Well TX
  c meant well M *Mary Shelley's alteration.*
8*a* 'Tis pity ["such intentions have] pave[d] Hell" TX
  b 'Tis pity "that such Meanings should pave Hell" TX, M

I almost lately have begun to doubt
    Whether Hell's pavement—if it be *so paved*—
Must not have latterly been quite worn out,
    Not by the numbers Good Intent hath saved,
But by the mass who go below without
    Those antient good intentions, which once shaved
And smoothed the brimstone of that street of Hell
Which bears the greatest likeness to Pall Mall.*

1   I almost [dou] lately . . .
2   so paved [out]
4   the numbers [their] Intent . . .
5*a* But [of] the Mass who go [to Hell] without TX
  b *Mary Shelley copied Byron's Tx deletions on M; Byron then restored on M his Tx substitutions.*
6*a* [A single good intention] which had shaved TX
  b Those antient good intentions which had shaved TX
  c *Mary Shelley copied the original Tx version on M, and Byron substituted the present text.*
7*a* [At least] the [sharp points] of that ["burning Marle"] TX
  b   [sharp stones] . . . TX
  c And smoothed the brimstone of that Street in Hell TX
  d *Mary Shelley on M wrote of Hell.*
8   Which [most may bear a] likeness to Pall Mall

Juan, by some strange chance, which oft divides
  Warrior from warrior in their grim career,
Like chastest wives from constant husbands' sides*
  Just at the close of the first bridal year,
By one of those odd turns of Fortune's tides,
  Was on a sudden rather puzzled here,
When, after a good deal of heavy firing,
He found himself alone, and friends retiring.

1a Juan, [no] *fragment*;   *b* Juan [who] by . . .
2   their [red] grim Career
4   [When on the] *fragment*
6   [Now found himself extremely] puzzled here
7   of [mutual] firing

28

I don't know how the thing occurred—it might
  Be that the greater part were killed or wounded,
And that the rest hàd faced unto the right
  About; a circumstance which has confounded
Caesar himself, who in the very sight
  Of his whole army, which so much abounded
In courage, was obliged to snatch a shield
And rally back his Romans to the field.*

1a I don't how . . . TX
 b I don't know how . . . M *Mary Shelley's addition.*
7a [snat] was compelled to . . . TX
 b   was obliged . . . M *Mary Shelley's alteration.*

Juan, who had no shield to snatch, and was
  No Caesar, but a fine young lad, who fought
He knew not why, arriving at this pass,
  Stopped for a minute, as perhaps he ought
For a much longer time; then, like an ass—
  (Start not, kind reader, since great Homer thought
This simile enough for Ajax,* Juan
Perhaps may find it better than a new one):—

3 why [when] arriving . . .
6 since [old] Homer . . .
8 may [like] it . . .

30

Then, like an ass, he went upon his way,
  And, what was stranger, never looked behind;
But seeing, flashing forward, like the day
  Over the hills, a fire enough to blind
Those who dislike to look upon a fray,
  He stumbled on, to try if he could find
A path to add his own slight arm and forces
To corps, the greater part of which were corses.

5 Those who [don't l] dislike . . .
7a–8a [A path to join the very valiant Corps]
    [A path to reach the remnants of the a] *Intended to write* army?
    [On which] [the] [he trod to] [f] [reach]
                    [join the few before]
  7b [His wa *sic?*] A path to [reach] add his own slight arm[s] . . .
    Intended to write way?
  8b Corpses TX, M

Perceiving then no more the commandant
  Of his own corps, nor even the corps, which had
Quite disappeared—the Gods know how! (I can't
  Account for every thing which may look bad
In history; but we at least may grant
  It was not marvellous that a mere lad,
In search of glory, should look on before,
Nor care a pinch of snuff about his corps) :—

5 In history—) [but no wonder a mere lad]
8a Nor [care a single damn about his] Corps
 b Nor [much dis] *fragment*

32

Perceiving nor commander nor commanded,
  And left at large, like a young heir, to make
His way to—where he knew not—single handed;
  As travellers follow over bog and brake
An "Ignis fatuus"; or as sailors stranded
  Unto the nearest hut themselves betake;
So Juan, following honour and his nose,
Rushed where the thickest fire announced most foes.*

1 Perceiving then Commander . . .
2 like a [yo] [sole] heir . . .
6a [Pursue a] [Cotta] [fisher's cottage light] *fragment*
 b Unto the nearest [hovel their way take]
 c   [shelter . . .]
7 following [Victory] and . . .

First draft of stanza 33 of Canto VIII (Courtesy of the Rare Books Collection of the University of Texas Library. Slightly reduced)

He knew not where he was, nor greatly cared,
    For he was dizzy, busy, and his veins
Filled as with lightning—for his Spirit shared
    The hour, as is the case with lively brains;
And where the hottest fire was seen and heard,
    And the loud cannon pealed his hoarsest strains,
He rushed, while Earth and Air were sadly shaken
By thy humane discovery, Friar Bacon!*

2–8   *Order of composition:*
    For he was dizzy—busy—[with] his [blood
    Lightening along his veins; and where he heard
    The liveliest fire, and saw the fiercest flood]
            [volleys . . .]
    [Of Friar Bacon's bright invention—shared]
            [mild discovery—shared]
    [By Turk and Christian equally, he could
    No longer now resist the attraction of Gunpowder
    But flew to where the pleasant noise grew louder]
           [the] [Mars' Orchestra played . . .]
7b He rushed [where] while . . .

And as he rushed along, it came to pass he
   Fell in with what was late the second column,
Under the orders of the General Lascy,*
   But now reduced, as is a bulky volume
Into an elegant extract (much less massy)
   Of heroism, and took his place with solemn
Air 'midst the rest, who kept their valiant faces
And levelled weapons still against the glacis.*

1 And as he [marched, by it] *fragment*
2 was [once] the . . .
4 But now [abridged a good deal—like a] volume
5–6 Into an elegant [abridgement]
                 extract [of which Class he
Believed himself] *fragment*
7–8 Air midst the rest who[se short breath and long faces
Kept always pushing onwards to the Glacis]

35

Just at this crisis up came Johnson too,
   Who had "retreated," as the phrase is when
Men run away much rather than go through
   Destruction's jaws into the devil's den;
But Johnson was a clever fellow, who
   Knew when and how "to cut and come again,"*
And never ran away, except when running
Was nothing but a valourous kind of cunning.

1a Just at this [time, our friend Johnson] too
 b Just at this crisis [Johnson came up] too
6   [Was well] Knew [how to time] *fragments*
8   a [valiant] kind . . .

And so, when all his corps were dead or dying,
  Except Don Juan,—a mere novice, whose
More virgin valour never dreamt of flying,
  From ignorance of danger, which indues
Its votaries, like Innocence relying
  On its own strength, with careless nerves and thews,—
Johnson retired a little, just to rally
Those who catch cold in "shadows of Death's valley."*

2   Juan [who] a mere . . .
4a [And a] *fragment*;   b From . . . which [Indues]
7   Johnson [retreated only] just to rally
8   Those who [dislike the] "Shadows . . .

37

And there, a little sheltered from the shot,
  Which rained from bastion, battery, parapet,
Rampart, wall, casement, house—for there was not
  In this extensive city, sore beset
By Christian soldiery, a single spot
  Which did not combat like the devil, as yet,—
He found a number of Chasseurs, all scattered
By the resistance of the chase they battered.

1   from the [fire]
7a of number . . .   TX;   b a number . . .   M   *Mary Shelley's*
                                                   alteration.

And these he called on; and, what's strange, they came
    Unto his call, unlike "the Spirits from
The vasty deep,"* to whom you may exclaim,
    Says Hotspur, long ere they will leave their home.
Their reasons were uncertainty, or shame
    At shrinking from a bullet or a bomb,
And that odd impulse, which in wars or creeds
Makes men, like cattle, follow him who leads.

4a Says Shakespeare . . .   TX
 b Says [Shakespeare] Hotspur . . .   M   *Byron's revision.*
5   The reason [partly was their] uncertainty . . .
7a And that [mechanic Impulse] which in wars and creeds   TX
 b And that odd Impulse . . .   TX   c or creeds   M   *Mary*
                                           Shelley's alteration.
8a Make . . .   TX;   b Makes . . .   M   *Mary Shelley's alteration.*

39

By Jove! he was a noble fellow, Johnson,
    And though his name, than Ajax or Achilles
Sounds less harmonious, underneath the sun soon
    We shall not see his likeness:* he could kill his
Man quite as quietly as blows the Monsoon
    Her steady breath (which some months the same
       still is):
Seldom he varied feature, hue, or muscle,
And could be very busy without bustle;

2 name [like] Ajax . . .
3 [Is] less harmonious, [be] underneath . . .   *Intended to write* beneath?
5 Man [with] quite . . .
6 [The] Her . . .
7 [And rarely] varied feature . . .

And therefore, when he ran away, he did so
   Upon reflection, knowing that behind
He would find others who would fain be rid so
   Of idle apprehensions, which like wind
Trouble heroic stomachs. Though their lids so
   Oft are soon closed, all heroes are not blind,
But when they light upon immediate death,
Retire a little, merely to take breath.

1 he did [it]
7 But when [they f] they light . . . *Intended to write* find?

41

But Johnson only ran off, to return
   With many other warriors, as we said,
Unto that rather somewhat misty bourn,*
   Which Hamlet tells us is a pass of dread.
To Jack howe'er this gave but slight concern:
   His soul (like Galvanism upon the dead)*
Acted upon the living as on wire,
And led them back into the heaviest fire.

1 ran [back] to return
6 His [Valour] (like . . .
7 Acted [& made *sic?*] upon . . .
8 And led them [headlong to] the heaviest fire

Egad! they found the second time what they
 The first time thought quite terrible enough
To fly from, malgré all which people say
 Of glory, and all that immortal stuff
Which fills a regiment (besides their pay,
 That daily shilling which makes warriors tough)—
They found on their return the self-same welcome,
Which made some *think*, and others *know*, a *Hell* come.

1*a* E[g]od! they . . . TX; *b* Ecod . . . TX
 c [Ecod] Egad . . . M *Byron's revision.*
3 [From which to fly] *fragment*
4 Of Glory, [Immortality] *fragment*
5 Which [forms] a regiment . . .
7 They found [the second time] the self . . .
8*a* Which make . . . TX
 b Which made . . . M *Mary Shelley's alteration.*

43

They fell as thick as harvests beneath hail,
 Grass before scythes, or corn below the sickle,*
Proving that trite old truth, that life's as frail
 As any other boon for which men stickle.
The Turkish batteries thrashed them like a flail
 Or a good boxer—into a sad pickle
Putting the very bravest, who were knocked
Upon the head, before their guns were cocked.

3 [And proved] *fragment*
6 *The punctuation of the 1823 edition (commas after* boxer *and* pickle)
 was confusing.
7 bravest,—[while the brave]

44

The Turks behind the traverses and flanks
 Of the next bastion, fired away like devils,
And swept, as gales sweep foam away, whole ranks:
 However, Heaven knows how, the Fate who levels

Towns, nations, worlds, in her revolving pranks,
   So ordered it, amidst these sulphury revels,
That Johnson and some few who had not scampered,
Reached the interior talus of the rampart.*

1*a* and [the] flanks   TX
 b *Mary Shelley on M wrote* the flanks *and Byron deleted* the.
2   like [fiends]
3   And swept [awa] [as sweeps the Gale] *fragment*
4*a* Fate which levels   TX
 b *Mary Shelley on M wrote* that levels, *and Byron changed it to* who
    levels.
6*a* that midst these . . .   TX
 b amidst these . . .   M   *Mary Shelley's alteration.*
7*a* Jack Johnson . . .   TX
 b [Jack] That Johnson . . .   M   *Byron's revision.*
8*a* [Had scaled] [Had gained] the interior [talus] . . .
 b [Climbed] . . .

45

First one or two, then five, six, and a dozen
   Came mounting quickly up, for it was now
All neck or nothing, as, like pitch or rosin,
   Flame was showered forth above as well's below,*
So that you scarce could say who best had chosen,
   The gentlemen that were the first to show
Their martial faces on the parapet,
Or those who thought it brave to wait as yet.

3*a* [for] like pitch and rosin   TX
 b as . . .   TX; *c* or rosin   M   *Mary Shelley's alteration.*
4*a* [It rained still flame] above . . .
 b   [down . . .]
5   [had] best had . . .
6   The Gentlemen [who] were
8   Or those who thought it [proudest] [valourous to]   *fragment*

But those who scaled,. found out that their advance
    Was favoured by an accident or blunder.
The Greek or Turkish Cohorn's ignorance*
    Had palisadoed in a way you'd wonder
To see in forts of Netherlands or France—
    (Though these to our Gibraltar must knock under)—
Right in the middle of the parapet
Just named, these palisades were primly set:*

5 To see in [any Christian] fort of Netherlands [of] France
8 were [duly] set

47

So that on either side some nine or ten
    Paces were left, whereon you could contrive
To march; a great convenience to our men,
    At least to all those who were left alive,
Who thus could form a line and fight again;
    And that which further aided them to strive
Was, that they could kick down the palisades,
Which scarcely rose much higher than grass blades.*

5 Who [could] thus could . . .
6 them [was] to strive
8a Which [were but two feet high] *fragment*
 b Which scarcely [were] much higher . . .

48

Among the first,—I will not say the *first,*
    For such precedence upon such occasions
Will oftentimes make deadly quarrels burst
    Out between friends as well as allied nations:
The Briton must be bold who really durst
    Put to such trial John Bull's partial patience,
As say that Wellington at Waterloo
Was beaten,—though the Prussians say so too;—

[136]

4   as [rival] nations
6a [Say Wellington at] *fragment*
 b Put [John Bull's] to such trial John Bull's [slender] patience
8a but the Prussians . . . TX
 b [but] though the . . . M *Byron's revision.*

49

And that if Blücher, Bulow, Gneisenau,*
    And God knows who besides in "au" and "ou,"
Had not come up in time to cast an awe
    Into the hearts of those who fought till now
As tigers combat with an empty craw,
    The Duke of Wellington had ceased to show
His orders, also to receive his pensions,*
Which are the heaviest that our history mentions.

4   Into the [hearts] [brave] hearts . . .
5   As tigers [battle] with . . .
7   His Orders [at the balls] also to receive . . .
8a that History mentions TX
 b that our History . . . M *Byron's revision.*

50

But never mind;—"God save the king!" and kings!
    For if *he* don't, I doubt if *men* will longer—
I think I hear a little bird, who sings
    The people by and bye will be the stronger:
The veriest jade will wince whose harness wrings
    So much into the raw as quite to wrong her
Beyond the rules of posting,*—and the Mob
At last fall sick of imitating Job:*

8a [grows] falls sick . . . TX; *b* falls sick . . . M

At first it grumbles, then it swears, and then,
    Like David, flings smooth pebbles 'gainst a giant;
At last it takes to weapons such as men
    Snatch when despair makes human hearts less pliant.
Then comes "the tug of war";—'twill come again,
    I rather doubt; and I would fain say "fie on't,"
If I had not perceived that Revolution
Alone can save the Earth* from Hell's pollution.

3 takes [up] to . . .
8 save all Earth . . . TX, M

51

52

But to continue;—I say not *the* first,
    But of the first, our little friend Don Juan
Walked o'er the walls of Ismail, as if nurst
    Amidst such scenes—though this was quite a new one
To him, and I should hope to *most*. The thirst
    Of Glory, which so pierces through and through one,
Pervaded him—although a generous creature,
As warm in heart as feminine in feature.

2   Don [Johnny]
5   most:—[accurst *sic?*]
7   [Led him on]—Although [he was the gentlest] Creature
8*a* As [kind] in heart as feminine of feature TX
 b As warm . . . TX; *c* in feature M *Mary Shelley's alteration.*

And here he was—who upon Woman's breast,
　　Even from a child, felt like a child; howe'er
The man in all the rest might be confest,
　　To him it was Elysium to be there;
And he could even withstand that awkward test
　　Which Rousseau points out to the dubious fair,
"Observe your lover when he *leaves* your arms";
But Juan never left them, while they had charms,

2　Even [as] a Child . . .
6a　Which Rousseau [preaches to the] dubious [lover]
　b　Which Rousseau [recommends to . . .]

54

Unless compelled by fate, or wave, or wind,
　　Or near relations, who are much the same.
But *here* he was!—where each tie that can bind
　　Humanity must yield to steel and flame:
And *he* whose very body was all Mind,
　　Flung here by Fate, or Circumstance, which tame
The loftiest, hurried by the time and place,
Dashed on like a spurred blood-horse in a race.

1a　Waves, or Winds　TX
　b　wave[s]—or wind[s]　M　*Byron's revision.*
3a　every [th] tie which binds　TX　*Intended to write* thing?
　b　*Mary Shelley copied the Tx version on M; Byron deleted part of it*
　　and substituted the present text.
5a　And He—whose [Mind was] *fragment*　TX
　b　And He—whose very body was all Mind's　TX
　c　　　　　　　　　　　　　　Mind['s]　M　*Byron's revision.*
6　Flung [th] here—by [lot], or . . .
7　hurried [on] by Time . . .
8　Dashed [like a blood] *fragment*

So was his blood stirred while he found resistance,
  As is the hunter's at the five-bar gate,
Or double post and rail,* where the existence
  Of Britain's youth depends upon their weight,
The lightest being the safest: at a distance
  He hated cruelty, as all men hate
Blood, until heated—and even there his own
At times would curdle o'er some heavy groan.

2 at the [bristling hedge]
3 [The] double . . .
7a even then his own TX
 b even there . . . M *Mary Shelley's alteration.*

56

The General Lascy,* who had been hard prest,
  Seeing arrive an aid so opportune
As were some hundred youngsters all abreast,
  Who came as if just dropped down from the moon,
To Juan, who was nearest him, addressed
  His thanks, and hopes to take the city soon,
Not reckoning him to be a "base Bezonian,"*
(As Pistol calls it) but a young Livonian.*

4a by the moon TX; b from the moon M *Mary Shelley's alteration.*
5 nearest him, [expressed]
7a Not [taking] him [for any] "base . . .
 b   [as . . .]
8 (As Pistol [saith]) but [for] a . . .

Juan, to whom he spoke in German, knew
   As much of German as of Sanscrit, and
In answer made an inclination to
   The General who held him in command;
For seeing one with ribbons, black and blue,
   Stars, medals, and a bloody sword in hand,
Addressing him in tones which seemed to thank,
He recognized an officer of rank.

1 Juan [who] to whom . . .
5a [He saw that he had] ribbands . . .
 b [And] seeing . . .
6 [And] medals . . .
7 [Although he] *fragment*
8 He [thought he was] an Officer . . .

58

Short speeches pass between two men who speak
   No common language; and besides, in time
Of war and taking towns, when many a shriek
   Rings o'er the dialogue, and many a crime
Is perpetrated ere a word can break
   Upon the ear, and sounds of horror chime
In like church bells, with sigh, howl, groan, yell, prayer,
There cannot be much conversation there.

1 between [all those] who speak
4 [Chimes with] the dialogue . . .
7a bells—[the howl—the yell—groan—sigh]—prayer! TX
 b bells—as sigh, howl—groan, yell—prayer! TX
 c bells—[as] with sigh . . . M *Byron's revision.*

And therefore all we have related in
   Two long octaves, passed in a little minute;
But in the same small minute, every sin
   Contrived to get itself comprised within it.
The very cannon, deafened by the din,
   Grew dumb, for you might almost hear a linnet,
As soon as thunder, 'midst the general noise
Of human Nature's agonizing voice!

1   all [who] we . . .
6a Grew also dumb—for you might hear a linnet TX
  b *Mary Shelley copied the Tx version on M and omitted* also.
    Byron did not insert almost *on M.*
7   As soon as [they a] midst . . .

60

The town was entered. Oh Eternity!—
   "God made the country, and man made the town,"
So Cowper says*—and I begin to be
   Of his opinion, when I see cast down
Rome, Babylon, Tyre, Carthage, Nineveh,
   All walls men know, and many never known;
And pondering on the present and the past,
To deem the woods shall be our home at last:—

1   The town was [taken] . . .
2   and [xxxx] man . . .
4   I see [th] cast down *Intended to write* thrown?
6a All walls [we know] and . . .
  b All walls [writ of] . . .
7   And [when] pondering . . .

Of all men, saving Sylla the Man-slayer,*
    Who passes for in life and death most lucky,
Of the great names which in our faces stare,
    The General Boon, back-woodsman of Kentucky,*
Was happiest amongst mortals any where;
    For killing nothing but a bear or buck, he
Enjoyed the lonely vigorous, harmless days
Of his old age in wilds of deepest maze.

1   Of all men [except] Sylla . . .
4   [Was] General Boon . . .
5   [The] happiest [to] [of all] mortals . . .
7a [Passed the long] lonely—vigorous [harmless—Patriarchal]
 b   harmless [years]
8   [Harmless] *fragment*

62

Crime came not near him—she is not the child
    Of Solitude; health shrank not from him—for
Her home is in the rarely-trodden wild,
    Where if men seek her not, and death be more
Their choice than life, forgive them, as beguiled
    By habit to what their own hearts abhor—
In cities caged. The present case in point I
Cite is, that Boon lived hunting up to ninety;*

1   not the [Growth]
3a [She is] [the] [Toil's daughter] *fragment*
 b Her home [was] in . . .
6   hearts [own *sic?*] abhor
7   [Nev] In cities Caged;—the [proof] *fragment*
8   [Press] is that . . .

And what's still stranger, left behind a name
 For which men vainly decimate the throng,
Not only famous, but of that *good* fame,
 Without which Glory's but a tavern song—
Simple, serene, the antipodes of shame,*
 Which hate nor envy e'er could tinge with wrong;
An active hermit, even in age the child
Of Nature, or the Man of Ross* run wild.

2a [That] which Men [often] vainly [seek in throngs]
 b For Which Men [so] . . .
5 Simple—serene—[and quite as free from] *fragment*
6 nor Envy [could not] [sh *sic?*] [tint] with wrong
 Intended to write shade?

'Tis true he shrank from men even of his nation,
 When they built up unto his darling trees,—
He moved some hundred miles off, for a station
 Where there were fewer houses and more ease;
The inconvenience of civilization
 Is, that you neither can be pleased nor please;
But where he met the individual man
He shewed himself as kind as mortal can.

1a shrank from [Men even from] his Nation TX
 b shrank from Crowds even of . . . TX, M
2 [into] his . . .
3a hundred leagues off [till] a Station TX
 b hundred leagues off for . . . TX, M

He was not all alone: around him grew
   A sylvan tribe of children of the chace,
Whose young, unwakened world was ever new,
   Nor sword nor sorrow yet had left a trace
On her unwrinkled brow, nor could you view
   A frown on Nature's or on human face;—
The free-born forest found and kept them free,
And fresh as is a torrent or a tree.

No revisions.

66

And tall and strong and swift of foot were they,
   Beyond the dwarfing city's pale abortions,
Because their thoughts had never been the prey
   Of care or gain: the green woods were their portions;
No sinking Spirits told them they grew grey,
   No Fashion made them apes of her distortions;
Simple they were, not savage; and their rifles,
Though very true, were not yet used for trifles.

6 No Fashion[s] made . . .

67

Motion was in their days, Rest in their slumbers,
   And Cheerfulness the handmaid of their toil;
Nor yet too many nor too few their numbers;
   Corruption could not make their hearts her soil;
The Lust which stings, the Splendour which encumbers,
   With the free foresters divide no spoil;
Serene, not sullen, were the solitudes
Of this unsighing people of the woods.

4 *Byron on Tx wrote* her soil, *which Mary Shelley on M changed to* the
soil. *Byron restored his original word.*
6 [Of] the . . .

So much for Nature:—by way of variety,
  Now back to thy great joys, Civilization!
And the sweet consequence of large society,
  War, Pestilence, the despot's desolation,
The kingly scourge, the Lust of Notoriety,
  The millions slain by soldiers for their ration,
The scenes like Catherine's boudoir at three-score,*
With Ismail's storm to soften it the more.

6 The [thousand Gates of] *fragment*
7 [and] threescore
8 With Ismail's Storm to [yield one] *fragment*

69

The town was entered: first one column made
  Its sanguinary way good—then another;
The reeking bayonet and the flashing blade
  Clashed 'gainst the scymitar, and babe and mother
With distant shrieks were heard Heaven to upbraid;—
  Still closer sulphury clouds began to smother
The breath of Morn and Man, where foot by foot
The maddened Turks their city still dispute.

1 The town was [taken] . . .
3 The [blo] reeking . . . *Intended to write* bloody.
6 [The] Still . . .
7–8 *Order of composition:*
  [The natural air, in wide or narrow streets/Which]
  [The air in every wide or narrow street]
  [The natural air, in . . .]
  [Which] The breath of Morn and Man, [as still dispute]
                              [where . . .]
  [The desperate Moslem]
  [The maddened Turks their City foot by foot]

Koutousow,* he who afterwards beat back
　　(With some assistance from the frost and snow)
Napoleon on his bold and bloody track,
　　It happened was himself beat back just now:
He was a jolly fellow, and could crack
　　His jest alike in face of friend or foe,
Though life, and death, and victory were at stake,
But here it seemed his jokes had ceased to take:

3 Napoleon [from] his . . .
5 He was a [lively Youth then] *fragment*
6 His [Joke] alike in face of friend [and] foe
8 But [now] it . . .

71

For having thrown himself into a ditch,*
　　Followed in haste by various grenadiers,
Whose blood the puddle greatly did enrich,
　　He climbed to' where the parapet appears;
But there his project reached its utmost pitch;
　　('Mongst other deaths the General Ribaupierre's
Was much regretted) for the Moslem Men
Threw them all down into the ditch again.

7 the Mussulmen　TX, M

And had it not been for some stray troops, landing
    They knew not where, being carried by the stream
To some spot, where they lost their understanding,
    And wandered up and down as in a dream,
Until they reached, as day-break was expanding,
    That which a portal to their eyes did seem,—
The great and gay Koutousow might have lain
Where three parts of his column yet remain.*

1 been that some . . .   TX, M
4 in [the] dream
5 Daybreak [seen] was . . .
6 [A Gate somewhat to their eyes Such *sic?*] did seem
7 Koutousow [and] might . . .
8 Where [he] three . . .

73

And scrambling round the rampart, these same troops,
    After the taking of the "Cavalier,"*
Just as Koutousow's most "Forlorn" of "Hopes"*
    Took like camelions some slight tinge of fear,
Opened the gate called "Kilia"* to the groups
    Of baffled heroes who stood shyly near,
Sliding knee-deep in lately frozen mud,
Now thawed into a marsh of human blood.

1*a* But scrambling . . .   TX;   *b* And . . .   M   *Mary Shelley's*
4   [Began to take a little] tinge of Fear   *alteration.*
5–6*a* Opened the Gate called "Kilia,"—[not as Opes
    The Gate of Paradise] *fragment*
6*b* heroes [which] stood [doubting] near
  c   [dubious] . . .
7*a* Sliding [whi] knee deep [in blood of their own companions]
  b   [in blood & frozen mud]
  c   [& mud late frozen]
8*a* [But melted now, by heat] of human blood
  b Now [slippery . . .]

The Kozaks, or if so you please, Cossacques—
   (I don't much pique myself upon orthography,*
So that I do not grossly err in facts,
   Statistics, tactics, politics and geography)—
Having been used to serve on horses' backs,
   And no great dilettanti in topography
Of fortresses, but fighting where it pleases
Their chiefs to order,—were all cut to pieces.*

1a The Kozaks—or [Cossacques—for] *fragment* TX
 b   if you so please—Cossacques TX
 c   if so you . . . M *Mary Shelley's alteration.*
3   not [greatly] err . . .
6a And [no great] dilettanti . . .
 b And [being] no great . . .
7   Of Fortresses, [which they had never seen]

75

Their column, though the Turkish batteries thundered
   Upon them, ne'ertheless had reached the rampart,*
And naturally thought they could have plundered
   The city, without being further hamper'd;
But as it happens to brave men, they blundered—
   The Turks at first pretended to have scampered,
Only to draw them 'twixt two bastion corners,*
From whence they sallied on those Christian scorners.

3   And [having] naturally . . .
4a further hampered TX
 b farther . . . M *Mary Shelley's alteration.*
7–8a [But] only to draw them [b] [in between two] Corners
    [Of bastions—]whence they sallied on these Scorners TX
 b From whence . . . these Christian . . . TX
 c   those . . . M *Mary Shelley's alteration.*

Then being taken by the tail—a taking
  Fatal to bishops* as to soldiers—these
Cossacques were all cut off as day was breaking,
  And found their lives were let at a short lease—
But perished without shivering or shaking,
  Leaving as ladders their heaped carcases,*
O'er which Lieutenant Colonel Yesouskoi
Marched with the brave battalion of Polouzki:—

1–2a Then being . . . tail—a [mode]
   Fatal to warriors as to women . . . TX
  b Fatal to bishops as to soldiers . . . M
   *Mary Shelley apparently refused to copy lines 1 and 2 on M and
   Byron wrote in the present text.*
 3a while day . . . TX; b as day . . . M *Mary Shelley's alteration.*
 6 Leaving [their] as . . .

This valiant man killed all the Turks he met,
  But could not eat them,* being in his turn
Slain by some Mussulmans, who would not yet,
  Without resistance, see their city burn.
The walls were won, but 'twas an even bet
  Which of the armies would have cause to mourn:
'Twas blow for blow, disputing inch by inch,
For one would not retreat, nor t'other flinch.

7a [For] blow for blow [in blood, and] inch . . .
 b [With] . . .
8 The one . . . TX, M

Another column also suffered much:*—
And here we may remark with the Historian,
You should but give few cartridges to such
Troops as are meant to march with greatest glory on:
When matters must be carried by the touch
Of the bright bayonet, and they all should hurry on,
They sometimes, with a hankering for existence,
Keep merely firing at a foolish distance.

No revisions.

79

A junction of the General Meknop's men*
(Without the General, who had fallen some time
Before, being badly seconded just then)
Was made at length with those who dared to climb
The death-disgorging rampart once again;
And though the Turk's resistance was sublime,
They took the bastion, which the Seraskier
Defended at a price extremely dear.

```
 1   [The] Junction . . .
2a   (Without their General who had [been] fallen . . .  TX
 b   (Without the general . . .  M   Mary Shelley's alteration.
 4   [Arrived] at length . . .
5a   The [oft disputed] rampart . . .
 b   The [still . . .]
7–8  [At last] the bastion [which] the Seraskier
     [In person fought] fragment
     [Fought, was] fragment
```

Juan and Johnson, and some volunteers
    Among the foremost, offered him good quarter,
A word which little suits with Seraskiers,
    Or at least suited not this valiant Tartar.
He died, deserving well his country's tears,
    A savage sort of military martyr.
An English naval officer, who wished
To make him prisoner, was also dished:

5 He [pe] died deserving [of] his . . . *Intended to write* perished?

81

For all the answer to his proposition
    Was from a pistol shot that laid him dead;*
On which the rest, without more intermission,
    Began to lay about with steel and lead—
The pious metals most in requisition
    On such occasions: not a single head
Was spared,—three thousand Moslems perished here,*
And sixteen bayonets pierced the Seraskier.

2 shot [which] laid . . .

82

The city's taken*—only part by part—
    And Death is drunk with gore: there's not a street
Where fights not to the last some desperate heart
    For those for whom it soon shall cease to beat.
Here War forgot his own destructive Art
    In more destroying Nature; and the heat
Of Carnage, like the Nile's sun-sodden Slime,*†
Engendered monstrous shapes of every Crime.

1 [and] part by part

A Russian officer, in martial tread
 Over a heap of bodies, felt his heel
Seized fast, as if 'twere by the serpent's head
 Whose fangs Eve taught her human seed to feel:
In vain he kicked, and swore, and writhed, and bled,
 And howled for help as wolves do for a meal—
The teeth still kept their gratifying hold,
As do the subtle snakes described of old.

3 Seized [on a sudden like] *fragment*
4 [Which] Whose fangs Eve [gave all] human seed to feel
6*a* And [called for succour as Wolves] *fragment*
 b And [roared for aid . . .] *fragment*
8*a* As do[th] the subtle Snake's denounced . . . TX
 b   snakes described . . . M *Mary Shelley's*
                  alteration.

84

A dying Moslem, who had felt the foot
 Of a foe o'er him, snatched at it, and bit
The very tendon, which is most acute—
 (That which some ancient Muse or Modern Wit
Named after thee, Achilles) and quite through't
 He made the teeth meet, nor relinquished it
Even with his life—for (but they lie) 'tis said
To the live leg still clung the severed head.

2*a* snatched at it—& [caught]
 b   [seized]
3 The very tendon [which the least may suit]
6 [not] relinquished it

However this may be, 'tis pretty sure
    The Russian officer for life was lamed,
For the Turk's teeth stuck faster than a skewer,
    And left him 'midst the invalid and maimed:
The regimental surgeon could not cure
    His patient, and perhaps was to be blamed
More than the head of the inveterate foe,
Which was cut off, and scarce even then let go.

5 [Perhaps] *fragment*
6 *Byron on Tx wrote* and perhaps was. *Mary Shelley on M wrote* and
was perhaps even. *Byron restored his original phrasing.*

86

But then the fact's a fact—and 'tis the part
    Of a true poet to escape from fiction
Whene'er he can; for there is little art
    In leaving verse more free from the restriction
Of truth than prose, unless to suit the mart
    For what is sometimes called poetic diction,
And that outrageous appetite for lies
Which Satan angles with, for souls, like flies.

1 tis the [duty]
2 Of a [good] poet . . .
3–4a Wheneer he can—for [what can be the beauty
    Of lying sincere *sic?* in verse than prose] *fragment Intended to
    write sincerely?*
4b [Of] leaving . . .
5 [is] unless . . .
8 *Three alternatives on Tx, the last of which is written in the margin:*
    Which most of <u>all</u> doth Man[ki] characterize
    Which Satan <u>angles</u> [there withal]—like flies
                        with for Souls . . .
    The twigs which Satan limes for human flies
    Mary Shelley copied only the present text on M.

The City's taken, but not rendered!—No!
    There's not a Moslem that hath yielded sword:
The blood may gush out, as the Danube's flow
    Rolls by the city wall; but deed nor word
Acknowledge aught of dread of death or foe:
    In vain the yell of victory is roared
By the advancing Muscovite—the groan
Of the last foe is echoed by his own.

2a Moslem who . . .   TX
 b Moslem that . . .   M   *Mary Shelley's alteration.*
3   The Blood [continues] may [stream down] as the Danube's flow
4   Rolls [past] the City . . .

88

The bayonet pierces and the sabre cleaves,
    And human lives are lavished every where,
As the year closing whirls the scarlet leaves
    When the stript forest bows to the bleak air,
And groans; and thus the peopled City grieves,
    Shorn of its best and loveliest, and left bare;
But still it falls with vast and awful splinters,
As Oaks blown down with all their thousand winters.

2-4 And human [breath is poured upon the air]
     As [Autumn winds disperse] the [yellow] leaves
     [And leave] the [Green] Forest . . .
 6   [Stripped] of it's best . . .
 7   But still it falls with [dignity] [might] *fragment*
 8   [Like] As . . .

It is an awful topic—but 'tis not
  My cue for any time to be terrific:
For checquered as is seen our human lot
  With good, and bad, and worse, alike prolific
Of melancholy merriment, to quote
  Too much of one sort would be soporific;*—
Without, or with, offence to friends or foes,
I sketch your world exactly as it goes.

1 awful [subj] topic . . .
2a My Cue for [any long time] *fragment*
  b My Cue for [a long period to be awful]
3a For [that] checquered . . .   TX
  b   checquered . . .   M   *Mary Shelley's spelling.*
  c   checker'd . . .   *In 1833 and in later editions. These varia-*
  tions will not be noted hereafter.
4 [And at its best and worst] alike prolific
5 [Of horrible or ludicrous] to quote
7a and foes TX;   b or foes M   *Mary Shelley's alteration.*

90

And one good action in the midst of crimes
  Is "quite refreshing," in the affected phrase*
Of these ambrosial, Pharisaic times,
  With all their pretty milk-and-water ways,
And may serve therefore to bedew these rhymes.
  A little scorched at present with the blaze
Of conquest and its consequences, which
Make Epic poesy so rare and rich.

2 [as] the affected . . .
3a [Which] Of these [most canting—servile]—Pharisaic times
  b   [our . . .]
4a [Goes when some person condescends to praise]
  b   [pert Pretender deals his . . .]
5 to ["refresh"] these rhymes
8 Make Epic [poet] Poesy . . .

Upon a taken bastion where there lay
   Thousands of slaughtered men, a yet warm group
Of murdered women, who had found their way
   To this vain refuge, made the good heart droop
And shudder;—while, as beautiful as May,
   A female child of ten years* tried to stoop
And hide her little palpitating breast
Amidst the bodies lulled in bloody rest.

5 [To think such thing should be] *fragment*
7 And hide [herself amidst the bodies from]

92

Two villainous Cossacques pursued the child
   With flashing eyes and weapons: matched with them
The rudest brute that roams Siberia's wild
   Has feelings pure and polished as a gem,—
The bear is civilized, the wolf is mild:
   And whom for this at last must we condemn?
Their natures? or their sovereigns, who employ
All arts to teach their subjects to destroy?

2*a* weapons,—[in their eyes]
 b   [with their hearts]
 c   [and] matched with <u>them</u>
6   must [be] we . . .

Their sabres glittered o'er her little head,
  Whence her fair hair rose twining with affright,
Her hidden face was plunged amidst the dead:
  When Juan caught a glimpse of this sad sight,
I shall not say exactly what he *said*,
  Because it might not solace "ears polite";*
But what he *did*, was to lay on their backs,
The readiest way of reasoning with Cossacques.

2 hair [lay] twining . . .
3 [While] Her . . .
5 I [do not know] exactly . . .
6 it [may] not . . .
8 [Some dozen sabre strokes] *fragment*

94

One's hip he slashed,* and split the other's shoulder,
  And drove them with their brutal yells to seek
If there might be chirurgeons who could solder
  The wounds they richly merited, and shriek
Their baffled rage and pain; while waxing colder
  As he turned o'er each pale and gory cheek,
Don Juan raised his little captive from
The heap a moment more had made her tomb.

1 One's [cheek] he slashed, and [sabred t'other's] shoulder
4 The[ir] wounds . . . merited,—[to speak]
5a while turning colder TX
 b while [turning] waxing . . . M *Byron's revision.*
7 raised [the] his . . .
8 [of] a moment . . .

And she was chill as they, and on her face
    A slender streak of blood announced how near*
Her fate had been to that of all her race;
    For the same blow which laid her Mother here,
Had scarred her brow, and left its crimson trace
    As the last link with all she had held dear;
But else unhurt, she opened her large eyes,
And gazed on Juan with a wild surprise.

2 A [little] streak . . .
4 ['Twas] the same . . .
5 [That] scarred . . .
6 last [token] with . . .
7 [And still] [her] [she was unhurt] *fragment*

96

Just at this instant, while their eyes were fixed
    Upon each other, with dilated glance,
In Juan's look, pain, pleasure, hope, fear, mixed
    With joy to save, and dread of some mischance
Unto his protégée; while her's, transfixed
    With infant terrors, glared as from a trance,
A pure, transparent, pale, yet radiant face,
Like to a lighted alabaster vase;*—

1   their. [faces] fixed
3a [And] Juan's [face]—pain,—[pleasure]—hope . . .
 b   [aspect] pain,—[joy] . . .
5   Unto his [infant] protegeè . . .
6   as [in] a trance
7a [Transparent—as an Alabaster Vase]
 b   [pale—pure]
 c A pure—[pal] transparent—pale—[imploring] face
 d   [spiritual] . . .
 e   [and] radiant . . .

Up came John Johnson: (I will not say "*Jack*,"
   For that were vulgar, cold, and common place
On great occasions, such as an attack
   On cities, as hath been the present case):
Up Johnson came, with hundreds at his back,
   Exclaiming:—"Juan! Juan! On, boy! brace
Your arm, and I'll bet Moscow to a dollar,
That you and I will win St. George's collar.*

2 that [is vul] vulgar . . .
3 [like to] an attack
6 [Up]—boy! . . .
7 and I [will] bet [London] to . . .

98

"The Seraskier is knocked upon the head,
   But the stone bastion still remains, wherein
The old Pacha sits among some hundreds dead,
   Smoking his pipe quite calmly 'midst the din
Of our artillery and his own: 'tis said
   Our killed, already piled up to the chin,
Lie round the battery; but still it batters,
And grape in volleys, like a vineyard, scatters.

3 sits [amidst] some . . .
5 and his own—[we have led]
8a And [with each] *fragment* TX
 b And [like a Vineyard—Grape—in volleys scatters] TX
 c *Present text on Tx.*
 d *Mary Shelley on M substituted* patters *for* scatters, *and Byron restored his original word.*

"Then up with me!"—But Juan answered, "Look
   Upon this child—I saved her—must not leave
Her life to chance; but point me out some nook
   Of safety, where she less may shrink and grieve,
And I am with you."—Whereon Johnson took
   A glance around—and shrugged—and twitched his
     sleeve
And black silk neckcloth—and replied, "You're right;
Poor thing! what's to be done? I'm puzzled quite."

1 [quoth] Juan answered . . .
4 may [grieve] shrink . . .
8 done?—[on such a Night]

100

Said Juan—"Whatsoever is to be
   Done, I'll not quit her till she seems secure
Of present life a good deal more than we."—
   Quoth Johnson—"*Neither* will I quite ensure;
But at the least *you* may die gloriously."—
   Juan replied—"At least I will endure
Whate'er is to be borne—but not resign
This child, who is parentless and therefore mine."

1 Said Juan "what[ever is] . . .
2a till I think her sure TX
 b *Mary Shelley copied the Tx version on M; Byron deleted a few*
   words and substituted the present text.
3   than [me]
4a Quoth Johnson—"that I scarcely will ensure TX
 b *Mary Shelley copied the Tx version on M; Byron deleted a few words*
   and substituted the present text.

Johnson said—"Juan, we've no time to lose;
  The child's a pretty child—a very pretty—
I never saw such eyes—but hark! now choose
  Between your fame and feelings, pride and pity;—
Hark! how the roar increases!—no excuse
  Will serve when there is plunder in a city;—
I should be loth to march without you, but,
By God! we'll be too late for the first cut."

4a Betwixt . . . pride or pity TX
 b Between . . . pride and pity M *Mary Shelley's alteration.*
6 [of] a City

102

But Juan was immoveable; until
  Johnson, who really loved him in his way,
Picked out amongst his followers with some skill
  Such as he thought the least given up to prey;
And swearing if the infant came to ill
  That they should all be shot on the next day;
But, if she were delivered safe, and sound,
They should at least have fifty roubles round;

3 Picked out [from out] his . . .
4 Such as he thought [humanest *sic?*] *fragment*
6 by the . . . TX, M
7 [And] if . . .
8a rubles . . . TX; b roubles . . . M

And all allowances besides of plunder
    In fair proportion with their comrades;—then
Juan consented to march on through thunder,
    Which thinned at every step their ranks of men:
And yet the rest rushed eagerly—no wonder,
    For they were heated by the hope of gain,
A thing which happens every where each day—
No Hero trusteth wholly to half-pay.

4 [the] ranks . . .
8 [From] [No Man trusteth wholly to] *fragments*

                104

And such is victory, and such is man!
    At least nine-tenths of what we call so;—God
May have another name for half we scan
    As human beings, or his ways are odd.
But to our subject: a brave Tartar Khan,—
    Or "*Sultan*," as the author (to whose nod
In prose I bend my humble verse)* doth call
This chieftain—somehow would not yield at all:

4   [or] his way [is] odd
6a Or "Sultan" as the [Manuscript whose *sic?*] *fragment*
  b   [volu] *fragment   Intended to write* volume.

But flanked by *five* brave sons (such is Polygamy,
   That she spawns warriors by the score, where none
Are prosecuted for that false crime bigamy)
   He never would believe the city won
While courage clung but to a single twig.—Am I
   Describing Priam's, Peleus', or Jove's son?*
Neither,—but a good, plain, old, temperate man,
Who fought with his five children in the van.*

2 score [and] [while] none

106

To *take* him was the point. The truly brave,
   When they behold the brave oppressed with odds,
Are touched with a desire to shield and save;—
   A mixture of wild beasts and demi-gods
Are they—now furious as the sweeping wave,
   Now moved with pity: even as sometimes nods
The rugged tree unto the summer wind,
Compassion breathes along the savage mind.

1 him—[the] was . . .
2 opprest . . .   TX, M
4 [Now like] Wild . . .
6 Now [touched] with pity . . .
7 The [stately] tree unto the [gentle] wind
8 [A] Compassion breath[ing] along . . .   *This line was written in the margin.*

But he would *not* be *taken,* and replied
    To all the propositions of surrender
By mowing Christians down on every side,
    As obstinate as Swedish Charles at Bender.*
His five brave boys no less the foe defied;
    Whereon the Russian pathos grew less tender,
As being a virtue, like terrestrial patience,
Apt to wear out on trifling provocations.

2 To [every] proposition . . .
5 *Byron on Tx wrote* defied; *Mary Shelley on M wrote* despised, *and*
Byron restored his original word.
6 [At which] the Russian [Pity] grew . . .
7 like [Celestial] Patience

108

And spite of Johnson and of Juan, who
    Expended all their Eastern phraseology
In begging him, for God's sake, just to show
    So much less fight as might form an apology
For *them* in saving such a desperate foe—
    He hewed away, like doctors of theology
When they dispute with sceptics; and with curses
Struck at his friends, as babies beat their nurses.

2*a* Expended all th[y Oriental knowledge]
 b   [phrases]
3–4*a* In begging him for Godsake, [to bring to
    As is the naval mode] *fragment*
 4*b* As much less . . . TX, M
7–8 When they dispute with [Infidels]—and [wounded]
    [Turned] at his friends, as [C] Babies . . . *Intended to write*
                             Children?

Nay, he had wounded, though but slightly, both
  Juan and Johnson; whereupon they fell,
The first with sighs, the second with an oath,
  Upon his angry Sultanship, pell-mell,
And all around were grown exceeding wroth
  At such a pertinacious Infidel,
And poured upon him and his sons like rain,
Which they resisted like a sandy plain

5a extremely wroth TX
  b exceeding wroth M *Mary Shelley's alteration.*
8 [While] they resisted like a [sto] sandy . . . *Intended to write*
   stony?

110

That drinks and still is dry. At last they perished—
  His second son was levelled by a shot;
His third was sabred; and the fourth, most cherished
  Of all the five, on bayonets met his lot;
The fifth, who, by a Christian mother nourished,
  Had been neglected, ill-used, and what not,
Because deformed, yet died all game and bottom,*
To save a sire who blushed that he begot him.

1 [Which] drinks . . .
2 His [old] [youngest] second son . . .
3 His third was [bayoneted, his] fourth . . .
4 five—[was sabred] on bayonets . . .
7a Because [a Hunchback—made his breast the Shield]
  b   [interposed his breast]
  c Because deformed, yet died [with th]
  d   all game and bottom
8 To save a Sire [ashamed] [he] [that he] begot him

The eldest was a true and tameless Tartar,
    As great a scorner of the Nazarene
As ever Mahomet picked out for a martyr,
    Who only saw the black-eyed girls in green,*
Who make the beds of those who won't take quarter
    On Earth, in Paradise; and when once seen,
Those Houris, like all other pretty creatures,
Do just whate'er they please, by dint of features.

1 His eldest [born]—a true and [trusty] Tartar
2a Scorner of the [Christian tribe]
 b   Nazarene[s]
4 [Could] only [see] the black . . .
5a [Who] make . . . TX
 b That make . . . TX
 c Who make . . . M   *Mary Shelley's alteration.*

112

And what they pleased to do with the young Khan
    In heaven, I know not, nor pretend to guess;
But doubtless they prefer a fine young man
    To tough old heroes, and can do no less;
And that's the cause no doubt why, if we scan
    A field of battle's ghastly wilderness,
For one rough, weather-beaten, veteran body,
You'll find ten thousand handsome coxcombs bloody.

1 with [the] Khan
2 know not—[though perhaps I] guess
3 [For] doubtless . . .
4a [In battle to Old Age and Ugliness]
 b To tough . . . do [not] no less
5 And that's the [reason doubtless] *fragment*
6 A Field of [Glory's boney] Wilderness
7 For [one tough] weather-beaten . . .

Your Houris also have a natural pleasure
 In lopping off your lately married men,
Before the bridal Hours have danced their measure,
 And the sad, second moon grows dim again,
Or dull Repentance hath had dreary leisure
 To wish him back a bachelor now and then.
And thus your Houri (it may be) disputes
Of these brief blossoms the immediate fruits.*

4 Moon [begins to lower]
5 [And] dull . . .
6a bachelor . . . TX; b batchelor . . . M
7a [And] And thus your Houri [(who can tell?) it suits] TX
 b *Present text on Tx.*
 c *Mary Shelley on M wrote* the young Houri, *and Byron restored his original words.*
8 Of these brief blossoms [to] [parta] [promote the] fruits

114

Thus the young Khan, with Houris in his sight,
 Thought not upon the charms of four young brides,
But bravely rushed on his first heavenly night.
 In short, howe'er *our* better Faith derides,
These black-eyed virgins make the Moslems fight,
 As though there were one Heaven and none besides—
Whereas, if all be true we hear of Heaven
And Hell, there must at least be six or seven.

3 But [rather prest] on . . .
5a These black-eyed Visions make your Moslem fight TX
 b *Mary Shelley on M wrote the present text; Byron did not correct her alteration of his original phrasing.*
6 were [a] Heaven

So fully flashed the phantom on his eyes,
    That when the very lance was in his heart,
He shouted "Allah!" and saw Paradise
    With all its veil of mystery drawn apart,
And bright Eternity without disguise
    On his soul, like a ceaseless sunrise, dart;—
With Prophets, Houris, Angels, Saints, descried
In one voluptuous blaze,—and then he died:

4 Veil of [tears] Mystery . . .
5 [The Beauty of all Creation] *fragment*
6a [Upon his Spirit like] *fragment*
  b On his Soul like [an] a . . .
7 With Prophets—[Saints]—Houris . . .
8 [In] [Like] In one [immortal Glance]; and . . .

116

But, with a heavenly rapture on his face,
    The good old Khan, who long had ceased to see
Houris, or aught except his florid race
    Who grew like Cedars round him gloriously—
When he beheld his latest hero grace
    The earth, which he became like a felled tree,
Paused for a moment from the fight, and cast
A glance on that slain son, his first and last.

2 The [poor] old Khan . . .
4 round him [happily]
5 When he beheld [the] his [last young] hero grace
6 The Earth [on] which he became [with dignity]

[169]

The soldiers, who beheld him drop his point,
  Stopped as if once more willing to concede
Quarter, in case he bade them not "aroint!"*
  As he before had done. He did not heed
Their pause nor signs: his heart was out of joint,
  And shook (till now unshaken) like a reed,
As he looked down upon his children gone,*
And felt—though done with life—he was alone.

2a [Advanced as] willing once more . . . TX
 b Stopped as if willing . . . TX
 c Stopt as if once more willing . . . M *Mary Shelley's alteration.*
3a aroint TX, M; b aroynt *In 1833 and in later editions.*
The manuscript variants for lines 5 and 8 are all fragmentary.
5   Their [gesture or their pause]
8a And felt, [that he must]
 b And felt, though done with life—he [was]
 c   [lived]

118

But 'twas a transient tremor;—with a spring
  Upon the Russian steel his breast he flung,
As carelessly as hurls the moth her wing
  Against the light wherein she dies: he clung
Closer, that all the deadlier they might wring,
  Unto the bayonets which had pierced his young;
And throwing back a dim look on his sons,
In one wide wound poured forth his soul at once.

2–3a [He dashed himself upon his foes &] flung
      [His breast, as doth the Moth] *fragment*
              [hurls . . .] *fragment*
 3b As [hurls the] [hu] carelessly . . .
 5a Closer as twere—however they might wring TX
  b *Mary Shelley copied the Tx version on M; Byron deleted it and
    substituted the present text.*
 7   back [one] dim . . .

'Tis strange enough—the rough, tough soldiers, who
    Spared neither sex nor age in their career
Of carnage, when this old man was pierced through,
    And lay before them with his children near,
Touched by the heroism of him they slew,
    Were melted for a moment; though no tear
Flowed from their blood-shot eyes, all red with strife,
They honoured such determined scorn of life.

7 their [fiery] eyes . . .

120

But the stone bastion still kept up its fire,*
    Where the chief Pacha calmly held his post:
Some twenty times he made the Russ retire,
    And baffled the assaults of all their host;
At length he condescended to enquire
    If yet the city's rest were won or lost;
And being told the latter, sent a Bey
To answer Ribas' summons to give way.

2   calmly [kept] his post
4   the [best] assaults . . .
6   If [the rest of the town] were won or lost
8a [To treat] *fragment*
 b [In] answer [to a] Summons [sent] to give way

In the mean time, cross-legged, with great sang froid,*
    Among the scorching ruins he sat smoking
Tobacco on a little carpet;—Troy
    Saw nothing like the scene around;—yet looking
With martial stoicism, nought seemed to annoy
    His stern philosophy; but gently stroking
His beard, he puffed his pipe's ambrosial gales,
As if he had three lives as well as tails.*

1a In the meantime, [cross-legged on the remains]
 b   [one] cross-legged with . . .
2 [Upon] the scorching . . .
3 [His pipe upon] a little carpet . . .
4 Saw nothing like the Scene [around him] *fragment*
5 With martial Stoicism, [now gently strokin]
6 [now] gently . . .
7 puffed [the] his . . .

122

The town was taken—whether he might yield
    Himself or bastion, little mattered now;
His stubborn valour was no future shield.
    Ismail's no more! The crescent's silver bow
Sunk, and the crimson cross glared o'er the field,
    But red with no *redeeming* gore: the glow
Of burning streets, like moonlight on the water,
Was imaged back in blood, the sea of slaughter.

2 [did not] little mattered now
3 no further shield TX, M
5a [Yields to the] *fragment*
 b [Shrink to the] *fragment*
 c [Sinks] and the [bloody] Cross . . .
6a [bl] gore . . . TX
 b *Mary Shelley on M wrote* blood *instead of* gore, *and Byron re-stored his original word.*

7–8   *Order of composition on Tx:*
       Of burning [Streets, the groan of] [bravest] [bravest men]
                           [groans . . .]
                   [and flow of ceaseless Slaughter]
       [Mirrored the Christian Flags—like] [like Moonlight]
                           [and] [as Moonbeams on the water]
       [Was imaged back in blood—the Sea of Slaughter]
       Of burning Cities, those full Moons of Slaughter
       Was imaged back in blood instead of Water
       *A marginal alternative gives the present text, which also appears on
       M.*

123

       All that the mind would shrink from of excesses;*
           All that the body perpetrates of bad;
       All that we read, hear, dream of man's distresses;
           All that the Devil would do if run stark mad;
       All that defies the worst which pen expresses;
           All by which Hell is peopled, or as sad
       As Hell—mere mortals who their power abuse,—
       Was here (as heretofore and since) let loose.

2   *Byron on Tx wrote* All that; *Mary Shelley on M wrote* And that,
     and Byron restored his original word.
3a   All that [the] we hear [or] read—dream . . .   TX
 b   we read, hear, dream . . .   *Mary Shelley's alteration.*
6a   All with [Evil in her] *fragment* TX
 b   All with which Hell is peopled or [less] sad   TX
 c   more sad   TX, M
7a   Than Hell—[when] Mortals [can] their power abuse   TX
 b   Than Hell—mere Mortals who . . .   TX, M
8   Was [heret] here . . .   *Intended to write* heretofore.

If here and there some transient trait of pity
    Was shown, and some more noble heart broke through
Its bloody bond, and saved perhaps some pretty
    Child, or an aged, helpless man or two—
What's this in one annihilated city,
    Where thousand loves, and ties, and duties grow?
Cockneys of London! Muscadins of Paris!*
Just ponder what a pious pastime war is:

3 [It] [The] It's bloody . . .
5 [amidst] one . . .
7a [Where fifty] *fragment*
 b [You Citizens] of London! [and] of Paris!
8a [Think—shall good reader] *fragment*
 b [Would you do less "pro focis et pro aris"]

Think how the joys of reading a Gazette
    Are purchased by all agonies and crimes:
Or if these do not move you, don't forget
    Such doom may be your own in after times.
Meantime the taxes, Castlereagh, and debt,*
    Are hints as good as sermons, or as rhymes.
Read your own hearts and Ireland's present story,
Then feed her famine fat with Wellesley's glory.*

4 [What] doom . . .
7 Read [England's too your] *fragment*

But still there is unto a patriot nation,
　　Which loves so well its country and its King,
A subject of sublimest exultation—
　　Bear it, ye Muses, on your brightest wing!
Howe'er the mighty locust, Desolation,
　　Strip your green fields, and to your harvests cling,
Gaunt Famine never shall approach the throne—
Though Ireland starve, great George weighs twenty
　　　stone.*

1a–2　Yet still there is a patriot [Consolation
　　　　For those who love their] Country and [their] King　TX
　　1b　*Present text on Tx except for* Yet still, *which Mary Shelley on M
　　　　altered to* But still.
　　3　A Subject of [complete congratulation]
　　4　Muses [with] on . . .
　　5　Howeer [Destruction may] *fragment*
　　8　weighs forty stone　TX, M

But let me put an end unto my theme:
　　There was an end of Ismail—hapless town!
Far flashed her burning towers o'er Danube's stream,
　　And redly ran his blushing waters down.
The horrid war-whoop and the shriller scream
　　Rose still; but fainter were the thunders grown:
Of forty thousand who had manned the wall,
Some hundreds breathed—the rest were silent all!*

　　3　[Red ran the wide and rapid Danub] *fragment*
　　5　[War-hoop] War-whoop . . .　TX, M
　　7a　[For six and thirty thousand brave defenders]　TX
　　　b　Of forty . . . her wall　TX
　　　c　　　　　　　the wall　M　*Mary Shelley's alteration.*

In one thing ne'ertheless 'tis fit to praise
   The Russian army upon this occasion,
A virtue much in fashion now-a-days,
   And therefore worthy of commemoration:
The topic's tender, so shall be my phrase—
   Perhaps the season's chill, and their long station
In winter's depth, or want of rest and victual,
Had made them chaste;—they ravished very little.

1 [I know] *fragment*
3 [As being a] Virtue . . .
4 worthy of [my] [a peroration]
6 [Whether] the Season's . . .

129

Much did they slay, more plunder, and no less
   Might here and there occur some violation
In the other line;—but not to such excess
   As when the French, that dissipated nation,
Take towns by storm: no causes can I guess,
   Except cold weather and commiseration;
But all the ladies, save some twenty score,
Were almost as much virgins as before.

1   and no [doubt]
2   [That] here and there occurr[ed] [a] some viol[ence]
3   not to [that] excess
5   [the] cause [I cannot] guess
6   [I hardly think it was] commiseration
7   some [fifty] score
8*a* [Were as much Virgins as they were] before
 b [Lived . . .]
 c [Were . . .]

Some odd mistakes too happened in the dark,
      Which showed a want of lanthorns, or of taste—
Indeed the smoke was such they scarce could mark
      Their friends from foes,—besides such things from
         haste
Occur, though rarely, when there is a spark
      Of light to save the venerably chaste:—
But six old damsels, each of seventy years,*
Were all deflowered by different Grenadiers.

4 things [in] haste
7a But six [old] damsels [aged] seventy years TX
 b But six poor damsels each of . . . TX
 c *Mary Shelley refused to copy lines 7–8 on M; Byron wrote in the
   present text.*

131

But on the whole their continence was great;
      So that some disappointment there ensued
To those who had felt the inconvenient state
      Of "single blessedness,"* and thought it good
(Since it was not their fault, but only fate,
      To bear these crosses) for each waning prude
To make a Roman sort of Sabine wedding,*
Without the expense and the suspense of bedding.

1 their [abstinence] was great
3 To those [who long had thought a single state]
4 thought [though rude]
5 [Yet] (since [t]was not . . .
6a [There was a good excuse] for [every] prude
 b To [share] these crosses) for each waning prude
7 of Sabine [marriage]

Some voices of the buxom middle-aged
　　Were also heard to wonder in the din
(Widows of forty were these birds long caged)
　　"Wherefore the ravishing did not begin!"*
But while the thirst for gore and plunder raged,
　　There was small leisure for superfluous sin;
But whether they escaped or no, lies hid
In darkness—I can only hope they did.

3　(Widows of forty—[who had been] long caged)
7*a* And whether . . .　TX;　*b* But whether . . .　M　*Mary Shelley's*
　　　　　　　　　　　　　　　　　　　　　　　　alteration.

133

Suwarrow now was conqueror—a match
　　For Timour or for Zinghis in his trade.
While mosques and streets, beneath his eyes, like thatch
　　Blazed, and the cannon's roar was scarce allayed,
With bloody hands he wrote his first dispatch;
　　And here exactly follows what he said:—
"Glory to *God* and to the Empress!" (*Powers*
Eternal!! such names mingled!) "Ismail's our's."*

1　*Byron on Tx wrote* now was; *Mary Shelley on M substituted* was a,
　and Byron restored his original words.
2　*Byron on Tx wrote* Zinghis, *which Mary Shelley on M changed to*
　Genghis, *and Byron restored his original spelling.*
5　he [made] his . . .
8　names [joined] mingled . . .

Methinks these are the most tremendous words,
  Since "Menè, Menè,† Tekel," and "Upharsin,"*
Which hands or pens have ever traced of swords.
  Heaven help me! I'm but little of a parson:
What Daniel read was short-hand of the Lord's,
  Severe, sublime; the Prophet wrote no farce on
The fate of Nations;—but this Russ so witty
Could rhyme, like Nero, o'er a burning city.*

3 ever [writ] of Swords
5 [And] Daniel [wr] *fragment   Intended to write* wrote?
6 [Serious and] sublime . . .

135

He wrote this Polar melody, and set it,
  Duly accompanied by shrieks and groans,
Which few will sing, I trust, but none forget it—
  For I will teach, if possible, the stones
To rise against Earth's tyrants. Never let it
  Be said that we still truckle unto thrones;—
But ye—our children's children! think how we
Showed *what things were* before the world was free!

2a [With due accom] *fragment   Intended to write* accompaniment.
 b Duly accompanied by [tears] and groans
6   still [bow down] unto thrones
8   [Strove] *fragment*

That hour is not for us, but 'tis for you:
  And as, in the great joy of your millennium,
You hardly will believe such things were true
  As now occur, I thought that I would pen you 'em;
But may their very memory perish too!—
  Yet if perchance remembered, still disdain you 'em
More than you scorn the savages of yore,
Who *painted* their *bare* limbs, but *not* with gore.*

3   things [are] true
6a Or if . . . TX;   *b* But if . . . M   *Mary Shelley's alteration.*
7a [As] More than [the] [painted] [earliest Savages] of yore TX
  b   [your] [the] your Savage Ancestors of yore TX
  *c Mary Shelley copied the final Tx version on M; Byron deleted part of
  it and substituted the present text.*

137

And when you hear historians talk of thrones,
  And those that sate upon them, let it be
As we now gaze upon the Mammoth's bones,*
  And wonder what old world such things could see,
Or hieroglyphics on Egyptian stones,*
  The pleasant riddles of Futurity—
Guessing at what shall happily be hid
As the real purpose of a Pyramid.

*Byron at first intended this to be the final stanza of the canto; beneath it
on Tx he wrote and later deleted "End of Canto 8ᵗʰ" and a date, part of
which was superscribed. The day and month are uncertain, but "Jʸ, A, 3"
and "1ˢᵗ" are all apparent, followed by "1822." The usual signature-
symbol is uncanceled.*

2   And [their things] that sate . . .
4   And [doubt how] *fragment*
5   Aegyptian . . . TX, M
7a Guessing [by] [what] [way of pastime what they meant]
  b Guessing [for] at what . . .

Reader! I have kept my word,—at least so far
    As the first Canto promised. You have now
Had sketches of love, tempest, travel, war—
    All very accurate, you must allow,
And *Epic,* if plain truth should prove no bar;
    For I have drawn much less with a long bow
Than my forerunners.*† Carelessly I sing,
But Phoebus lends me now and then a string,

This and the following three stanzas were afterthoughts written on the
same matrix leaf with the preceding several stanzas.

4   accurate as you . . .   TX, M
5*a*   if [you] plain truth[s such ever are]   TX
  b   truth should prove no bar   TX
  c   *Mary Shelley on* M *wrote* truths shall; *Byron deleted only* shall *and*
       wrote should.
6   fore-runners; [yet while] carelessly . . .

139

With which I still can harp, and carp, and fiddle.
    What further hath befallen or may befall
The hero of this grand poetic riddle,
    I by and bye may tell you, if at all:
But now I choose to break off in the middle,†
    Worn out with battering Ismail's stubborn wall,
While Juan is sent off with the dispatch,
For which all Petersburgh is on the watch.*

2   befal   *In 1823 edition.*
6   Worn[t] out . . .
8*a* Petersburg . . .   TX;   *b* Petersburgh . . .   M   *Mary Shelley's*
                                                    spelling.

This special honour was conferred, because
    He had behaved with courage and humanity;—
Which *last*, men like, when they have time to pause
    From their ferocities produced by vanity.
His little captive gained him some applause
    For saving her amidst the wild insanity
Of carnage,—and I think he was more glad in her
Safety, than his new order of St. Vladimir.*

3 [For people like the last when] *fragment*
4*a* the ferocities ... TX; *b* their ferocities ... M   *Mary Shelley's*
7 Of Carnage—and [her fair and infant grace]   *alteration.*

141

The Moslem orphan went with her protector,
    For she was homeless, houseless, helpless; all
Her friends, like the sad family of Hector,*
    Had perished in the field or by the wall:
Her very place of birth was but a spectre
    Of what it had been; there the Muezzin's call
To prayer was heard no more!—And Juan wept,
And made a vow to shield her, which he kept.

On the last page of Tx below this stanza Byron wrote "End of Canto 8th
J^y A—1822" *and his usual signature-symbol.*

7 [but] Juan [made] wept

Canto IX

1

Oн, Wellington!* (or "Vilainton"*—for Fame
    Sounds the heroic syllables both ways;
France could not even conquer your great name,
    But punned it down to this facetious phrase—
Beating or beaten she will laugh the same)—
    You have obtained great pensions and much praise;
Glory like yours should any dare gainsay,
Humanity would rise, and thunder "Nay!"*

Cantos IX, X, and XI were published in one volume by John Hunt on August 29, 1823.

    All manuscript readings are taken from Y (Yale manuscript), the original first draft, except those noted as Tx (Texas manuscript), a first draft fragment earlier intended for use in Canto III.

    The first draft of this and the following seven stanzas appears on Tx fragment. A fair copy of these eight stanzas in the hand of the Countess Guiccioli exists on Y. On Tx above the first stanza is the date, "July 10th 1819." The same date appears on the Y fair copy of the first eight stanzas.

1*a* Vilainton . . . *Tx, Y, 1823, and 1833 editions.*
 b Villainton . . . *In 1837 and in later editions.*
3 [thy] great name TX
5 She [always] laugh[s] the same) TX
6 [Thou has] obtained . . . TX
7 yours [who] should . . . TX
8*a* rise and [answer] TX
 b rise and thunder—Ney! TX
 c *The Countess Guiccioli misread Ney and copied it on Y as* ray. *Byron corrected it to* Ney *and then altered it to* Nay.

[183]

I don't think that you used Kinnaird quite well
    In Marinêt's affair*—in fact 'twas shabby,
And like some other things won't do to tell
    Upon your tomb in Westminster's old abbey.
Upon the rest 'tis not worth while to dwell,
    Such tales being for the tea hours of some tabby;*
But though your years as *man* tend fast to zero,
In fact your Grace is still but a *young Hero*.

1 K—n—rd *In 1823 edition.*
6 Such talk being . . . TX, Y

3

Though Britain owes (and pays you too) so much,*
    Yet Europe doubtless owes you greatly more:
You have repaired Legitimacy's crutch,*—
    A prop not quite so certain as before:
The Spanish, and the French, as well as Dutch,
    Have seen, and felt, how strongly you *restore;*
And Waterloo has made the world your debtor—
(I wish your bards would sing it rather better).*

4 [And propp] *fragment* TX *Intended to write* propped.
5 [The Spain] The Spanish . . . TX
6 Have seen [how] & felt how . . . TX
8 I wish you bards . . . Y

4

You are "the best of cut-throats":*—do not start;
    The phrase is Shakspeare's, and not misapplied:—
War's a brain-spattering, windpipe-slitting art,
    Unless her cause by Right be sanctified.
If you have acted *once* a generous part,
    The World, not the World's masters, will decide,
And I shall be delighted to learn who,
Save you and yours, have gained by Waterloo?

2 Shakespeare's . . . TX
3 [For] War's [at best] *fragment* TX
5 If [yours] ha[s been so let mankind decide] TX
6*a* [My] The World,—[and] not . . . TX; *b* [and] not . . . Y

5

I am no flatterer—you've supped full of flattery:*
    They say you like it too—'tis no great wonder:
He whose whole life has been assault and battery,
    At last may get a little tired of thunder;
And swallowing eulogy much more than satire, he
    May like being praised for every lucky blunder;*
Called "Saviour of the Nations"—not yet saved,
And Europe's Liberator*—still enslaved.

3*a* He who [has] *fragment* TX
 b He whose [long] life . . . TX
5 And [liking] eulogy . . . TX
6 May [gorge on] praise for . . . TX
8 And [see his statue raised—& print engraved] TX

6

I've done. Now go and dine from off the plate
    Presented by the Prince of the Brazils,*
And send the sentinel before your gate
    A slice or two from your luxurious meals:*
He fought, but has not fed so well of late.
    Some hunger too they say the people feels:—
There is no doubt that you deserve your ration,
But pray give back a little to the nation.

1 [Yet you're a noble fellow and but wait] TX
5 so well as late TX, Y
8 But [not at the expence of a whole nation] TX

I don't mean to reflect—a man so great as
　　You, my Lord Duke! is far above reflection.
The high Roman fashion too of Cincinnatus,*
　　With modern history has but small connection:
Though as an Irishman you love potatoes,
　　You need not take them under your direction;
And half a million for your Sabine farm*
Is rather dear!—I'm sure I mean no harm.

*This and the following stanza are written crosswise on Tx.
No revisions.*

8

Great men have always scorned great recompenses:
　　Epaminondas saved his Thebes, and died,
Not leaving even his funeral expenses:*
　　George Washington had thanks and nought beside,*
Except the all-cloudless Glory (which few men's is)
　　To free his country: Pitt too had his pride,*
And, as a high-soul'd Minister of State, is
Renowned for ruining Great Britain gratis.

No revisions.

Never had mortal Man such opportunity,
  Except Napoleon, or abused it more:
You might have freed fall'n Europe from the Unity
  Of Tyrants, and been blest from shore to shore:
And *now*—What *is* your fame? Shall the Muse tune it
    ye?
  Now—that the rabble's first vain shouts are o'er?
Go, hear it in your famished Country's cries!
Behold the World! and curse your victories!

This stanza and the following one Byron added in his own hand to
the Countess Guiccioli's fair copy of the first eight.
  No revisions on stanza 9.

10

As these new Cantos touch on warlike feats,
  To *you* the unflattering Muse deigns to inscribe
Truths that you will not read in the Gazettes,
  But which, 'tis time to teach the hireling tribe
Who fatten on their Country's gore and debts,
  Must be recited, and—without a bribe.
You *did great* things; but not being *great* in mind,
Have left *undone* the *greatest*—and mankind.

2 To you—[this one unflattering Muse inscribes]
3 Truths [which] you . . .

Death laughs*—Go ponder ò'er the skeleton
    With which men image out the unknown thing
That hides the past world, like to a set sun
    Which still elsewhere may rouse a brighter spring,—
Death laughs at all you weep for:—look upon
    This hourly dread of all, whose *threatened sting*
Turns life to terror, even though in its sheath!
Mark! how its lipless mouth grins without breath!

Byron originally regarded this as the first stanza of the canto. It is numbered "1" on Y. Hence the Y first draft begins here.

1   Death laughs, Go, [look upon] the Skeleton
2   With which [they] image out . . .
3a [Which] hides [from] [him] [us as Night the Set Sun]
 b That hides [life] . . .
4   Which [still] [yet] still elsewhere . . .
5a Death laughs; [you dare not; Go and] Look upon
 b   at all you [dare not] . . .
7a [Stings in] life [with apprehension in its sheath]
 b   [even within it's sheath]
 c Turns life to terror [Even] Ere it quits it's sheath

12

Mark! how it laughs and scorns at all you are!
    And yet *was* what you are: from *ear* to *ear*
It *laughs not*—there is now no fleshy bar
    So called; the Antic long hath ceased to *hear*,
But still he *smiles;* and whether near or far
    He strips from man that mantle (far more dear
Than even the tailor's) his incarnate skin,
White, black, or copper—the dead bones will grin.

1 Mark! how it scoffs and scorns . . .
3 It [grins] not . . .
6-7 *Order of composition:*
    [You strip] [the] [from Man his Mantle (which is] dear
                         [the Earth's] . . .
    [Though beautiful in youth)] his [carnal] Skin—
    [Though dearest . . .]

He strips from Man [the] Mantle (much more dear
                    that . . .
Than even the tailor's . . .

13

And thus Death laughs,—it is sad merriment,
    But still it *is* so; and with such example
Why should not Life be equally content,
    With his Superior, in a smile to trample
Upon the nothings which are daily spent
    Like bubbles on an ocean much less ample
Than the eternal deluge, which devours
Suns as rays—worlds like atoms—years like hours?

4 [From] his Superior? [to] in a smile . . .
8 Suns [like to Atoms] *fragment*

14

"To be or not to be! that is the question,"
    Says Shakespeare, who just now is much in fashion.*
I am neither Alexander nor Hephaestion,*
    Nor ever had for *abstract* fame much passion;
But would much rather have a sound digestion,
    Than Buonaparte's cancer:*—could I dash on
Through fifty victories to shame or fame,
Without a stomach—what were a good name?

2 Says Shakespeare [and] who . . . the fashion
6 Cancer; [though] I dash on
7 Through [pleasures thick and thin to fame or shame]
8a [A] [S] [Stomachs] *fragment*
 b Without . . . what [is] a good name?

"Oh dura ilia messorum!"*—"Oh
    Ye rigid guts of reapers!"—I translate
For the great benefit of those who know
    What Indigestion is—that inward fate
Which makes all Styx through one small liver flow.
    A peasant's sweat is worth his Lord's estate:
Let *this* one toil for bread—*that* rack for rent,
He who sleeps best, may be the most content.

2 "Ye [iron] Guts of reapers!" [in] I translate—
5*a* all [Hell] through one . . .
 b Styx though . . .   *Misprint in 1823 edition.*
8 best [shall] may be. . . .

16

"To be or not to be?"—Ere I decide,
    I should be glad to know that which *is being?*
'Tis true we speculate both far and wide,
    And deem, because we *see,* we are *all-seeing:*
For my part, I'll enlist on neither side,
    Until I see both sides for once agreeing.
For me, I sometimes think that Life is Death,*
Rather than Life a mere affair of breath.

1 [bef] ere I decide *Intended to write* before.
6 see both [neither] sides . . .
7*a* [For whether Life] *fragment*
 b [By G—d] I sometimes . . .

"Que sçais-je?" was the motto of Montaigne,*
  As also of the first Academicians:†
That all is dubious which Man may attain,
  Was one of their most favourite positions.
There's no such thing as certainty, that's plain
  As any of Mortality's Conditions:
So little do we know what we're about in
This world, I doubt if doubt itself be doubting.*

3   all is [doubtful] which Man . . .
4   one of [its] most . . .
5   no such [cert] thing as Certainty . . .
6a [You cannot] *fragment*
 b [And one] of our Mortality's . . .
7   [You can't be sure even] *fragment*
8   doubt itself [is] doubting

18

It is a pleasant voyage perhaps to float,
  Like Pyrrho, on a sea of speculation;*
But what if carrying sail capsize the boat?
  Your wise men don't know much of navigation;
And swimming long in the abyss of thought
  Is apt to tire: a calm and shallow station
Well nigh the shore, where one stoops down and gathers
Some pretty shell,* is best for moderate bathers.

1   [This] a pleasant . . .
3   But what if [Something should upset] the boat?
5   And [soon tire] swimming in the Abyss . . .
6   a calm and [quiet] station
7   [Upon] the shore where one [picks up] *fragment*
8   is best for [timi] moderate . . .

"But Heaven," as Cassio says, "is above all,*—
   No more of this then,—let us pray!" We have
Souls to save, since Eve's slip and Adam's fall,
   Which tumbled all mankind into the grave,
Besides fish, beasts, and birds. "The Sparrow's fall
   Is special providence,"* though how it gave
Offence, we know not; probably it perched
Upon the tree which Eve so fondly searched.

3 [Souls to be] [Alas! Since Eve's] *fragments*
5 Besides [the birds, and beast]—"the Sparrow's fall
6 though [they] gave
7–8 Offence . . . probably [they perched]
   Upon the tree [of Knowledge while Eve searched]
       which Eve [for] so [vainly] searched

20

Oh, ye immortal Gods! what is Theogony?
   Oh, thou too mortal Man! what is Philanthropy?
Oh, World! which was and is, what is Cosmogony?
   Some people have accused me of Misanthropy;
And yet I know no more than the mahogany
   That forms this desk, of what they mean;—
      *Lykanthropy**
I comprehend, for without transformation
Men become wolves on any slight occasion.

6 Which forms my desk . . .
7 I [understand—for wolves and men] *fragment*

But I, the mildest, meekest of mankind,
    Like Moses, or Melancthon,* who have ne'er
Done any thing exceedingly unkind,—
    And (though I could not now and then forbear
Following the bent of body or of mind)
    Have always had a tendency to spare,—
Why do they call me misanthrope? Because
They hate me, not I them:—And here we'll pause.

2*a* Like Moses—[who was "very meek"] *fragment*
 b   or like Cobbett* who have neer
4   [But] though . . .
6   [Yet] always had . . .

22

'Tis time we should proceed with our good poem,
    For I maintain that it is really good,
Not only in the body, but the proem,
    However little both are understood
Just now,—but by and by the Truth will show 'em*
    Herself in her sublimest attitude:
And till she doth, I fain must be content
To share her Beauty and her Banishment.

4*a* However [both be little] understood
 b However little both [be] . . .
6   [The] Herself . . .
7   And till she doth—I [am Content to] *fragment*

Our Hero (and, I trust, kind reader! your's)—
  Was left upon his way to the chief City
Of the immortal Peter's polished boors,
  Who still have shown themselves more brave than
    witty.
I know its mighty Empire now allures
  Much flattery—even Voltaire's,* and that's a pity.
For me, I deem an absolute Autocrat
Not a Barbarian, but much worse than that.

1 I trust [ye] reader! . . .
6 [Each] Much flattery . . .
7a For me—I [look upon your] Autocrat
 b   deem [your] absolute . . .
8 [As still a mere Barbarian, and scarce] that

24

And I will war, at least in words (and—should
  My chance so happen—deeds) with all who war
With Thought;*—and of Thought's foes by far most
    rude,
  Tyrants and Sycophants have been and are.
I know not who may conquer: if I could
  Have such a prescience, it should be no bar
To this my plain, sworn, downright detestation
Of every despotism in every nation.

2 My chance so [bend] happen . . .
3a With thought[s]—and [that midst the] *fragment*
 b   and of Thought's [tramplers]
 c   and of [such warrior's the most] rude
4 [Are Despots] *fragment*
6 Have such a [knowl] prescience . . . *Intended to write* knowledge.
7a To [what I think and say] *fragment*
 b To this my plain [downright sworn] detestation
8 Of every [king that ever curst a] Nation

It is not that I adulate the people:
   Without *me*, there are Demagogues enough,*
And Infidels, to pull down every steeple
   And set up in their stead some proper stuff.
Whether they may sow Scepticism to reap Hell,
   As is the Christian dogma rather rough,
I do not know;—I wish men to be free*
As much from mobs as kings—from you as me.

1 that I [care much for] the people
3 And [Priests] infidels . . .
5 Whether the [latter] sow . . .
6 Christian [doctrine] rather [rough]
8 As much from [them as Kings] *fragment*

26

The consequence is, being of no party,*
   I shall offend all parties:—never mind!
My words, at least, are more sincere and hearty
   Than if I sought to sail before the wind. ·
He who has nought to gain can have small art: he
   Who neither wishes to be bound nor bind,
May still expatiate freely, as will I,
Nor give my voice to Slavery's Jackall cry.

1   is [that]—being . . .
8a [Though Priests and Slaves may join in the servile cry]
 b Nor join my voice to Slavery's Jackal Cry
 c jackal . . .   *In 1833 and in later editions. This variation will not be noted hereafter.*

That's an appropriate simile; *that Jackall;* —
    I've heard them in the Ephesian ruins howl*
By night, as do that mercenary pack all,
    Power's base purveyors, who for pickings prowl,
And scent the prey their masters would attack all.
    However, the poor Jackalls are less foul
(As being the brave Lions' keen providers)
Than human Insects, catering for Spiders.

3   as doth that . . .
4   [The] Power's base purveyors who [in legion] prowl
5   [But] And scent . . .
6a [But for less] *fragment*
 b However . . . Jackal [is] less foul
7   (As being the [brave] Lion's [small] providers)
8a [Whereas the others hunt for regal] Spiders
 b [Whereas your modern monarchs are mere] Spiders
 c [Whereas you are] insects catering for Spiders

28

Raise but an arm! 'twill brush their web away,
    And without *that,* their poison and their claws
Are useless. Mind, good People! what I say —
    (Or rather Peoples) — *go on* without pause!
The web of these Tarantulas each day
    Increases, till you shall make common cause:
None, save the Spanish Fly and Attic Bee,
As yet are strongly stinging to be free.

6   Encreases — [though the flies] make . . .
7   Except the Spanish Fly . . .
8   Which still are strongly [fluttering] stinging . . .

Don Juan, who had shone in the late slaughter,
    Was left upon his way with the dispatch,
Where Blood was talked of as we would of Water;
    And carcases that lay as thick as thatch
O'er silenced cities, merely served to flatter
    Fair Catherine's pastime,—who looked on the match
Between these nations as a main of cocks,
Wherein she liked her own to stand like rocks.

3 as you would . . .
5 Oer [house] silenced cities, [made] merely . . .
7–8 Between [your Turk and Russian as a Main
    Of Cocks]—wherein her own [should] *fragment*

30

And there in a *kibitka** he rolled on,
    (A cursed sort of carriage without springs,
Which on rough roads leaves scarcely a whole bone)
    Pondering on glory, chivalry, and kings,
And orders, and on all that he had done—
    And wishing that post horses had the wings
Of Pegasus—or, at the least, post chaises
Had feathers, when a traveller on deep ways is.

1 on a Kibitka . . .
3 leaves [not a] whole bone
5 and [upon] all that . . .
7 Of Pegasus—[and that] *fragment*

At every jolt—and they were many—still
   He turned his eyes upon his little charge,
As if he wished that she should fare less ill
   Than he, in these sad highways left at large
To ruts, and flints, and lovely Nature's skill,
   Who is no paviour, nor admits a barge
On *her* canals, where God takes sea and land,
Fishery and farm, both into his own hand.

1   [But] every jolt . . .
4   left at [charge]
5   To ruts, and [rocks], and lovely . . .
6   [She] is no . . .
7a On her Canals [but leave both Sea and land]
  b   [lets . . .]

32

At least he pays no rent, and has best right
   To be the first of what we used to call
"Gentlemen Farmers"—a race worn out quite,
   Since lately there have been no rents at all,*
And "gentlemen" are in a piteous plight,
   And "farmers" can't raise Ceres from her fall.
She fell with Buonaparte:*—What strange thoughts
Arise, when we see Emperors fall with oats!

6   And "farmers" can't raise [sad Ceres] *fragment*
7   [Who] fell . . . what [a thought!]
8a [When blood ceased] *fragment*
  b Rise when we see that [Con] [Conquerors] *fragment*
  c   that Emperors fall . . .

But Juan turned his eyes on the sweet child
    Whom he had saved from slaughter—what a trophy!
Oh! ye who build up monuments, defiled
    With gore, like Nadir Shah,* that costive Sophy,
Who, after leaving Hindostan a wild,
    And scarce to the Mogul a cup of coffee
To soothe his woes withal, was slain—the sinner!
Because he could no more digest his dinner;*—

3   build up [Statues all] defiled
5   after [making] Hindostan . . .
6a And [leaving Asia scarce a] cup of Coffee
  b And scarce[ly] to the Mogul a . . .
7–8a To soothe his woes withal [went mad—and was
    Killed because what he swallowed would not pass]
  8b [Slain because . . .]

34

Oh ye! or we! or he! or she! reflect,
    That *one* life saved, especially if young
Or pretty, is a thing to recollect
    Far sweeter than the greenest laurels sprung
From the manure of human clay, though decked
    With all the praises ever said or sung:
Though hymned by every harp, unless within
Your Heart joins Chorus, Fame is but a din.

1   we—or She—or He—reflect
4   than the [bright] greenest . . .
6a With [Garlands round by every nation hung]
  b With all the [flatteries] ever said or sung
7   Though [sung] by every harp . . .
8   Your heart sings chorus; [tis a] Fame is . . .

Oh, ye great Authors luminous, voluminous!
  Ye twice ten hundred thousand daily scribes,
Whose pamphlets, volumes, newspapers illumine us!
  Whether you're paid by Government in bribes,
To prove the public debt is not consuming us—
  Or, roughly treading on the "Courtier's kibes"*
With clownish heel, your popular circulation
Feeds you by printing half the realm's Starvation;—

1 great [Writers]—luminous . . .
4 paid by [Despotism's] bribes
5 [Or] To prove [that] the public . . .
6 Or roughly [tread] treading . . .
7 heel—[the] your [daily] Circulation
8a [Drains further shillings] *fragment*
 b Feeds you by [daily pointing out] *fragment*

36

Oh, ye great Authors!—"Apropos des bottes"*—
  I have forgotten what I meant to say,
As sometimes have been greater Sages' lots;—
  'Twas something calculated to allay
All wrath in barracks, palaces, or cots:
  Certes it would have been but thrown away,
And that's one comfort for my lost advice,
Although no doubt it was beyond all price.

4 Twas something [moderate] *fragment*
5 All [an] [nervousness *sic?* whether in] *fragment*
8 Although no doubtless it was . . .

But let it go:—it will one day be found
　　With other relics of "a former world,"
When this world shall be *former*, underground,
　　Thrown topsy-turvy, twisted, crisped, and curled,
Baked, fried, or burnt, turned inside-out, or drowned,
　　Like all the worlds before, which have been hurled
First out of and then back again to Chaos,
The Superstratum which will overlay us.

4　[Turned] topsy turvy . . .
5　fried or burned, [or] turned . . .
7　back [to] again to . . .
8*a*　[Making all Nature labour *sic?*] *fragment*
　b　[As Monsieur] *fragment*
　c　Or the Substrata which [la] will overlay us

38

So Cuvier says;*—and then shall come again
　　Unto the new Creation, rising out
From our old crash, some mystic, ancient strain
　　Of things destroyed and left in airy doubt:
Like to the notions we now entertain
　　Of Titans, Giants, fellows of about
Some hundred feet in height, *not* to say *miles*,
And Mammoths, and your winged Crocodiles.

2　Creation rising [forth]
3　some [faint] ancient strain
4　Of [aged] things . . .
6–8　Of Titans—[Adamites] Giants—fellows of about
　　Some hundred feet in height, [as well as years]
　　And Mammoths [and also] winged Crocodiles

[201]

Think if then George the Fourth should be dug up!
　　How the new worldlings of the then new East
Will wonder where such animals could sup!
　　(For they themselves will be but of the least:
Even worlds miscarry, when too oft they pup,
　　And every new Creation hath decreased
In size, from overworking the material—
Men are but maggots of some huge Earth's burial.)

```
3    wonder [how] such animals . . .
4    [And] For they . . .
6    And [each succeeding] fragment
8a   [And every] fragment
 b   Men are but [worms of] some huge [old] Earth's burial
```

40

How will—to these young people, just thrust out
　　From some fresh Paradise, and set to plough,
And dig, and sweat, and turn themselves about,
　　And plant, and reap, and spin, and grind, and sow,
Till all the Arts at length are brought about,
　　Especially of war and taxing,—how,
I say, will these great relics, when they see 'em,
Look like the monsters of a new Museum?

```
1     How will [the new] young People . . .
2-3   From some [new] Paradise and set to [dig]
      And [plough] & sweat . . .
4a    And plant—& reap—& [sow & fight] fragment
 b                   and [set sic?] spin and till and sow
5     [Until quite civilized by War] fragment
7     I say [how] will . . .
8a    [Become] the Monsters of a new Museum
 b    [Show] like . . .
```

But I am apt to grow too metaphysical:
     "The time is out of joint,"*—and so am I;
I quite forget this poem's merely quizzical,
     And deviate into matters rather dry.
I ne'er decide what I shall say, and this I call
     Much too poetical. Men should know why
They write, and for what end; but, note or text,
I never know the word which will come next.

2   "The times are out of joint" . . .
4a And [grow] into matters . . .
 b And [wander] . . .
5a [Though deep enough] *fragment*
 b I neer [know what's next to come] and this I call
6   [all] men should . . .

42

So on I ramble, now and then narrating,
     Now pondering:—it is time we should narrate:
I left Don Juan with his horses baiting—
     Now we'll get o'er the ground at a great rate.
I shall not be particular in stating
     His journey, we've so many tours of late:
Suppose him then at Petersburgh;* suppose
That pleasant capital of painted Snows;*

5 I [never was] particular . . .

Suppose him in a handsome uniform;
   A scarlet coat, black facings, a long plume,
Waving, like sails new shivered in a storm,
   Over a cocked hat in a crowded room,
And brilliant breeches, bright as a Cairn Gorme,*
   Of yellow cassimere we may presume,
White stockings drawn, uncurdled as new milk,
O'er limbs whose symmetry set off the silk:

2 a long [feather]
3*a* [In a Cocked hat] [A large Cocked hat] *fragments*
 b Waving like [a white] sail shivered . . .
4 Over a [large] cocked hat . . .
5 And [breeches dazzling] as . . .
6 Casimire . . . Y *This spelling was also used in 1833 and in some later editions without the capitalization. A few editions print* casimere.
7*a* [White s] *fragment*
 b White stockings drawn [all] unruffled as new milk
8 Oer limbs [which mightily] set off . . .

44

Suppose him sword by side, and hat in hand,
   Made up by Youth, Fame, and an Army tailor—
That great Enchanter, at whose rod's command
   Beauty springs forth, and Nature's self turns paler,
Seeing how Art can make her work more grand,
   (When she don't pin men's limbs in like a jailor)—
Behold him placed as if upon a pillar! He
Seems Love turned a Lieutenant of Artillery!

1 and [right *sic?*] hat in hand
2*a* [In all the glow of Nature] *fragment*
 b [Set off] by Youth . . .
3 [As brilliantly as if an] *fragment*
4 springs [up] and . . .
6*a* [Behold him] *fragment*; *b* Jailer Y; *c* gaoler *In 1833 and in later editions. This common variation will not be noted hereafter.*
7 Behold him placed [in Youth and Glory's pillory]
8 [Like] Love [as] a Lieutenant . . .

[204]

His Bandage slipped down into a cravat;
 His Wings subdued to epaulettes; his Quiver
Shrunk to a scabbard, with his Arrows at
 His side as a small sword, but sharp as ever;
His Bow converted into a cocked hat;
 But still so like, that Psyche were more clever
Than some wives (who make blunders no less stupid)
If She had not mistaken him for Cupid.

3 Scabbard—[where his arrows sat]
4*a* [Pruned to a sword but sharp no doubt] as ever
 b His side [though] as . . .
7 blunders [quite as] stupid

46

The courtiers stared, the ladies whispered, and
 The Empress smiled; the reigning favourite
  frowned—
I quite forget which of them was in hand
 Just then, as they are rather numerous found,*
Who took by turns that difficult command
 Since first her Majesty was singly crowned:*
But they were mostly nervous six-foot fellows,*
All fit to make a Patagonian jealous.

2 The Empress smiled, [while all the Orloff] frowned
3*a* [A numerous family of favourites]
 b [A nervous family to whose heart or hand]
4 [Mild Catherine owed the chance of being crown'd]
5*a* Who took by turns [upon them to] command
 b   that [duty to] . . .
8 [And] fit . . .

Juan was none of these, but slight and slim,
  Blushing and beardless; and yet ne'ertheless
There was a something in his turn of limb,
  And still more in his eye, which seemed to express
That though he looked one of the Seraphim,
  There lurked a Man beneath the Spirit's dress.
Besides, the Empress sometimes liked a boy,
And had just buried the fair faced Lanskoi.*

1 none of those . . .
3 in his [shape and] limb
5a That though he [was a sort] of Seraphim
 b   [seemed] one of the . . .
6 There was a Man beneath [his] the Spirit's dress
8a And [almost died for] the [scarce-fledged] Lanskoi
 b And had just buried the   smooth-faced . . .

48

No wonder then that Yermoloff, or Momonoff,
  Or Scherbatoff, or any other off*
Or on, might dread her Majesty had not room enough
  Within her bosom (which was not too tough)
For a new flame; a thought to cast of gloom enough
  Along the aspect whether smooth or rough
Of him who, in the language of his station,
Then held that "high official situation."

1 Yermdoff . . . sic?
3 Majesty had room enough
7 who [was] in . . .

Oh, gentle ladies! should you seek to know
    The import of this diplomatic phrase,
Bid Ireland's Londonderry's Marquess* show
    His parts of speech; and in the strange displays
Of that odd string of words, all in a row,
    Which none divine, and every one obeys,
Perhaps you may pick out some queer *no*-meaning,
Of that weak wordy harvest the sole gleaning.

2 [That] the [meaning] of this . . .
3 [Go—] [ask of] [bid Lord] Londonderry *fragment*
5 Of [his] that . . .
7 some [stra] queer . . .   *Intended to write* strange.
8 Of that [sad wordy] harvest . . .

50

I think I can explain myself without
    That sad inexplicable beast of prey—
That Sphinx, whose words would ever be a doubt,
    Did not his deeds unriddle them each day—
That monstrous Hieroglyphic—that long Spout
    Of blood and water, leaden Castlereagh!
And here I must an anecdote relate,
But luckily of no great length or weight.

4a Did not his [actions] unriddle . . .
  b   [acts] . . .
5   That Monstrous [Mystagogue]—that [mere] spout
8   [The greater part] *fragment*

An English lady asked of an Italian,
    What were the actual and official duties
Of the strange thing some Women set a value on,
    Which hovers oft about some married Beauties,
Called "Cavalier Servente"?*—a Pygmalion
    Whose statues warm (I fear, alas! too true 'tis)
Beneath his Art. The dame, pressed to disclose them,
Said—"Lady, I beseech you to *suppose them*."

2*a* [The function] *fragment*
 b What were [the real functions of the duties]
3   Of that strange . . .
4   Which hovers often about married beauties
6   Whose [labours] [Staut] Statues warm . . .
7*a* Beneath [his ceaseless touches, the Hesperian]
 b Beneath his [chisel] the dame prest to disclose them

52

And thus I supplicate your supposition,
    And mildest, Matron-like interpretation
Of the Imperial Favourite's Condition.
    'Twas a high place, the highest in the nation*
In fact, if not in rank; and the suspicion
    Of any one's attaining to his station,
No doubt gave pain, where each new pair of shoulders,
If rather broad, made stocks rise and their holders.

2 And mildest [modestest] interpretation
4 highest of the Nation
6 Of any one's aspiring to . . .
7 No doubt gave [umbrage unto one who] *fragment*
8 If [new and] broad . . .

Juan, I said, was a most beauteous Boy,
    And had retained his boyish look beyond
The usual hirsute seasons which destroy,
    With beards and whiskers and the like, the fond
Parisian aspect which upset old Troy
    And founded Doctors' Commons:—I have conned
The history of divorces, which, though chequered,
Calls Ilion's the first damages on record.

3 hirsute [years which] destroy
5 upset [all] Troy
6–8 [And Greece and bound fair Helen in a bond
    Stronger than Matrimony;] *fragment*
    Stronger [than Marriage!] *fragment*
    The History of [Marriage]—which though [Checque] checquered
    Calls [these] the [earliest] damages on record

54

And Catherine, who loved all things (save her lord,
    Who was gone to his place) and passed for much,
Admiring those (by dainty dames abhorred)
    Gigantic Gentlemen, yet had a touch
Of Sentiment; and he She most adored
    Was the lamented Lanskoi,* who was such
A lover as had cost her many a tear,
And yet but made a middling grenadier.

3a [Adored *sic?*] *fragment*
 b Admiring [that you modest] dames abhorred
 c Admiring those by [delicate] . . .
5   and [him] she most . . .
6a Was the [deceased] Lanskoi [whose] *fragment*
 b Was the [late buried] . . . *fragment*
8   And yet had made . . .

Oh, thou "teterrima Causa" of all "belli"*—
　　Thou gate of Life and Death—thou nondescript!
Whence is our exit and our entrance,—well I
　　May pause in pondering how all Souls are dipt
In thy perennial fountain:—how man *fell*, I
　　Know not, since Knowledge saw her branches stript
Of her first fruit; but how he falls and rises
Since, Thou hast settled beyond all surmises.

3 Whence [are] our Exit . . .
4 May pause in pondering [over all] *fragment*
5 perrennial . . . *Misprint in 1823 edition.*
6 since [the] Knowledge . . .
7 [Know not at first but how he] falls and rises
8 [Just] Since . . .

Some call thee "the worst Cause of war," but I
　　Maintain thou art the *best:* for after all
From thee we come, to thee we go, and why
　　To get at thee not batter down a wall,
Or waste a world? Since no one can deny
　　Thou dost replenish worlds both great and small:
With, or without thee, all things at a stand
Are, or would be, thou Sea of Life's dry Land!

3 From thee we [spring]—to thee we [tend] and why—
7–8 *Order of composition:*
　　[Thou Riddle—which all read—none understand]
　　[Without thee Earthless were Lifeless] *fragment*
　　[Thou Riddle without whom Earth's Ashes end]
　　[Dark Riddle of all Life! Earth's lifeless end]
　　With—or without thee—all things at a Stand!
　　Are, or would be thou [Ocean—which doth make] sand
　　　　　　　　　Sea which lavest Life's sand

Catherine, who was the grand Epitome
   Of that great Cause of war, or peace, or what
You please (it causes all the things which be,
   So you may take your choice of this or that)—
Catherine, I say, was very glad to see
   The handsome herald, on whose plumage sat
Victory;* and, pausing as she saw him kneel
With his dispatch, forgot to break the seal.

No revisions.

58

Then recollecting the whole Empress, nor
   Forgetting quite the woman (which composed
At least three parts of this great whole) she tore
   The letter open with an air which posed
The Court, that watched each look her visage wore,
   Until a royal smile at length disclosed
Fair weather for the day. Though rather spacious,
Her face was noble, her eyes fine, mouth gracious.*

5 The Court—[which] watched . . .

Great joy was her's, or rather joys; the first
    Was a ta'en city—thirty thousand slain.
Glory and triumph o'er her aspect burst,
    As an East Indian Sunrise on the main.
These quenched a moment her Ambition's thirst—
    So Arab Deserts drink in Summer's rain:
In vain!—As fall the dews on quenchless sands,
Blood only serves to wash Ambition's hands!

2 A taken city . . .
3 oer her [vision] burst
5 These [her Ambiti] quenched . . .
6 [As] Arab deserts [are by] Summer's Rain
7 In vain—as [sink] the [rain within] *fragment*

60

Her next amusement was more fanciful;
    She smiled at mad Suwarrow's rhymes,* who threw
Into a Russian couplet rather dull
    The whole gazette of thousands whom he slew.
Her third was feminine enough to annul
    The shudder which runs naturally through
Our veins, when things called Sovereigns think it best
To kill, and Generals turn it into jest.

7a [One's] veins—when [Sovereign's think it] *fragment*
  b Our veins—when [Men] called Sovereigns . . .

The two first feelings ran their course complete,
    And lighted first her eye and then her mouth:
The whole Court looked immediately most sweet,
    Like flowers well watered after a long drouth:—
But when on the Lieutenant at her feet
    Her Majesty, who liked to gaze on youth
Almost as much as on a new dispatch,
Glanced mildly, all the world was on the watch.

2a her [glance] and then . . .
 b her [mouth] . . .
3   [So that] *fragment*
6a who liked [the looks of] Youth
 b who liked [to look] [g] [on] . . .
7   a fresh dispatch

62

Though somewhat large, exuberant, and truculent,
    When *wroth;* while *pleased,* she was as fine a figure
As those who like things rosy, ripe, and succulent,
    Would wish to look on, while they are in vigour.
She could repay each amatory look* you lent
    With interest, and in turn was wont with rigour
To exact of Cupid's bills the full amount
At sight, nor would permit you to discount.

2 as fine a [woman]
5 [Well she repaid] *fragment*
6 With interest—and [indeed was used] with rigour
7 To exact [the payment of Dan Cupid's bills]
8 At Sight,—[which] [nor would permit y] *fragment*

With her the latter, though at times convenient,
　　Was not so necessary; for they tell
That she was handsome, and though fierce *looked* lenient,
　　And always used her favourites too well.
If once beyond her boudoir's precincts in ye went,
　　Your "Fortune" was in a fair way "to swell
A Man," as Giles says;* for though she would widow all
Nations, she liked Man as an individual.

1　[This] With her . . .
2　Was not so [incommodious] for [she really]
3a　[Was voluptuous and though fierce looked lenient]
 b　[Was very handsome and though . . .]
 c　[Extremely handsome . . .]
4　her favourites [genteelly]
6　[Your fortune was in a fair way to Swell—I]
7　[You as] (Sir Giles says) for though she [could] widow all

64

What a strange thing is man!* and what a stranger
　　Is woman! What a whirlwind is her head,
And what a whirlpool full of depth and danger
　　Is all the rest about her! Whether wed,
Or widow, maid, or mother, she can change her
　　Mind like the wind; whatever she has said
Or done, is light to what she'll say or do;—
The oldest thing on record, and yet new!

5　Maid—or Neither, She can . . .
7　Or done is [little] light . . .
8　& [still] New!

Oh Catherine! (for of all interjections
    To thee both *oh!* and *ah!* belong of right
In love and war) how odd are the connections
    Of human thoughts, which jostle in their flight!
Just now *your's* were cut out in different sections:
    First Ismail's capture caught your fancy quite;
Next of new knights, the fresh and glorious hatch;
And *thirdly,* he who brought you the dispatch!

2   belong by right
3   how [strange] are . . .
4   which [jumble] jostle in . . .
5   Just now [you] were . . .
7–8*a* [And 2dly your Glory and the batch/Of new] *fragment*
8*b* And thirdly—him who . . .

66

Shakspeare talks of "the Herald Mercury*
    New lighted on a Heaven-kissing hill";
And some such visions crossed her Majesty,
    While her young Herald knelt before her still.
'Tis very true the hill seemed rather high
    For a Lieutenant to climb up; but skill
Smoothed even the Simplon's steep,* and by God's
        blessing,
With Youth and Health all kisses are "heaven-kissing."

1   Shakespeare . . .
7*a* [Makes mountains passable] and by [heaven's] blessing
 b Smoothed even the Simplon's [Mount] and by God's . . .

Her Majesty looked down, the Youth looked up—
    And so they fell in love:—She with his face,
His grace, his God-knows-what: for Cupid's cup
    With the first draught intoxicates apace,
A quintessential laudanum or "black drop,"*
    Which makes one drunk at once, without the base
Expedient of full bumpers; for the eye
In love drinks all life's fountains (save tears) dry.

4   With [a few drops] intoxicates . . .
8a [Immortal] *fragment*
  b In love drinks [every] fountain . . .
  c   all [Earth's] fountains . . .

68

He, on the other hand, if not in love,
    Fell into that no less imperious passion,
Self-love—which, when some sort of Thing above
    Ourselves, a singer, dancer, much in fashion,
Or dutchess, princess, Empress, "deigns to prove,"
    ('Tis Pope's phrase)* a great longing, tho' a rash one,
For one especial person out of many,
Makes us believe ourselves as good as any.

5a Or [Princess—Empress] Or [Countess] *fragments*
  b Or Dutchess . . .;   c duchess . . . *In 1833 and in later editions.*
  This common variation will not be noted hereafter.
8   ourselves [the best] of Any

Besides, he was of that delighted age
 Which makes all female ages equal*—when
We don't much care with whom we may engage
 As bold as Daniel in the Lion's den,
So that we can our native Sun assuage
 In the next Ocean, which may flow just then,
To make a twilight in, just as Sol's heat is
Quenched in the lap of the salt Sea, or Thetis.

5 we may our native [fire] assuage
6 In [some] the next . . .
7a twilight in,—[we all have read]
 b   [as] just as . . .
8a Quenched [as Lamps were *sic?*] *fragment*
 b Quenched in the lap . . . Seas . . .

70

And Catherine (we must say thus much for Catherine)
 Though bold and bloody, was the kind of thing
Whose temporary passion was quite flattering,
 Because each lover looked a sort of king,
Made up upon an amatory pattern,
 A royal husband in all save the *ring*—
Which, being the damn'dest part of matrimony,
Seemed taking out the sting to leave the honey.

4 lover [seemed] a sort . . .
5 [Oer whom an Empress her Crown Jewels scattering]
6a [Married with something better than a ring]
 b [Was wed with . . .]
 c [Made him her] husband in all . . .

And when you add to this, her womanhood
    In its meridian,* her blue eyes, or grey*—
(The last, if they have soul, are quite as good,
    Or better, as the best examples say:
Napoleon's, Mary's (Queen of Scotland)* should
    Lend to that colour a transcendant ray;
And Pallas also sanctions the same hue,
Too wise to look through Optics black or blue)—

2   blue eyes—[which then]
3   if [well *sic?*] they . . .
4   Or better—[being livelier] *fragment*
5*a* [Pallas'] *fragment*; *b* Napoleon's Mary['s] . . .
6*a* [Give] to that Colour [Fashion's] a transcendent ray
 b transcendent . . . *In 1833 and in later editions.*
8   [By far too wise to gaze with] *fragment*

72

Her sweet smile, and her then majestic figure,
    Her plumpness, her imperial condescension,
Her preference of a boy to men much bigger,
    (Fellows whom Messalina's self would pension)*
Her prime of life, just now in juicy vigour,
    With other *extras*, which we need not mention,—
All these, or any one of these, explain
Enough to make a stripling very vain.

In the manuscript margin Byron wrote "Empress Semptress," obviously a reminder of a rhyme he later wanted to use (see stanza 77).

1*a* [Her figure—and her vigour and her rigour]
 b Her sweet smile—and her [figure and her vigour]
2   Her plumpness [and her] her imperial . . .

And that's enough, for love is vanity,
    Selfish in its beginning as its end,
Except where 'tis a mere Insanity,
    A Maddening Spirit which would strive to blend
Itself with Beauty's frail Inanity,
    On which the passion's self seems to depend:
And hence some heathenish philosophers
Make Love the Main Spring* of the Universe.

2a [In all Intrigue's beginning, as their end,]
 b [In its sincere beginning—or dull end]
 c [A Self] Selfish . . .
3   where it is mere . . .
7   hence [your] some . . .

74

Besides Platonic love, besides the love
    Of God, the love of Sentiment, the loving
Of faithful pairs—(I needs must rhyme with dove,
    That good old steam-boat* which keeps verses
        moving
'Gainst Reason—Reason ne'er was hand-and-glove
    With rhyme, but always leant less to improving
The sound than sense)—besides all these pretences
To Love, there are those things which Words name
        Senses;—

4   old [refuge] Steam-boat which . . .
5a Gainst [sense and reason who] fragment
 .b Gainst [ryh] [reason's tide who was never] fragment
6   leant more to improving
7   all those pretences
8a To Love, there [also] are those [damned] fragment
 b   are those things [some call the Senses]

Those movements, those improvements in our bodies
　　Which make all bodies anxious to get out
Of their own sand-pits to mix with a Goddess,
　　For such all Women are at first no doubt.
How beautiful that moment! and how odd is
　　That fever which precedes the languid rout
Of our Sensations! What a curious way
The whole thing is of clothing souls in clay!

3a　Of their own [prison] to mix . . .
　b　Of their own Sand pit . . .
4　Women are [th] just then no doubt
5　how odd [tis]
6　which precede[d] . . .
7a　Of [that sad heavy dreary drowsy deadly] drear
　b　Of such sensations in the drowsy drear
8a　After, which shadows [the first—Say—a year]
　b　　　　　　　　　　　　the—Say—second year

76

The noblest kind of Love is Love Platonical,
　　To end or to begin with; the next grand
Is that which may be christened Love Canonical,
　　Because the clergy take the thing in hand;
The third sort to be noted in our Chronicle
　　As flourishing in every Christian land,
Is, when chaste Matrons to their other ties
Add what may be called *Marriage in Disguise.*

This stanza does not appear on Y.

Well, we won't analyze—our story must
   Tell for itself: the Sovereign was smitten,
Juan much flattered by her love, or lust;—
   I cannot stop to alter words once written,
And the two are so mixed with human dust,
   That he who *names one*, both perchance may hit on:
But in such matters Russia's mighty Empress
Behaved no better than a common Sempstress.

5   And the two [things] are so mixed [up with] dust
6*a* That he who names one [upon both] may hit on
 b   [we]
 c   both [belike] may hit on
7   But [Russia's Empress] [Juan] [Russia's] *fragments*

78

The whole Court melted into one wide whisper,
   . And all lips were applied unto all ears!
The elder ladies' wrinkles curled much crisper
   As they beheld; the younger cast some leers
On one another, and each lovely lisper
   Smiled as she talked the matter o'er; but tears
Of rivalship rose in each clouded eye
Of all the standing army who stood by.

1   The whole court [now] melted into wide whisper
2   And all [mouths] were applied . . .
3   wrinkles [waxed] much crisper
5*a*–6*a* [Upon each] other [as] [they] [we gaze on Hesper
        They gazed upon this rising Star] [but tears]
5*b*–6*b* On one another and each [go] blooming lisper
        Smiled as she talked [about it all] *fragment*
                  [it over] *fragment*
                  the matter oer; but tears
7*a* [Came to the eyes] *fragment*
 b [Came thick and warm *sic?* into] [the] each clouded eye

[221]

All the Ambassadors of all the Powers
   Inquired, Who was this very new young man,
Who promised to be great in some few hours?
   Which is full soon (though life is but a span)
Already they beheld the silver showers
   Of rubles rain, as fast as specie can,
Upon his cabinet, besides the presents
Of several ribbons and some thousand peasants.*

4 Which is [not long] though life . . .
5 the [golden] showers

80

Catherine was generous,—all such ladies are:
   Love, that great opener of the heart and all
The ways that lead there, be they near or far,
   Above, below, by turnpikes great or small,—
Love—(though she had a cursed taste for war,
   And was not the best wife,* unless we call
Such Clytemnestra; though perhaps 'tis better
That one should die, than two drag on the fetter)*—

1 all [Harlots] are—
2 Love [which] that grand opener . . .
3 The ways which lead . . .
8 That [both] one should die—than [both endure] the fetter

81

Love had made Catherine make each lover's fortune;
   Unlike our own half-chaste Elizabeth,
Whose avarice all disbursements did importune,
   If History, the grand liar, ever saith
The truth; and though Grief her old age might shorten,
   Because she put a favourite to death,*
Her vile, ambiguous method of flirtation,
And Stinginess, disgrace her Sex and Station.

[CANTO IX]

1   Catherine make [her] lovers' fortune[s]
3*a* Whose passion [every bill at sight] importune[s]
  b   all disbursements did . . .
4   [At] If History the Liar . . .
5*a* and though her [old Life] [old Age] shorten[s]
  b and though her Grief her days might . . .
6   she puts . . .
8   And Avarice—disgust a polished Nation

82

But when the levee rose, and all was bustle
   In the dissolving Circle, all the nations'
Ambassadors began as 'twere to hustle
   Round the young man with their congratulations.
Also the softer silks were heard to rustle
   Of gentle dames, among whose recreations
It is to speculate on handsome faces,
Especially when such lead to high places.

2 In the departing circles . . .
7 It is to [look] [criticize all] handsome faces

83

Juan, who found himself, he knew not how,
   A general object of attention, made
His answers with a very graceful bow
   As if born for the Ministerial trade.
Though modest, on his unembarrassed brow
   Nature had written "gentleman." He said
Little, but to the purpose; and his manner
Flung hovering Graces o'er him like a banner.

1 Juan—who [all at once] *fragment*
3 with [many a] graceful bow
4 for the [diplomatic] trade
7 Little;—but [that was to the] *fragment*
8 Flung [floating] graces . . .

[223]

An order from her Majesty consigned
　Our young Lieutenant to the genial care
Of those in office: all the World looked kind
　(As it will look sometimes with the first stare,
Which Youth would not act ill to keep in mind)
　As also did Miss Protasoff* then there,
Named from her mystic office "l'Eprouveuse,"
A term inexplicable to the Muse.

1　A [Message] from . . .
3　the world [like] looked kind
4　will sometimes do with . . .
5　[As] Youth would not [do] act . . .
6a　[And not be dazzled by its early glare]
　b　[He] As also did Miss Protasof . . .
7a　[A] [Call] *fragment*
　b　Named from [virtuous] office . . .

85

With *her* then, as in humble duty bound,
　Juan retired,—and so will I, until
My Pegasus shall tire of touching ground.
　We have just lit on a "Heaven-kissing hill,"
So lofty that I feel my brain turn round,
　And all my fancies whirling like a mill;
Which is a signal to my nerves and brain,
To take a quiet ride in some green lane.

*On the last page of the Y first draft below this stanza (numbered 74 on
the manuscript) Byron wrote his signature-symbol and "End of Canto 9ᵗʰ
Augᵗ–Septʳ 1822."*
4　We have just [alighted] *fragment*
5　brain turn[ed] round
8　[To leave] [To pause in rhyme] *fragments*

Canto X

1

WHEN Newton saw an apple fall,* he found
    In that slight startle from his contemplation—
'Tis *said* (for I'll not answer above ground
    For any sage's creed or calculation)—
A mode of proving that the earth turned round
    In a most natural whirl called "Gravitation";
And this is the sole mortal who could grapple,
Since Adam, with a fall, or with an apple.

4   For any Sage's [su] [mode of] Calculation   *Intended to write* subject?
5   A [way] of proving . . .
6*a* In a most natural [whirling of rotation]
  b   [mode]—called "Gravitation"
7   And thus . . .
3   Since Adam—[gloriously against an] Apple

Man fell with apples, and with apples rose,
    If this be true; for we must deem the mode
In which Sir Isaac Newton could disclose
    Through the then unpaved stars the turnpike road,
A thing to counterbalance human woes;*
    For ever since immortal man hath glowed
With all kinds of mechanics, and full soon
Steam-engines will conduct him to the Moon.*

2 for [I] must deem the [way]
4 [To the then unploughed] stars . . .
6 [And] ever . . .

3

And wherefore this exordium?—Why, just now,
    In taking up this paltry sheet of paper,
My bosom underwent a glorious glow,
    And my internal Spirit cut a caper:
And though so much inferior, as I know,
    To those who, by the dint of glass and vapour,
Discover stars, and sail in the wind's eye,
I wish to do as much by Poesy.

3a I felt [myself all] in a glorious glow
  b I felt my bosom in . . .
4a And my internal Spirit [in] a caper
  b   [gave] . . .

In the Wind's Eye I have sailed, and sail; but for
 The stars, I own my telescope is dim;
But at the least I have shunned the common shore,
 And leaving land far out of sight, would skim
The Ocean of Eternity:* the roar
 Of breakers has not daunted my slight, trim,
But *still* sea-worthy skiff; and she may float
Where ships have foundered, as doth many a boat.

3 But at the [best] I have [left] the common shore
4*a* And [leaving] land far . . .
 b And [shun] [shunning] land . . .

5

We left our hero, Juan, in the *bloom*
 Of favouritism, but not yet in the *blush;* —
And far be it from my *Muses* to presume
 (For I have more than one Muse at a push)
To follow him beyond the drawing-room:
 It is enough that Fortune found him flush
Of youth, and vigour, beauty, and those things
Which for an instant clip Enjoyment's wings.

1 [Our hero—Juan—was left] in the <u>bloom</u>
2 [And] Of . . .
3 And far [be't] from my <u>Muses</u> to presume[s]

But soon they grow again and leave their nest.
   "Oh!" saith the Psalmist,* "that I had a dove's
Pinions to flee away, and be at rest!"†
   And who, that recollects young years and loves,—
Though hoary now, and with a withering breast,
   And palsied Fancy, which no longer roves
Beyond its dimmed eye's sphere,—but would much
     rather
Sigh like his son, than cough like his grandfather?

1a grow again and [fly away]
 b   [flee away]
4   And who [that hath or had a heart in breast]
5   [Aged] hoary [head] and [the now] withering breast
6   [The] palsied . . .
7a Beyond [it's eyesight—but would wish] much rather
 b Beyond [it's curtailed eye's sight]—but would [wish]
 c Beyond [it's contained . . .]
8   [To sigh instead of Coughing—and crying—"pish!"]

7

But sighs subside, and tears (even widows') shrink,
   Like Arno in the summer, to a shallow,*
So narrow as to shame their wintry brink,
   Which threatens inundations deep and yellow!
Such difference doth a few months make.* You'd think
   Grief a rich field which never would lie fallow;
No more it doth,—its ploughs but change their boys,
Who furrow some new soil to sow for joys.

1   But Sighs [will pass]—and tears . . .
2   in the Summer—[in]to [channels]
4a Which [menace] [und] [inundations to all their Annals]
 b Which [threatens an inundation . . .]
8a [To try] [To follow other] *fragments*
 b Who . . . new [field in] to sow . . .
 c   [land] . . .

But coughs will come when sighs depart—and now
    And then before sighs cease; for oft the one
Will bring the other, ere.the lake-like brow
    Is ruffled by a wrinkle, or the Sun
Of life reach ten o'clock: and while a glow,
    Hectic and brief as summer's day nigh done,
O'erspreads the cheek which seems too pure for clay,
Thousands blaze, love, hope, die—how happy they!—

2   before [they do]—for oft . . .
3   [oer] the lake-like brow
5a–6a Of [youth] reached nine o'clock; [and so was begun
     Life] *fragment*
  5b Of [Life] reached . . .   [and scarce begun]
5c–6b Of Youth reached nine o'clock; and [with] a glow
     Hectic [and transitory] *fragment*
  5d reach'd . . . *In 1833 and in some later editions.*
  7   seems [too p] too pure . . .
  8a [They blaze—love—hope and die]—how happy they!
   b [Youth] [Youth blazes—loves, hopes—dies] . . .

9

But Juan was not meant to die so soon.
    We left him in the focus of such Glory
As may be won by favour of the Moon
    Or ladies' fancies—rather transitory
Perhaps; but who would scorn the month of June,
    Because December, with his breath so hoary,
Must come? Much rather should he court the ray,
To hoard up warmth against a wintry day.

8a To [lay up] warmth . . .; b To [hord] up . . .

Besides, he had some qualities which fix
　　Middle-aged ladies even more than young:
The former know what's what;* while new-fledged
　　　chicks
　　Know little more of Love than what is sung
In rhymes, or dreamt (for Fancy will play tricks)
　　In visions of those skies from whence Love sprung.
Some reckon women by their Suns or Years,
I rather think the Moon should date the dears.

2　[Elderly ladies—even far] more than young
3a　The former know what's what; [the l] *fragment   Intended*
　　to write latter?
　b　　　　　　　　　　　　while [scarce] fledged [chick]
6　[In the] ['Twixt] [Between their teen] *fragments*
7a　[Most Sages reckon women by their] years
　b　[Some people] reckon . . .
8　I rather think [their] Moon should date the [Dears]

11

And why? Because She's changeable and chaste.
　　I know no other reason, whatsoe'er
Suspicious people, who find fault in haste,
　　May choose to tax me with; which is not fair,
　　Nor flattering to "their temper or their taste,"
　　As my friend Jeffrey writes with such an air:*
However, I forgive him, and I trust
He will forgive himself;—if not, I must.

2　other reasons . . .
3　[Malicious] people who find . . .
4　which is [un]fair
5　[And] Nor . . .
6a　Jeffrey . . . *S, 1833, and later editions.*
　b　Jeffery . . . *In 1823 edition.*
7　forgive him, and [resist] I trust
8　himself—[at] if not . . .

Old enemies who have become new friends
　　Should so continue—'tis a point of honour;
And I know nothing which could make amends
　　For a return to hatred: I would shun her
Like garlic, howsoever she extends
　　Her hundred arms and legs, and fain outrun her.
Old flames, new wives, become our bitterest foes—
Converted foes should scorn to join with those.

2*a* tis a [point] of honour
 b tis a [debt] . . .
5   As long's I can however she extends
7   Old [friends,] new Wives . . .
8   [But generous] *fragment*

                              13

This were the worst desertion:—renegadoes,
　　Even shuffling Southey, that incarnate lie,
Would scarcely join again the "reformadoes,"*
　　Whom he forsook to fill the Laureate's sty:
And honest men, from Iceland to Barbadoes,
　　Whether in Caledon or Italy,
Should not veer round with every breath, nor seize,
To pain, the moment when you cease to please.

1   This were the worst [of renegades] . . .
2*a* Even Southey's [self] [that essence of all] *fragment*
 b Even [the rogue] Southey that Incarnate Lie
4   When he forsook [for] to . . . [Stye]
5*a* And [honourable men] *fragment*
 b And honest men from [Brit] *fragment*
6*a* [Though] [In] *fragment*;   *b* Whether in [Edinburgh] or Italy

The lawyer and the critic but behold
   The baser sides of literature and life,
And nought remains unseen, but much untold,
   By those who scour those double vales of strife.
While common men grow ignorantly old,
   The lawyer's brief is like the surgeon's knife,
Dissecting the whole inside of a question,
And with it all the process of digestion.

This stanza was written crosswise on the manuscript.

3 And [many parts of both remain] untold

15

A legal broom's* a moral chimney-sweeper,
   And that's the reason he himself's so dirty:
The endless soot* bestows a tint far deeper
   Than can be hid by altering his shirt; he
Retains the sable stains of the dark creeper,
   At least some twenty-nine do out of thirty,
In all their habits:—Not so *you,* I own;
As Caesar wore his robe you wear your gown.

This stanza does not appear on the manuscript.

16

And all our little feuds, at least all *mine,*
   Dear Jeffrey, once my most redoubted foe,*
(As far as rhyme and criticism combine
   To make such puppets of us things below)
Are over. Here's a health to "Auld Lang Syne"!
   I do not know you, and may never know
Your face,—but you have acted on the whole
Most nobly, and I own it from my soul.

[CANTO X]

1a [But never mind our feuds—at] least all <u>mine</u>
  b [With decency; our feuds] at least . . .
2a [My] Jeffrey . . . s; b Jeffery . . . *In 1823 edition.*
6 know [thee] and . . .
7 Your face—[you mine]—you have . . .

17

And when I use the phrase of "Auld Lang Syne"!
  'Tis not addressed to you—the more's the pity
For me, for I would rather take my wine
  With you, than aught (save Scott) in your proud city.
But somehow,—it may seem a schoolboy's whine,
  And yet I seek not to be grand nor witty,—
But I am half a Scot by birth, and bred
A whole one, and my heart flies to my head,—

3 rather [drink] my wine
5 But Something—it may . . .

18

As "Auld Lang Syne" brings Scotland, one and all,*
  Scotch plaids, Scotch snoods, the blue hills, and
    clear streams,
The Dee, the Don, Balgounie's Brig's *black wall,*
  All my boy feelings, all my gentler dreams
Of what I *then dreamt,* clothed in their own pall,
  Like Banquo's offspring;*—floating past me seems
My childhood in this childishness of mine:
I care not—'tis a glimpse of "Auld Lang Syne."

1 [And] "Auld lang Syne" . . .
2 Scotch [men]—Scotch [lasses]—Blue hills . . .
5 dream[ed] . . .

[233]

And though, as you remember, in a fit
    Of wrath and rhyme, when juvenile and curly,
I railed at Scots to shew my wrath and wit,
    Which must be owned was sensitive and surly,
Yet 'tis in vain such sallies to permit,
    They cannot quench young feelings fresh and early:
I "*scotched,* not killed,"* the Scotchman in my blood,
And love the land of "mountain and of flood."*

3 to show my rage and wit
4 Which, [I allow] was sensitive . . .
5 sallies [we] permit
6 They [could] cannot . . .

20

Don Juan, who was real or ideal,—
    For both are much the same, since what men think
Exists when the once thinkers are less real
    Than what they thought, for mind can never sink,*
And 'gainst the body makes a strong appeal;
    And yet 'tis very puzzling on the brink
Of what is called Eternity, to stare,
And know no more of what is here than there:—

1 [Our] Juan . . .
2 what [we] think
3 the [warm] thinkers . . .
4 Than what they thought [and they thought] *fragment*

Don Juan grew a very polished Russian—
  How we won't mention, *why* we need not say:
Few youthful minds can stand the strong concussion
  Of any slight temptation in their way:
But *his* just now were spread as is a cushion
  Smoothed for a monarch's seat of honour: gay
Damsels, and dances, revels, ready money,
Made ice seem Paradise, and winter sunny.

4 Of [all] any [small] temptation . . .
5 But His just now were [manifold a] *fragment*
7*a* [Damsels, great Wealth, and illustrious Orders]
 b Damsels, [and Rubles and Chivalric Orders].
 c Damsels, [and Orders and ready Money]
 d Damsels, and dances—[revels]—revels, ready Money
8*a* [Made even a Moscow Winter] *fragment*
 b [Made] [Pert] [Pert] [Petersburgh] *fragments*
 c Made Ice seem [Pard] Paradise; and [Ice] *fragment*

22

The favour of the Empress was agreeable;
  And though the duty waxed a little hard,
Young people at his time of life should be able
  To come off handsomely in that regard.
He now was growing up like a green tree, able
  For love, war, or ambition, which reward
Their luckier votaries, till old Age's tedium
Make some prefer the circulating medium.*

2 duty [was] a little hard
5 like a [fair] tree . . .
6 For love, [or] war,—[the two things] which reward
7*a* Their luckier votaries—till [Life's gr] *Intended to write* gray?
 b   [wan]
 c   [old] Age's tedium

About this time, as might have been anticipated,
    Seduced by youth and dangerous examples,
Don Juan grew, I fear, a little dissipated;
    Which is a sad thing, and not only tramples
On our fresh feelings, but—as being participated
    With all kinds of incorrigible samples
Of frail humanity—must make us selfish,
And shut our souls up in us like a shell-fish.

5 On our [best] feelings . . .
7 [makes] make us selfish
8 And shut our [hearts] up . . .

24

This we pass over. We will also pass
    The usual progress of intrigues between
Unequal matches, such as are, alas!
    A young Lieutenant's with a *not old* Queen,
But one who is not so youthful as she was
    In all the royalty of sweet seventeen.
Sovereigns may sway materials, but not matter,
And wrinkles (the d—d democrats) won't flatter.

3 Unequal Matches,—[as must be] alas!
4 A young Lieutenant [and a] <u>not old</u> Queen
6–8 *Order of composition:*
    [Some thirty years before at fair eighteen]
    [Or Seven and twenty—but it] [is] [does not matter]
                [which . . .]
    [Wrinkles—those damndest democrats—wont]
    [Wrinkles—those deadly democrats wont flatter]
    [Do what we will] *fragment*
    [Though Sovereigns] *fragment*
    In all the royalty of sweet seventeen
    Sovereigns [may] may sway [Men] Materials, but not Matter,
    And Wrinkles—the [d—d] democrats! won't flatter.

And Death, the sovereign's Sovereign, though the great
   Gracchus of all mortality, who levels
With his *Agrarian* laws, the high estate
   Of him who feasts, and fights, and roars, and revels,
To one small grass-grown patch (which must await
   Corruption for its crop) with the poor devils
Who never had a foot of land till now—
Death's a reformer, all men must allow.

1 Sovereign—[and] the great
5 To one small grass-grown [little] *fragment*
7 [Of him who neer had foot] of land till now
8 [Death is a Radical] *fragment*

26

He lived (not Death, but Juan) in a hurry
   Of waste, and haste, and glare, and gloss, and glitter,
In this gay clime of bear-skins black and furry—
   Which (though I hate to say a thing that's bitter)
Peep out sometimes, when things are in a flurry,
   Through all the "purple and fine linen,"* fitter
For Babylon's than Russia's royal harlot—
And neutralize her outward show of Scarlet.

3–4   [Like many publications of John Murray
      That modest bibliopole] *fragment*
  7a [For Bable's] [Bable's] [Bable] *fragments*
   b For [Babel's than for] Russia's . . .
  8 And neutralize [the] outward . . .

And this same state we won't describe: we could
    Perhaps from hearsay, or from recollection;
But getting nigh grim Dante's "obscure wood,"*
    That horrid equinox, that hateful section
Of human years,* that half-way house, that rude
    Hut, whence wise travellers drive with circumspection
Life's sad post-horses o'er the dreary frontier
Of age, and looking back to youth, give *one* tear;—

1 And this same [Life] we . . .
4*a* That horrid [time of Life] that hateful [sect] section
  b   [tide . . .]
5–6 Of Human years [when] that half-way house, that rude
    Hut, where we travellers bait with dim reflection
7 [The] Life's [sad horses] sad post horses . . .

I won't describe*—that is, if I can help
    Description; and I won't reflect—that is,
If I can stave off thought, which, as a whelp
    Clings to its teat, sticks to me through the abyss
Of this odd labyrinth; or as the kelp
    Holds by the rock; or as a lover's kiss
Drains its first draught of lips:—but, as I said,
I *won't* philosophize, and *will* be read.

2–3*a* Description—and I won't reflect—[for that
    Is worse and I will] *fragment*
  3*b* [For] If I can stave off Thought, which [like] a whelp
  4 Clings to its [dam]—sticks . . .
  7*a* [To a] [new Misst] first [lip but as I said of late] *Intended to write* Mistress.
  b [Sucks] it's first draught of lips . . .
  8*a* [I will not moralize—but] *fragment*
  b I['ll not] philosophize, and will [narrate]

Juan, instead of courting courts, was courted,
    A thing which happens rarely: this he owed
Much to his youth, and much to his reported
    Valour; much also to the blood he showed,
Like a race-horse; much to each dress he sported,
    Which set the beauty off in which he glowed,
As purple clouds befringe the sun; but most
He owed to an old woman and his post.

1   Juan [was] instead . . .
3   and [more] to his reported
5a [In all his movements] *fragment*
 b Like [a true race] *fragment*
 c Like a race horse, much to [the] each . . .
6   Which set [his] the Beauty off [with] which . . .
7   As purple Clouds [set off] the Sun . . .

30

He wrote to Spain:—and all his near relations,
    Perceiving he was in a handsome way
Of getting on himself, and finding stations
    For cousins also, answered the same day.
Several prepared themselves for emigrations;
    And, eating ices, were o'erheard to say,
That with the addition of a slight pelisse,
Madrid's and Moscow's climes were of a-piece.

1   to Spain—[to] and all . . .
4a For [all his Cousins]; answered the [next] day
 b For [many] Cousins . . .
6   [And bought up Maps] *fragment*

His Mother, Donna Inez, finding too
    That in the lieu of drawing on his banker,
Where his assets were waxing rather few,
    He had brought his spending to a handsome anchor,—
Replied, "that she was glad to see him through
    Those pleasures after which wild youth will hanker;
As the sole sign of man's being in his senses
Is, learning to reduce his past expenses.

3 [While] his . . .
7 As the sole [of M] sign of [Young] Man's being . . .
8 Is [when he learns to limit his] expences

32

"She also recommended him to God,
    And no less to God's Son, as well as Mother;
Warned him against Greek-worship, which looks odd
    In Catholic eyes; but told him too to smother
Outward dislike, which don't look well abroad:
    Informed him that he had a little brother
Born in a second wedlock; and above
All, praised the Empress's *maternal* love.

2 And [also] to God's . . .
5 <u>Outward</u> [aver *sic?*] dislike, which [is as] well abroad   *Intended to write* aversion?
7 Born in a [recent] wedlock . . .
8 All, [begged] [bade] praised . . .

"She could not too much give her approbation
  Unto an Empress, who preferred young men
Whose age, and, what was better still, whose nation
  And climate, stopped all scandal (now and then):—
At home it might have given her some vexation;
  But where thermometers sunk down to ten,
Or five, or one, or zero, she could never
Believe that virtue thawed before the river."

2   Unto a [Sovereign] who . . .
4   And Climate—stopped [the Lion Scandal's den]
7a–8 Or five . . . zero—[till the Ice
        Cracked, she need *sic?* neer believe in thaws for Vice]
7b   Or five . . . zero—She would never

                                34

Oh for a *forty-parson-power* to chaunt*
  Thy praise, Hypocrisy! Oh for a hymn
Loud as the Virtues thou dost loudly vaunt,
  Not practise! Oh for trumps of cherubim!
Or the ear-trumpet of my good old aunt,*
  Who, though her spectacles at last grew dim,
Drew quiet consolation through its hint,
When she no more could read the pious print.

4   [And never practise, Oh] trumps . . .
5   Or [for the] trumpet . . .
6   Who, through . . . *Misprint in 1823 edition.*
7   [Sensed *sic?* out the due responses by] it's hint

She was no hypocrite at least, poor soul,
　　But went to heaven in as sincere a way
As any body on the Elected Roll,
　　Which portions out upon the judgment day
Heaven's freeholds, in a sort of doomsday scroll,
　　Such as the conqueror William did repay
His knights with, lotting others' properties
Into some sixty thousand new knights' fees.*

7a His knights—[dividing] others' properties
 b　　　　　　　　　　　 other's . . .   *Misprint in 1823 edition.*

36

I can't complain, whose ancestors are there,*
　　Erneis, Radulphus—eight-and-forty manors
(If that my memory doth not greatly err)
　　Were their reward for following Billy's banners;
And though I can't help thinking 'twas scarce fair
　　To strip the Saxons of their *hydes*, like tanners;*
Yet as they founded churches with the produce,
You'll deem, no doubt, they put it to a good use.

1 We can't complain; [my] Ancestors . . .
5 And [yet] I . . .
6 [Stripping] the Saxons . . .
7–8 [And humbly] [that] [hope that the same God which hath given
　Us land on earth] [would] [will do no less in heaven]

The gentle Juan flourished, though at times
He felt like other plants called Sensitive,*
Which shrink from touch, as monarchs do from rhymes,
Save such as Southey can afford to give.
Perhaps he longed, in bitter frosts, for climes
In which the Neva's ice* would cease to live
Before May-day: perhaps, despite his duty,
In royalty's vast arms he sighed for beauty:

2 He felt like plants, [which] *fragment*
5 Perhaps he [sighed], in [very] bitter . . .
7 perhaps [he found his] Duty
8 [Would sometimes have changed Royalty for Beauty]

                          38

Perhaps—but, sans perhaps, we need not seek
For causes young or old: the canker-worm
Will feed upon the fairest, freshest cheek,
As well as further drain the withered form:
Care, like a house-keeper, brings every week
His bills in, and however we may storm,
They must be paid: though six days smoothly run,
The seventh will bring blue devils* or a dun.

1 Perhaps—but d—n perhaps . . .
4 [And] As [yet] as further . . .

I don't know how it was, but he grew sick:
    The Empress was alarmed, and her physician
(The same who physicked Peter)* found the tick
    Of his fierce pulse betoken a condition
Which augured of the dead, however *quick*
    Itself, and showed a feverish disposition;
At which the whole court was extremely troubled,
The Sovereign shocked, and all his medicines doubled.

1 I don't know it was—but he grew [pale]
7 whole Court were extremely ...

40

Low were the whispers, manifold the rumours:*
    Some said he had been poisoned by Potemkin;
Others talked learnedly of certain tumours,
    Exhaustion, or disorders of the same kin;
Some said 'twas a concoction of the humours,
    Which with the blood too readily will claim kin;
Others again were ready to maintain,
" 'Twas only the fatigue of last campaign."

7 [The Doctors] *fragment*

41

But here is one prescription out of many:*
    "Sodae-Sulphat. ℥vj. ʒſs. Mannae optim.
Aq. fervent. F. ʒiſs. ℥ij. tinct. Sennae
    Haustus." (And here the surgeon came and cupped
    him)
"R. Pulv. Com. gr. iij. Ipecacuanhae"
    (With more beside, if Juan had not stopped 'em).
"Bolus Potassae Sulphuret. sumendus,
Et Haustus ter in die capiendus."

[CANTO X]

1   But here is [Doctor Rogeson's *sic?* prescription]
          [the] one prescription out of many
2   ℥vi [et] Mannae . . .
4   Haustus—(and here the[y also bled &] cupped him)
5*a* [Potassae Supertast ℥ij] *fragment*
 b Rx Pulv. Com. [grains] gr. iii . . .
6   stopped [him]

42

This is the way physicians mend or end us,
    Secundum artem: but although we sneer
In health—when ill, we call them to attend us,
    Without the least propensity to jeer:
While that "hiatus maxime deflendus,"*
    To be filled up by spade or mattock, 's near,
Instead of gliding graciously down Lethe,
We tease mild Baillie, or soft Abernethy.*

1 physicians [end or] mend or end us
6 Spade and Mattock's near
8 [They] teaze . . .

43

Juan demurred at this first notice to
    Quit; and though Death had threatened an ejection,
His youth and constitution bore him through,
    And sent the doctors in a new direction.
But still his state was delicate: the hue
    Of health but flickered with a faint reflection
Along his wasted cheek, and seemed to gravel
The Faculty—who said that he must travel.

1*a* Juan [got well—which is] [and] *fragment*
 b Juan demurred to this . . .
4   And sent [the Spectre] the Doctors . . .
5–6 But still his [Health] was delicate; the hue
    Of Health [still wavered] with [but] faint reflection

[245]

The climate was too cold they said for him,
Meridian-born, to bloom in. This opinion
Made the chaste Catherine look a little grim,
Who did not like at first to lose her minion:
But when she saw his dazzling eye wax dim,
And drooping like an eagle's with clipt pinion,
She then resolved to send him on a mission,
But in a style becoming his condition.

2a Meridian-born to [flourish in this nation]
 b   [flower in . . .]
4 [But she was a Philosopher, whose Caution]
5a But She [was a Philosopher] *fragment*
 b But when She saw [him wax so pale and slim]
8 But with a train becoming . . .

45

There was just then a kind of a discussion,
A sort of treaty or negociation
Between the British cabinet and Russian,
Maintained with all the due prevarication
With which great states such things are apt to push o_
Something about the Baltic's navigation,
Hides, train-oil, tallow, and the rights of Thetis,*
Which Britons deem their "uti possidetis."

1 There was just then, a [secret charge of trust]
2a negociation   s;   b negotiation   *In 1833 and in later editions*
3a Between [Great Britain's] Cabinet *fragment*
 b Between the British [and] *fragment*
 c   [Monarch] *fragment*
7 [Iron, and hides, train oil, and tallow] *fragment*

So Catherine, who had a handsome way
    Of fitting out her favourites, conferred
This secret charge on Juan, to display
    At once her royal splendour, and reward
His services. He kissed hands the next day,
    Received instructions how to play his card,
Was laden with all kinds of gifts and honours,
Which showed what great discernment was the donor's.

3 [A] secret . . .
4 [Her own munificence and] reward
5 His services; [appointed] hands . . .
7 Was [loaded] laden with all kinds of [handsome] *fragment*

47

But she was lucky, and luck's all. Your Queens
    Are generally prosperous in reigning;
Which puzzles us to know what Fortune means.
    But to continue: though her years were waning,
Her climacteric teased her like her teens;
    And though her dignity brooked no complaining,
So much did Juan's setting off distress her,
She could not find at first a fit successor.

4   her [days] were waning
5a [She was as amatory as in] her teens
 b   [amorous as if] . . .
 c Her Climacteric plagued her like . . .
7   [She really liked her Spaniard] *fragment*
8   She [tried ten days nor found a] fit Successor

But Time the comforter will come at last;
   And four-and-twenty hours, and twice that number
Of candidates requesting to be placed,
   Made Catherine taste next night a quiet slumber:—
Not that she meant to fix again in haste,
   Nor did she find the quantity encumber,
But always choosing with deliberation,
Kept the place open for their emulation.

3   Of Candidates [all pressing] to be placed
4   Made Catherine [have] next . . .
5   to [choose] again in haste
7*a* [For she was used to act] *fragment*
  b   [to pick from] *fragment*
  c But always [picking with discernment] [deliberation]

49

While this high post of honour's in abeyance,
   For one or two days, reader, we request
You'll mount with our young hero the conveyance
   Which wafted him from Petersburgh: the best
Barouche, which had the glory to display once
   The fair Czarina's Autocratic crest,
(When, a new Iphigene, she went to Tauris)
Was given to her favourite,* and now *bore his.*

2 For [two or three] days . . .
6 [Her] The fair . . .
7 When, [like] a new . . .

A bull-dog, and a bull-finch, and an ermine,
  All private favourites of Don Juan; for
(Let deeper sages the true cause determine)
  He had a kind of inclination,* or
Weakness, for what most people deem mere vermin—
  Live animals: an old maid of threescore
For cats and birds more penchant ne'er displayed,
Although he was not old, nor even a maid;—

1 A [Secretary—lap dog and a bull dog—and]
5 Weakness for what [many] people . . .
7 [For] cats and [dogs] more penchant [scarce] betrayed
8 nor yet a maid

51

The animals aforesaid occupied
  Their station: there were valets, secretaries,
In other vehicles; but at his side
  Sat little Leila,* who survived the parries
He made 'gainst Cossaque sabres, in the wide
  Slaughter of Ismail. Though my wild Muse varies
Her note, she don't forget the infant girl
Whom he preserved—a pure and living pearl.

4 Sate little Leila [owing to] the parries
6 my [m]ild [varies]

Poor little thing! She was as fair as docile,
    And with that gentle, serious character,
As rare in living beings as a fossile
    Man, 'midst thy mouldy Mammoths, "grand
        Cuvier!"*
Ill fitted with her ignorance to jostle
    With this o'erwhelming world, where all must err:
But she was yet but ten years old, and therefore
Was tranquil, though she knew not why or wherefore.

1 as fair [and] docile
3 As rare midst living . . .
4 Man, [a]midst [all] thy Mammoths, Cuvier!
5 Ill fitted was her . . .   *S, 1833, and later editions.*
7 was [still] but . . .
8 nor wherefore

53

Don Juan loved her, and she loved him, as
    Nor brother, father, sister, daughter love.
I cannot tell exactly what it was;
    He was not yet quite old enough to prove
Parental feelings, and the other class,
    Called brotherly affection could not move
His bosom,—for he never had a sister:
Ah! if he had, how much he would have missed her!

2 sister [mother] love
5 [nor] that other class
6 affections . . .

And still less was it sensual; for besides
　　That he was not an ancient debauchee,
(Who like sour fruit, to stir their veins' salt tides,
　　As Acids rouse a dormant Alkali)
Although ('twill happen as our planet guides)
　　His youth was not the chastest that might be,
There was the purest platonism at bottom
Of all his feelings—only he forgot 'em.

3–4　([To] like sour fruit, to [sharpen up the tides
　　Of their salt veins and] [their] [stir their stagnancy]
　　　　　　　　[and their sad shallow seas])
　　As Acids rouse the dormant Alkalie)
　5　happen as [our Star presides]
　6　that [may] be
　7　There was [a longing] Platonism . . .
　8　feelings—[until] he . . .

55

Just now there was no peril of temptation;
　　He loved the infant orphan he had saved,
As Patriots (now and then) may love a nation;
　　His pride too felt that she was not enslaved,
Owing to him;—as also her salvation
　　Through his means and the church's might be paved.
But one thing's odd, which here must be inserted,
The little Turk refused to be converted.

No revisions.

'Twas strange enough she should retain the impression
    Thro' such a scene of change, and dread, and
        slaughter;
But though three bishops told her the transgression,
    She showed a great dislike to holy water:
She also had no passion for confession;
    Perhaps she had nothing to confess:—no matter;
Whate'er the cause, the church made little of it—
She still held out that Mahomet was a prophet.

2 Through . . .
3 bishops [showed] her . . .
4 to holy [daughter]
5 She also [showed] no . . .
6 Perhaps [because she had naught to confess]

57

In fact, the only Christian she could bear
    Was Juan, whom she seemed to have selected
In place of what her home and friends once *were*.
    He *naturally* loved what he protected:
And thus they formed a rather curious pair;
    A guardian green in years, a ward connected
In neither clime, time, blood, with her defender;
And yet this want of ties made their's more tender.

2 Was Juan—[and] she . . .
3a In place of [all] her Friends and [Country] were
 b In place of what her Friends and Home once were
6 A Guardian [of nineteen], a Ward . . .
7a In neither clime—[age—tongue—] with . . .
 b   [years . . .]

They journeyed on through Poland and through
    Warsaw,
  Famous for mines of salt and yokes of iron:
Through Courland also, which that famous farce saw
    Which gave her dukes the graceless name of "Biron."*
'Tis the same landscape which the modern Mars saw
    Who marched to Moscow, led by Fame, the Syren!
  To lose by one month's frost some twenty years
  Of conquest, and his guard of grenadiers.

4*a* [Which] gave . . . ; *b* That gave . . .
6 Siren s *This spelling without the capitalization is used in 1833 and in later editions.*
7 To lose by one Month's frost [five lustrous years]

Let not this seem an anti-climax:—"Oh!
   My Guard! my Old Guard!"* exclaimed that God
     of Clay.—
Think of the Thunderer's falling down below
   Carotid-artery-cutting Castlereagh!*—
Alas! that glory should be chilled by snow!
   But should we wish to warm us on our way
Through Poland, there is Kosciusko's name*
Might scatter fire through ice, like Hecla's flame.

1a Let not this . . .
  b Let this not . . . *In 1833 and in later editions.*
3–4 [Who now that he is dead has not a foe]
    [Who now his dust is . . .]
    [Who states a *sic?*] *fragment*
    [The last expired in cut throat] Castlereagh
  8 *In the following order of composition, the first two attempts are*
    fragments:
    [A Talisman]
    [Might]
    [Which burns more bright in ice,] like Hecla's flame
    [Which gathers] fire [from] ice . . .
    [Which vomits] . . .
    Might scatter[s] fire through ice . . .

60

From Poland they came on through Prussia Proper,
   And Koningsberg the capital, whose vaunt,
Besides some veins of iron, lead, or copper,
   Has lately been the great Professor Kant.*
Juan, who cared not a tobacco-stopper
   About philosophy, pursued his jaunt
To Germany, whose somewhat tardy millions
Have princes who spur more than their postillions.

2a And [changing horses] *fragment*
  b Konigsberg . . . s; c Königsberg *In 1833 and in later editions.*
  The spelling of the 1823 edition, Koningsberg, *can be found in gazet-*
  teers of Byron's day and afterward.

7a [As fast as] *fragment*
 b [Through] Germany—[as fast] *fragment*
 c To Germany—[that] whose . . .
8a Have [Tyrants much more quick] than their postillions
 b postilions *In 1833 and in later editions. This variation will not be noted hereafter.*

61

And thence through Berlin, Dresden, and the like,
    Until he reached the castellated Rhine:*—
Ye glorious Gothic scenes! how much ye strike
    All phantasies, not even excepting mine:
A grey wall, a green ruin, rusty pike,
    Make my soul pass the equinoctial line
Between the present and past worlds, and hover
Upon their airy confine, half-seas-over.

No revisions.

62

But Juan posted on through Manheim, Bonn,
    Which Drachenfels frowns over like a spectre
Of the good feudal times for ever gone,
    On which I have not time just now to lecture.
From thence he was drawn onwards to Cologne,
    A city which presents to the inspector
Eleven thousand Maidenheads of bone,*
The greatest number Flesh hath ever known.

1a Manheim . . . *S, 1833 edition, and contemporary gazetteers.*
 b Mannheim *In 1903 and in other modern editions.*
2 Which Drakenfels [hangs] over . . .
5 he [trotted] was drawn . . .
6 presents to [our Conjecture]
7 Eleven thousand [virgin skulls] *fragment*
8 number [that was] ever known

From thence to Holland's Hague and Helvoetsluys,*
   That water land of Dutchmen and of ditches,
Where juniper expresses its best juice,
   The poor man's sparkling substitute for riches.
Senates and sages have condemned its use*—
   But to deny the mob a cordial which is
Too often all the clothing, meat, or fuel
Good government has left them, seems but cruel.

2 That [lovely] land . . .
4 substitute [vinta] for riches *Intended to write* vintage.
5 [Of which] *fragment*
6 But [why] deny . . .

64

Here he embarked, and with a flowing sail
   Went bounding for the island of the free,
Towards which the impatient wind blew half a gale:
   High dashed the spray, the bows dipped in the sea,
And sea-sick passengers turned somewhat pale;
   But Juan, seasoned as he well might be
By former voyages, stood to watch the skiffs
Which passed, or catch the first glimpse of the cliffs.

3*a* [To] which . . .; *b* Toward which . . .
4 the spray—[her] bows dipped . . .
6 But Juan [who was] seasoned . . .

At length they rose, like a white wall along
   The blue sea's border; and Don Juan felt—
What even young strangers feel a little strong
   At the first sight of Albion's chalky belt—
A kind of pride that he should be among
   Those haughty shop-keepers,* who sternly dealt
Their goods and edicts out from pole to pole,
And made the very billows pay them toll.

7 Their [edicts and] goods and edicts . . .

66

I have no great cause to love that spot of earth,
   Which holds what *might have been* the noblest nation;
But though I owe it little but my birth,
   I feel a mixed regret and veneration
For its decaying fame and former worth.
   Seven years (the usual term of transportation)
Of absence lay one's old resentments level,
When a man's country's going to the devil.

1a I have no . . . s;   b I've no . . .   *In 1833 and in later editions.*
4 [A mixture of] regret . . .
5 For [all] it's . . .
7a Of Absence [form feelings] *fragment*
  b   [feeling so far cannot level]

67 [CANTO X]

Alas! could She but fully, truly, know
 How her great name is now throughout abhorred;
How eager all the earth is for the blow
 Which shall lay bare her bosom to the sword;
How all the nations deem her their worst foe,
 That worse than *worst of foes*, the once adored
False friend, who held out freedom to mankind,
And now would chain them, to the very mind;—

2 through [earth] abhorred
4 lay [her] bare her . . .
7*a* False friend—[that held out Freedom's name in vain]
 b   [that taking Freedom's . . .]
 c   who hold out Freedom [and Men]
 d   [as a bait]
8 *Three fragments:*
 a [Rose up to grasp it]
 b [To chain the world]
 c [To lure the world to chains]

68

Would she be proud, or boast herself the free,
 Who is but first of slaves? The nations are
In prison,—but the jailor, what is he?
 No less a victim to the bolt and bar.
Is the poor privilege to turn the key
 Upon the captive, freedom? He's as far
From the enjoyment of the earth and air
Who watches o'er the chain, as they who wear.

3 In [dungeons] prison . . .
6 Upon [your kind] [the true freedom] *fragment*

Don Juan now saw Albion's earliest beauties,—
    Thy cliffs, *dear* Dover! harbour, and hotel;
Thy custom-house, with all its delicate duties;
    Thy waiters running mucks at every bell;*
Thy packets, all whose passengers are booties
    To those who upon land or water dwell;
And last, not least, to strangers uninstructed,
Thy long, long bills, whence nothing is deducted.

4 at every bell[s]
6 To those who [on the] land or [sea may] dwell
7 And [most of all] to Strangers . . .
8 long bill . . .

70

Juan, though careless, young, and magnifique,
    And rich in rubles, diamonds, cash, and credit,
Who did not limit much his bills per week,
    Yet stared at this a little, though he paid it,—
(His Maggior Duomo, a smart, subtle Greek,
    Before him summed the awful scroll and read it):
But doubtless as the air, though seldom sunny,
Is free, the respiration's worth the money.

3 [And] Who . . .
4 [And] Yet . . .
5 His [steward a subtle] *fragment*
6a [With] [Had] *fragments*
 b Before him summed the awful [document] and read it
7 [And] But . . .

On with the horses! Off to Canterbury!
    Tramp, tramp, o'er pebble, and splash, splash, thro'
        puddle;
Hurrah! how swiftly speeds the post so merry!
    Not like slow Germany, wherein they muddle
Along the road,* as if they went to bury
    Their fare; and also pause besides, to fuddle
With "schnapps"—sad dogs! whom "Hundsfot" or
        "Ferflucter"*
Affect no more than lightning a conductor.

    4   Not like [dull] Germany . . .
7a–8a   With [Scnapes]
        With "Schnapps"—[and spite of all the "dogs" and "logs"]
                            [of "damn em"]
        [Launched at their heads—jog—jog—jog—jog—jog—jog]
    7b   With "Schnapps"—sad dogs whom "Hundsfot [Sacrament]
    c   "Ferfluktor"
    d   Verflucter   In 1833 and in later editions.
    8b   Affect no more than Lightning a Conductor
7e–8c   Alternative couplet:
        With Schnapps—Democritus would cease to smile
        By German postboys driven a German Mile

72

Now there is nothing gives a man such spirits,
    Leavening his blood as Cayenne doth a curry,
As going at full speed—no matter where its
    Direction be, so 'tis but in a hurry,
And merely for the sake of its own merits:
    For the less cause there is for all this flurry,
The greater is the pleasure in arriving
At the great *end* of travel—which is driving.

    2   [Stirring] his blood . . .
    4   Direction be—[so all are] in a hurry
    5   [Especially when there's no cause] *fragment*

They saw at Canterbury the Cathedral;
    Black Edward's helm, and Becket's bloody stone,*
Were pointed out as usual by the Bedral,
    In the same quaint, uninterested tone:—
There's Glory again for you, gentle reader! All
    Ends in a rusty casque, and dubious bone,*
Half-solved into those sodas or magnesias,
Which form that bitter draught, the human species.

1–2 [At] Canterbury [they saw] the Cathedral
     [An ancient building which extremely] *fragment*
  5 There's Glory [for you] . . .
  7 Half solved into ⌈some⌉ Sodas [of] Magnesias
 8*a* With [which formed] that bitter draught . . .
  b With form that . . .

74

The effect on Juan was of course sublime:
    He breathed a thousand Cressys,* as he saw
The casque, which never stooped, except to Time.
    Even the bold Churchman's tomb excited awe,
Who died in the then great attempt to climb
    O'er kings, who *now* at least *must talk* of law,
Before they butcher. Little Leila gazed,
And asked why such a structure had been raised:

  3 That Casque which . . .
  5 Who died [for Tithes] *fragment*
  6 now [must] at least must . . .
  8 And [now *sic?*] asked . . .

And being told it was "God's house," she said
　He was well lodged, but only wondered how
He suffered Infidels in his homestead,
　The cruel Nazarenes, who had laid low
His holy temples in the lands which bred
　The True Believers;—and her infant brow
Was bent with grief that Mahomet should resign
A mosque so noble, flung like pearls to swine.

2–3　[Twas fit that here as in the holy land
　　　Of Mecca he should be well lodged] *fragment*
　　　[Of Mecca his Apartments should] *fragment*
　6　[His] true . . .
　7a　[Flushed] with [a pious fury to survey]
　　b　　　　　　　[wrath to see the Heavens resign]

76

On, on! through meadows, managed like a garden,
　A Paradise of hops and high production:
For after years of travel by a Bard in
　Countries of greater heat but lesser suction,
A green field is a sight which makes him pardon
　The absence of that more sublime construction,
Which mixes up vines, olives, precipīces,
Glaciers, volcanos, oranges, and ices.

4　Countries [more] of . . .
5　[The pushed *sic?* up feelings] *fragment*
6　The absence of that [beautiful destruction]
7a　[Which] [Such as] *fragments*
　b　Which mixes up Vines—[Precipices] . . .
8　[Volcanos] *fragment*

And when I think upon a pot of beer—
    But I won't weep!—and so drive on, postillions!
As the smart boys spurred fast in their career,
    Juan admired these highways of free millions;
A country in all senses the most dear
    To foreigner or native, save some silly ones,
Who "kick against the pricks"* just at this juncture,
And for their pains get only a fresh puncture.

2a But—I won't weep—[Come postboys! anon]
 b   [Come postboys! Whirl along]
3   spurred [on] in . . .
5   A Country [of] in . . .
6   To foreigner & native . . .
7–8 Who [may] "kick against the pricks" [of higher stations]
    [And for their pains get smarter puncturations]

78

What a delightful thing's a turnpike road!
    So smooth, so level, such a mode of shaving
The earth, as scarce the eagle in the broad
    Air can accomplish, with his wide wings waving.
Had such been cut in Phaeton's time, the God
    Had told his son to satisfy his craving
With the York mail;—but onward as we roll,
"Surgit amari aliquid"*—the toll!

2 mode of [clearing]
5 Had [they] been . . .
7 [By driving] the York Mail;—but [Ah! my sinking Soul]
8 ['tis] the toll!

Alas! how deeply painful is all payment!
 Take lives, take wives, take aught except men's purses.
As Machiavel shows those in purple raiment,*
 Such is the shortest way to general curses.
They hate a murderer much less than a claimant
 On that sweet ore which every body nurses:—
Kill a man's family, and he may brook it,
But keep your hands out of his breeches' pocket.

2a Take lives—take [every thing]—except . . .
 b   [any thing] . . .
5a [Much sooner] *fragment*
 b They hate a [parricide] much less . . .
6a On that sweet ore [Earth's] *fragment*
 b   [xxxx] *fragment*
 c   which [all Mankind so] nurses
 d   which every [man so] . . .
7a Kill a man's family—[himself—a father]
 b   [sire]

80

So said the Florentine: ye Monarchs, hearken
 To your instructor. Juan now was borne,
Just as the day began to wane and darken,
 O'er the high hill which looks with pride or scorn
Toward the great city:—ye who have a spark in
 Your veins of Cockney spirit, smile or mourn,
According as you take things well or ill—
Bold Britons, we are now on Shooter's Hill!*

1   ye Monarchs [listen]
2a [He was your Master of your stupid college]
 b [He is the . . .]
4   [To] that high . . .
5   [Oer] the . . .
7a According [to your] *fragment*
 b According as you take things well or [kill]

> The sun went down, the smoke rose up, as from
>   A half-unquenched volcano, o'er a space
> Which well beseemed the "Devil's drawing-room,"*
>   As some have qualified that wondrous place.
> But Juan felt, though not approaching *home*,
>   As one who, though he were not of the race,
> Revered the soil, of those true sons the mother,
> Who butchered half the earth, and bullied t'other.*

5   felt [as if] not . . .
6   [As one who might] *fragment*
7   *Three fragments:*
  a Revered the Soil—[which]
  b   [whose Sons twere]
  c   [Sons of their]
8   [Butchered one half the] [of] [earth] and bullied t'other

82

> A mighty mass of brick, and smoke, and shipping,
>   Dirty and dusky, but as wide as eye
> Could reach, with here and there a sail just skipping
>   In sight, then lost amidst the forestry
> Of masts; a wilderness of steeples peeping
>   On tiptoe, through their sea-coal canopy;
> A huge, dun cupola, like a foolscap crown
> On a fool's head—and there is London Town!

All the manuscript variants for this stanza are fragments except that for line 7.

2   [All black all gloom]
5*a* Of Masts—[a steeple here and]
  b   [gothic tower or]
6   [As if] on tiptoe through their [chimneyed]
7–8 A huge dun Cupola—like a Foolscap [crowning
     A kindred brain]

But Juan saw not this: each wreath of smoke
  Appeared to him but as the magic vapour
Of some alchymic furnace, from whence broke
  The wealth of worlds (a wealth of tax and paper):
The gloomy clouds, which o'er it as a yoke
  Are bowed, and put the sun out like a taper,
Were nothing but the natural atmosphere,
Extremely wholesome, though but rarely clear.

1 each [puff] of Smoke
3 furnace—[and the] from whence broke
4 The [Wine] Wealth of Worlds [as light from out a taper]
6 [Were] bowed and [makes] the Sun out . . .
8 but [seldom] clear

84

He paused—and so will I; as doth a crew
  Before they give their broadside. By and bye,
My gentle countrymen, we will renew
  Our old acquaintance:* and at least I'll try
To tell you truths *you* will not take as true,
  Because they are so:—a male Mrs. Fry,*
With a soft besom will I sweep your halls,
And brush a web or two from off the walls.

6–7 Because they are [true—Oh virtuous Mrs. Fry!
Hath never brushed your prison walls with gen] [mild] *Intended
to write* gentle.

85

Oh, Mrs. Fry! Why go to Newgate?† Why
  Preach to poor rogues? And wherefore not begin
With Carlton, or with other houses?* Try
  Your hand at hardened and imperial sin.
To mend the people's an absurdity,
  A jargon, a mere philanthropic din,

        Unless you make their betters better:—Fie!
        I thought you had more religion, Mrs. Fry.

3*a* With C—t—on—or . . . s;   *b* C—lt—n . . .   *In 1823 edition.*
5   people's [mere] absurdity
7*a* Fie   s;   *b* Fy!   *In 1833 and in some later editions.*
8   more [courage] Mrs. Fry

86

        Teach them the decencies of good threescore;
          Cure them of tours, Hussar and Highland dresses;
        Tell them that youth once gone returns no more;
          That hired huzzas redeem no land's distresses;
        Tell them Sir William Curtis* is a bore,
          Too dull even for the dullest of excesses—
        The witless Falstaff of a hoary Hal,
        A fool whose bells have ceased to ring at all;—

5 Tell them—Sir W—ll—m C—t—s . . .   *S and 1823 edition.*

87

        Tell them, though it may be perhaps too late
          On life's worn confine, jaded, bloated, sated,
        To set up vain pretences of being great,
          'Tis not so to be good; and be it stated,
        The worthiest kings have ever loved least state;
          And tell them—but you won't, and I have prated
        Just now enough; but by and bye I'll prattle
        Like Roland's horn in Roncesvalles' battle.*

On the last page of S below this stanza Byron wrote his usual signature-symbol and "Genoa O^{ctre} 6th (or 5th?) 1822. End of Canto 10th."
8*a* [Like to a Roman Trumpet ere a battle]
  b [Like an old . . .]

Canto XI

1

WHEN Bishop Berkeley said "there was no matter,"*
    And proved it—'twas no matter what he said:
They say his system 'tis in vain to batter,
    Too subtle for the airiest human head;
And yet who can believe it! I would shatter
    Gladly all matters, down to stone or lead,
Or adamant, to find the World a spirit,
And wear my head, denying that I wear it.

For the date of publication see p. 183 of this volume.

    All manuscript readings are taken from S (Sterling manuscript), Byron's first draft. On the first page of S above the first stanza is the date, "Octr 6th 1822."

  3 I hear his System . . .
  4 To subtle . . .
6–8 Most willingly all [ever] seen or read
                 matters . . .
    To know myself and all besides mere Spirit
    [Would this d—d headache suffer me to bear it]

What a sublime discovery 'twas to make the
    Universe universal Egotism!
That all's ideal—*all ourselves:* I'll stake the
    World (be it what you will) that *that's* no Schism.
Oh, Doubt!—if thou be'st Doubt, for which some take
      thee,
    But which I doubt extremely—thou sole prism
Of the Truth's rays, spoil not my draught of spirit!
Heaven's brandy,—though our brain can hardly bear it.

This stanza does not appear on S.

3

For ever and anon comes Indigestion,
    (Not the most "dainty Ariel")* and perplexes
Our soarings with another sort of question:
    And that which after all my spirit vexes,
Is, that I find no spot where man can rest eye on,
    Without confusion of the sorts and sexes,
Of being, stars, and this unriddled wonder,
The World, which at the worst's a glorious blunder—

1   But ever . . .
3   My soarings . . .
6   Without great doubts [of] on all the sorts . . .
7*a* [Of Worlds and Species—Matters—Souls, and body]
  b   [Matter—Soul . . .]
  c Of Beings—[Worlds]—and this [eternal] Wonder
8   The [Universe]—which . . .

If it be Chance; or if it be according
　　To the Old Text, still better:—lest it should
Turn out so, we'll say nothing 'gainst the wording,
　　As several people think such hazards rude:
They're right; our days are too brief for affording
　　Space to dispute what *no one* ever could
Decide, and *every body one day* will
Know very clearly—or at least lie still.

1　[and] it be according
5*a*　[I am quite of their opinion—and am hoarding]
　b　They are right . . .

5

And therefore will I leave off metaphysical
　　Discussion, which is neither here nor there:
If I agree that what is, is; then this I call
　　Being quite perspicuous and extremely fair.
The truth is, I've grown lately rather phthisical:*
　　I don't know what the reason is—the air
Perhaps; but as I suffer from the shocks
Of illness, I grow much more orthodox.

5 The truth is—I [have] grown lately rather Ptisical

The first attack at once proved the Divinity;
　　(But *that* I never doubted, nor the Devil);
The next, the Virgin's mystical virginity;
　　The third, the usual Origin of Evil;
The fourth at once established the whole Trinity
　　On so uncontrovertible a level,
That I devoutly wished the three were four,
On purpose to believe so much the more.

3 The [next] [second—cleared] the Virgin's [pure] Virginity
6 [So firmly] *fragment*

7

To our theme:—The man who has stood on the
　　Acropolis,
　　And looked down over Attica; or he
Who has sailed where picturesque Constantinople is,
　　Or seen Tombuctoo, or hath taken tea
In small-eyed China's crockery-ware metropolis,
　　Or sat amidst the bricks of Nineveh,
May not think much of London's first appearance—
But ask him what he thinks of it a year hence?

1 [Now to our theme] [Now to our theme] [He who] *fragments*
3a Who [hath] sailed [up] where . . .; b Who'th sailed . . .
4a Tombuctu . . . S.
 b *Tombuctoo . . . In 1823 edition.*
 c *Timbuctoo . . . In 1833 and later editions.*
5 [Within the walls of] China's . . .
6a [Or Rome on Tiber—Naples on the Sea]
 b [Or Babel's bricks] *fragment*
7 much of [the] London's . . .

Don Juan had got out on Shooter's Hill;*
    Sunset the time, the place the same declivity
Which looks along that vale of good and ill
    Where London streets ferment in full activity;
While every thing around was calm and still,
    Except the creak of wheels, which on their pivot he
Heard,—and that bee-like, bubbling, busy hum
Of cities, that boils over with their scum:—

1 [Oh while] Don Juan [paused] on . . .
2 that same . . .
4 Where London['s Scene] ferment[s] in . . .
7–8 [He] heard, and that [inexplicable hum]
    Of [City] Cities which boil[s] over . . .

9

I say, Don Juan, wrapt in contemplation,
    Walked on behind his carriage, o'er the summit,
And lost in wonder of so great a nation,
    Gave way to't, since he could not overcome it.
"And here," he cried, "is Freedom's chosen station;
    Here peals the people's voice, nor can entomb it
Racks, prisons, inquisitions; resurrection
Awaits it, each new meeting or election.

2 Walked [by his carriage side—just on] the [crest]
4 Gave way [to it] . . .
6a [And yonder] [domes] [dome like Freedom's Cap]
 b Here [is] the People's . . .

"Here are chaste wives, pure lives; here people pay
    But what they please; and if that things be dear,
'Tis only that they love to throw away
    Their cash, to show how much they have a-year.
Here laws are all inviolate; none lay
    Traps for the traveller; every highway's clear:
Here"—he was interrupted by a knife,
With "Damn your eyes! your money or your life!"

1 wives [purel] pure lives . . .
2 things are dear
5 Here [all the] laws are all . . .
6 the traveller[s] . . .

11

These freeborn sounds proceeded from four pads,
    In ambush laid, who had perceived him loiter
Behind his carriage; and, like handy lads,
    Had seized the lucky hour to reconnoitre,
In which the heedless gentleman who gads
    Upon the road, unless he prove a fighter,
May find himself within that Isle of riches
Exposed to lose his life as well as breeches.

1–3 These free born . . . four [Minions]
     [Of the Fair Moon] who had perceived him [loit] loiter
     [Some way] behind his carriage[s] *fragment*
     Byron later in stanza 14 used the image he canceled here.
4   Had seized the [lucky point] to . . .
5a [In which] *fragment*;   b [To] which . . .
6   Upon [a journey] unless . . .

Juan, who did not understand a word
    Of English, save their shibboleth, "God damn!"*
And even that he had so rarely heard,
    He sometimes thought 'twas only their "Salam,"
Or "God be with you!"—and 'tis not absurd
    To think so; for half English as I am
(To my misfortunè) never can I say
I heard them wish "God with you," save that way;—

1 [Who] *fragment*
2 save—[that] Shibboleth . . .
3 he [knew] so rarely heard
4 He [knew not if twere] *fragment*
8 To have heard them . . .

13

Juan yet quickly understood their gesture,
    And being somewhat choleric and sudden,
Drew forth a pocket-pistol from his vesture,
    And fired it into one assailant's pudding—
Who fell, as rolls an ox o'er in his pasture,
    And roared out, as he writhed his native mud in,
Unto his nearest follower or henchman,
"Oh Jack! I'm floored by that 'ere bloody Frenchman!"

2 coleric . . .
3 Drew forth [some] pocket-pistol[s] from . . .
4 And fired [one] into [the] Assailant's . . .
7 follower and henchman
8 I'm [doubled by this] bloody . . .

On which Jack and his train set off at speed,
   And Juan's suite, late scattered at a distance,
Came up, all marvelling at such a deed,
   And offering, as usual, late assistance.
Juan, who saw the Moon's late minion bleed*
   As if his veins would pour out his existence,
Stood calling out for bandages and lint,
And wished he had been less hasty with his flint.

6 As if [within] *fragment*
7 [Was] calling . . .

15

"Perhaps," thought he, "it is the country's Wont
   To welcome foreigners in this way: now
I recollect some innkeepers who don't
   Differ, except in robbing with a bow,
In lieu of a bare blade and brazen front.
   But what is to be done? I can't allow
The fellow to lie groaning on the road:
So take him up; I'll help you with the load."

1 "Perhaps [he thought,] it is the Country's [custom]
2 in this way, [or]
3 I recollect [few] Innkeepers . . .
4 [Receive one much] *fragment*
5a In lieu of [a] bare [steel] blade, . . .
  b   [the] . . .
6 But what [shall I do]—I . . .

But ere they could perform this pious duty,
 The dying man cried, "Hold! I've got my gruel!
Oh! for a glass of *max!* * We've miss'd our booty—
 Let me die where I am!" And as the fuel
Of life shrunk in his heart, and thick and sooty
 The drops fell from his death-wound, and he drew ill
His breath,—he from his swelling throat untied
A kerchief, crying "Give Sal that!"—and died.

3 [God d—n you lads I've missed a handsome] booty
5 shrunk in his [veins] and . . .
6 The drops fell from his [wound] *fragment*
8 A [handkerchief, cried]—"Give Sal that" . . .

17

The cravat stained with bloody drops fell down
 Before Don Juan's feet: he could not tell
Exactly why it was before him thrown,
 Nor what the meaning of the man's farewell.
Poor Tom was once a kiddy upon town,
 A thorough varmint, and a *real* swell,
Full flash,* all fancy, until fairly diddled,
His pockets first, and then his body riddled.

1 The [kerchief] stained . . .
4 Nor [if] the . . .
5 once a [knowing one in] town
6 *Three fragments:*
 a [Not a mere] [p] [flas]
 b [A thorough]
 c [Not a mere kiddy—but] a <u>real</u> swell
7 [All] flash—all [flas] fancy . . .
8 and [now] his body . . .

Don Juan, having done the best he could
   In all the circumstances of the case,
As soon as "Crowner's 'quest" allowed,* pursued
   His travels to the capital apace;—
Esteeming it a little hard he should
   In twelve hours' time, and very little space,
Have been obliged to slay a freeborn native
In self-defence:—this made him meditative.

8 In self defence;—[and he grew more] meditative

19

He from the world had cut off a great man,
   Who in his time had made heroic bustle.
Who in a row like Tom could lead the van,
   Booze in the ken,* or at the spellken hustle?
Who queer a flat? Who (spite of Bow-street's ban)
   On the high toby-spice so flash the muzzle?
Who on a lark, with black-eyed Sal (his blowing)
So prime, so swell, so nutty, and so knowing?

3 Who [at a fight] like Tom . . .

20

But Tom's no more—and so no more of Tom.
   Heroes must die; and by God's blessing 'tis
Not long before the most of them go home.—
   Hail! Thamis, hail! Upon thy verge it is
That Juan's chariot, rolling like a drum
   In thunder, holds the way it can't well miss,
Through Kennington and all the other "tons,"
Which make us wish ourselves in town at once;—

5 [Our] Chariot . . .
6 [It] thunder[s] *fragment*

Through Groves, so called as being void of trees,
　　(Like *lucus* from *no* light) ;* through prospects named
Mount Pleasant, as containing nought to please,
　　Nor much to climb; through little boxes framed
Of bricks, to let the dust in at your ease,
　　With "To be let," upon their doors proclaimed;
Through "Rows" most modestly called "Paradise,"*
Which Eve might quit without much sacrifice;—

　　3　Mounts . . . *Misprint in 1823 edition. Byron wrote* Mount *on* S.
　　4　to [mount]—through . . .
　　5　[As twere of] *fragment*
7a–8a　[And here and there some more celestial row]
　　　　　　　　　　　　[snug . . .]
　　　　[Called "Paradise"] *fragment*
7b–8b　Through [Rows called "Paradise" by way of showing
　　　　Good Christians that to which they all are going]

22

Through coaches, drays, choked turnpikes, and a whirl
　　Of wheels, and roar of voices and confusion;
Here taverns wooing to a pint of "purl,"*
　　There mails fast flying off like a delusion;
There barber's blocks with periwigs in curl
　　In windows; here the lamplighter's infusion
Slowly distilled into the glimmering glass,
(For in those days we had not got to gas) :*—

　　3　[Of Life and motion; that] *fragment*
　　5a　There [Ball] Barbers blocks with [pery] [perig] periwigs . . .
　　b　perriwigs . . . *In 1823 edition.*
　　6　In windows,—[with] lamplighters' [xxxx] infusion
　　7　[Distilling into the rekindling] glass

Through this, and much, and more, is the approach
  Of travellers to mighty Babylon:
Whether they come by horse, or chaise, or coach,
  With slight exceptions, all the ways seem one.
I could say more, but do not choose to encroach
  Upon the guide-book's privilege. The Sun
Had set some time, and night was on the ridge
Of twilight, as the party crossed the bridge.

1 Through this and much [more] *fragment*
3 [At least] *fragment*
8 as [they] crossed . . .

24

That's rather fine, the gentle sound of Thamis—
  Who vindicates a moment too his stream—
Though hardly heard through multifarious "damme's."
  The lamps of Westminster's more regular gleam,
The breadth of pavement, and yon shrine where Fame is
  A spectral resident—whose pallid beam
In shape of moonshine hovers o'er the pile—
Make this a sacred part of Albion's Isle.

2   a moment to . . .
3a   Though hardly heard [amidst the so] *fragment*
 b   midst multifarious "dammes"
5–6 The breadth . . . and [that spot] where Fame is
     A [constant] resident . . .
7   Moonshine [hovers oer yon] pile
8   Make this a sacred [portion of] *fragment*

The Druid's groves are gone—so much the better:
 Stone-Henge* is not—but what the devil is it?—
But Bedlam still exists* with its sage fetter,
 That madmen may not bite you on a visit;
The Bench* too seats or suits full many a debtor;
 The Mansion House too (though some people quiz
  it)*
To me appears a stiff yet grand erection;
But then the Abbey's worth the whole collection.

2 Stone-Henge—[but] is . . .
5 The Bench too [handsomely] seats [if] or . . .
7a To me [rears an imposing grand erection]
 b To me appears a [most grand and stiff erection]
 c   a stiff [but] grand . . .

26

The line of lights too up to Charing Cross,
 Pall Mall,* and so forth, have a coruscation
Like gold as in comparison to dross,
 Matched with the Continent's illumination,
Whose cities Night by no means deigns to gloss:
 The French were not yet a lamp-lighting nation,
And when they grew so—on their new-found lanthorn,
Instead of wicks, they made a wicked man turn.*

1 The line of [lamps] too . . .
3a [Beyond the Continental cities] *fragment*
 b Like Gold . . . with dross
4 [When] matched with [foreign land's i] *fragment* **Intended to
write** illumination.
7a And when they [grew upon their] *fragment*
 b   [were] [tis] *fragment*
 c   grew so [upon] . . .

A row of gentlemen along the streets
　　Suspended, may illuminate mankind,
As also bonfires made of country seats;*
　　But the old way is best for the purblind:
The other looks like phosphorus on sheets,
　　A sort of Ignis-fatuus* to the mind,
Which, though 'tis certain to perplex and frighten,
Must burn more mildly ere it can enlighten.

2–4　Suspended—may [enlighten all] mankind
　　　[With other revolutionary feats]
　　　[With early . . .]
　　　[But such improvements are b] *fragment　Intended to write* best?
　　　[But hardly serve to] *fragment*
　　　[As for] *fragment*
　　6　[An] [A meteoric] *fragment*

28

But London's so well lit, that if Diogenes
　　Could recommence to hunt his *honest man*,
And found him not amidst the various progenies
　　Of this enormous city's spreading spawn,
'Twere not for want of lamps to aid his dodging his
　　Yet undiscovered treasure. What *I* can,
I've done to find the same throughout life's journey,
But see the world is only one attorney.

2–4　[Were to set out] to [seek] his <u>honest man</u>
　　　[He would not find him in the Cockneys' progenys]
　　　Of [oergrown London's] *fragment*
　5a　lamps to [help] in dodging his
　　b　　　　aid in dodging his　*Here the manuscript seems preferable*
　　　to the printed text.
　6　treasure; [all] <u>I</u> can
　7a　I've done [and <u>do</u> to make the same discovery]
　　b　I've done to [find] the same [upon my] *fragment*
　　c　I've done to find the same [on various] journey[s]
　8a　[But all the World is but One vast Attorney]
　　b　But see [Mankind is but one vast Attorney]

Over the stones still rattling, up Pall Mall,
    Through crowds and carriages, but waxing thinner
As thundered knockers broke the long-sealed spell
    Of doors 'gainst duns, and to an early dinner
Admitted a small party as night fell,—
    Don Juan, our young diplomatic sinner,
Pursued his path, and drove past some Hotels,
St. James's Palace, and St. James's "Hells."*

2 but [rather] waxing . . .
3 As [thundering] knockers . . .
4 [to] and to . . .
7 and [passed by] some hotels

30

They reached the hotel: forth streamed from the front
      door
    A tide of well-clad waiters, and around
The mob stood, and as usual, several score
    Of those pedestrian Paphians,* who abound
In decent London when the daylight's o'er;
    Commodious but immoral, they are found
Useful, like Malthus,* in promoting marriage:—
But Juan now is stepping from his carriage

*The present version of this stanza does not appear on S. See the rejected
stanza (p. 313 of this volume) for which Byron substituted the present text.*

Into one of the sweetest of hotels,*
    Especially for foreigners—and mostly
For those whom favour or whom fortune swells,
    And cannot find a bill's small items costly.
There many an envoy either dwelt or dwells,
    (The den of many a diplomatic lost lie)
Until to some conspicuous square they pass,
And blazon o'er the door their names in brass.

1 'Twas one of the delightfullest hotels
5 There many a [Minister still] dwelt or [dwells]
7–8 *Order of composition:*
    Until [they found in some conspicuous square]
    And [in some conspicuous square—their name]
    [On a brass plate was given to knocks and Fame]
    [Beneath a knocker was up held to fame]

32

Juan, whose was a delicate commission,
    Private, though publicly important, bore
No title to point out with due precision
    The exact affair on which he was sent o'er.
'Twas merely known that on a secret mission
    A foreigner of rank had graced our shore,
Young, handsome, and accomplished, who was said
(In whispers) to have turned his Sovereign's head.

3 No [outer title which could] *fragment*
6 A Foreigner of [qu] rank . . .   *Intended to write* quality?
8 [To] (In whispers) . . .

Some rumour also of some strange adventures
    Had gone before him, and his wars and loves;
And as romantic heads are pretty painters,
    And, above all, an Englishwoman's roves
Into the excursive, breaking the indentures
    Of sober reason, wheresoe'er it moves,
He found himself extremely in the fashion,
Which serves our thinking people for a passion.

2 Had gone before him, of his [loves and wars]
4–5 [And ladies like a little spice of Mars
    Of course] *fragment*
6 Of [poor dull] Reason . . .
8 Which serves our [colder clime instead of] passion

34

I don't mean that they are passionless, but quite
    The contrary; but then 'tis in the head;
Yet as the consequences are as bright
    As if they acted with the heart instead,
What after all can signify the site
    Of ladies' lucubrations? So they lead
In safety to the place for which you start,
What matters if the road be head or heart?

3a [But as] the . . .;   b [But then] the . . .
6a Of [ladies lucubrations or] [they] [the path they tread]
 b Of [fair Philosophy or where tis they tread?]
7 [If you arrive at that] for which . . .

Juan presented in the proper place,
    To proper placemen, every Russ credential;
And was received with all the due grimace,
    By those who govern in the mood potential;*
Who, seeing a handsome stripling with smooth face,
    Thought (what in state affairs is most essential)
That they as easily might *do* the youngster,
As hawks may pounce upon a woodland songster.

1   presented [his] in . . .
2   To proper placemen [his credential] *fragment*
3a [As also to his bankers] *fragment*
 b And was received with [every] due . . .
5   a handsome [youngster] with . . .
6   [Saw] (what in . . .
7a [A] [It would be no hard task to do a youngster]
7b–8a [Twould be as slight a task to <u>do</u> a youngster
    As for a hawk to] *fragment*
7c That they . . . <u>do</u> a youngster
8b As Hawks may <u>pounce</u> upon a [for] *fragment* *Intended to write*
    forest.

36

They erred, as aged men will do; but by
    And by we'll talk of that; and if we don't,
'Twill be because our notion is not high
    Of politicians and their double front,
Who live by lies, yet dare not boldly lie:
    Now what I love in women is, they won't
Or can't do otherwise than lie, but do it
So well, the very truth seems falsehood to it.

2   or if . . .
3a [It] 'Twill be [from the extreme contempt] *fragment*
 b   because [we think contemptuously]
7a [Lie and yet never can get out the truth]
 b Or can't do otherwise than lie—[forsooth!]
8   [And yet think] [all] [lies are—or should be—the truth]

And, after all, what is a lie? 'Tis but
    The truth in masquerade; and I defy
Historians, heroes, lawyers, priests to put
    A fact without some leaven of a lie.
The very shadow of true Truth would shut
    Up annals, revelations, poesy,
And prophecy—except it should be dated
Some years before the incidents related.

2 [A false attempt at Truth]—and I defy
4 without the leaven . . .
6 Revelations—[philop] poesy
7 except it [be related]

38

Praised be all liars and all lies! Who now
    Can tax my mild Muse with misanthropy?
She rings the world's "Te Deum," and her brow
    Blushes for those who will not:—but to sigh
Is idle; let us like most others bow,
    Kiss hands, feet, any part of Majesty,
After the good example of "Green Erin,"*
Whose Shamrock now seems rather worse for wearing.

3 She [lauds] sings the World's "te deum,"—[with a sigh]
5 like [the] others bow
6-8 [Kiss] Kiss hands—or feet—or—what men by and bye
    Will kiss not in sad metaphor—but earnest—
    Unless on Tyrant's Sterns—we turn the Sternest.

Don Juan was presented, and his dress
    And mien excited general admiration—
I don't know which was most admired or less:
    One monstrous diamond drew much observation,
Which Catherine in a moment of "ivresse"*
    (In love or brandy's fervent fermentation)
Bestowed upon him, as the public learned;
And, to say truth, it had been fairly earned.

3a [The last—'tis said drew from] *fragment*
 b I don't know which was [most] admired . . .
6 fervent [animation]
7 [Presented] Bestowed upon . . .
8 truth, [the] it had been [really] earned

40

Besides the Ministers and underlings,
    Who must be courteous to the accredited
Diplomatists of rather wavering kings,
    Until their royal riddle's fully read,
The very clerks,—those somewhat dirty springs
    Of office, or the House of Office, fed
By foul corruption into streams,—even they
Were hardly rude enough to earn their pay.

2 Who must be [civil] to . . .
8 Were [almost] hardly . . .

And insolence no doubt is what they are
 Employed for, since it is their daily labour,
In the dear offices of peace or war;
 And should you doubt, pray ask of your next
  neighbour,
When for a passport, or some other bar
 To freedom, he applied (a grief and a bore)
If he found not this spawn of tax-born riches,
Like lap-dogs, the least civil sons of b—s.

1*a* [As that no] doubt is what they [ea] [make] *Intended to write*
 b   [toil]   earn?
2 their [greatest] labour
4*a*–5*a* [A sneer or short reply unto their neighbour
  Who asks his very Servants'] *fragment*
 4*b* [If you demur]—pray—ask of your [next] neighbour
 5*b* [If] for . . .
6 To Freedom—[you] he applied . . .
7*a* [He did not find] *fragment*
 b [He found not] *fragment*
 c [If he did not] [found] [th] [these salaried]
 d   [slaves feed from his riches]
 e   [slav]
 f   [salaried slaves of taxes]
8*a* [Or poverty] [the riches] *fragment*
 b Like lap-dogs,—the [most] least civil sons of b—tch—s.

42

But Juan was received with much "empressement":*—
 These phrases of refinement I must borrow
From our next neighbour's land, where, like a chessman,
 There is a move set down for joy or sorrow*
Not only in mere talking, but the press. Man
 In islands is, it seems, downright and thorough,
More than on continents—as if the sea
(See Billingsgate)* made even the tongue more free.

2–3*a* [For] phrases of [politeness] I must [use
 The language] *fragment*

3*b* neighbour's [tongue] where . . .
4*a* There is a [regular Move] for Joy . . .
  b There is a [set-down Move] . . .
5 Not only [for] mere . . .

43

And yet the British "Damme" 's rather Attic:*
  Your Continental oaths are but incontinent,
And turn on things which no Aristocratic
  Spirit would name, and therefore even I won't anent*
This subject quote; as it would be schismatic
  In politesse, and have a sound affronting in't:—
  But "Damme" 's quite ethereal, though too daring—
  Platonic blasphemy, the soul of swearing.

1 [There's something even in] "Damme's"—[democratic]
3 And turn on [filt] [filthy] things which no [true Attic]
4 Spirit would [quote]—and therefore . . .
5*a* [This Subject thought tis apropos] *fragment*
  b [This Subject adduce]—[bring to bear] *fragment*
  c [This Subject quote,] [My] [M] [although like Ship in pratique]
  d   [although Pantisocratic]
6*a* [In the opinions which I am apt to sp] *fragment   Intended to write*
    specify?
  b [In all things gainst which I must set my front anent]
  c [In most . . .]
  d [Gainst] Politesse,—[for which I bear the brunt anent]
  e   [the . . .]
7*a* But—"Damme's" [simple—dashing—free—and] dareing
  b But—"Damme's" quite etherial, [boundless], dareing
8 [The purest] blasphemy . . .

For downright rudeness, ye may stay at home;
　For true or false politeness (and scarce *that*
Now) you may cross the blue deep and white foam—
　The first the emblem (rarely though) of what
You leave behind—the next of much you come
　To meet. However, 'tis no time to chat
On general topics: poems must confine
Themselves to Unity, like this of mine.

1　For [honest] rudeness—[we] may stay at home
2a　For false politeness—(and [even scarce] *fragment*
　b　　　　　　　　　　　　[now scarce even] that
3a　Now,—) [we may cross the channel] *fragment*
　b　Now,—) Ye may cross the blue deep . . .
4　The first the emblem [probably] (rarely though) of what
7　About such general matters—but particular
8a　A poem [should be much more] perpendicular
　b　A poem's progress should be perpendicular

45

In the Great World,—which being interpreted
　Meaneth the West or worst end of a city,
And about twice two thousand people bred
　By no means to be very wise or witty,
But to sit up while others lie in bed,
　And look down on the universe with pity,—
Juan, as an inveterate Patrician,
Was well received by persons of condition.

1　In the great world which [means] *fragment*
2　Meaneth the West End of a smoky City
4a　[Up to be neither very wise nor] witty
　b　By no means to be [either] wise or witty
5　[Some] [Born] to sit up while others in bed
6　And look [upon] the . . .
7　[Don] Juan . . .

First draft of stanzas 43 and 44 of Canto XI, numbered "42" and "43" by Byron on the manuscript (Courtesy of Sir Louis Sterling. Reduced one-half)

He was a bachelor, which is a matter
    Of import both to Virgin and to Bride;
The former's hymeneal hopes to flatter;
    And (should she not hold fast by love or pride)
'Tis also of some moment to the latter:
    A rib's a thorn in a wed Gallant's side,
Requires decorum, and is apt to double
The horrid sin—and what's still worse, the trouble.

1   which is a [point]
2a Of [great importance] both to [maids] and [brides]
 b Of [much . . .]
 c Of import both to virgin[s] and to bride
3   [Besides a fine young fellow] *fragment*
4a And (should She [have a turn to step aside)]
 b   like to range a little wide)
6   A [wife's] a [deep *sic?*] thorn in a [lover's] side
7   [And] Requires . . .

47

But Juan was a bachelor—of arts,
    And parts, and hearts: he danced and sung, and had
An air as sentimental as Mozart's
    Softest of melodies; and could be sad
Or cheerful, without any "flaws or starts,"*
    Just at the proper time; and though a lad,
Had seen the world—which is a curious sight,
And very much unlike what people write.

5a Or cheerful [at the proper time] *fragment*
 b   [with any] "flaws or starts"

Fair virgins blushed upon him; wedded dames
  Bloomed also in less transitory hues;
For both commodities dwell by the Thames,
  The painting and the painted; youth, ceruse,
Against his heart preferred their usual claims,
  Such as no gentleman can quite refuse;
Daughters admired his dress, and pious mothers
Enquired his income, and if he had brothers.

1 Fair virgins [smiled] upon him— . . .
2a [Blushed too but it was hidden by their rouge]
 b   [as much as] *fragment*
 c   [beneath their rouge's rival hues]
4a [The true and artificial] *fragment*
 b [The natural and the prepared ceruse]
5a [His heart had a variety of claims]
 b [Upon] his heart . . .
6 can [all] refuse
7 dress [while] and pious . . .

49

The milliners who furnish "drapery Misses"*
  Throughout the season, upon speculation
Of payment ere the honeymoon's last kisses
  Have waned into a crescent's coruscation,
Thought such an opportunity as this is,
  Of a rich foreigner's initiation,
Not to be overlooked,—and gave such credit,
That future bridegrooms swore, and sighed, and paid it.

2 [In spangles for] *fragment*
3 [That ere] the Honey Moon [has with waning] kisses
4 Have [dwindled to] a Crescent's . . .
5 Thought such as an . . .
8 That [many a] Bridegroom . . .

The Blues, that tender tribe, who sigh o'er sonnets,
　And with the pages of the last Review
Line the interior of their heads or bonnets,*
　Advanced in all their azure's highest hue:
They talked bad French of Spanish, and upon its
　Late authors asked him for a hint or two;
And which was softest, Russian or Castilian?
And whether in his travels he saw Ilion?

5a They talked bad French of Spanish . . . s
 b 　　　　　　　　　　or . . . *In 1833 and in later editions. This slight change destroys Byron's witty point.*

51

Juan, who was a little superficial,
　And not in literature a great Drawcansir,*
Examined by this learned and especial
　Jury of matrons, scarce knew what to answer:
His duties warlike, loving, or official,
　His steady application as a dancer,
Had kept him from the brink of Hippocrene,*
Which now he found was blue instead of green.

2 And not [of very literary] *fragment*
7 from [these] the brink . . .
8 [Which is not quite so] *fragment*

52

However, he replied at hazard, with
　A modest confidence and calm assurance,
Which lent his learned lucubrations pith,
　And passed for arguments of good endurance.
That prodigy, Miss Araminta Smith,*
　(Who at sixteen translated "Hercules Furens"
Into as furious English) with her best look,
Set down his sayings in her common-place book.

2*a* confidence . . .   *S, 1833, and later editions.*
  b confidance . . .   *In 1823 edition.*
4 indurance
8 Set [his] down . . .

53

Juan knew several languages—as well
    He might—and brought them up with skill, in time
To save his fame with each accomplished belle,
    Who still regretted that he did not rhyme.
There wanted but this requisite to swell
    His qualities (with them) into sublime:
Lady Fitz-Frisky, and Miss Maevia Mannish,
Both longed extremely to be sung in Spanish.

1 [What] Juan knew—[were] languages . . .
2 He might—and brought [skifully] *fragment*
3 To save his fame with [every litera] *fragment*
4 ryhme   *Misprint in 1823 edition.*

54

However, he did pretty well, and was
    Admitted as an aspirant to all
The Coteries; and, as in Banquo's glass,*
    At great assemblies or in parties small,
He saw ten thousand living authors pass,*
    That being about their average numeral;
Also the eighty "greatest living poets,"
As every paltry magazine can show *it's.*

5 He saw [the whole] *fragment*
8 As every mighty Magazine . . .

In twice five years the."greatest living poet,"
　　Like to the champion in the fisty ring,
Is called on to support his claim, or show it,
　　Although 'tis an imaginary thing.
Even I—albeit I'm sure I did not know it,
　　Nor sought of foolscap subjects to be king,—
Was reckoned, a considerable time,
The grand Napoleon of the realms of rhyme.

2a　Like to the [Champion's title]—in the [ring]
　b　　　　　Champion[s] in the fisty ring
3　[Hath oft been called upon] *fragment*
5　Even I—[although] I'm . . .
6a　Nor [wished of such frail realms to be the] king
　b　Nor sought of [such] foolscap . . .
8　[A proper Potentate] of the realms . . .

56

But Juan was my Moscow,* and Faliero
　　My Leipsic, and my Mont Saint Jean seems Cain:
"La Belle Alliance" of dunces down at zero,*
　　Now that the Lion's fall'n, may rise again:
But I will fall at least as fell my hero;
　　Nor reign at all, or as a *monarch* reign;*
Or to some lonely isle of Jailors go,
With turncoat Southey for my turnkey Lowe.*

This stanza was written crosswise on S.
2　Jean [my] Cain
6　a Monarch again
8　With turnkey Southey for my Hudson Lowe

Sir Walter reigned before me; Moore and Campbell*
  Before and after; but now grown more holy,
The Muses upon Sion's hill must ramble,
  With poets almost clergymen, or wholly;
And Pegasus hath a psalmodic amble
  Beneath the very Reverend Rowley Powley,*
Who shoes the glorious animal with stilts,
A modern Ancient Pistol—by the hilts!*

Lines 5–7 were omitted in the 1823 edition and were first printed in 1833.

1–2   [Scott was my predecessor]—Moore—and Campbell
     [Had each their turn, like me]; but now more holy
  5   [They're lately gotten] a Psalmodic amble
  6a Beneath the reverend [Poet] [Mr] [rider] [Mr]
    b   [good George Croly]
    c Beneath the reverend Cambyses Croly
7–8a [Whose Strains—whateer they be—surpass at least
      The howling Hebrews of Cybele's priest]   *Byron used this deleted*
      line when he wrote the next stanza.
  8b "by these Hilts!"

58

Still he excels that artificial hard
  Labourer in the same vineyard,* though the vine
Yields him but vinegar for his reward,—
  That neutralised dull Dorus of the Nine;
That swarthy Sporus, neither man nor bard;
  That ox of verse, who *ploughs* for every line:—
Cambyses' roaring Romans beat at least
The howling Hebrews of Cybele's priest.—

This stanza was written crosswise on S. It was omitted in the 1823 edition
and was first printed in 1837.

1 [But still he beats] that artificial, hard
5 That swarthy Sporus neither [man who] *fragment*

Then there's my gentle Euphues;* who, they say,
  Sets up for being a sort of *moral me;*
He'll find it rather difficult some day
  To turn out both, or either, it may be.
Some persons think that Coleridge hath the sway;
  And Wordsworth has supporters, two or three;
  And that deep-mouthed Boeotian, "Savage Landor,"*
Has taken for a swan rogue Southey's gander.

1–4 Then there's my gentle Barry—[and the late
John Keats—who was killed off by one Critique
Just as he really promised something great
If not intelligible] *fragment*
Byron used these lines when he began the next stanza.
 6a [For] Wordsworth—[there's as usual] two or three
  b   [there are sometimes] . . .
 7 And that [divine Boeotian] "Savage Landor"
 8 [Mistaking] for a Swan [poor] Southey's Gander

60

John Keats, who was killed off by one critique,*
  Just as he really promised something great,
If not intelligible,—without Greek
  Contrived to talk about the Gods of late,
Much as they might have been supposed to speak.
  Poor fellow! His was an untoward fate:—
  'Tis strange the mind, that very fiery particle,*
Should let itself be snuffed out by an Article.

1 John Keats who was killed off [at the] *fragment*
7–8 *Order of composition:*
  [An early victim to those paper pellets
  To] [And weakly Mind to let] *fragment*
  Tis strange the Mind [should let such phrases quell it's
  Internal fires with idle] *fragment*
  [Chief Impulse with a few frail paper pellets]

Tis strange the Mind that [all celestial] Particle
            very fiery . . .
Should let itself be [put] out by an Article
            snuffed . . .

61

The list grows long of live and dead pretenders
    To that which none will gain—or none will know
The Conqueror at least; who, ere time renders
    His last award, will have the long grass grow
Above his burnt-out brain, and sapless cinders.
    If I might augur, I should rate but low
Their chances;—they're too numerous, like the thirty
Mock tyrants,* when Rome's annals waxed but dirty.

1   dead [Competitors]
2   [For] that . . . [as] none . . .
3   The Conqueror—who, [long] ere . . .
4   [shall] will have . . .
5   [Over his busy] brain . . .
7a Their chances;—[xxxx] they're too numerous . . .
  b   [there mock monarchs like the]
8   Mock [monarchs,] when Rome's Annals [grew] but dirty

62

This is the literary *lower* Empire,
    Where the Praetorian bands take up the matter;*—
A "dreadful trade," like his who "gathers samphire,"*
    The insolent soldiery to soothe and flatter,
With the same feelings as you'd coax a vampire.
    Now, were I once at home, and in good satire,
I'd try conclusions with those Janizaries,*
And show them *what* an intellectual war is.

2 Where the [a] Praetorian bands [decide] the matter

I think I know a trick or two, would turn
    Their flanks;—but it is hardly worth my while
With such small gear to give myself concern:
    Indeed I've not the necessary bile;
My natural temper's really aught but stern,
    And even my Muse's worst reproof's a smile;
And then she drops a brief and modern curtsy,
And glides away, assured she never hurts ye.

4–7 Indeed [I have not got sufficient] Bile
    [As from my great great humour you may learn
    My Muse's worst reproof's a gentle] smile
    And then She drops a [slight] and modern curtsy
  8 away, [and] assured . . .

63
64

My Juan, whom I left in deadly peril
    Amongst live poets and blue ladies, past
With some small profit through that field so sterile.
    Being tired in time, and neither least nor last
Left it before he had been treated very ill;
    And henceforth found himself more gaily classed
Amongst the higher spirits of the day,
The sun's true son, no vapour, but a ray.

3 [Through the Ordeal and profit] *fragment*

His morns he passed in business—which dissected,
　　Was like all business, a laborious nothing,
That leads to lassitude, the most infected
　　And Centaur-Nessus garb of mortal clothing,*
And on our sophas makes us lie dejected,
　　And talk in tender horrors of our loathing
All kinds of toil, save for our country's good—
Which grows no better, though 'tis time it should.

1　[Day] [Morn after Morn in] Business . . .
3–4　[Which] leads to lassitude the most [expected
　　And truly very pleasant] mortal cloathing
5a　[While on] our Sofas [we can] lie dejected
　b　[Which] And on our Sofas . . .
7　All kinds of [acts] [acts] save . . .
8　Which [got] grows . . .

66

His afternoons he passed in visits, luncheons,
　　Lounging, and boxing; and the twilight hour
In riding round those vegetable puncheons
　　Called "Parks," where there is neither fruit nor flower
Enough to gratify a bee's slight munchings;
　　But after all it is the only "bower,"
(In Moore's phrase)* where the fashionable fair
Can form a slight acquaintance with fresh air.

2 Lounging—and [yawning]—and . . .
7 [As Moore would call it—where the] *fragment*
8 Can [make] form [the] a slight . . .

Then dress, then dinner, then awakes the world!
    Then glare the lamps, then whirl the wheels, then roar
Through street and square fast flashing chariots, hurled
    Like harnessed meteors; then along the floor
Chalk mimics painting;* then festoons are twirled;
    Then roll the brazen thunders of the door,
Which opens to the thousand happy few
An earthly Paradise of "Or Molu."*

  2 Then [flash] the . . .
  3 [the] fast-flashing . . .
4–5 Like harnessed Meteors; [all St. James's oer
    Their floors are chalked,] [then] [and] then . . .
  7 to two thousand . . .
  8 [A Paradise] *fragment*

68

There stands the noble Hostess, nor shall sink
    With the three-thousandth curtsey; there the Waltz,
The only dance which teaches girls to think,*
    Makes one in love even with its very faults.
Saloon, room, hall o'erflow beyond their brink,
    And long the latest of arrivals halts,
'Midst royal dukes and dames condemned to climb,
And gain an inch of staircase at a time.

  1 Hostess—[till She drops]
  3 which [makes young ladies] think
5a Saloon, [and] room, hall [are crowded to the brink]
  b   oerflow [xxxx] beyond . . .
  6 And long the latest [arrived] *fragment*
  7 *Four fragments:*
    [Upon the] [In the climbed]
    [Jostled with royal dukes] [Jostled]

Thrice happy he, who, after a survey
  Of the good company, can win a corner,
A door that's *in,* or boudoir *out* of the way,
  Where he may fix himself, like small "Jack Horner,"
And let the Babel round run as it may,
  And look on as a mourner, or a scorner,
Or an approver, or a mere spectator,
Yawning a little as the night grows later.

2 can [gain] win . . .
3a A door[way—or a] boudoir out [of] o' the way
  b A door that's in—or boudoir out o' the way
4 like snug "Jack Horner"

70

But this won't do, save by and by; and he
  Who, like Don Juan, takes an active share,
Must steer with care through all that glittering sea
  Of gems and plumes, and pearls and silks, to where
He deems it is his proper place to be;
  Dissolving in the waltz to some soft air,
Or proudlier prancing with mercurial skill
Where Science marshals forth her own quadrille.

2 active [part]
3 with skill through [all] that all glittering Sea
4 plumes—and silks, and pearls, to where
7 Or [triumphing] proudlier prancing with [mech] . . . *Intended to
   write* mechanical?
8 marshals out . . .

Or, if he dance not, but hath higher views
    Upon an heiress or his neighbour's bride,
Let him take care that that which he pursues
    Is not at once too palpably descried.
Full many an eager gentleman oft rues
    His haste: impatience is a blundering guide
Amongst a people famous for reflection,
Who like to play the fool with circumspection.

1 he [deign] not . . .
6 His haste—[for] impatience . . .
7 [We are] a people . . .
8 [And] Who . . .

72

But, if you can contrive, get next at supper;
    Or, if forestalled, get opposite and ogle:—
Oh, ye ambrosial moments! always upper
    In mind, a sort of sentimental bogle,*
Which sits for ever upon Memory's crupper,
    The ghost of vanished pleasures once in vogue! Ill
Can tender souls relate the rise and fall
Of hopes and fears which shake a single ball.

3–4 Oh ye [delightful] moments [now] upper
    [In Sentimental memories] *fragment*
  5 Which [haunts] sits . . .
  7 Souls [recall] relate . . .

But these precautionary hints can touch
  Only the common run, who must pursue,
And watch, and ward; whose plans a word too much
  Or little overturns; and not the few
Or many (for the number's sometimes such)
  Whom a good mien, especially if new,
Or fame, or name, for wit, war, sense, or nonsense,
Permits whate'er they please, or *did* not long since.

4 [the] and not . . .
7 name—for [wit or war]—or nonsense—

74

Our hero, as a hero, young and handsome,
  Noble, rich, celebrated, and a stranger,
Like other slaves of course must pay his ransom
  Before he can escape from so much danger
As will environ a conspicuous man. Some
  Talk about poetry, and "rack and manger,"*
And ugliness, disease, as toil and trouble,—
I wish they knew the life of a young noble.*

3 [Could not] *fragment*
4 Before he [could] escape . . .
5-6 As [must] environ [such a conspicuous man;] some
    Talk [of the pangs] *fragment*
7 disease;—[and death]—trouble

They are young, but know not youth—it is anticipated;
    Handsome but wasted, rich without a sou;
Their vigour in a thousand arms is dissipated;
    Their cash comes *from*, their wealth goes *to* a Jew;*
Both senates see their nightly votes participated
    Between the tyrant's and the tribunes' crew;*
And having voted, dined, drank, gamed, and whored,
The family vault receives another lord.

2a Handsome, but [it is blàse], rich . . .
 b   [wasted] . . .
 c   "blàsè," . . .
3 Their [he] vigour in [some] thousand . . . *Intended to write* health?
5 [The] Senate see[s] their . . .
6 [Betwixt a] Tyrant's [&] the . . .
7 voted, [drank] drunk . . .

See p. 314 for two canceled stanzas that appear after this one on the manuscript.

76

"Where is the world?" cries Young at *eighty*.* "Where
    The world in which a man was born?" Alas!
Where is the world of *eight* years past?* *'Twas there*—
    I look for it—'tis gone,* a Globe of Glass!
Cracked, shivered, vanished, scarcely gazed on, ere
    A silent change dissolves the glittering mass.
Statesmen, chiefs, orators, queens, patriots, kings,
And dandies, all are gone on the wind's wings.

2 The World [when] in which . . .
5 [Shivered] And frailer, since without a breath of air
7 Statesmen—[and] Chiefs, [and] Orators—[and kings]

Where is Napoleon the Grand? God knows:
  Where little Castlereagh? The devil can tell:
Where Grattan, Curràn, Sheridan, all those*
  Who bound the bar or senate in their spell?
Where is the unhappy Queen, with all her woes?
  And where the Daughter, whom the Isles loved well?
Where are those martyred Saints the Five per Cents?
And where—oh where the devil are the Rents!

1*a* Where is [Napoleon—this alone] God knows
  b Where is [the grand Napoleon] . . .
2 And where Lord Castlereagh . . .
3 Where Grattan [Whitbread] Sheridan . . .
4 Senate [with] their spell?
7 [And] Where are ten thousand lovely innocents?

78

Where's Brummell?* Dished. Where's Long Pole
    Wellesley? 'Diddled.
  Where's Whitbread? Romilly? Where's George
    the Third?
Where is his will?* (That's not so soon unriddled.)
  And where is "Fum" the Fourth, our "royal bird"?*
Gone down it seems to Scotland,* to be fiddled
  Unto by Sawney's violin,† we have heard:
"Caw me, caw thee"*—for six months hath been hatching
This scene of royal itch and loyal scratching.

1*a* Brummell . . . *S and 1903 edition;* *b* Brummel . . . *In 1823,*
  1833, and some modern editions.
3 [Where's Charlotte? (that's not easily own'd)]
6 [Upon] by [loyal] Sawney [as we've] heard
8 This Scene of royal [and of] loyal scratching

Where is Lord This? And where my Lady That?
　　The Honourable Mistresses and Misses?
Some laid aside like an old opera hat,
　　Married, unmarried, and remarried: (this is
An evolution oft performed of late).
　　Where are the Dublin shouts—and London hisses?
Where are the Grenvilles?*† Turned as usual. Where
My friends the Whigs? Exactly where they were.

7 Where [is the] are . . .

80

Where are the Lady Carolines and Franceses?*
　　Divorced or doing thereanent. Ye annals
So brilliant, where the list of routs and dances is,—
　　Thou Morning Post, sole record of the pannels
Broken in carriages, and all the phantasies
　　Of fashion,—say what streams now fill those channels?
Some die, some fly, some languish on the Continent,
Because the times have hardly left them *one* tenant.

1 Carolines and [Fannys]
3 So brilliant—where the list of [night] *fragment*
4 Post—historian of the pannels
6 Of Fashion—[other] Streams now . . .
7 [Many of which diverge unto the] Continent

81

Some who once set their caps at cautious Dukes,*
　　Have taken up at length with younger brothers:
Some heiresses have bit at sharpers' hooks;
　　Some maids have been made wives, some merely
　　　　mothers;
Others have lost their fresh and fairy looks:
　　In short, the list of alterations bothers:

There's little strange in this, but something strange is
The unusual quickness of these common changes.

This stanza was written crosswise on S.
1 Some who have set their caps and curls at Dukes

82

Talk not of seventy years as age! in seven
    I have seen more changes, down from monarchs to
The humblest individual under heaven,
    Than might suffice a moderate century through.
I knew that nought was lasting, but now even
    Change grows too changeable, without being new:
Nought's permanent among the human race,
Except the Whigs *not* getting into place.

4 suffice a [handsome] Century through
5 nought was [permanent] but even

83

I have seen Napoleon, who seemed quite a Jupiter,
    Shrink to a Saturn. I have seen a Duke*
(No matter which) turn politician stupider,
    If that can well be, than his wooden look.
But it is time that I should hoist my "blue Peter,"*
    And sail for a new theme:—I have seen—and shook
To see it—the King hissed, and then carest;*
But don't pretend to settle which was best.

Stanzas 83–85 do not appear on S.

I have seen the landholders without a rap—
    I have seen Johanna Southcote—I have seen
The House of Commons turned to a tax-trap—
    I have seen that sad affair of the late Queen*—
I have seen crowns worn instead of a fool's-cap—
    I have seen a Congress doing all that's mean*—
I have seen some nations like o'erloaded asses
Kick off their burthens*—meaning the high classes.

85

I have seen small poets, and great prosers, and
    Interminable—*not eternal*—speakers—
I have seen the Funds at war with house and land*—
    I've seen the Country Gentlemen turn squeakers*—
I've seen the people ridden o'er like sand*
    By slaves on horseback—I have seen malt liquors
Exchanged for "thin potations"* by John Bull—
I have seen John half detect himself a fool.—

86

But "Carpe diem,"* Juan, "Carpe, carpe!"
    To-morrow sees another race as gay
And transient, and devoured by the same harpy.
    "Life's a poor player,"—then "play out the play,*
Ye villains!" and above all keep a sharp eye
    Much less on what you do than what you say:
Be hypocritical, be cautious, be
Not what you *seem*, but always what you *see*.

1*a* ["Carpe diem"—Carpe"—Juan while you can]
  b Then "Carpe . . .
3   transient—[all] devoured . . .
8   [A Scoundrel and you'll have good company]

But how shall I relate in other Cantos
    Of what befell our hero in the land,
Which 'tis the common cry and lie to vaunt as
    A moral country? But I hold my hand—
For I disdain to write an Atalantis;*
    But 'tis as well at once to understand,
You are *not* a moral people, and you know it
Without the aid of too sincere a poet.

3 cry [of] and lie . . .
4 but I'll hold . . .
5a [Else I could tell ye] *fragment*
 b For I [would] disdain . . .
7 *Four fragments:*
 a [That there is not an]
 b [That you are not a moral people]
 c [There's not a Vice and not a]
 d   [nor Meanness]
8 aid of [an unflattering] poet

88

What Juan saw and underwent, shall be
    My topic, with of course the due restriction
Which is required by proper courtesy;
    And recollect the work is only fiction,
And that I sing of neither mine nor me,
    Though every scribe, in some slight turn of diction,
Will hint allusions never *meant*. Ne'er doubt
This—when I speak, I *don't hint*, but *speak out.*

1 underwent—[and whether]
5a And [I sing neither] *fragment*
 b And that I neither sing of mine [or] nor me
6 Though every [idiot] [envious] scribe . . .
7a [Or] Will hunt allusions never meant; [and] doubt
 b   nor doubt
8a This—[reader—when I mean] *fragment*
 b This—when I speak—I don't [speak]—but speak out

Whether he married with the third or fourth
    Offspring of some sage, husband-hunting Countess,
Or whether with some virgin of more worth
    (I mean in Fortune's matrimonial bounties)
He took to regularly peopling Earth,
    Of which your lawful awful wedlock fount is,—
Or whether he was taken in for damages,
For being too excursive in his homages,—

4 I mean in [weight of] *fragment*
6 Of [whether] which your lawful Wedlock the true fount is

90

Is yet within the unread events of time.
    Thus far, go forth, thou Lay! which I will back
Against the same given quantity of rhyme,
    For being as much the subject of attack
As ever yet was any work sublime,
    By those who love to say that white is black.
So much the better!—I may stand alone,
But would not change my free thoughts for a throne.*

*On the last page of S below this stanza (numbered 86 on the manuscript)
Byron wrote his signature-symbol and the date, "Octr 17th 1822."*
7a So much the better—I [should blush to be]
  b   [would] stand alone
8   [In] But . . .

Rejected Stanzas

29

At length the boys drew up before a door
    From whence poured forth a tribe of well-clad waiters
(While on the pavement many a hungry w—re—
    With which this Moralest of cities caters
For Gentlemen whose passions may boil oer
    Stood as the unpacking gathered more spectators)
And Juan found himself in an extensive
Apartment;—fashionable but expensive.

This stanza, numbered 29 by Byron on S, is not deleted. At some time after the completion of the first draft of Canto XI, Byron substituted for this stanza the one now numbered 30 in the 1823 text.

6   [Of the unpacking stood the sad spectators]
8*a* Apartment;—[so handsome] *fragment*
  b   fashionable [and] expensive

[That is, if same lordship has an ancestor
    Of rank enough to set in stone or lead,
Far easier though for the good town of Manchester*
    To find retorts [sic?] for innocent blood shed
By butchers in her streets, than for the staunchest, or
    Proudest of Parian Patrician (bred
They know not how) the one half the present case
Of peers, to prove their title no disgrace.]

This stanza and the next one are completely canceled on S and were originally intended to follow stanza 75, numbered on the manuscript 74.

1a–2a [Juan, as a Voluptuary was new
       Although he had known pleasure in excess]
  1b [That is, if] [the] [same lordship has] [a family] [ancestor]
  2b [Entitled to be] *fragment*
  3 [Far easier twere] [though . . .]
  5 [streets,] [as] [than . . .]
  6 [Proudest of] [those] [Parian . . .]
  7 [They know not where . . .]

[76]

[Bankers—Contractors—Borough Mongers—Bullies
    Scotch with blue green ribbons—Irish with a blue:*
Some, for having turned converted [sic?] Cullies,*
    Others for other dirty work gone through
Dukes—fools by birth, while Clogher's Bishop*† sullies
    The law, at least until the Bench revert to true
Plain simple fornication—nor behold
The Senate which Tiberius met* of old—]

1 [Bankers—Contractors]—[Bullies—Borough mongers]
2 [Scotch] [for blue . . .] [Irish for . . .]
3 [Some, silenced Cuckolds . . .]
5 [Dukes—fools by birth,] [and bishops who]
6 [until the Bench] [turn back]

Canto XII

1

OF all the barbarous Middle Ages, that
   Which is the most barbarous is the middle age
Of man; it is—I really scarce know what;
   But when we hover between fool and sage,
And don't know justly what we would be at,—
   A period something like a printed page,
Black letter upon foolscap, while our hair
Grows grizzled, and we are not what we were,—

Cantos XII, XIII, and XIV were published in one volume by John Hunt on December 17, 1823.

   All manuscript readings are taken from S (Sterling manuscript), the original first draft.

1   Of all the [middle ages] *fragment*
3   Of Man [which seems]—I really . . .
7   Black letter[s] upon fools cap—[neither white]
8*a* [Is] grizzled—[and our heads are neither here nor there]
  b   [which we think is hardly fair]

Too old for youth,—too young, at thirty-five,
    To herd with boys, or hoard with good threescore,—
I wonder people should be left alive;
    But since they are, that epoch is a bore:
Love lingers still, although 'twere late to wive;
    And as for other love, the illusion's o'er;
And money, that most pure imagination,*
Gleams only through the dawn of its creation.

7 pure [of] Imagination

3

Oh Gold! Why call we misers miserable?*
    Theirs is the pleasure that can never pall;
Theirs is the best bower-anchor, the chain cable
    Which hold fast other pleasures great and small.
Ye who but see the saving man at table,
    And scorn his temperate board, as none at all,
And wonder how the wealthy can be sparing,
Know not what visions spring from each cheese-paring.

2   which can . . .
4a [Without which] other pleasures [are but] small   s
 b   [were but] . . .   s
 c Which hold fast other pleasures great or small   s
 d Which hold . . . and small   In 1823 edition.
 e Which holds . . .   In 1833 and in later editions.
5   Ye—who but see the [old Gentleman at ta] fragment
7   how the [rich man] can . . .

Love or lust makes man sick, and wine much sicker;
    Ambition rends, and gaming gains a loss;
But making money, slowly first, then quicker,
    And adding still a little through each cross
(Which *will* come over things) beats love or liquor,
    The gamester's counter, or the statesman's *dross*.
Oh Gold! I still prefer thee unto paper,
Which makes bank credit like a bark of vapour.*

2   Ambition [tears]—and Gaming[s] gain a loss
5   Which will occur in things . . .
6   The [Statesman's] counter . . .
7*a* [For Fame is dross or worse—and at the last]
  b [I say dross—or if you prefer—say] paper
8*a* [For since Steam Engines' F] *fragment   Intended to write* Fame?
  b [But since Steam Engines praise and honour Vapour]
  c [Although that's] *fragment*
  d Which makes Bank Credit like a Bark of Vapour
     John Hunt misread the manuscript as bank of vapour, *but Byron corrected the proof sheets and wrote Hunt about the phrase on April 24, 1823 (cf. "Byroniana und Anderes aus dem Englischen Seminar in Erlangen," 1912, p. 23). It is correctly printed in the 1823, 1833, and 1837 editions, but the 1903 and some other modern editions print* bank of vapour.

Who hold the balance of the world? Who reign
    O'er Congress, whether royalist or liberal?
Who rouse the shirtless patriots of Spain?*†
    (That make old Europe's journals squeak and gibber*
    all.)
Who keep the world, both old and new, in pain
    Or pleasure? Who make politics run glibber all?
The shade of Bonaparte's noble daring?—
Jew Rothschild, and his fellow Christian Baring.*

1 Who hold[s] the . . .
2a Oer Congress[es and] royalist[s and] liberal[s]?
 b Oer Congress whether [the] royalist . . .
3 Who [can put up] the shirtless . . .
4 [Who] make [all] Europe's . . .
5 both new and old in pain
6a Or pleasure? [and] make . . .
 b   what make . . .
7 The Shade of Buonaparte—[nor you are owing]
8a [No—twere] Jew Rothschild and [the] Christian Baring
 b [No—they] [tis] . . .

6

Those, and the truly liberal Lafitte,*
    Are the true lords of Europe. Every loan
Is not a merely speculative hit,
    But seats a nation or upsets a throne.
Republics also get involved a bit;
    Columbia's stock hath holders not unknown
On 'Change; and even thy silver soil, Peru,*
Must get itself discounted by a Jew.

4a But seats—[or casts a king down from his throne]
 b   [or beats . . .]
 c But seats a Nation or [beats down] a throne
5a [Even your republics are a little bit]
 b Republics also get involved [a bit] [a bit] [a bit]
7 On Change—and [the Great Fount of] *fragment*

Why call the miser miserable? as
   I said before: the frugal life is his,
Which in a saint or cynic ever was
   The theme of praise: a hermit would not miss
Canonization for the self-same cause,
   And wherefore blame gaunt Wealth's austerities?
Because, you'll say, nought calls for such a trial;—
Then there's more merit in his self-denial.

2 I said before;—[he leads] the frugal life
6 Then wherefore . . .

8

He is your only poet;—passion, pure
   And sparkling on from heap to heap, displays
Possess'd, the ore, of which *mere hopes* allure
   Nations athwart the deep: the golden rays
Flash up in ingots from the mine obscure;
   On him the diamond pours its brilliant blaze,
While the mild emerald's beam shades down the dyes
Of other stones, to soothe the miser's eyes.

1   only Poet,—[Fancy] pure
3   Possest [by him—what] *fragment*
6–7*a* The Diamond [makes with its radiant] blaze
     [The] Emerald's [mild] Green [softens] down the dyes
  b While the mild Emerald's Green shades . . .

The lands on either side are his: the ship
   From Ceylon, Inde, or far Cathay, unloads
For him the fragrant produce of each trip;
   Beneath his cars of Ceres groan the roads,
And the vine blushes like Aurora's lip;
   His very cellars might be kings' abodes;
While he, despising every sensual call,
Commands—the intellectual lord of all.

3 of [its] trip
7 While he [unmoved]—despising . . .

10

Perhaps he hath great projects in his mind,
   To build a college, or to found a race,*
A hospital, a church,—and leave behind
   Some dome surmounted by his meagre face:
Perhaps he fain would liberate mankind
   Even with the very ore which makes them base:
Perhaps he would be wealthiest of his nation,
Or revel in the joys of calculation.

3 A hospital—[or Sect]—and . . .

But whether all, or each, or none of these
   May be the hoarder's principle of action,
The fool will call such mania a disease:—
   What is his *own?*—Go look at each transaction,
Wars, revels, loves—do these bring men more ease
   Than the mere plodding through each "vulgar
      fraction"?*
Or do they benefit mankind? Lean Miser!
Let spendthrifts' heirs enquire of yours—who's wiser?

3 The fool [may] call [his] Mania . . .

12

How beauteous are rouleaus! how charming chests,
   Containing ingots, bags of dollars, coins
(Not of old Victors, all whose heads and crests
   Weigh not the thin ore where their visage shines,
But) of fine unclipt gold, where dully rests
   Some likeness, which the glittering cirque confines,
Of modern, reigning, sterling, stupid stamp:—
Yes! ready money *is* Aladdin's lamp.*

1 [Ye beautiful] Rouleaus! [ye iron Caskets!]
2a [Ye Bars,—ye Ingots—ye beloved] Coins
 b [Of . . .]   [immortal Coins!]
3 Not [of] old Victors—[all] whose [real] heads [in baskets]
4 [Were not worth one whereer their profile] shines
6a [The dull profile the] glittering Cirque confines
 b Some [plain profile the] . . .
7 Of modern reigning—sterling [Sovereign]—stamp
8a [Yet] [only] [each and all are like] Aladdin's lamp
 b [All Hail! for each is an] Aladdin's lamp
 c [Yet after all you bear] Aladdin's lamp

"Love rules the camp,* the court, the grove,"—"for
　　Love
　　Is Heaven, and Heaven is Love":—so sings the bard;
Which it were rather difficult to prove,
　　(A thing with poetry in general hard).
Perhaps there may be something in "the grove,"
　　At least it rhymes to "Love"; but I'm prepared
To doubt (no less than Landlords of their rental)
If "courts" and "camps" be quite so sentimental.

5a [First—except pigeons] *fragment*
　b [First save in case of pigeons—how the Grove]
6–7a [At least in a cold country may award] [award]
　　　　　　　　　　　　　　　　　[reward]
　　[A Paradise] *fragment*
7b To doubt, [with] (no less . . .

14

But if Love don't, *Cash* does, and Cash alone:
　　Cash rules the grove, and fells it too besides;
Without cash, camps were thin, and courts were none;
　　Without cash, Malthus tells you, "take no brides."*
So Cash rules Love the ruler, on his own
　　High ground, as Virgin Cynthia sways the tides;
And as for "Heaven being Love," why not say honey
Is wax? Heaven is not Love, 'tis Matrimony.

6 High ground—[as chaste] Cynthia . . .

Is not all love prohibited whatever,
  Excepting marriage? which is love no doubt
After a sort; but somehow people never
  With the same thought the two words have helped
    out:
Love may exist *with* marriage, and *should* ever,
  And marriage also may exist without;
But love *sans* banns is both a sin and shame,
And ought to go by quite another name.

4 [Have with the same] [h] [thought helped th two words out]
7 But Love sans banns [is an illegal] *fragment*

16

Now, if the "court" and "camp" and "grove" be not
  Recruited all with constant married men,
Who never coveted their neighbour's lot,
  I say *that* line's a lapsus of the pen;—
Strange too in my "buon camerado" Scott,
  So celebrated for his morals, when
My Jeffrey held him up as an example*
To me;—of which these morals are a sample.

3 Who never [envied yet] their . . .
5 [Quite] Strange too in my [Moral] "buon' . . .
6 for his moral [pen]
7–8 *Order of composition:*
    [Held up to me by Jeffrey as] example
    [Of Which] *fragment*
    [With profit—as you'll soon see by] a sample
    My [pious] Jeffrey held . . .

Well, if I don't succeed, I *have* succeeded,
  And that's enough; succeeded in my youth,
The only time when much success is needed:
  And my success produced what I in sooth
Cared most about; it need not now be pleaded—
  Whate'er it was, 'twas mine: I've paid, in truth,
Of late, the penalty of such success,
But have not learned to wish it any less.

6 What [that] it was . . .

18

That suit in Chancery,*—which some persons plead
  In an appeal to the unborn, whom they,
In the faith of their procreative creed,
  Baptize Posterity, or future clay,—
To me seems but a dubious kind of reed
  To lean on for support in any way;
Since odds are that Posterity will know
No more of them, than they of her, I trow.

*An entire first draft of this stanza is deleted. See the rejected stanza, p. 357
of this volume. The following readings belong to the rewritten version.*
1   some fellows plead
3   In [their all Christian] procreative Creed
5   but a [doubt] dubious . . .
7a [If] Since [we shall either know nought] *fragment*
 b Since [the] Odds are [we shall know none] *fragment*

19

Why, I'm Posterity—and so are you;
  And whom do we remember? Not a hundred.
Were every memory written down all true,
  The tenth or twentieth name would be but blundered:
Even Plutarch's lives have but picked out a few,
  And 'gainst those few your annalists have thundered;

And Mitford* in the nineteenth century
Gives, with Greek truth, the good old Greek the lie.

3a [If] every Memory [were written] true
 b Were every Memory [but] written down all true
5   [And] Even . . .

20

Good People all, of every degree,
   Ye gentle readers and ungentle writers,
In this twelfth Canto 'tis my wish to be
   As serious as if I had for inditers
Malthus and Wilberforce:*—the last set free
   The Negroes, and is worth a million fighters;
While Wellington has but enslaved the whites,
And Malthus does the thing 'gainst which he writes.*

4 Inditors

21

I'm serious—so are all men upon paper;
   And why should I not form my speculation,
And hold up to the sun my little taper?*
   Mankind just now seem wrapt in meditation
On Constitutions and Steam-boats of vapour;
   While sages write against all procreation,
Unless a man can calculate his means
Of feeding brats the moment his wife weans.

3 my [spa] little Taper?   *Intended to write* sparse?
7 a Man [could] calculate . . .

That's noble! That's romantic! For my part,
  I think that "Philo-genitiveness"* is—
(Now here's a word quite after my own heart,
  Though there's a shorter a good deal than this,
If that politeness set it not apart,
  But I'm resolved to say nought that's amiss)—
I say, methinks that "Philo-genitiveness"
Might meet from men a little more forgiveness.

3 Now [that's] a word . . .
4 deal [of] this

23

And now to business. Oh, my gentle Juan!
  Thou art in London—in that pleasant place*
Where every kind of mischief's daily brewing
  Which can await warm youth in its wild race.
'Tis true that thy career is not a new one;
  Thou are no novice in the headlong chase
Of early life; but this is a new land
Which foreigners can never understand.

No revisions.

What with a small diversity of climate,
 Of hot or cold, mercurial or sedate,
I could send forth my mandate like a primate
 Upon the rest of Europe's social state;
But thou art the most difficult to rhyme at,
 Great Britain, which the Muse may penetrate:
All countries have their "Lions,"* but in thee
There is but one superb menagerie.

2   Of Hot [and] Cold . . .
4a [Up] Upon [such] [few *sic?*] [European national *sic?* state]
 b   [most . . .]
6   [Bold] Britain . . .

                    25

But I am sick of politics. Begin,
 "*Paulo Majora.*"* Juan, undecided
Amongst the paths of being "taken in,"
 Above the ice had like a skaiter glided:
When tired of play, he flirted without sin
 With some of those fair creatures who have prided
Themselves on innocent tantalization,
And hate all vice except its reputation.

2–3 "Paulo Majora."—Juan [was divided/Between] *fragment*
 4a Skaiter . . . s; b skater . . . *In 1833 and in later editions. This
     variation will not be noted hereafter.*
 5a [He played and paid: made love without much sin]
  b When tired of play, [and] flirted . . .
 6   who [long] prided
 7a Themselves [on seldom yielding to temptation]
  b   [on rarely . . .]
  c   [on simple . . .]
 8   [the] it's reputation

But these are few, and in the end they make
    Some devilish escapade or stir, which shows
That even the purest people may mistake
    Their way through Virtue's primrose paths of snows;
And then men stare, as if a new ass spake
    To Balaam,* and from tongue to ear o'erflows
Quick silver Small Talk, ending (if you note it)
With the kind world's Amen!—"Who would have
      thought it?"

3   the [chastest] people . . .
4   Virtue's [purest] path . . .
5a [Oh Virtue! thou! but for the virtues sake]
  b And then folks stare . . .
6–7a [Like] Balaam['s]—and [through all saloons there goes
     The pleasant Small Talk] *fragment*
  7b Quick Silver Small Talk—ending [(as they] note it)
    c   [(if you] . . .
    d   [prithee] . . .

27

The little Leila, with her orient eyes
    And taciturn Asiatic disposition,
(Which saw all Western things with small surprise,
    To the surprise of people of condition,
Who think that novelties are butterflies
    To be pursued as food for inanition)
Her charming figure and romantic history
Became a kind of fashionable mystery.

.1 Leilah . . . *This variation will not be noted hereafter.*
3 with [sli] small surprise *Intended to write* slight?
6 To be [run after] as food . . .
7 Her [pr] charming figure and [her curious] history *Intended to write*
pretty?

The women much divided—as is usual
  Amongst the sex in little things or great.
Think not, fair creatures, that I mean to abuse you all—
  I have always liked you better than I state:
Since I've grown moral, still I must accuse you all
  Of being apt to talk at a great rate;
And now there was a general sensation
Amongst you, about Leila's education.

3 Think not fair [things!] that I mean . . .
6–7a Of being apt [to run at a great rate
    Before the Wind] *fragment*
  7b And now [you had] there was . . .

29

In one point only were you settled—and
  You had reason;—'twas that a young Child of Grace,
As beautiful as her own native land,
  And far away, the last bud of her race,
Howe'er our friend Don Juan might command
  Himself for five, four, three, or two years' space,
Would be much better taught beneath the eye
Of Peeresses whose follies had run dry.

1 On one . . . ye settled—and
4 [And bright eyed as] [And] [Like] *fragments*
6a Himself [just now in four or five] years' space
  b Himself for [two three four or five] ·. . .
7–8 Would be much better [educated by
    Some Countesses] whose Follies . . .

So first there was a generous emulation,
　　And then there was a general competition
To undertake the orphan's education.
　　As Juan was a person of condition,
It had been an affront on this occasion
　　To talk of a subscription or petition;
But sixteen dowagers, ten unwed she sages,
Whose tale belongs to "Hallam's Middle Ages,"*

5　[It would have been] [There was] *fragments*
7a But sixteen Dowagers,—[and twelve heirless]
　b　　　　　　　　　　ten [unmarried Sages]

31

And one or two sad, separate wives, without
　　A fruit to bloom upon their withering bough,
Begged to bring *up* the little girl, and "*out*,"—
　　For that's the phrase that settles all things now,
Meaning a virgin's first blush at a rout,
　　And all her points as thorough-bred to show:
And I assure you, that like virgin honey
Tastes their first season (mostly if they have money).

2 A fruit to [blooming] upon . . .
3 [Who] Begged . . .
6 [The] [By whom—and how—she hath been bred] to show

How all the needy honourable misters,
　　Each out-at-elbow peer, or desperate dandy
The watchful mothers and the careful sisters
　　(Who, by the by, when clever, are more handy
At making matches, where " 'tis gold that glisters,"*
　　Than their *he* relatives) like flies o'er candy
Buzz round "*the* Fortune" with their busy battery,
To turn her head with waltzing and with flattery!

2 [The] out at Elbow peer[s—the] desperate dand[ies]
4 Who by the way [and] when clever . . .
6 flies [round] candy
7 Buzz round "the [spoilt—bewildered] *fragment*
8 [And] turn . . .

33

Each aunt, each cousin hath her speculation;
　　Nay, married dames will now and then discover
Such pure disinterestedness of passion,
　　I've known them court an heiress for their lover.*
"Tantaene!"* Such the virtues of high station!
　　Even in the hopeful Isle, whose outlet's "Dover":
While the poor rich wretch, object of these cares,
Has cause to wish her sire had had male heirs.

1 hath her [separate notion]
2a dames [such a time] discover
 b dames [at such . . .]
3 [Their own] disinterestedness . . .
5 [But this is but] *fragment*
6 hopeful [land] Isle—whose . . .

Some are soon bagged, but some reject three dozen.
　　'Tis fine to see them scattering refusals
And wild dismay o'er every angry cousin
　　(Friends of the party) who begin accusals,
Such as—"Unless Miss (Blank) meant to have chosen
　　Poor Frederick, why did she accord perusals
To his billets? *Why* waltz with him? Why, I pray,
Look *yes* last night and yet say *no* to-day?

1 reject [by] dozen[s]
2 [I like] to see . . .
3 dismay [amongst the] angry cousin[s]
4 who [have now] accusals

35

"Why?—Why?—Besides, Fred. really was *attached;*
　　'Twas not her fortune—he has enough without:
The time will come she'll wish that she had snatched
　　So good an opportunity, no doubt:—
But the old marchioness some plan has hatched,
　　As I'll tell Aurea at to-morrow's rout:
And after all poor Frederick may do better—
Pray did you see her answer to his letter?"

3 she'll wish[ed] that . . .
5 But [that] old [Lady] Marchioness . . .
6 As I [shall] tell [Mr Casca] at . . .
7 [Pray have y] *fragment*

Smart uniforms and sparkling coronets
 Are spurned in turn, until her turn arrives,
After male loss of time, and hearts, and bets
 Upon the sweepstakes for substantial wives:
And when at last the pretty creature gets
 Some gentleman who fights, or writes, or drives,
It soothes the awkward squad of the rejected,
To find how very badly she selected.

3 [Besides the] loss of time . . .
4 [Of] Upon . . .
8 To find [at last] how badly . . .

37

For sometimes they accept some long pursuer,
 Worn out with importunity; or fall
(But here perhaps the instances are fewer)
 To the lot of him who scarce pursued at all.
A hazy widower turned of forty's sure*
 (If 'tis not vain examples to recall)
To draw a high prize: now, howe'er he got her, I
See nought more strange in this than t'other lottery.

1 they [elect] accept some . . .
3 But here [I own] the instances are [fewer]
4 who [not] pursued at all
5 [A drunken Gentleman of Forty's] sure
6a [If he goes after dinner to a ball]
 b [If he can hiccup nonsense at a ball]
 c [Whateer astonishment this seems to call]
7a [To make the very best of] [For] *fragments*
 b To draw [the very best of these fair prizes]
8a [And show how very useful to advise is]
 b [Which shows how very useful good advice is]

I, for my part—(one "modern instance" more,
   "True 'tis a pity, pity 'tis, 'tis true")*
Was chosen from out an amatory score,
   Albeit my years were less discreet than few;
But though I also had reformed before
   Those became one who soon were to be two,
I'll not gainsay the generous public's voice,
That the young lady made a monstrous choice.

1a I[f] for my part—([one grievous] instance more
 b   ([one usual *sic?*] . . .
 c   [hear]
3   Was chosen [out of better than a] score
4   [Tis true] my years . . .
5   [And then] I also . . .
8   [That there was never yet so bad a] choice

39

Oh, pardon me digression—or at least
   Peruse! 'Tis always with a moral end
That I dissert, like Grace before a feast:
   For like an aged aunt, or tiresome friend,
A rigid guardian, or a zealous priest,
   My Muse by exhortation means to mend
All people, at all times and in most places;
Which puts my Pegasus to these grave paces.

1a Oh pardon me digression . . . s
 b   my digression *In 1833 and in later editions.*
2   tis alway with . . .
3   That I [digress]—like . . .
4   [To] For . . .
5   a [stricter] priest
6a [As these my] exhortation[s],—[tis to] mend
 b My Muse by exhortation . . . *S, 1833, and later editions.*
 c   exhortion . . . *Misprint in 1823 edition.*
8   [I] put my Pegasus [upon his] paces

But now I'm going to be immoral; now
  I mean to show things really as they are,
Not as they ought to be: for I avow,
  That till we see what's what in fact, we're far
From much improvement with that virtuous plough
  Which skims the surface, leaving scarce a scar
Upon the black loam long manured by Vice,
Only to keep its corn at the old price.

4 we [know] what's what . . .
5 that [moral] plough
6 Which [but turns up] the surface—leaving scarce a [scarce]
7 Upon [that] black . . .
8a [Only to keep it's Corn up to the price]
 b [To keep it's Corn-bill to the old price]

41

But first of little Leila we'll dispose;
  For like a day-dawn she was young and pure,
Or, like the old comparison of snows,*
  Which are more pure than pleasant to be sure.
Like many people every body knows,
  Don Juan was delighted to secure
A goodly guardian for his infant charge,
Who might not profit much by being at large.

7 A[n] goodly [Tutor] Guardian . . .

Besides, he had found out that he was no tutor:
　(I wish that others would find out the same)*
And rather wished in such things to stand neuter,
　For silly wards will bring their guardians blame:
So when he saw each ancient dame a suitor
　To make his little wild Asiatic tame,
Consulting "the Society for Vice
Suppression,"* Lady Pinchbeck was his choice.

1a found out that he was . . .　s
　b found out he was　*In 1833 and in later editions.*
5　he [found] each . . .

43

Olden she was—but had been very young;
　Virtuous she was—and had been, I believe:
Although the world has such an evil tongue
　That—but my chaster ear will not receive
An echo of a syllable that's wrong:
　In fact, there's nothing makes me so much grieve
As that abominable tittle tattle,
Which is the cud eschewed*† by human cattle.

4–5　That—but I will not listen, by your leave
　　Unto a single syllable . . .
　8　Cud [of] eschewed . . .

44

Moreover I've remarked (and I was once
　A slight observer in a modest way)
And so may every one except a dunce,
　That ladies in their youth a little gay,
Besides their knowledge of the world, and sense
　Of the sad consequence of going astray,
Are wiser in their warnings 'gainst the woe
Which the mere passionless can never know.

1 [Besides—I have] remarked . . .
2 A [shrewd] observer . . .
7a [Though] [Are always] *fragments*
 b Are [milder] in their . . .

45

While the harsh Prude indemnifies her virtue
   By railing at the unknown and envied passion,
Seeking far less to save you than to hurt you,
   Or what's still worse, to put you out of fashion,—
The kinder veteran* with calm words will court you,
   Entreating you to pause before you dash on;
Expounding and illustrating the riddle
Of Epic Love's beginning, end, and middle.

1 While the [fierce] Prude . . .
4 [And trying how] *fragment*
6 [Of] [And beg of] you to pause . . .
8 [Of] [Lov] *fragment*

46

Now whether it be thus, or that they are stricter,
   As better knowing why they should be so,
I think you'll find from many a family picture,
   That daughters of such mothers as may know
The world by experience rather than by lecture,
   Turn out much better for the Smithfield Show*
Of vestals brought into the marriage mart,
Than those bred up by prudes without a heart.

2 [Than] As . . .
4 as [well] know
7 Of [Virgins] brought . . .
8 Than those [of] bred . . .

I said that Lady Pinchbeck* had been talked about—
  As who has not, if female, young, and pretty?
But now no more the ghost of Scandal stalked about;
  She merely was deemed amiable and witty,
And several of her best bon-mots were hawked about;
  Then she was given to charity and pity,
And passed (at least the latter years of life)
For being a most exemplary wife.

4 She merely [passed for] amiable . . .

48

High in high circles, gentle in her own,
  She was the mild reprover of the young
Whenever—which means every day—they'd shown
  An awkward inclination to go wrong.
The quantity of good she did's unknown,
  Or at the least would lengthen out my song:—
In brief, the little orphan of the East
Had raised an interest in her which encreased.

8 interest [for] her . . .

49

Juan too was a sort of favourite with her,
  Because she thought him a good heart at bottom,
A little spoiled, but not so altogether;
  Which was a wonder, if you think who got him,
And how he had been tossed, he scarce knew whither:
  Though this might ruin others, it did *not* him,
At least entirely, for he had seen too many
Changes in youth, to be surprised at any.

3 spoilt . . .
5 And how he had [proved the extremes] *fragment*

And these vicissitudes tell best in youth;
　　For when they happen at a riper age,
People are apt to blame the Fates, forsooth,
　　And wonder Providence is not more sage.
Adversity is the first path to truth:
　　He who hath proved war, storm, or woman's rage,
Whether his winters be eighteen or eighty,
Hath won the experience which is deemed so weighty.

2a　For when they happen [to an aged person]
　b　　　　　　　　　　[when the Mind is]
6　proved—Storm—War—[and] Woman's rage

51

How far it profits is another matter.—
　　Our hero gladly saw his little charge
Safe with a lady, whose last grown-up daughter
　　Being long married, and thus set at large,
Had left all the accomplishments she taught her
　　To be transmitted, like the Lord Mayor's barge,*
To the next comer; or—as it will tell
More Muse-like—say like Cytherea's shell.*

2　Our hero [having seen] his . . .
3　Safe with a[n ancient] Lady . . .
4a　[Had] long [been] married—[and] left at large
　b　　　　　　　　　　[that is]—left . . .
5　[And therefore left her] *fragment*
7a　[All carved and gilded] or—as it will tell
　b　Painted and Gilded—or . . .
8　More [Muse-like] [Musel] Muse-like . . .

I call such things transmission; for there is
  A floating balance of accomplishment
Which forms a pedigree from Miss to Miss,
  According as their minds or backs are bent.
Some waltz; some draw; some fathom the abyss
  Of metaphysics; others are content
With music; the most moderate shine as wits,
While others have a genius turned for fits.

1 I [talk of such] transmission . . .
2 A [Certain quantum] of Accomplishment
7 With [playing; well,] the most moderate . . .

53

But whether fits, or wits, or harpsichords,
  Theology, Fine Arts, or finer stays
May be the baits for gentlemen or lords,
  With regular descent, in these our days
The last year to the new transfers its hoards;
  New vestals claim men's eyes with the same praise
Of "elegant" *et cetera,* in fresh batches—
All matchless creatures and yet bent on matches.

2   [Or Metaphysics]—Fine Arts . . .
3a May be the [traps for their connubial] Lords
 b   baits [to attract . . .]
4   In regular . . .
6   New [Misses] claim . . .
7a [And elegant accomplished lovely] *fragment*
 b [Of . . .] *fragment*
8   and [all] yet . . .

But now I will begin my poem.—'Tis
   Perhaps a little strange, if not quite new,
That from the first of Cantos up to this
   I've not begun what we have to go through.
These first twelve books are merely flourishes,
   Preludios, trying just a string or two
Upon my lyre, or making the pegs sure;
   And when so, you shall have the overture.

6 Preludios—trying [if a String's amiss]
7*a* Upon [my fiddle—seeing if all's sure]
 b Upon my kit; [screwing] [and] [the] [pegs secure] [sure]
 c   [on the]

55

My Muses do not care a pinch of rosin
   About what's called success, or not succeeding:
Such thoughts are quite below the strain they have
      chosen;
   'Tis a "great moral lesson"* they are reading.
I thought, at setting off, about two dozen
   Cantos would do; but at Apollo's pleading,
If that my Pegasus should not be foundered,
   I think to canter gently through a hundred.

2 About [their] what's . . .
5 I thought at [first] setting [out] about two dozen
6 Cantos would [be] [hold] do . . .

Don Juan saw that microcosm on stilts,
    Yclept the Great World; for it is the least,
Although the highest: but as swords have hilts
    By which their power of mischief is encreased,
When man in battle or in quarrel tilts,
    Thus the low world,* north, south, or west, or east,
Must still obey the high—which is their handle,
Their moon, their sun, their gas, their farthing candle.

4 power of [action] is increased
5 in [combat] battle . . .
6 Thus the low World both North—South—West and East
8 Their [torch—their] Moon—their Sun . . .

57

He had many friends who had many wives, and was
    Well looked upon by both, to that extent
Of friendship which you may accept or pass,
    It does nor good nor harm; being merely meant
To keep the wheels going of the higher class,
    And draw them nightly when a ticket's sent:
And what with masquerades, and fêtes, and balls,
For the first season such a life scarce palls.

4 [Which] does nor good nor harm—[and's] merely meant

58

A young unmarried man, with a good name
    And fortune, has an awkward part to play;
For good society is but a game,
    "The royal game of Goose,"* as I may say,
Where every body has some separate aim,
    An end to answer, or a plan to lay—
The single ladies wishing to be double,
The married ones to save the virgins trouble.

2 And [good looks]—has . . .
8 save the[m so much] trouble

59

I don't mean this as general, but particular
    Examples may be found of such pursuits:
Though several also keep their perpendicular
    Like poplars, with good principles for roots;
Yet many have a method more *reticular*—
    "Fishers for men,"* like Sirens with soft lutes;
For talk six times with the same single lady,
And you may get the wedding dresses ready.

3   [But] Several . . .
5   [But others] have a method . . .
6*a* "Fishers [for] Men" . . .;   *b* "Fishers of . . .
7   [Or] [Talk—sing—or dance] six times with [an unmarried] lady
8*a* [Tis time the wedding dresses were got] ready
 b And you [will find] the wedding . . .

60

Perhaps you'll have a letter from the mother,
    To say her daughter's feelings are trepanned;
Perhaps you'll have a visit from the brother,
    All strut and stays and whiskers, to demand
What "your intentions are"?—One way or other
    It seems the virgin's heart expects your hand;
And between pity for her case and yours,
You'll add to Matrimony's list of cures.

2 feelings are [involved]
4 [All Gentlemen with whiskers]—-to demand
6 [Between] *fragment*

I've known a dozen weddings made even *thus,*
　　And some of them high names: I have also known
Young men who—though they hated to discuss
　　Pretensions which they never dreamed to have
　　　　shown—
Yet neither frightened by a female fuss,
　　Nor by mustachios moved, were let alone,
And lived, as did the broken-hearted fair,
In happier plight than if they formed a pair.

4 they never [meant] to . . .
5 [Were] neither [to be] frightened . . .
6 Nor [moved by grim Mustachios]—let alone
8 In happ[y] plight . . .

62

There's also nightly, to the uninitiated,
　　A peril—not indeed like love or marriage,
But not the less for this to be depreciated:
　　It is—I meant and mean not to disparage
The show of virtue even in the vitiated—
　　It adds an outward grace unto their carriage—
But to denounce the amphibious sort of harlot,
"*Couleur de rose,*" who's neither white nor scarlet.

2 A[nother] peril . . .
4 mean [nev] not to . . .
6–8 It adds [a sort of Grace] unto their carriage
　　　But [these are cold Coquettes—a sort of] Harlot
　　　"Couleur de Rose" [nor white being] *fragment*

Such is your cold coquette, who can't say "No,"
　　And won't say "Yes," and keeps you on and off-ing,
On a lee shore, till it begins to blow—
　　Then sees your heart wrecked with an inward scoffing
This works a world of sentimental woe,
　　And sends new Werters* yearly to their coffin;
But yet is merely innocent flirtation,
Not quite adultery, but adulteration.

3–7　[Like a] Lee shore, [until it comes on] to blow
　　[And] then [will wreck you with a world of] scoffing
　　[Most young beginners may be taken so
　　But those who have been a little used to roughing
　　Know how to end this half and half] Flirtation
　6b　to the Coffin

64

"Ye Gods, I grow a talker!"* Let us prate.
　　The next of perils, though I place it *stern*est,
Is when, without regard to "Church or State,"
　　A wife makes or takes love in upright earnest.
Abroad, such things decide few women's fate—
　　(Such, early traveller! is the truth thou learnest)—
But in Old England when a young bride errs,
Poor thing! Eve's was a trifling case to her's.

3　to "Church and State"
4　A [wedded Dame] *fragment*
5　decide [not woman's] fate
7　But [here] in . . .
8　a trivial case to hers

For 'tis a low, newspaper, humdrum, law-suit
  Country, where a young couple of the same ages
Can't form a friendship but the world o'erawes it.
  Then there's the vulgar trick of those d—d damages!
A verdict—grievous foe to those who cause it!—
  Forms a sad climax to romantic homages;
Besides those soothing speeches of the pleaders,
And evidences which regale all readers!

1 a [curst] Newspaper . . .
2 where [warm young people] of the same ages
4 [And there's that] *fragment*
6 [Makes] a sad . . .
7 those [pleasin] soothing . . .

66

But they who blunder thus are raw beginners;
  A little genial sprinkling of hypocrisy
Has saved the fame of thousand splendid sinners,
  The loveliest Oligarchs of our Gynocrasy;*
You may see such at all the balls and dinners,
  Among the proudest of our Aristocracy,
So gentle, charming, charitable, chaste—
And all by having *tact* as well as taste.

4a Gynocrasy s; b gynocracy *In 1833 and in later editions.*

67

Juan, who did not stand in the predicament
  Of a mere novice, had one safeguard more;
For he was sick—no, 'twas not the word *sick* I meant—
  But he had seen so much good love before,
That he was not in heart so very weak;—I meant
  But thus much, and no sneer against the shore
Of white cliffs, white necks, blue eyes, bluer stockings,
Tithes, taxes, duns, and doors with double knockings.*

3 [But] he . . .
7–8 Of white cliffs—[and white bosoms—and blue eyes
And stockings; virtues, loves, and chastities]

68

But coming young from lands and scenes romantic,
  Where lives not law-suits must be risked for Passion,
And Passion's self must have a spice of frantic,
  Into a country where 'tis half a fashion,
Seemed to him half commercial, half pedantic,
  Howe'er he might esteem this moral nation;
Besides (alas! his taste—forgive and pity!)
At first he did not think the women pretty.

2a Where [Loves] not . . . passion
 b *The 1823 edition misprints* Passions.
4 Into a climate where . . .
5 Seemed [so rather formal and] pedantic
6 [He much esteemed this great & glorious] nation
8 [The] At first he . . .

69

I say at *first*—for he found out at *last*,
  But by degrees, that they were fairer far
Than the more glowing dames whose lot is cast
  Beneath the influence of the Eastern star.*
A further proof we should not judge in haste;
  Yet inexperience could not be his bar
To taste:—the truth is, if men would confess,
That novelties *please* less than they *impress*.

5a [Which proves that one should never] judge in haste
 b   [rarely] . . .
6a [And yet 'twas not his fault] *fragment*
 b Yet . . . be [his] [a] bar
7–8 To [his good] Taste,—the truth is [neither more nor less]
That Novelties [don't please; they but] impress

Though travelled, I have never had the luck to
    Trace up those shuffling negroes, Nile or Niger,
To that impracticable place Timbuctoo,
    Where Geography finds no one to oblige her
With such a chart as may be safely stuck to—
    For Europe ploughs in Afric like *"bos piger"*;*
But if I *had been* at Timbuctoo, there
    No doubt I should be told that black is fair.*

1   [For my part] I have never had the luck to
2   Trace up [that Negro—the strange] *fragment*
3a [Up to their sources] *fragment*; *b* [Timbucktoo]
4a [But should a Lady ask me to] oblige her
  b [Nor till a Lady . . .]
  c [While] Geography finds . . .
5–6 [By] [Though many thousands both of pith and pluck too
                    [hundreds . . .]
    Have done their best] *fragment*
    [Have ventured past the Jaws of Moor and Tiger]
    [And] Europe ploughs . . .
    Canceled manuscript marginal note on line 6: "By particular license
    positively for this time at [the] particular desire etc. to be pro-
    nounced 'tydger.' Such is what Gifford calls the 'wicked necessity of
    rhyming.' "
8   black was fair

71

It is. I will not swear that black is white;
    But I suspect in fact that white is black,
And the whole matter rests upon eye-sight.*
    Ask a blind man, the best judge. You'll attack
Perhaps this new position—but I'm right;
    Or if I'm wrong, I'll not be ta'en aback:—
He hath no morn nor night, but all is dark
Within; and what sees't thou? A dubious spark.

2   But [by the Gods I swear] that White is black
4   [And every body sees that what they lack]

6*a* [For both our prejudices he must back]
 b [For all . . .]
8   what [see all?]—a dubious spark

72

But I'm relapsing into metaphysics,
  That labyrinth, whose clue is of the same
Construction as your cures for hectic phthisics,
  Those bright moths fluttering round a dying flame:
And this reflection brings me to plain physics,
  And to the beauties of a foreign dame,
Compared with those of our pure pearls of price,
Those Polar summers, *all* sun, and some ice.*

3*a* Construction as [a cure for Het] Hectic Ptisicks
 b   our Cures for . . .
4   [Those flies that flutter] round . . .
7   our [cold] Pearls . . .
8*a* [Like Polar Summers] *fragment*
 b [Above all Sunshine, and below half Ice]
 c [Like] Polar Summer[s] all Sun . . .

73

Or say they are like virtuous mermaids, whose
  Beginnings are fair faces, ends mere fishes;—
Not that there's not a quantity of those
  Who have a due respect for their own wishes.
Like Russians rushing from hot baths to snows*
  Are they, at bottom virtuous even when vicious:
They warm into a scrape, but keep of course,
As a reserve, a plunge into remorse.

1 [Like] [P] [Arctic Summers—or like Mermaids]—whose
3 there [are] not . . .
6 Are they, [even] at . . . vitious
7 They [plunge] into a Scrape . . .

But this has nought to do with their outsides.
 I said that Juan did not think them pretty
At the first blush; for a fair Briton hides
 Half her attractions—probably from pity—
And rather calmly into the heart glides,
 Than storms it as a foe would take a city;
But once there (if you doubt this, prithee try)
She keeps it for you like a true ally.

3 At the first blush [because our fair Girls hide]
4 Half [of their charms—most] probably from pity
5 And rather [into the heart] *fragment*
7a But once there—[Chase her if you can;]
 b   [it is scarce removeably, *sic?*]
 c   [(few have felt this more than I)]

75

She cannot step as does an Arab barb,
 Or Andalusian girl from mass returning,*
Nor wear as gracefully as Gauls her garb,
 Nor in her eye Ausonia's* glance is burning;
Her voice, though sweet, is not so fit to warb-
 le those bravuras (which I still am learning
To like, though I have been seven years in Italy,
And have, or had, an ear that served me prettily);—

1 She [does not] step as doth . . .
6 -le [those grand bravuras I'm still] learning
8 ear which served . . .

She cannot do these things, nor one or two
　　Others, in that off-hand and dashing style
Which takes so much—to give the devil his due,—
　　Nor is she quite so ready with her smile,
Nor settles all things in one interview,
　　(A thing approved as saving time and toil) ;—
But though the soil may give you time and trouble,
Well cultivated, it will render double.

1　and one . . .
3　Which takes [at once] to give . . .
5　[But] Nor . . .
6a [Which settles me] [Which neertheless] *fragments*
　b [A thing which sav] *fragment　Intended to write* saves.

77

And if in fact she takes to a *"grande passion,"*
　　It is a very serious thing indeed :
Nine times in ten 'tis but caprice or fashion,
　　Coquetry, or a wish to take the lead,
The pride of a mere child with a new sash on,
　　Or wish to make a rival's bosom bleed;
But the tenth instance will be a Tornado,
For there's no saying what they will or may do.

6　Or wish to [hurt] a rival *fragment*
7a [is] a tornado;　b will a tornado
8　For [once] there's . . .

[351]

The reason's obvious: if there's an eclât,
    They lose their caste at once, as do the Parias;
And when the delicacies of the law
    Have filled their papers with their comments various,
Society, that china without flaw,
    (The hypocrite!) will banish them like Marius,*
To sit amidst the ruins of their guilt:
For Fame's a Carthage not so soon rebuilt.

4   the Papers . . .
5   Society, [like] China [bears no] flaw
6   (The Hypocrite!) will [shut them full] *fragment*
7a [Amidst the] *fragment*
 b [To sit upon the ruins of their Guilt]
 c [To sit] [Amidst the ruins of their Name]

79

Perhaps this is as it should be;—it is
    A comment on the Gospel's "Sin no more,
And be thy sins forgiven":*—but upon this
    I leave the saints to settle their own score.
Abroad, though doubtless they do much amiss,
    An erring woman finds an opener door
For her return to Virtue—as they call
That Lady who should be at home to all.

1   is [at] [at] as it . . .
8   who [is not] at home . . .

80

For me, I leave the matter where I find it,
    Knowing that such uneasy Virtue leads
People some ten times less in fact to mind it,
    And care but for discoveries and not deeds.
And as for Chastity, you'll never bind it
    By all the laws the strictest lawyer pleads,

But aggravate the crime you have not prevented,
By rendering desperate those who had else repented.

2a Knowing that such [outrageous] *fragment*
 b   such uneasy Virtue[s] lead
3   People [in fact] ten times . . .
4   And [only] care [for the] discovery [not the] deed
6   [By all the lawyers that will ever plead]
7   But [merely] aggravate . . .
8   desperate [her], who . . .

81

But Juan was no casuist, nor had pondered
    Upon the moral lessons of mankind:
Besides, he had not seen of several hundred
    A lady altogether to his mind.
A little *"blâsé"*—'tis not to be wondered
    At, that his heart had got a tougher rind:
And though not vainer from his past success,
No doubt his sensibilities were less.

No revisions.

82

He also had been busy seeing sights—
    The Parliament and all the other houses;
Had sate beneath the gallery at nights,
    To hear debates whose thunder *roused* (not *rouses*)
The world to gaze upon those northern lights
    Which flashed as far as where the musk-bull browses:*
He had also stood at times behind the throne—
But Grey was not arrived, and Chatham gone.*

1 [B] [And] He also . . .
5 The world [which] to [listen] *fragment*
6 the Musk Ox browses

[353]

He saw however at the closing session,
    That noble sight, when *really* free the nation,
A king in constitutional possession
    Of such a throne as is the proudest station,
Though despots know it not—till the progression
    Of freedom shall complete their education.
'Tis not mere splendour makes the show august
To eye or heart—it is the people's trust.

1   He saw however—[though he did] *fragment*
3   constitutional [procession]
5   [perhaps] progression
6a Of [Man's opinions forms] their education
 b Of Freedom [will] complete . . ··
7–8a [And] [Tis not the Splendour of the Show which] must
                             [can or] must
    [Content the eye] *fragment*
8b To eye or heart, [tis] the [sacred] trust
 c   [but 'tis] [it] *fragment*

84

There too he saw (whate'er he may be now)
    A Prince, the prince of princes, at the time*
With fascination in his very bow,
    And full of promise, as the spring of prime.
Though royalty was written on his brow,
    He had *then* the grace too, rare in every clime,
Of being, without alloy of fop or beau,
A finished gentleman from top to toe.

2 Princes—[of that] time
6 He had [the grace] *fragment*

And Juan was received, as hath been said,
    Into the best society: and there
Occurred what often happens, I'm afraid,
    However disciplined and *debonnaire*:—
The talent and good humour he displayed,
    Besides the marked distinction of his air,
Exposed him, as was natural, to temptation,
Even though himself avoided the occasion.

1*a* And [thus for what] *fragment*
 b And Juan was as hath been said received
4 [Although he had really grown] *fragment*
5 [But] [if he] [that which him befell] *fragment*

86

But what, and where, with whom, and when, and why,
    Is not to be put hastily together;
And as my object is morality
    (Whatever people say) I don't know whether
I'll leave a single reader's eyelid dry,
    But harrow up his feelings till they wither,
And hew out a huge monument of pathos,
As Philip's son proposed to do with Athos.*

1 where—[and] with whom . . .
5 [That] I [shall the] *fragment*
6 [When the pathetic] [For now] *fragments*
8 to do [of] Athos

Here the twelfth Canto of our introduction
    Ends. When the body of the book's begun,
You'll find it of a different construction
    From what some people say 'twill be when done:
The plan at present's simply in concoction.
    I can't oblige you, reader! to read on;
That's your affair, not mine: a real spirit
Should neither court neglect nor dread to bear it.

Byron at first ended the canto with this stanza, below which on S he wrote his usual signature-symbol and the date, "10ᵇʳᵉ 7ᵈ 1822." ("10ᵇʳᵉ" is Byron's abbreviation for "December.")

4a From what some people [think is to b] *fragment*
  b   ['twill be] *fragment*
7   not mine—[a man of Spirit]
8   Should [neth] neither . . .

88

And if my thunderbolt not always rattles,
    Remember, reader! you have had before
The worst of tempests and the best of battles
    That e'er were brewed from elements or gore,
Besides the most sublime of—Heaven knows what else—
    An Usurer could scarce expect much more—
But my best Canto, save one on Astronomy,
Will turn upon "Political Economy."*

Stanzas 88–89 do not appear on S.

That is your present theme for popularity:
   Now that the Public Hedge hath scarce a stake,
It grows an act of patriotic charity
   To show the people the best way to break.
My plan (but I, if but for singularity,
   Reserve it) will be very sure to take.
Mean time read all the National-Debt sinkers,*
And tell me what you think of your great thinkers.

Rejected Stanza

[18]

[That suit in Chancery—(I have a Chancery Suit
   In right good earnest—also an Appeal*
Before the Lords—whose Chancellor's more acute
   In law than equity—as I can feel—
Because my Cases put his Lordship to't—
   And—though no doubt tis for the Public weal,
His Lordship's Justice—seems not that of Solomon—
Not that I deem our Chief Judge is a hollow man—)]

This canceled first draft follows stanza 17 on the manuscript.

5 [Because I'm a republican] *fragment*
7 Justice—[is not] that . . .

Canto XIII

1

I NOW mean to be serious;—it is time,
   Since laughter now-a-days is deemed too serious.
A jest at Vice by Virtue's called a crime,
   And critically held as deleterious:
Besides, the sad's a source of the sublime,
   Although when long a little apt to weary us;
And therefore shall my lay soar high and solemn
As an old temple dwindled to a column.

For the date of publication see p. 315 of this volume.
   *All manuscript readings are taken from Tn (Thorne manuscript),
Byron's first draft.*
   On the first page of the manuscript above the first stanza is the date,
"Fʸ 12ᵗʰ 1823."

2 Since Laughter, [it appears,] is deemed . . .
3 And jests at Vice . . .
8 As [oer a fallen City a] *fragment*

The Lady Adeline Amundeville
  ('Tis an old Norman name, and to be found
In pedigrees by those who wander still
  Along the last fields of that Gothic ground)—
Was high-born, wealthy by her father's will,
  And beauteous, even where beauties most abound,
In Britain—which of course true patriots find
The goodliest soil of Body and of Mind.

3 who [ponder] still
4 [The] Along . . .
8 The [only] soil [for] of Body or of Mind

3

I'll not gainsay them; it is not my cue;
  I leave them to their taste, no doubt the best:
An eye's an eye, and whether black or blue,
  Is no great matter, so 'tis in request:
'Tis nonsense to dispute about a hue—
  The kindest may be taken as a test.
The fair sex should be always fair, and no man,
Till thirty, should perceive there's a plain woman.

7 [And] The . . .

And after that serene and somewhat dull
   Epoch, that awkward corner turned for days
More quiet, when our Moon's no more at full,
   We may presume to criticise or praise;
Because indifference begins to lull
   Our passions, and we walk in Wisdom's ways;
Also because the figure and the face
Hint, that 'tis time to give the younger place.

2 turned [to steadier days]
3 [When] More quiet—when our Moon's [no longer] full
7 Also—because—[though] [th] [although with] *fragment*

5

I know that some would fain postpone this era,
   Reluctant as all placemen to resign
Their post; but theirs is merely a chimera,
   For they have passed life's equinoctial line:
But then they have their claret and madeira
   To irrigate the dryness of decline;
And County Meetings and the Parliament,
And debt, and what not, for their solace sent.

3 their's *In 1823 edition;* theirs, TN *and in 1833 and later editions.*
4a [Which I used] *fragment*
 b For they have passed [the] Equinoctial line
5 [Of Life's] [be] [and on't there] *fragment*
6a To [gently smoothe] the [progress] of decline
 b To liquify the dryness . . .

6

And is there not Religion, and Reform,
   Peace, War, the taxes, and what's called the "Nation"?
The struggle to be Pilots in a storm?*
   The landed and the monied speculation?
The joys of mutual hate, to keep them warm,
   Instead of love, that mere hallucination?

[360]

      Now hatred is by far the longest pleasure;
      Men love in haste, but they detest at leisure.

4 or the monied . . .
7 the [truest] pleasure
8 they can hate at leisure

7

      Rough Johnson, the great moralist, professed,
        Right honestly, "he liked an honest hater"*—
      The only truth that yet has been confest
        Within these latest thousand years or later.
      Perhaps the fine old fellow spoke in jest:—
        For my part, I am but a mere spectator,
      And gaze where'er the palace or the hovel is,
      Much in the mode of Goethe's Mephistopheles;

5 fellow [was] in jest
8 Metistophiles

8

      But neither love nor hate in much excess;
        Though 'twas not once so. If I sneer sometimes,
      It is because I cannot well do less,
        And now and then it also suits my rhymes.
      I should be very willing to redress
        Men's wrongs, and rather check than punish crimes,
      Had not Cervantes in that too true tale
      Of Quixote, shown how all such efforts fail.

6 Man's wrongs . . .

First draft of stanzas 10 and 11 of Canto XIII (Courtesy of Mrs. Landon K. Thorne. Somewhat reduced)

Of all tales 'tis the saddest*—and more sad,
　　Because it makes us smile: his hero's right,
And still pursues the right;—to curb the bad,
　　His only object, and 'gainst odds to fight,
His guerdon: 'tis his virtue makes him mad!
　　But his adventures form a sorry sight;—
A sorrier still is the great moral taught
By that real Epic unto all who have thought.

1　and [most] sad
3　the right;—[and therefore's]
5a　His guerdon—[and therefore] *fragment*
　b　His guerdon—[a Philosopher gone] mad
　c　His guerdon—[and] 'tis his Virtue makes [him] mad
6　[But] [And] But his adventures [make] a sorry sight
8　By that great Epic . . .

10

Redressing injury, revenging wrong,
　　To aid the damsel and destroy the caitiff;
Opposing singly the united strong,
　　From foreign yoke to free the helpless native;—
Alas! Must noblest views, like an old song,
　　Be for mere Fancy's sport a theme creative?
A jest, a riddle, Fame through thin and thick sought?
And Socrates himself but Wisdom's Quixote?

1–2　*Order of composition:*
　　　[He who will combat Evil long in Use
　　　Is told he fights with Windmills] *fragment*
　　　Redressing injur[ies]—revenging wrong
　　　[Relieving damsels—and destroying] Caitiff[s]
　4　From foreign [Despots—helpl] [helping hopeless] native[s]
　5　Alas! must [views like these] like an old Song
　7a　A jest—or riddle Fame through thin and thick sought　TN
　　b　　　　　　　　　　　　　　　thick and thin . . .　*In 1833*
　　　and in some later editions.

Cervantes smiled Spain's Chivalry away;
   A single laugh demolished the right arm
Of his own country;—seldom since that day
   Has Spain had heroes. While Romance could charm,
The world gave ground before her bright array;
   And therefore have his volumes done such harm,
That all their glory, as a composition,
Was dearly purchased by his land's perdition.

3a Of his own Country—[which] since that Day
 b   [never] . . .
4a–8 Has Spain had Heroes;—[once her whole Array
     Was such—while yet Romance had all her charms]
     And therefore [though no Volume grave or gay
     Deserves more] [praise] [Glory as a] Composition
     [Yet was it] purchased . . .
4b Has Spain had Heroes;—while Romance [had] charm
7b That all [the] Glory . . .
 c That all [it's] . . .

12

I'm "at my old Lunes"*—digression, and forget
   The Lady Adeline Amundeville;
The fair most fatal Juan ever met,
   Although she was not evil, nor meant ill;
But Destiny and Passion spread the net,
   (Fate is a good excuse for our own will)
And caught them;—what do they *not* catch, methinks?
But I'm not Oedipus, and life's a Sphinx.

5 But Destiny or Passion . . .
7 And caught—[what] them . . .

I tell the tale as it is told, nor dare
  To venture a solution: "*Davus sum!*"*
And now I will proceed upon the pair.
  Sweet Adeline, amidst the gay world's hum,
Was the Queen-Bee, the glass of all that's fair;*
  Whose charms made all men speak, and women dumb.
The last's a miracle, and such was reckoned,
And since that time there has not been a second.

No revisions.

                    14

Chaste was she, to detraction's desperation,
  And wedded unto one she had loved well;
A man known in the councils of the nation,
  Cool, and quite English; imperturbable,
Though apt to act with fire upon occasion;
  Proud of himself and her, the world could tell
Nought against either, and both seemed secure—
She in her virtue, he in his hauteur.

No revisions.

                    15

It chanced some diplomatical relations,
  Arising out of business, often brought
Himself and Juan in their mutual stations
  Into close contact. Though reserved, nor caught
By specious seeming, Juan's youth, and patience,
  And talent, on his haughty spirit wrought,
And formed a basis of esteem, which ends
In making men what Courtesy calls friends.

4 though [not] reserved . . .
8 In making [most] men [the things which are called] friends

And thus Lord Henry, who was cautious as
   Reserve and pride could make him, and full slow
In judging men—when once his judgment was
   Determined, right or wrong, on friend or foe,
Had all the pertinacity pride has,
   Which knows no ebb to its imperious flow,
And loves or hates, disdaining to be guided,
Because its own good pleasure hath decided.

2 [Genius] and Pride . . .
4 [Decided]—right or wrong—of friend . . .

17

His friendships therefore, and no less aversions,
   Though oft well founded, which confirmed but more
His prepossessions, like the laws of Persians
   And Medes,* would ne'er revoke what went before.
His feelings had not those strange fits, like tertians,
   Of common likings, which make some deplore
What they should laugh at—the mere ague still
Of Men's regard, the fever or the chill.

6 make [men] deplore
7–8 What they should laugh at—[the now hot or cold
   Advances] [which] [or repulses, they behold]

18

" 'Tis not in mortals to command success;*
   But *do you more*, Sempronius—*don't* deserve it";
And take my word, you won't have any less:
   Be wary, watch the time, and always serve it;
Give gently way, when there's too great a press;
   And for your conscience, only learn to nerve it,—
For, like a racer or a boxer training,
'Twill make, if proved, vast efforts without paining.

[366]

4 [Bear a bold brow] [and] [for your bosom nerve] it
7 For [tis] like . . .

19

Lord Henry also liked to be superior,
    As most men do, the little or the great;
The very lowest find out an inferior,
    At least they think so, to exert their state
Upon: for there are very few things wearier
    Than solitary Pride's oppressive weight,
Which mortals generously would divide,
By bidding others carry while they ride.

5 are [few] very few . . .
7 Which [people general] generously . . .

20

In birth, in rank, in fortune likewise equal,
    O'er Juan he could no distinction claim;
In years he had the advantage of time's sequel;
    And, as he thought, in country much the same—
Because bold Britons have a tongue and free quill,
    At which all modern nations vainly aim;
And the Lord Henry was a great debater,
So that few members kept the House up later.

1a in fortune—[almost so]
 b in fortune—[also] equal
6 all [old] modern . . .

These were advantages: and then he thought—
  It was his foible, but by no means sinister—
That few or none more than himself had caught
  Court mysteries, having been himself a minister:
He liked to teach that which he had been taught,
  And greatly shone whenever there had been a stir;
And reconciled all qualities which grace man,
Always a Patriot, and sometimes a Placeman.*

2a It was his foible—[having been Ambassador]
 b   [a minister]
4   [The mystery of Courts] *fragment*

22

He liked the gentle Spaniard for his gravity;
  He almost honoured him for his docility,
Because, though young, he acquiesced with suavity,
  Or contradicted but with proud humility.
He knew the world, and would not see depravity
  In faults which sometimes show the soil's fertility,
If that the weeds o'erlive not the first crop,—
For then they are very difficult to stop.

3 he [con] acquiesced . . .   *Intended to write* concurred?

23

And then he talked with him about Madrid,
  Constantinople, and such distant places;
Where people always did as they were bid,
  Or did what they should not with foreign graces.
Of coursers also spake they: Henry rid
  Well, like most Englishmen, and loved the races;
And Juan, like a true-born Andalusian,
Could back a horse,* as despots ride a Russian.

2 such [foreign] places
5 Of [horses] also . . .

24

And thus acquaintance grew, at noble routs,
    And diplomatic dinners, or at other—
For Juan stood well both with Ins and Outs,
    As in Freemasonry a higher brother.*
Upon his talent Henry had no doubts,
    His manner showed him sprung from a high mother;
And all men like to show their hospitality
To him whose breeding marches with his quality.

6   [And his demeanour showed a high bred] Mother
8a To [one] whose breeding marches   TN
  b   matches . . .   *In 1833 and in later editions.*

25

At Blank-Blank Square;—for we will break no squares*
    By naming streets: since men are so censorious,
And apt to sow an author's wheat with tares,*
    Reaping allusions private and inglorious,
Where none were dreamt of, unto love's affairs,
    Which were, or are, or are to be notorious,
That therefore do I previously declare,
Lord Henry's mansion was in Blank-Blank Square.

1 [At] In . . .
2 for Men . . .
3 And apt to [make allusions] *fragment*
4 [Making] allusions . . .
6 Which [are] were . . .
7 [And] therefore . . .
8 Lord Henry [had] *fragment*

Also there bin another pious reason*
    For making squares and streets anonymous;
Which is, that there is scarce a single season
    Which doth not shake some very splendid house
With some slight heart-quake of domestic treason—
    A topic Scandal doth delight to rouse:
Such I might stumble over unawares,
Unless I knew the very chastest Squares.

1a Also [I have] another pious reason
 b Also there be . . .
2 For making Streets and Squares anonymous
4 not [make] some . . . house
5 slight [species] of domestic treason
6 [Which] *fragment*
7 [And therefore] *fragment*

27

'Tis true, I might have chosen Piccadilly,*
    A place where peccadillos are unknown;
But I have motives, whether wise or silly,
    For letting that pure sanctuary alone.
Therefore I name not square, street, place, until I
    Find one where nothing naughty can be shown,
A vestal shrine of innocence of heart:
Such are—but I have lost the London Chart.

8 Such [are] there are—but I've lost . . .

28

At Henry's mansion then, in Blank-Blank Square,
    Was Juan a *recherché*, welcome guest,
As many other noble Scions were;
    And some who had but talent for their crest;
Or wealth, which is a passport every where;
    Or even mere fashion, which indeed's the best

[CANTO XIII]

> Recommendation;—and to be well drest
> Will very often supersede the rest.

No revisions.

29

> And since "there's safety in a multitude
>   Of counsellors,"* as Solomon has said,
> Or some one for him, in some sage, grave mood;—
>   Indeed we see the daily proof displayed
> In Senates, at the Bar, in wordy feud,
>   Where'er collective wisdom can parade,
> Which is the only cause that we can guess
> Of Britain's present wealth and happiness;—

1 But [as] "there's . . .
3 for him [doubtless] in some . . .
4 [We] Indeed we . . .
5 [at] or the bar . . .

30

> But as "there's safety grafted in the number
>   Of Counsellors" for men,—thus for the sex
> A large acquaintance lets not Virtue slumber;
>   Or should it shake, the choice will more perplex—
> Variety itself will more encumber.
>   'Midst many rocks we guard more against wrecks;
> And thus with women: howsoe'er it shocks some's
> Self-love, there's safety in a crowd of coxcombs.

1 But as "there's safety in [a Multitude]
3 [A numerous Circle] let not [Virtue] slumber
4 Or [if it should]—the Choice . . .
5–6 [The slightest Obstacle which may encumber
    The path down hill is something gained]
7a–8 And thus [for Woman] howsoeer it shocks some's
    [Safety lies in a Multitude of] Coxcombs
7b shock *In 1823 edition.*

But Adeline had not the least occasion
  For such a shield, which leaves but little merit
To virtue proper, or good education.
  Her chief resource was in her own high spirit,
Which judged mankind at their due estimation;
  And for coquetry, she disdained to wear it:
Secure of admiration, its impression
Was faint, as of an every-day possession.

1 had not [occasion for]
2 [This paltry] shield which . . .
8 Was—[no more] as of . . .

32

To all she was polite without parade;
  To some she showed attention of that kind
Which flatters, but is flattery conveyed
  In such a sort as cannot leave behind
A trace unworthy either wife or maid;—
  A gentle, genial courtesy of mind,
To those who were or passed for meritorious,
Just to console sad Glory for being glorious;

2 showed [an] attention . . .
3 but [no more] is Flattery conveyed
5 A [sin] trace . . .
6a [Unless a] *fragment*
 b [Not even in fools—who—howsoever blind]
8 [In wit or war] [And tis this] *fragments*

Which is in all respects, save now and then,
　　A dull and desolate appendage. Gaze
Upon the Shades of those distinguished men,
　　Who were or are the puppet-shows of praise,
The praise of persecution. Gaze again
　　On the most favoured; and amidst the blaze
Of sunset halos o'er the laurel-browed,
What can ye recognize?—A gilded cloud.

3　Upon the [tale] of those . . .
5　The Praise [chequered] *fragment*
7*a* [Which gilds their] *fragment*
　b [Which kindles Sunlike] oer the laurel-browed
8*a* [The light's not theirs] *fragment*
　b What can you recognize . . .

34

There also was of course in Adeline
　　That calm Patrician polish in the address,
Which ne'er can pass the equinoctial line
　　Of any thing which Nature would express;
Just as a Mandarin finds nothing fine,—
　　At least his manner suffers not to guess
That any thing he views can greatly please.
Perhaps we have borrowed this from the Chinese—

2　That [Polish of Indifference]—in the [manner]
7–8*a* That anything [is new to a Chinese
　　And such is Europe's fashionable Ease.]
　8*b* Perhaps we borrowed this . . .

Perhaps from Horace: his "*Nil admirari*"*
    Was what he called the "Art of Happiness";
An art on which the artists greatly vary,
    And have not yet attained to much success.
However, 'tis expedient to be wary:
    Indifference *certes* don't produce distress;
And rash Enthusiasm in good society
Were nothing but a moral Inebriety.

2 the [road] Art of . . .
4 attained [with] much success

36

But Adeline was not indifferent: for
    (*Now* for a common place!) beneath the snow,
As a Volcano holds the lava more
    Within—*et caetera.* Shall I go on?—No!
I hate to hunt down a tired metaphor:
    So let the often used volcano go.
Poor thing! How frequently, by me and others,
It hath been stirred up till its smoke quite smothers.

1 indifferent—[and] for
4 et cetera . . .

I'll have another figure in a trice:—
  What say you to a bottle of champagne?
Frozen into a very vinous ice,
  Which leaves few drops of that immortal rain,
Yet in the very centre, past all price,
  About a liquid glassful will remain;
And this is stronger than the strongest grape
Could e'er express in its expanded shape:

1a [I've got a better Similie than that]
 b   [this]
 c [I've got a Similie that worth *sic?* it twice]
 d I'll have [a better] figure in a [trice]
 6 About a Glass-full—[liquid] will remain
 8 Could ever form in . . .

                        38

'Tis the whole spirit brought to a quintessence;
  And thus the chilliest aspects may concentre
A hidden nectar under a cold presence.
  And such are many—though I only meant her,
From whom I now deduce these moral lessons,
  On which the Muse has always sought to enter:—
And your cold people are beyond all price,
When once you have broken their confounded ice.

 2 And thus the [coldest] aspects [will] concentre
 3 A hidden [wine below an icy] presence
 4 though I merely [mean] her
 5 those moral lessons
 7a [And put to flight] *fragment*
  b And these cold . . .
 8a [That is to those who can break through the Ice]
  b [Though less to those who skait then break the ice]
  c When once you have [through] broken . . .
  d When once you've broken . . . *In some modern editions.*

But after all they are a North-West Passage
    Unto the glowing India of the soul;
And as the good ships sent upon that message
    Have not exactly ascertained the Pole
(Though Parry's efforts look a lucky presage)*
    Thus gentlemen may run upon a shoal;
For if the Pole's not open, but all frost,
(A chance still) 'tis a voyage or vessel lost.

5 Though [this we hope—has been reserved for this age]
6 Thus Gentlemen may [al] [sometimes play the fool]

And young beginners may as well commence
    With quiet cruizing o'er the ocean woman;
While those who are not beginners, should have sense
    Enough to make for port, ere Time shall summon
With his grey signal flag: and the past tense,
    The dreary *"Fuimus"** of all things human,
Must be declined, while life's thin thread's spun out
Between the gaping heir and gnawing gout.

1 And [thereof] young . . .
2a With [the first warm] crui[z]ing [to] the Ocean, Woman TN
  b With quiet cruising oer . . . TN
  c   cruising . . . *In 1833 and in later editions.*
7 while [the] threads . . .
8 Between [our duteous Offspring—and the] Gout

But Heaven must be diverted: its diversion
  Is sometimes truculent—but never mind:
The world upon the whole is worth the assertion
  (If but for comfort) that all things are kind:
And that same devilish doctrine of the Persian,
  Of the two Principles,* but leaves behind
As many doubts as any other doctrine
Has ever puzzled Faith withal, or yoked her in.

2 Is [rather] truculent . . .
4 (If but for comfort) [to think all things] kind

42

The English winter—ending in July,
  To recommence in August—now was done.
'Tis the postillion's Paradise: wheels fly;
  On roads, East, South, North, West, there is a run.
But for post horses who finds sympathy?
  Man's pity's for himself, or for his son,
Always premising that said son at college
Has not contracted much more debt than knowledge.

3 [A blest hour for postilions;—Chariots] fly!
4 South—[and] North . . .
6a [His] pity's for himself . . . TN
 b Man's pity's . . . TN;   c Man's pity . . . *Misprint in 1823 edition.*
7 that [the] Son . . .
8 Has [spent] not contracted . . .

The London winter's ended in July—
　　Sometimes a little later. I don't err
In this: whatever other blunders lie
　　Upon my shoulders, here I must aver
My Muse a glass of Weatherology;
　　For Parliament is our Barometer:
Let Radicals its other acts attack,
Its sessions form our only almanack.

1 The [Engl] London winter's . . .
2 [I do not] *fragment*
5–7 [The strict correctness] of Weatherology
For Parliament is our thermometer
[The] [The very Season rises and subsides]
8 It's Sessions [are] form . . .

44

When its quicksilver's down at zero,—lo!
　　Coach, chariot, luggage, baggage, equipage!
Wheels whirl from Carlton palace to Soho,*
　　And happiest they who horses can engage;
The turnpikes glow with dust; and Rotten Row*
　　Sleeps from the chivalry of this bright age;
And tradesmen, with long bills and longer faces,
Sigh—as the postboys fasten on the traces.

2 [The] Coach—[the] Chariot—luggage—baggage—[all]
5 The turnpikes [reek] glow . . .

They and their bills, "Arcadians both,"* are left
　　To the Greek Kalends* of another session.
Alas! to them of ready cash bereft,
　　What hope remains? Of *hope* the full possession,
Or generous draft, conceded as a gift,
　　At a long date—till they can get a fresh one,—
Hawked about at a discount, small or large;—
Also the solace of an overcharge.

2 To the Greek [Calends] of . . .

46

But these are trifles. Downward flies my Lord
　　Nodding beside my Lady in his carriage.
Away! away! "Fresh horses!" are the word,
　　And changed as quickly as hearts after marriage;
The obsequious landlord hath the change restored;
　　The postboys have no reason to disparage
Their fee; but ere the watered wheels* may hiss hence,
The ostler pleads for a small reminiscence.

2 in his [Chariot]
5 hath his change . . .
6a [The Post boys touch their hats] *fragment*
 b The Post boys [hath] no reason . . .
8a pleads for a small . . .   TN
 b pleads too for a reminiscence   *In 1833 and in later editions.*

'Tis granted; and the valet mounts the dickey*—
 That gentleman of lords and gentlemen;
Also my lady's gentlewoman, tricky,
 Tricked out, but modest more than poet's pen
Can paint, *"Cosi Viaggino i Ricchi"*!*
 (Excuse a foreign slipslop now and then,
If but to show I've travell'd; and what's travel,
Unless it teaches one to quote and cavil?)

1 Dicky
2 Lords [of] and . . .
3 my Lady's [Woman]—Gentlewoman . . .
4*a* And tricked out—[finer than a] poet's pen
 b And tricked out—Modest more than . . .
5 [And thus] [Tis thus] *fragments*
7 show that I [have] travelled . . .

48

The London winter and the country summer
 Were well nigh over. 'Tis perhaps a pity,
When Nature wears the gown that doth become her,
 To lose those best months in a sweaty city,
And wait until the nightingale grows dumber,
 Listening debates not very wise or witty,
Ere Patriots their true *country* can remember;—
But there's no shooting (save grouse) till September.

3*a* [To lose those months in towns] *fragment*
 b gown which doth . . .
6 [He] Listening . . . wise nor witty
7*a* [Before] [Ere Patriots] [that theres] *fragments*
 b   their own <u>Country</u> . . .
8*a* But [then—there is no Shooting] till September
 b But there's [not] no Shooting . . .

I've done with my tirade. The world was gone;
　　The twice two thousand, for whom earth was made,
Were vanished to be what they call alone,—
　　That is, with thirty servants for parade,
As many guests or more; before whom groan
　　As many covers, duly, daily laid.
Let none accuse Old England's hospitality—
Its quantity is but condensed to quality.

7a Let [not] accuse . . . Hospitality TN; b hopitality *Misprint in
　　1823 edition.*
8　[Although its] quantity . . .

50

Lord Henry and the Lady Adeline
　　Departed, like the rest of their compeers,
The peerage, to a mansion very fine;
　　The Gothic Babel of a thousand years.
None than themselves could boast a longer line,
　　Where Time through heroes and through beauties
　　　　steers;
And oaks, as olden as their pedigree,
Told of their sires, a tomb in every tree.

2 Departed [with] the . . .

A paragraph in every paper told
    Of their departure: such is modern fame:
'Tis pity that it takes no further hold
    Than an advertisement, or much the same;
When, ere the ink be dry, the sound grows cold.
    The Morning Post was foremost to proclaim—
"Departure, for his country seat, to-day,
    Lord H. Amundeville and Lady A.

1 paper [spoke]
3 farther . . . *In 1833 and in later editions.*
5 ink is dry . . .
6 The Morning Post [the first] to proclaim

"We understand the splendid host intends
    To entertain, this autumn, a select
And numerous party of his noble friends;
    Midst whom we have heard, from sources quite
        correct,
The Duke of D— the shooting season spends,
    With many more by rank and fashion decked;
Also a foreigner of high condition,
The Envoy of the secret Russian Mission."

1 the [noble] host . . .
4 [Of] whom . . .
6 With [all] many . . .
7 Also [the] a foreigner . . .

And thus we see—who doubts the Morning Post?
  (Whose articles are like the "Thirty Nine,"*
Which those most swear to who believe them most)—
  Our gay Russ Spaniard was ordained to shine,
Decked by the rays reflected from his host,
  With those who, Pope says, "greatly daring dine."*
'Tis odd, but true,—last war the News abounded
More with these dinners than the killed or wounded;—

2 [Our young Russ-Spaniard was in high request]
4 Our young Russ-Spaniard . . .
8 these diners than the killed and wounded

54

As thus: "On Thursday there was a grand dinner;
  Present, Lords A. B. C."—Earls, dukes, by name
Announced with no less pomp than victory's winner:
  Then underneath, and in the very same
Column: Date, "Falmouth. There has lately been here
  The Slap-Dash Regiment, so well known to fame;
Whose loss in the late action we regret:
The vacancies are filled up—see Gazette."

2 Lords A—B C [D]" . . .
3 pomp[s] . . .
6 The Dash-Dash-Regiment—[to recruit] *fragment*
7a [Was much] *fragment*
 b Whose loss in the late action [has been great]

To Norman Abbey whirled the noble pair,*—
  An old, old monastery once, and now
Still older mansion, of a rich and rare
  Mixed Gothic, such as Artists all allow
Few specimens yet left us can compare
  Withal: it lies perhaps a little low,
Because the monks preferred a hill behind,
To shelter their devotion from the wind.

3 [An] older . . .
4*a*–5*a* Mixed Gothic—such as [Artists might compare]
                [Architects . . .]
    [With all such relics and fin] *fragment* *Intended to write* find?
4*b*–5*b* Mixed Gothic—such as Artists [might] allow
    Few Specimens yet left us—[could] compare
6 it [lay] perhaps . . .
8 [As] To . . .

56

It stood embosom'd in a happy valley,
  Crown'd by high woodlands, where the Druid oak*
Stood like Caractacus in act to rally
  His host,* with broad arms 'gainst the thunder-stroke;
And from beneath his boughs were seen to sally
  The dappled foresters—as day awoke,
The branching stag swept down with all his herd,*
To quaff a brook which murmured like a bird.

1 It stood [then in the bosom of a] valley
2 Woodlands [of] the Druid Oak
6 [The Stag and all his herd] *fragment*
7 The [Stag with branched horns and] all his herd

Before the mansion lay a lucid lake,*
   Broad as transparent, deep, and freshly fed
By a river, which its soften'd way did take
   In currents through the calmer water spread
Around: the wild fowl nestled in the brake
   And sedges, brooding in their liquid bed:
The woods sloped downwards to its brink, and stood
With their green faces fix'd upon the flood.

3 it's [gentle] way . . .
6 sedges [which] brooding . . .

58

Its outlet dash'd into a steep cascade,*
   Sparkling with foam, until again subsiding
Its shriller echoes—like an infant made
   Quiet—sank into softer ripples, gliding
Into a rivulet; and thus allay'd
   Pursued its course, now gleaming, and now hiding
Its windings through the woods; now clear, now blue,
According as the skies their shadows threw.

1a dashed into a steep Cascade   TN
 b   deep . . .   *In 1833 and in later editions.*
2 [Fo] Sparkling . . .
3 It's shriller Echo . . .
4 [Quit]—sank into the [smooth] ripples gliding
7 now clear, now [hue]

A glorious remnant of the Gothic pile,
  (While yet the church was Rome's) stood half apart
In a grand Arch, which once screened many an aisle.
  These last had disappear'd—a loss to Art:
The first yet frowned superbly o'er the soil,
  And kindled feelings in the roughest heart,
Which mourn'd the power of time's or tempest's march,
In gazing on that venerable Arch.

1 A [goodly] remnant . . .
5 yet [looked] frowned . . .
6 And [wakened] feelings . . .
7 Which [sympathized with] Time's [and] Tempest's march
8 that [high and haughty] Arch

60

Within a niche, nigh to its pinnacle,
  Twelve saints had once stood sanctified in stone;*
But these had fallen, not when the friars fell,
  But in the war which struck Charles from his throne,
When each house was a fortalice—as tell
  The annals of full many a line undone,—
The gallant Cavaliers,* who fought in vain
For those who knew not to resign or reign.

2 Twelve Saints had [stood] and [clasped their hands] in Stone
3 when the [Convent] fell
6 The annals of [the Cavaliers] full many a [line] undone

But in a higher niche, alone, but crown'd,
　　The Virgin Mother of the God-born child,*
With her son in her blessed arms, look'd round,
　　Spared by some chance when all beside was spoil'd;
　She made the earth below seem holy ground.
　　This may be superstition, weak or wild,
But even the faintest relics of a shrine
Of any worship, wake some thoughts divine.

1　niche—alone—[supreme]
4a　[And made the earth below seem holy gr] *fragment*　*Intended*
　　to write ground.
　b　Spared by some [favor *sic?* fifty Statues] spoiled
8　Of [whatsoever] worship—wakes some . . .

62

A mighty window, hollow in the centre,
　　Shorn of its glass of thousand colourings,
Through which the deepen'd glories once could enter,
　　Streaming from off the sun like seraph's wings,
Now yawns all desolate: now loud, now fainter,
　　The gale sweeps through its fretwork, and oft sings
The owl his anthem, where the silenced quire
Lie with their hallelujahs quench'd like fire.

2　[Now shorn of all its Glass of thousand hues] [tints]
3　Through the [Streaming] Glories once would enter
4　the sun[-beams] like . . .
5　Now—yawn[ed] all desolate; [and] loud—[or] fainter
6　The Gale [rushed] through . . .
8a　[With their quenched Halleluiahs] *fragment*
　b　Lie . . . Halleluiahs . . .

But in the noontide of the Moon, and when
    The wind is winged from one point of heaven,
There moans a strange unearthly sound, which then
    Is musical—a dying accent driven
Through the huge Arch,* which soars and sinks again.
    Some deem it but the distant echo given
Back to the Night wind by the waterfall,
And harmonized by the old choral wall:

1   the [stillness] of the Moon . . .
2*a* The Wind is [in one] *fragment*
 b The Wind is [waning in] one point of [Axis *sic?*]
3   There [is] a strange . . .
8   [Which] And harmonized by the [old gray] Choral wall

64

Others, that some original shape, or form
    Shaped by decay perchance, hath given the power
(Though less than that of Memnon's statue,* warm
    In Egypt's rays, to harp at a fixed hour)
To this grey ruin, with a voice to charm.
    Sad, but serene, it sweeps o'er tree or tower:
The cause I know not, nor can solve; but such
The fact:—I've heard it,—once perhaps too much.*

1 some [peculiar]—shape . . .
2 Shaped [only] by Decay hath given the Power
4 [To] Aegypt's . . .
5 [Which] this . . .
6 tree and tower
7 [the] but such

Amidst the court a Gothic fountain play'd,*
    Symmetrical, but deck'd with carvings quaint—
Strange faces, like to men in masquerade,
    And here perhaps a monster, there a Saint:
The spring gush'd through grim mouths, of granite
        made,
    And sparkled into basins, where it spent
Its little torrent in a thousand bubbles,
Like man's vain glory, and his vainer troubles.

2 with [faces] quaint
5 The [Stream] gushed . . .
6 And [spa] [bubbled] into basins . . .

66

The mansion's self was vast and venerable,
    With more of the monastic than has been
Elsewhere preserved: the cloisters still were stable,
    The cells too and refectory, I ween:
An exquisite small chapel* had been able,
    Still unimpair'd, to decorate the scene;
The rest had been reform'd, replaced, or sunk,
And spoke more of the baron than the monk.

4 The Cells—[the] and the refectory . . .
7 The rest had been [converted]—[dest] replaced . . . *Intended to
write* destroyed.

Huge halls, long galleries, spacious chambers,* join'd
    By no quite lawful marriage of the Arts,
Might shock a Connoisseur; but when combined,
    Form'd a whole which, irregular in parts,
Yet left a grand impression on the mind,
    At least of those whose eyes are in their hearts.
We gaze upon a Giant for his stature,
Nor judge at first if all be true to Nature.

4 Formed a [grand] whole, [which] irregular . . .
7 [As] We . . .

68

Steel Barons, molten the next generation
    To silken rows of gay and garter'd Earls,
Glanced from the walls* in goodly preservation;
    And Lady Marys blooming into girls,
With fair long locks, had also kept their station:
    And Countesses mature in robes and pearls:
Also some beauties of Sir Peter Lely,
Whose drapery hints we may admire them freely.

1 [Bold] Barons—[softened] the next . . .
3 walls in [confessed *sic?*] preservation
4 And [blooming] Lady Marys blooming . . .
8a Whose Drapery [bade] us to admire . . .
 b Whose Drapery tells us to admire . . .

Judges in very formidable ermine
     Were there, with brows that did not much invite
The accused to think their Lordships would determine
     His cause by leaning much from might to right:
Bishops, who had not left a single sermon;
     Attornies-General, awful to the sight,
As hinting more (unless our judgments warp us)
Of the "Star Chamber" than of "Habeas Corpus."*

2   brows which did . . .
3   The [Cul] accused . . . *Intended to write* Culprit.
4*a* His cause by [leaning too much to the Right]
 b His cause by [much mistaking Might for Right] [Right]
6   Attorney Generals . . .

70

Generals, some all in armour, of the old
     And iron time, ere Lead had ta'en the lead;
Others in wigs of Marlborough's martial fold,
     Huger than twelve of our degenerate breed:
Lordlings with staves of white, or keys of gold:*
     Nimrods, whose canvas scarce contain'd the steed;
And here and there some stern high Patriot stood,
Who could not get the place for which he sued.

4*a* [Which need a Marlborough for excuse indeed]
 b *The present text was written in the manuscript margin.*
6   [Prouder of such a toy than of their breed] [Breed]

But ever and anon, to soothe your vision,
　　Fatigued with these hereditary glories,
There rose a Carlo Dolce or a Titian,*
　　Or wilder groupe of savage Salvatore's:*
Here danced Albano's boys,* and here the sea shone
　　In Vernet's ocean lights;* and there the stories
Of martyrs awed, as Spagnoletto* tainted
His brush with all the blood of all the sainted.

4a [Albano's] *fragment*
　b Or wilder groupe of [dark Salvator Rosa's]
　c 　　　　　　　　savage Salvatore's Rose's
　In the Tn margin Byron wrote the following note on this line: "Salvatore Rosa, 'the wicked necessity of rhyming' obliges me to adapt the name to the verse."
5a Here danced Albano's [Children] *fragment*
　b 　　　　　　　Boys, and there the Sea shone
7 [where] Spagnoletto tainted
8 His brush with [blood of all enduring] Sainted

72

Here sweetly spread a landscape of Lorraine;*
　　There Rembrandt* made his darkness equal light,
Or gloomy Caravaggio's gloomier stain*
　　Bronzed o'er some lean and stoic Anchorite:—
But lo! a Teniers* woos, and not in vain,
　　Your eyes to revel in a livelier sight:
His bell-mouthed goblet makes me feel quite Danish*
Or Dutch with thirst—What ho! a flask of Rhenish.

1a Lorraine　TN;　b Loraine　*Misprint in 1823 edition.*
2 There Rembrandt [from the] Darkness . . .
3 [And] gloomy . . .
4 [Revealed] some [lone] and Stoic . . .
5 [And] lo! a Teniers [to revive] *fragment*
6a Your eyes to [feast upon] a livelier sight
　b Your eyes to revel on . . .
7–8 His bell-mouthed Goblet—[and his laughing groupe
　　Provoke my thirst—what—ho! of wine a Stoup!]

Oh, reader! If that thou canst read,—and know,
    'Tis not enough to spell, or even to read,
To constitute a reader; there must go
    Virtues of which both you and I have need.
Firstly, begin with the beginning—(though
    That clause is hard); and secondly, proceed;
Thirdly, commence not with the end—or, sinning
In this sort, end at least with the beginning.

2 read[er]

74

But, reader, thou hast patient been of late,
    While I, without remorse of rhyme, or fear,
Have built and laid out ground at such a rate,
    Dan Phoebus takes me for an auctioneer.
That Poets were so from their earliest date,
    By Homer's "Catalogue of Ships,"* is clear;
But a mere modern must be moderate—
I spare you then the furniture and plate.

4 [That] Phoebus . . .
5 [And] That poets . . . the earliest date
7 But [I] a [modern] mere modern . . .
8 I spare you then then . . .

The mellow Autumn came, and with it came
    The promised party, to enjoy its sweets.
The corn is cut, the manor full of game;
    The pointer ranges, and the sportsman beats
In russet jacket:—lynx-like is his aim,
    Full grows his bag, and wonder*ful* his feats.
Ah, nutbrown Partridges! Ah, brilliant Pheasants!
And ah, ye Poachers!—'Tis no sport for peasants.

1 Autumn came [the] and . . .
3 The Corn [was] cut . . .
4 the [Sports] beats
5 [Alas! ye Partridges] *fragment*
7 [Alas! ye] *fragment*
8 [there's] no sport . . .

76

An English autumn, though it hath no vines,
    Blushing with Bacchant coronals along
The paths, o'er which the far festoon entwines
    The red grape in the sunny lands of song,
Hath yet a purchased choice of choicest wines;
    The Claret light, and the Madeira strong.
If Britain mourn her bleakness, we can tell her
The very best of vineyards is the cellar.

4   [It's broad leaves] in the sunny . . .
5a Hath yet [at night the very best of] wines
 b Hath yet purchased [a] choice . . .
6   [And] The Claret . . .

Then, if she hath not that serene decline,
  Which makes the Southern Autumn's day appear
As if 'twould to a second spring resign
  The season, rather than to winter drear,—
Of in-door comforts still she hath a mine,—
  The sea-coal fires, the earliest of the year;*
Without doors too she may compete in mellow,
As what is lost in green is gained in yellow.

2–3a Which make the Southern Autumn [rather seem
    A second Spring] *fragment*
  3b As if . . . Spring [refine]
  4 The Season,—[and not announce a falling year]
5–6a [Yet within doors she hath a chosen] mine
    [Of Comfort] *fragment*
  6b And Sea-Coal . . .
  8 And what . . . [she] gained . . .

78

And for the effeminate *villeggiatura**—
  Rife with more horns than hounds—she hath the chase,
So animated that it might allure a
  Saint from his beads to join the jocund race;
Even Nimrod's self might leave the plains of Dura,*
  And wear the Melton jacket* for a space:—
If she hath no wild boars, she hath a tame
Preserve of Bores, who ought to be made game.

7 hath [the] tame
8a [Within doors—Preserved] *fragment*
  b [Preserved within doors—why not make them Game?]

The noble guests, assembled at the Abbey,*
 Consisted of—we give the sex the pas—
The Duchess of Fitz-Fulke; the Countess Crabbey;
 The ladies Scilly, Busey;—Miss Eclât,
Miss Bombazeen, Miss Mackstay, Miss O'Tabbey,
 And Mrs. Rabbi, the rich banker's squaw;
Also the Honourable Mrs. Sleep,
Who look'd a white lamb, yet was a black sheep:

2 Consisted of—[a Sort] we give the [fair sex first]
3*a* Scquabbey TN; *b* Crabby *In 1833 and in later editions.*
5*a* O'Tabbey TN; *b* O'Tabby *In 1833 and in later editions.*

80

With other Countesses of Blank—but rank;
 At once the "lie"* and the "*élite*" of crowds;
Who pass like water filtered in a tank,
 All purged and pious from their native clouds;
Or paper turned to money by the Bank:
 No matter how or why, the passport shrouds
The "*passée*" and the passed; for good society
Is no less famed for tolerance than piety:

1 [The] Countesses of . . .
2 the "Elite" of [Fashion]

81

That is, up to a certain point; which point
 Forms the most difficult in punctuation.
Appearances appear to form the joint
 On which it hinges in a higher station;
And so that no explosion cry "Aroint
 Thee, Witch!"* or each Medea has her Jason;*
Or (to the point with Horace and with Pulci)
"*Omne tulit punctum, quae miscuit utile dulci.*"*

2 [Form] [Is of] the most . . .
6 Thee Witch [or] [and send Medea to her Jason]
7 Or (to [come to the point like my friend Pulci]

82

I can't exactly trace their rule of right,
    Which hath a little leaning to a lottery.
I've seen a virtuous woman put down quite
    By the mere combination of a Coterie;
Also a So-So Matron* boldly fight
    Her way back to the world by dint of plottery,
And shine the very *Siria** of the spheres,
Escaping with a few slight, scarless sneers.

5 Also—a Vicious matron [put to flight]
6 to the World by [fear or flattery]
8 Escaping [only] with . . .

83

I have seen more than I'll say:—but we will see
    How our *villeggiatura* will get on.
The party might consist of thirty-three
    Of highest caste—the Brahmins of the ton.*
I have named a few, not foremost in degree,
    But ta'en at hazard as the rhyme may run.
By way of sprinkling, scatter'd amongst these,
There also were some Irish absentees.*

1 I have seen—[no matter what—we now shall] see
3 might [be] consist . . .
4 Bramins . . .
5 I have named [not those—the] foremost [of] degree

There was Parolles too, the legal bully,*
    Who limits all his battles to the bar
And senate: when invited elsewhere, truly,
    He shows more appetite for words than war.
There was the young bard Rackrhyme, who had newly
    Come out and glimmer'd as a six-weeks' star.
There was Lord Pyrrho* too, the great freethinker;
And Sir John Pottledeep, the mighty drinker.

1a There was [too Henry Bobab*] *fragment*   *Intended to write* Bobadil.
  b There was Parolles too the [great] legal bully
3   And [knew how far where he] *fragment*
5   Rackrhime . . .

85

There was the Duke of Dash,* who was a—duke,
    "Aye, every inch a" duke;* there were twelve peers
Like Charlemagne's*—and all such peers in look
    And intellect, that neither eyes nor ears
For commoners had ever them mistook.
    There were the six Miss Rawbolds—pretty dears!
All song and sentiment; whose hearts were set
Less on a convent than a coronet.

3   and all [so like] in look
4–5 And intellect—that [if you studied years
    You never would have for Commoners] *fragment*
7   All Song, and Sentiment; [and gems to be set]

86

There were four Honourable Misters, whose
    Honour was more before their names than after;
There was the preux Chevalier de la Ruse,*
    Whom France and Fortune lately deign'd to waft here,
Whose chiefly harmless talent was to amuse;
    But the clubs found it rather serious laughter,

Because—such was his magic power to please—
The dice seem'd charm'd too with his repartees.

4a Whom France [had condescended] *fragment*
 b Whom France and Fortune . . . to waft[ed] here
6 [Though] But . . .
7 his [wondrous] power . . .
8 charmed [before] too . . .

87

There was Dick Dubious* the metaphysician,
    Who loved philosophy and a good dinner;
Angle, the *soi-disant* mathematician;
    Sir Henry Silvercup, the great race-winner.
There was the Reverend Rodomont Precisian,
    Who did not hate so much the sin as sinner;
And Lord Augustus Fitz-Plantagenet,
Good at all things, but better at a bet.

6 Who did not hate [Sin so much as the] Sinner

88

There was Jack Jargon the gigantic guardsman;
    And General Fireface,* famous in the field,
A great tactician, and no less a swordsman,
    Who ate, last war, more Yankees than he kill'd.
There was the waggish Welch Judge, Jefferies
        Hardsman,*
    In his grave office so completely skill'd,
That when a culprit came for condemnation,
He had his Judge's joke for consolation.

This stanza was written crosswise on Tn. No revisions.

Good company's a chess-board—there are kings,
    Queens, bishops, knights, rooks, pawns; the world's
        a game;
Save that the puppets pull at their own strings;
    Methinks gay Punch hath something of the same.
My Muse, the butterfly hath but her wings,
    Not stings, and flits through ether without aim,
Alighting rarely:—were she but a hornet,
Perhaps there might be vices which would mourn it.

3a [Only the Puppets pull their strings] *fragment*
  b [Excepting that the Puppets . . .]
5   the Butterfly, [with] hath . . .
7   [Perchin] Alighting rarely were she but a [Wasp]

90

I had forgotten—but must not forget—
    An Orator, the latest of the session,*
Who had deliver'd well a very set
    Smooth speech, his first and maidenly transgression
Upon debate: the papers echoed yet
    With this *debût*, which made a strong impression,
And rank'd with what is every day display'd—
"The best first speech that ever yet was made."

3a Who had [arisen and in] a very set
  b   [made] . . .
5   [On S] *fragment*
6a With this [essay] which made . . . TN
  b With this debut . . . TN;   c With his . . . *In 1833 and in later editions.*
8   [Viz.] "The best first Speech that [was] ever made"

Proud of his "Hear hims!" proud too of his vote
　And lost virginity of oratory,
Proud of his learning (just enough to quote)
　He revel'd in his Ciceronian glory:
With memory excellent to get by rote,
　With wit to hatch a pun or tell a story,
Graced with some merit and with more effrontery,
"His Country's pride," he came down to the country.

1　Proud of [this] his . . .
6　With wit to [tell a somewhat tedious] story
7a　[He came down] *fragment*
　b　[With all his laurels growing upon one tree]
　c　[With all Earth's laurels growing on his tree]

92

These also were two wits by acclamation,
　Longbow from Ireland, Strongbow from the Tweed,*
Both lawyers and both men of education;
　But Strongbow's wit was of more polish'd breed:
Longbow was rich in an imagination,
　As beautiful and bounding as a steed,
But sometimes stumbling over a potatoe,—
While Strongbow's best things might have come from
　　Cato.

5　Longbow was [wealthier in] imagination
7　But sometimes stumbled . . .

Strongbow was like a new-tuned harpsichord;
    But Longbow wild as an Aeolian harp,*
With which the winds of heaven can claim accord;
    And make a music, whether flat or sharp.
Of Strongbow's talk you would not change a word;
    At Longbow's phrases you might sometimes carp:
Both wits—one born so, and the other bred,
This by his heart—his rival by his head.

  5 [Weigh] *fragment*
7–8 [In short the last was born—the first was] bred
    [A Wit] *fragment*

94

If all these seem an heterogeneous mass
    To be assembled at a country seat,
Yet think, a specimen of every class
    Is better than an humdrum *tête-à-tête.*
The days of Comedy are gone, alas!
    When Congreve's fool could vie with Moliere's *bête:**
Society is smooth'd to that excess,
That manners hardly differ more than dress.

  1 a heterogeneous . . .
  4 a humdrum . . .
  6 could [rival] Moliere's béte

95

Our ridicules are kept in the back-ground—
    Ridiculous enough, but also dull;
Professions too are no more to be found
    Professional; and there is nought to cull
Of folly's fruit: for, though your fools abound,
    They're barren and not worth the pains to pull.
Society is now one polish'd horde,
Form'd of two mighty tribes, the *Bores* and *Bored.*

```
3 too [have] are . . .
4–5 Professional—[all classes mostly pull
     At the same oar—and] though [you] fools abound
  6 They are barren and not worth the [toil] to pull
```

96

But from being farmers, we turn gleaners,* gleaning
    The scanty but right-well thrashed ears of truth;
And, gentle reader! when you gather meaning,
    You may be Boaz, and I—modest Ruth.
Further I'd quote, but Scripture intervening,
    Forbids. A great impression in my youth
Was made by Mrs. Adams, where she cries
"That Scriptures out of church are blasphemies."*

```
2a well-threshed . . . TN;  b thresh'd . . . In 1833 and in later
     editions.
3   And [all such] gentle reader! when [I have a] meaning
4   You [should] be . . .
7   when she cries
```

97

But what we can we glean in this vile age
    Of chaff, although our gleanings be not grist.
I must not quite omit the talking sage,
    Kit-Cat, the famous conversationist,*
Who, in his common-place book, had a page
    Prepared each morn for evenings. "List, oh list!"—
"Alas, poor Ghost!"*—What unexpected woes
Await those who have studied their *bon mots!*

```
1–2 But what . . . this ripe age
     Of Chaff—though what we glean may not be Grist
  3 not quite [not] omit . . .
```

Firstly, they must allure the conversation
   By many windings to their clever clinch;
And secondly, must let slip no occasion,
   Nor *bate* (abate) their hearers of an *inch*,
But take an ell—and make a great sensation,
   If possible: and thirdly, never flinch
When some smart talker puts them to the test,
But seize the last word, which no doubt's the best.

4 Nor bate (read bait) their hearers . . .
7 [Even though they writhe] *fragment*

99

Lord Henry and his Lady were the hosts;
   The party we have touch'd on were the guests:
Their table was a board to tempt even ghosts
   To pass the Styx for more substantial feasts.
I will not dwell upon ragoûts or roasts,
   Albeit all human history attests,
That happiness for Man—the hungry sinner!—
Since Eve ate apples, much depends on dinner.*

1 Lady [had *sic?*] were . . .
2 [The Guests were more or less] *fragment*
3 a [feast] to tempt . . .
5 Ragouts and Roasts

Witness the lands which "flow'd with milk and honey,"
    Held out unto the hungry Israelites:
To this we have added since, the love of money,
    The only sort of pleasure which requites.
Youth fades, and leaves our days no longer sunny;
    We tire of Mistresses and Parasites;
But oh, Ambrosial Cash! Ah! who would lose thee?
When we no more can use, or even abuse thee!

No revisions.

101

The gentlemen got up betimes to shoot,*
    Or hunt: the young, because they liked the sport—
The first thing boys like, after play and fruit:
    The middle-aged, to make the day more short;
For *ennui* is a growth of English root,*
    Though nameless in our language:—we retort
The fact for words, and let the French translate
That awful yawn which sleep can not abate.

3 The first things boys . . .
4 The middle-aged [because] to make . . .
6 [Although] Though . . .

The elderly walked through the library,
  And tumbled books, or criticised the pictures,
Or sauntered through the gardens piteously,
  And made upon the hot-house several strictures,
Or rode a nag, which trotted not too high,
  Or on the morning papers read their lectures,
Or on the watch their longing eyes would fix,
Longing at sixty for the hour of six.

2 critizized . . .
5 Or [watched] rode . . .

103

But none were "*gêné*":* the great hour of union
  Was rung by dinner's knell; till then all were
Masters of their own time—or in communion,
  Or solitary, as they chose to bear
The hours, which how to pass is but to few known.
  Each rose up at his own, and had to spare
What time he chose for dress, and broke his fast
When, where, and how he chose for that repast.

2 [Was dinner-time—til then the Whole World] were
7 chose [for] dress[ing] and . . .
8 [In his] [own] [room—if such he] chose for [his] repast

104

The ladies—some rouged, some a little pale—
  Met the morn as they might. If fine, they rode,
Or walked; if foul, they read, or told a tale,
  Sung, or rehearsed the last dance from abroad;
Discussed the fashion which might next prevail,
  And settled bonnets by the newest code,
Or cramm'd twelve sheets into one little letter,
To make each correspondent a new debtor.

2 [Had Music—walking—riding—books—and talk]
4 [Or] Sung . . .
8 To [leave their] Correspondent[s not a] debtor

105

For some had absent lovers, all had friends.
   The earth has nothing like a She epistle,*
And hardly heaven—because it never ends.
   I love the mystery of a female missal,
Which, like a creed, ne'er says all it intends,
   But full of cunning as Ulysses' whistle,
When he allured poor Dolon:*—you had better
Take care what you reply to such a letter.

2   The Earth hath nothing . . .
6a [A sort of Rose entwining with a thistle]
 b [But] [sounds] [comes upon you like a Robber's whistle]
 c But full of wisdom as . . .
8   reply to [any] letter

106

Then there were billiards; cards too, but *no* dice;—
   Save in the Clubs no man of honour plays;—
Boats when 'twas water, skaiting when 'twas ice,
   And the hard frost destroy'd the scenting days:
And angling too, that solitary vice,
   Whatever Isaac Walton sings or says:*
The quaint, old, cruel coxcomb, in his gullet
Should have a hook, and a small trout to pull it.

No revisions.

With evening came the banquet and the wine;
    The *conversazione;* the duet,
Attuned by voices more or less divine,
    (My heart or head aches with the memory yet).
The four Miss Rawbolds in a glee would shine;
    But the two youngest loved more to be set
Down to the harp—because to music's charms
They added graceful necks, white hands and arms.

4 [to] the memory yet
6 two younger loved . . .
8 necks, [and] hands . . .

108

Sometimes a dance (though rarely on field days,
    For then the gentlemen were rather tired)
Display'd some sylph-like figures in its maze:
    Then there was small-talk ready when required;
Flirtation—but decorous; the mere praise
    Of charms that should or should not be admired.
The hunters fought their fox-hunt o'er again,
And then retreated soberly—at ten.

1 [The] Sometimes a daunce . . .
5 [and] mere praise

109

The politicians, in a nook apart,
    Discuss'd the world, and settled all the spheres;
The wits watched every loop-hole for their art,
    To introduce a *bon mot* head and ears:
Small is the rest of those who would be smart,
    A moment's good thing may have cost them years
Before they find an hour to introduce it,
And then, even *then,* some bore may make them lose it.

2 Discussed [the past and future parliament]
4 bon mot [by] head . . .

110

But all was gentle and aristocratic
   In this our party; polish'd, smooth and cold,
As Phidian forms* cut out of marble Attic.
   There now are no 'Squire Westerns as of old;
And our Sophias are not so emphatic,
   But fair as then, or fairer to behold.
We have no accomplish'd blackguards, like Tom Jones,
But gentlemen in stays, as stiff as stones.

5 [But] our . . .
6 But fair as [ever], or . . .

111

They separated at an early hour;
   That is, ere midnight—which is London's noon:
But in the country ladies seek their bower
   A little earlier than the waning Moon.
Peace to the slumbers of each folded flower—
   May the rose call back its true colours soon!
Good hours of fair cheeks are the fairest tinters,
And lower the price of rouge—at least some winters.

On the last page of Tn below this stanza Byron wrote his usual signature-symbol and the date, "F^y 19th 1823."

6a colours . . . TN; *b* colour . . . *In 1833 and in later editions.*
7a [Some] [earling] [early rising—exercise] *fragment*
 b [Good hours and care will soon restore the tint, or]
 c Good Hours of fair cheeks [is] the fairest tinters

Canto XIV

1

IF from great Nature's or our own abyss
    Of thought, we could but snatch a certainty,
Perhaps mankind might find the path they miss—
    But then 'twould spoil much good philosophy.
One system eats another up,* and this
    Much as old Saturn ate his progeny;*
For when his pious consort gave him stones
In lieu of sons, of these he made no bones.

For the date of publication see p. 315 of this volume.

    All manuscript readings are taken from B (Berg manuscript), Byron's first draft. On the first page of the manuscript above the first stanza is the curious date, "F^y 23, 1814." The year should have been 1823.

1 [We] from [out] Great Nature's . . .
2 Of Thought [—could gather aught like] Certainty
3*a* ['Twould] [These—what are called Men] *fragments*
 b Perhaps [the] Mankind . . .

But System doth reverse the Titan's breakfast,
    And eats her parents, albeit the digestion
Is difficult, Pray tell me, can you make fast,
    After due search, your faith to any question?
Look back o'er ages, ere unto the stake fast
    You bind yourself, and call some mode the best one.
Nothing more true than *not* to trust your senses;
And yet what are your other evidences?

2 parents—[although then] digestion
7 [And] Nothing . . .

3

For me, I know nought;* nothing I deny,
    Admit, reject, contemn; and what know *you,*
Except perhaps that you were born to die?
    And both may after all turn out untrue.
An age may come, Font of Eternity,
    When nothing shall be either old or new.
Death, so call'd, is a thing which makes men weep,
And yet a third of life is pass'd in sleep.

4 And [that] both . . .
7 Death—so called,['s but a precedent] *fragment*
8 And yet [one hal] a third . . .

A sleep without dreams, after a rough day
    Of toil, is what we covet most; and yet
How clay shrinks back from more quiescent clay!
    The very Suicide that pays his debt
At once without instalments (an old way
    Of paying debts, which creditors regret)
Lets out impatiently his rushing breath,
Less from disgust of life than dread of death.

1 [The] Sleep . . . after a [long] day

5

'Tis round him, near him, here, there, every where;*
    And there's a courage which grows out of fear,
Perhaps of all most desperate, which will dare
    The worst to *know* it:—when the mountains rear
Their peaks beneath your human foot, and there
    You look down o'er the precipice, and drear
The gulf of rock yawns,—you can't gaze a minute
Without an awful wish to plunge within it.

2 grows [of] out . . .
4 The worst to <u>know</u> it,—when the [huge] *fragment*
7 The Gulph of rocks . . .

6

'Tis true, you don't—but, pale and struck with terror,
 Retire: but look into your past impression!
And you will find, though shuddering at the mirror
 Of your own thoughts, in all their self confession,
The lurking bias, be it truth or error,
 To the *unknown;** a secret prepossession,
To plunge with all your fears—but where? You know
  not,
And that's the reason why you do—or do not.

1*a* struck by [Nature]; *b* struck by terror

7

But what's this to the purpose? you will say.
 Gent. Reader, nothing; a mere speculation,
For which my sole excuse is—'tis my way,
 Sometimes *with* and sometimes without occasion
I write what's uppermost, without delay;
 This narrative is not meant for narration,
But a mere airy and fantastic basis,*
To build up common things with common places.

No revisions.

You know, or don't know, that great Bacon saith,*
    "Fling up a straw, 'twill show the way the wind blows";
And such a straw, borne on by human breath,
    Is Poesy, according as the mind glows;
A paper kite, which flies 'twixt life and death,
    A shadow which the onward Soul behind throws:
And mine's a bubble not blown up for praise,
But just to play with, as an infant plays.

1   [Bac] that great Bacon [says]
2a show the Wind['s direction]
 b show which way the Wind blows
7   not [flung] up for praise

9

The world is all before me,* or behind;
    For I have seen a portion of that same,
And quite enough for me to keep in mind;—
    Of passions too, I have proved enough to blame,
To the great pleasure of our friends, mankind,
    Who like to mix some slight alloy with fame:
For I was rather famous in my time,
Until I fairly knock'd it up with rhyme.

5   friends [and kind]
7   was [very] famous . . .
8   with [your] Rhyme

10

I have brought this world about my ears, and eke
    The other; that's to say, the Clergy—who
Upon my head have bid their thunders break
    In pious libels by no means a few.
And yet I can't help scribbling once a week,
    Tiring old readers, nor discovering new.

In youth I wrote, because my mind was full,
And now because I feel it growing dull.

2 the [Clerly] Clergy . . .
4 In [pamphlets]—pious libels . . .

11

But "why then publish?"*—There are no rewards
    Of fame or profit, when the world grows weary.
I ask in turn,—why do you play at cards?
    Why drink? Why read?—To make some hour less
        dreary.
It occupies me to turn back regards
    On what I've seen or ponder'd, sad or cheery;
And what I write I cast upon the stream,
To swim or sink—I have had at least my dream.

4 [Or] Why drink . . . some hour [less weary]
5 to turn [my] back . . .
8 [for] I have . . .

12

I think that were I *certain* of success,
    I hardly could compose another line:
So long I've battled either more or less,
    That no defeat can drive me from the Nine.
This feeling 'tis not easy to express,
    And yet 'tis not affected, I opine.
In play, there are two pleasures for your choosing—
The one is winning, and the other losing.

8 The [first] is winning—and the [next is] losing

Besides, my Muse by no means deals in fiction:*
    She gathers a repertory of facts,
Of course with some reserve and slight restriction,
    But mostly sings of human things and acts—
And that's one cause she meets with contradiction;
    For too much truth, at first sight, ne'er attracts;
And were her object only what's call'd glory,
With more ease too she'd tell a different story.

2 [But] gathers . . .
4 But mostly [she turns] of human . . .
5 And that's [the] Cause . . .
7 object [merely] what's . . .

14

Love, war, a tempest*—surely there's variety;
    Also a seasoning slight of lucubration;
A bird's-eye view too of that wild, Society;
    A slight glance thrown on men of every station.
If you have nought else, here's at least satiety
    Both in performance and in preparation;
And though these lines should only line portmanteaus,*
Trade will be all the better for these Cantos.

3 A bird's eye view too of [what's called] *fragment*
7 [For] though . . .

15

The portion of this world which I at present
    Have taken up to fill the following sermon,
Is one of which there's no description recent:
    The reason why, is easy to determine:
Although it seems both prominent and pleasant,
    There is a sameness in its gems and ermine,
A dull and family likeness through all ages,
Of no great promise for poetic pages.

2*a* Have [taen upon me for] *fragment*
 b Have [taen upon me to dissect] *fragment*
 c Have taken up to fill the following [lecture]

16

With much to excite, there's little to exalt;
　Nothing that speaks to all men and all times;
A sort of varnish over every fault;
　A kind of common-place, even in their crimes:
Factitious passions, wit without much salt,
　A want of that true nature which sublimes
Whate'er it shows with truth; a smooth monotony
Of character, in those at least who have got any.

No revisions.

17

Sometimes indeed, like soldiers off parade,
　They break their ranks and gladly leave the drill;
But then the roll-call draws them back afraid,
　And they must be or seem what they were: still
Doubtless it is a brilliant masquerade;
　But when of the first sight you have had your fill,
It palls—at least it did so upon me,
This Paradise of Pleasure and *Ennui.*

2*a* [They break out into Virtue] *fragment*
 b They break their ranks and [wander where they will]
8　The Paradise . . .

When we have made our love, and gamed our gaming,
    Drest, voted, shone, and, may be, something more;
With dandies dined; heard senators declaiming;
    Seen beauties brought to market by the score;
Sad rakes to sadder husbands chastely taming;
    There's little left but to be bored or bore.
Witness those *"ci-devant jeunes hommes"** who stem
The stream, nor leave the world which leaveth them.

1 When [one] has made [one's] love . . .
5 husbands [sadly] taming
6 to [bor] be bored . . .
8 nor [dare] the world . . .

19

'Tis said—indeed a general complaint—
    That no one has succeeded in describing
The *Monde*, exactly as they ought to paint.
    Some say, that Authors only snatch, by bribing
The porter, some slight scandals strange and quaint,
    To furnish matter for their moral gibing;
And that their books have but one style in common—
My lady's prattle, filter'd through her woman.

4 only [know] by bribing
5 some [distorted] slight scandals . . .

20

But this can't well be true, just now; for writers
    Are grown of the *Beau Monde* a part potential:
I've seen them balance even the scale with fighters,
    Especially when young, for that's essential.
Why do their sketches fail them as inditers
    Of what they deem themselves most consequential—
The *real* portrait of the highest tribe?
'Tis that, in fact, there's little to describe.

[418]

1   But this can not be true . . .
5a Why [then do they so] fail [in] [as the] inditers
 b Why do . . . fail then as . . .
7   The real [outlines] portrait . . .

21

"*Haud ignara loquor*": these are *Nugae*, "*quarum*
   Pars parva *fui*,"* but still Art and part.
Now I could much more easily sketch a harem,
   A battle, wreck, or history of the heart,
Than these things; and besides, I wish to spare 'em,
   For reasons which I choose to keep apart.
"*Vetabo Cereris sacrum qui volgarit*"*—
   Which means that vulgar people must not share it.

1   there are [matters] "quarum
3a Now—I could [easily sketch off a] haram
 b   [easier . . .]
7   vulgaret *In 1823 edition.*
_____

22

And therefore what I throw off is ideal—
   Lower'd, leaven'd, like a history of Freemasons;*
Which bears the same relation to the real,
   As Captain Parry's voyage may do to Jason's.
The grand Arcanum's not for men to see all;
   My music has some mystic diapasons;
And there is much which could not be appreciated
   In any manner by the uninitiated.

2   [Or] Lowered—[heightened]—like a history . . .
3a [From] which [you] [know] *fragment*
 b [From] which [you no more gather what is] real
4a [Nor of the Arnogautic voyage of Jason's]
 b [Nor from the Argonautic . . .]
6   [The] Music hath . . .

Alas! Worlds fall—and Woman, since she fell'd
The World (as, since that history, less polite
Than true, hath been a creed so strictly held)
Has not yet given up the practice quite.
Poor Thing of Usages! Coerc'd, compell'd,
Victim when wrong, and martyr oft when right,
Condemn'd to child-bed, as men for their sins
Have shaving too entailed upon their chins,—

2 (as [in] that . . .
3 Creed so [strongly] held
5 Poor Thing—[from] *fragment*
6a [The general victim whether wrong or right]
 b Victim when wrong, and [sacrifice when right]
7–8a [Condemned to Child-bearing as Men to Shaving
 Which] [by] [daily plague's enough to set] *Byron probably
 intended to complete this line with* one raving.
 8b Have Shaving [visited] upon their Chins

24

A daily plague, which in the aggregate
May average on the whole with parturition.
But as to women, who can penetrate
The real sufferings of their she condition?
Man's very sympathy with their estate
Has much of selfishness and more suspicion.
Their love, their virtue, beauty, education,
But form good housekeepers, to breed a nation.

2 May [vie upon] the whole . . .
8 [To] form . . . [and] breed . . .

All this were very well and can't be better;
　　But even this is difficult, Heaven knows!
So many troubles from her birth beset her,
　　Such small distinction between friends and foes,
The gilding wears so soon from off her fetter,
　　That—but ask any woman if she'd choose
(Take her at thirty, that is) to have been
Female or male? a school-boy or a Queen?

1　All this [is] very well . . .
7a–8a [Take her at thirty—that is to be born
　　Female or male] *fragment*
　　Byron twice wrote the present text of line 7 and of the first three
　　words of line 8. He deleted the first of these attempts.
　8b Female or Male? a [ploughboy] or a Queen?

26

"Petticoat Influence"* is a great reproach,
　　Which even those who obey would fain be thought
To fly from, as from hungry pikes a roach;
　　But, since beneath it upon earth we are brought
By various joltings of life's hackney coach,
　　I for one venerate a petticoat—
A garment of a mystical sublimity,
No matter whether russet, silk, or dimity.*

4　But since beneath it [into life] we are brought
5a　[Into] [The] [By the World's Strand] [Throu] *fragments*
　b　By [that which may be deemed] Life's hackney Coach
6a　I for one [must respect] a petticoat
　b　　　　　[much respect] . . .
7–8 *Order of composition:*
　　[And though—by no means overpowered with riches]
　　[Would gladly place beneath] [it's l] [it my last rag of breeches]
　　[Would risk to please it my last rag of breeches]
　　A Garment of a mystical sublimity
　　[Whether composed] [Trimmed, or untrimmed] *fragments*
　　No matter whether [satin] silk—or dimity
　　　　　　　　　russet . . .

Much I respect, and much I have adored,
  In my young days, that chaste and goodly veil,
Which holds a treasure, like a Miser's hoard,
  And more attracts by all it doth conceal—
A golden scabbard on a Damasque sword,
  A loving letter with a mystic seal,
A cure for grief—for what can ever rankle
Before a petticoat and peeping ancle?

3a Which [holds a treasure] like a Miser's [hold]
 b Which [folds a treasure] . . .
4   [Which] more attracts . . .
6   with a [pretty] Seal
7   can [eer] rankle

28

And when upon a silent, sullen day,
  With a Sirocco, for example, blowing,
When even the sea looks dim with all its spray,
  And sulkily the river's ripple's flowing,
And the sky shows that very ancient gray,
  The sober, sad antithesis to glowing,—
'Tis pleasant, if *then* any thing is pleasant,
To catch a glimpse even of a pretty peasant.

3   looks [sulky] dim . . .
5   And the Sky [hath] shows . . .
7   Tis Pleasant—if [that] <u>then</u> anything . . .
8a To [meet along the road a pretty peasant]
 b To snatch a glimpse [though of a pretty peasant]
 c   even of a pretty peasant

We left our heroes and our heroines
   In that fair clime which don't depend on climate,
Quite independent of the Zodiac's signs,
   Though certainly more difficult to rhyme at,
Because the sun and stars, and aught that shines,
   Mountains, and all we can be most sublime at,
Are there oft dull and dreary as a *dun*—
Whether a sky's or tradesman's, is all one.

1   heros . . .
5   and [all] that shines
7*a* Are·[dull and dreary] *fragment*
 b Are there [ofttimes] dull and dreary as a [dun]
8   Whether [the] Sky's . . .

30

And in-door life is less poetical;
   And out of door hath showers, and mists, and sleet,
With which I could not brew a pastoral.
   But be it as it may, a bard must meet
All difficulties, whether great or small,
   To spoil his undertaking or complete,
And work away like spirit upon matter,
Embarrass'd somewhat both with fire and water.

1*a* And indoor Life . . .   B
 b An in-door . . . *In 1833 and in later editions.*
8*a* [Of which the most intractable] *fragment*
 b [And when Fire for] *fragment*
 c [Puzzled a good deal] both with fire and water

Juan—in this respect at least like saints—
   Was all things unto people of all sorts,
And lived contentedly, without complaints,
   In camps, in ships, in cottages, or courts—
Born with that happy soul which seldom faints,
   And mingling modestly in toils or sports.
He likewise could be most things to all women,
Without the coxcombry of certain *She* Men.

2–3 "Was all things to all men" and could comport
Himself—contentedly . . .

32

A fox-hunt to a foreigner is strange;
   'Tis also subject to the double danger
Of tumbling first, and having in exchange
   Some pleasant jesting at the awkward stranger:
But Juan had been early taught to range
   The wilds, as doth an Arab turn'd Avenger,
So that his horse, or charger, hunter, hack,
Knew that he had a rider on his back.

7 [And Ch] So that . . .

33

And now in this new field, with some applause,
   He clear'd hedge, ditch, and double post, and rail,
And never *craned,** and made but few *"faux pas,"*
   And only fretted when the scent 'gan fail.
He broke, 'tis true, some statutes of the laws
   Of hunting—for the sagest youth is frail;
Rode o'er the hounds, it may be, now and then,
And once o'er several Country Gentlemen.

2 He cleared both hedge and double post . . .

4a Was [also patient] when . . .
 b Was only fretted . . .
6   the [wisest] Youth . . .

34

But on the whole, to general admiration
    He acquitted both himself and horse: the 'squires
Marvell'd at merit of another nation;
    The boors cried "Dang it! who'd have thought it?"—
    Sires,
The Nestors* of the sporting generation
    Swore praises, and recall'd their former fires;
The Huntsman's self relented to a grin,
And rated him almost a whipper-in.*

1   [the] general . . .
5   [Who had seen their] *fragment*
6   Swore praises, [such the laurels] *fragment*
7–8 [The sulky Huntsman grimly said "the Frenchman"
    Was almost worthy to become his henchman]

35

Such were his trophies;—not of spear and shield,
    But leaps, and bursts, and sometimes fox's brushes;
Yet I must own,—although in this I yield
    To patriot sympathy a Briton's blushes,—
He thought at heart like courtly Chesterfield,
    Who, after a long chase o'er hills, dales, bushes,
And what not, though he rode beyond all price,
Ask'd next day, "If men ever hunted *twice?*"*

4   [With] patriot . . .
5   like [gay] Lord Chesterfield
7   And what not—though he [had ridden like a Centaur]
8a [When called next day declined the rough adventure]
 b   [same . . .]

He also had a quality uncommon
　　To early risers after a long chase,
Who wake in winter ere the cock can summon
　　December's drowsy day to his dull race,—
A quality agreeable to woman,
　　When her soft, liquid words run on apace,
Who likes a listener, whether Saint or Sinner,—
He did not fall asleep just after dinner.*

1 [Asking "if people ever did this twice"]
*Byron wrote this line before he canceled the couplet of the preceding
stanza. Then he went back to stanza 35 and wrote a new couplet in
which he used a revised version of his first attempt at the first line of
stanza 36.*
3 Who [rise] in winter ere the Cocks can summon
4 [Day to which by no] *fragment*

37

But, light and airy, stood on the alert,
　　And shone in the best part of dialogue,
By humouring always what they might assert,
　　And listening to the topics most in vogue;
Now grave, now gay, but never dull or pert;
　　And smiling but in secret—cunning rogue!
He ne'er presumed to make an error clearer;—
In short, there never was a better hearer.

1 But light and [lively] stood . . .
　　　　　　[gently] . . .
2 [He] shone . . .
7 [He] [At any slight mistakes] *fragment*

And then he danced;—all foreigners excel
  The serious Angles in the eloquence
Of pantomime;—he danced, I say, right well,
  With emphasis, and also with good sense—
A thing in footing indispensable:
  He danced without theatrical pretence,
Not like a ballet-master in the van
Of his drill'd nymphs, but like a gentleman.

1, 3, 6 daunced . . .
  5 indispenseable
  8 Of his [chaste choir] but like . . .

39

Chaste were his steps, each kept within due bound,
  And elegance was sprinkled o'er his figure;
Like swift Camilla, he scarce skimm'd the ground,*
  And rather held in than put forth his vigour;
And then he had an ear for music's sound,
  Which might defy a Crotchet Critic's rigour.
Such classic *pas—sans* flaws—set off our hero,
He glanced like a personified Bolero;*

1 steps—[but] [and] kept . . .
2 And [Grace] was sprinkled [over all] his figure
8 He [looked] like . . .

Or, like a flying Hour before Aurora,
    In Guido's famous fresco,* which alone
Is worth a tour to Rome, although no more a
    Remnant were there of the old world's sole throne.
The *"tout ensemble"* of his movements wore a
    Grace of the soft Ideal, seldom shown,
And ne'er to be described; for to the dolour
Of bards and prosers, words are void of colour.

4 World's [grand] throne

41

No marvel then he was a favourite;
    A full-grown Cupid, very much admired;*
A little spoilt, but by no means so quite;
    At least he kept his vanity retired.
Such was his tact, he could alike delight
    The chaste, and those who are not so much inspired.
The Duchess of Fitz-Fulke, who loved *"tracasserie,"*
Began to treat him with some small *"agaçerie."**

No revisions.

42

She was a fine and somewhat full-blown blonde,
    Desirable, distinguish'd, celebrated
For several winters in the grand, *grand Monde.*
    I'd rather not say what might be related
Of her exploits, for this were ticklish ground;
    Besides there might be falsehood in what's stated:
Her late performance had been a dead set
At Lord Augustus Fitz-Plantagenet.

3 in the [grandest] grand grand "Monde"
4 [I'd pause not to] say what . . .

5 exploits [which might be] ticklish . . .
7 Her late[st] performance . . .

43

    This noble personage began to look
      A little black upon this new flirtation;
    But such small licences must lovers brook,
      Mere freedoms of the female corporation.
    Woe to the man who ventures a rebuke!
      'Twill but precipitate a situation
    Extremely disagreeable, but common
    To calculators when they count on woman.

3 But [these] small licenses . . .
4 [These] freedoms . . .
8 To [most who calculate upon a] woman

44

    The circle smil'd, then whisper'd, and then sneer'd;
      The misses bridled, and the matrons frown'd;
    Some hoped things might not turn out as they fear'd;
      Some would not deem such women could be found;
    Some ne'er believed one half of what they heard;
      Some look'd perplex'd, and others look'd profound;
    And several pitied with sincere regret
    Poor Lord Augustus Fitz-Plantagenet.

5 [Others never] believed half . . .

But what is odd, none ever named the Duke,
　Who, one might think, was something in the affair.
True, he was absent, and 'twas rumour'd, took
　But small concern about the when, or where,
Or what his consort did: if he could brook
　Her gaieties, none had a right to stare:
Theirs was that best of unions, past all doubt,
Which never meets, and therefore can't fall out.

6a Her gaieties [no Stranger needs] *fragment*
　b Her gaieties none have a right to stare
7　past a doubt

46

But, oh that I should ever pen so sad a line!
　Fired with an abstract love of virtue, she,
My Dian of the Ephesians, Lady Adeline,
　Began to think the Duchess' conduct free;
Regretting much that she had chosen so bad a line,
　And waxing chiller in her courtesy,
Looked grave and pale to see her friend's fragility,
For which most friends reserve their sensibility.

3 [That] Dian of [the Dianas]—Lady Adeline

47

There's nought in this bad world like sympathy:
　'Tis so becoming to the soul and face;
Sets to soft music the harmonious sigh,
　And robes sweet Friendship in a Brussels lace.
Without a friend, what were humanity,
　To hunt our errors up with a good grace?
Consoling us with—"Would you had thought twice!
Ah! if you had but follow'd my advice!"

3 the harmonic sigh

4 And robes [our] Friendship . . .
5 [How] Without . . .
6 To hint our errors . . .
7 [And cry] [To shake the head] *fragments*

48

Oh, Job! you had two friends:* one's quite enough,
    Especially when we are ill at ease;
They are but bad pilots when the weather's rough,
    Doctors less famous for their cures than fees.
Let no man grumble when his friends fall off,
    As they will do like leaves at the first breeze:
When your affairs come round, one way or t'other,
Go to the coffee-house, and take another.*

2–3 [Of all I ever had and there were many
    As the World goes] *fragment*

49

But this is not my maxim: had it been,
    Some heart-aches had been spared me; yet I care not—
I would not be a tortoise in his screen
    Of stubborn shell, which waves and weather wear not.
'Tis better on the whole to have felt and seen
    That which humanity may bear, or bear not:
'Twill teach discernment to the sensitive,
    And not to pour their ocean in a sieve.

8 their [water] on a Sieve

Of all the horrid, hideous notes of woe,
    Sadder than owl-songs or the midnight blast,
Is that portentous phrase, "I told you so,"
    Utter'd by friends, those prophets of the past,
Who, 'stead of saying what you now should do,
    Own they foresaw that you would fall at last,
And solace your slight lapse 'gainst *"bonos mores,"**
With a long memorandum of old stories.

Byron made some marginal jottings here which he deleted: "Mem. B. D.
B. S. Hypocondria Nightingale memory *sic?*"

2 Sadder than [Screech-Owls] or . . .
6 [They own that you are fairly dished] at last
8 [By] a long . . .

51

The Lady Adeline's serene severity
    Was not confined to feeling for her friend,
Whose fame she rather doubted with posterity,
    Unless her habits should begin to mend;
But Juan also shared in her austerity,
    But mix'd with pity, pure as e'er was penn'd:
His inexperience moved her gentle ruth,
And (as her junior by six weeks) his youth.

7 [She felt] *fragment*
8 [Also (he was six weeks her Junior] *fragment*

52

These forty days' advantage of her years—
    And her's were those which can face calculation,
Boldly referring to the list of peers
    And noble births, nor dread the enumeration—
Gave her a right to have maternal fears
    For a young gentleman's fit education,

> Though she was far from that leap year, whose leap,
> In female dates, strikes Time all of a heap.

3 [Behold] *fragment*
4 And [peerage dates] nor dread . . .
6 [Of] a young . . .
7 [She yet] was far from that [grand] Year . . .

53

> This may be fixed at somewhere before thirty—
>   Say seven-and-twenty; for I never knew
> The strictest in chronology and virtue
>   Advance beyond, while they could pass for new.
> Oh, Time! Why dost not pause? Thy scythe, so dirty
>   With rust, should surely cease to hack and hew.
> Reset it; shave more smoothly, also slower,
> If but to keep thy credit as a mower.

5 [And] Oh! . . .
6 With rust—[sure] should . . .
7a [If but to polish it] *fragment*
 b [If but to set its edge to a fresh polish]
 c Reset it—[cut] more . . .
8 to [save] thy Credit . . .

54

> But Adeline was far from that ripe age,
>   Whose ripeness is but bitter at the best:
> 'Twas rather her experience made her sage,
>   For she had seen the world, and stood its test,
> As I have said in—I forget what page;
>   My Muse despises reference, as you have guess'd
> By this time;—but strike six from seven-and-twenty,
> And you will find her sum of years in plenty.

No revisions.

At sixteen she came out; presented, vaunted,
  She put all coronets into commotion:
At seventeen too the world was still enchanted
  With the new Venus of their brilliant ocean:
At eighteen, though below her feet still panted
  A hecatomb of suitors with devotion,
She had consented to create again
That Adam, called "the Happiest of Men."

1   came out; [and was presented]
2   [And] put all . . .
3   At seventeen the World was still inchanted
4   [Their Venus was b] *fragment*
5-6 *Order of composition:*
     At Eighteen [she with due demur had granted
     Her hand] *fragment*
     [To one of Seventy Suitors his promotion]
     At Eighteen though [before her there still] panted
                   [benea] below her feet [there] still panted
     A Hecatomb of Suitors [for promotion]
                   with devotion
7a   [Yet strange to say] *fragment*
 b   She had consented to [renew] again
8   [On] That [Centau] Adam called . . .

56

Since then she had sparkled through three glowing winters,
  Admired, adored; but also so correct,
That she had puzzled all the acutest hinters,
  Without the apparel of being circumspect:
They could not even glean the slightest splinters
  From off the marble, which had no defect.
She had also snatch'd a moment since her marriage
To bear a son and heir—and one miscarriage.

3   puzzled [even] the . . .
5   [Though] They . . .
7a   [Also she h] *fragment*
 b   [And] she had [found out time too] since her marriage

Fondly the wheeling fire-flies flew around her
    Those little glitterers of the London night;
But none of these possess'd a sting to wound her—
    She was a pitch beyond a coxcomb's flight.
Perhaps she wish'd an aspirant profounder;
    But whatsoe'er she wished, she acted right;
And whether coldness, pride, or virtue, dignify
A Woman, so she's good, what does it signify?

5 wished [for] an . . .
6 wished—she [did quite] right
7 And whether [pride or coldness] *fragment*

58

I hate a motive like a lingering bottle,
    Which with the landlord makes too long a stand,
Leaving all claretless the unmoistened throttle,
    Especially with politics on hand;
I hate it, as I hate a drove of cattle,
    Who whirl the dust as Simooms whirl the sand;
I hate it, as I hate an argument,
A Laureate's ode, or servile Peer's "Content."*

3 claret-less the [thirsty] throttle
6 Simoom whirl[s] the Sand
8 servile [Lord's] "Content!"

'Tis sad to hack into the roots of things,
    They are so much intertwisted with the earth:
So that the branch a goodly verdure flings,
    I reck not if an acorn gave it birth.
To trace all actions to their secret springs
    Would make indeed some melancholy mirth;
But this is not at present my concern,
And I refer you to wise Oxenstiern.*

2 interwisted . . .
3 So that the[ir] branch[es] . . .
4 gave [them] birth
5 To trace all [moti] actions . . .   *Intended to write* motions.
7 [Such] But . . .

60

With the kind view of saving an *eclât*,
    Both to the Duchess and diplomatist,
The Lady Adeline, as soon's she saw
    That Juan was unlikely to resist—
(For foreigners don't know that a *faux pas*
    In England ranks quite on a different list
From those of other lands unblest with Juries,
Whose verdict for such sin a certain cure is);—

1   saving [from] Eclat
7   From that of . . .
8a [Whose verdict] *fragment*
  b [Who are the causes that our moral] [pure] [is]
  c Whose Verdict for [all] Sin . . .

The Lady Adeline resolved to take
    Such measures as she thought might best impede
The further progress of this sad mistake.
    She thought with some simplicity indeed;
But innocence is bold even at the stake,
    And simple in the world, and doth not need
Nor use those palisades by dames erected,
Whose virtue lies in never being detected.

3   farther . . . *In 1833 and in later editions.*
4   [And this] with some . . .
7*a* [Those] Nor use [those palisades] erected
 b   [those formal palisades] erected
8*a* ⌊By ladies who may fear to be⌋ detected
 b Whose Virtue lies in [rarely being] detected

62

It was not that she fear'd the very worst:
    His Grace was an enduring, married man,
And was not likely all at once to burst
    Into a scene, and swell the clients' clan
Of Doctors' Commons; but she dreaded first
    The magic of her Grace's talisman,*
And next a quarrel (as he seemed to fret)
With Lord Augustus Fitz-Plantagenet.

2 His Grace—[the] [had been a patient] married man
3 likely [at] all at . . .
7 And [secondly] a quarrel . . .

Her Grace too pass'd for being an Intrigante,
    And somewhat *méchante** in her amorous sphere;
One of those pretty, precious plagues, which haunt
    A lover with caprices soft and dear,
That like to *make* a quarrel, when they can't
    Find one, each day of the delightful year;
Bewitching, torturing, as they freeze or glow,
And—what is worst of all—won't let you go;

1 Intriguante

64

The sort of thing to turn a young man's head,
    Or make a Werter* of him in the end.
No wonder then a purer soul should dread
    This sort of chaste *liaison* for a friend;
It were much better to be wed or dead,
    Than wear a heart a woman loves to rend.
'Tis best to pause, and think, ere you rush on,
If that a *"bonne fortune"* be really *"bonne."*

4 This sort of [a] liaison . . .
7 you [go] on

65

And first, in the o'erflowing of her heart,
    Which really knew or thought it knew no guile,
She called her husband now and then apart,
    And bade him counsel Juan. With a smile
Lord Henry heard her plans of artless art
    To wean Don Juan from the Siren's wile;
And answer'd, like a Statesman or a Prophet,
In such guise that she could make nothing of it.

4 [To counsel her] *fragment*
6 Siren's [smile]

Firstly, he said, "he never interfered
  In any body's business but the king's":
Next, that "he never judged from what appear'd,
  Without strong reason, of those sorts of things":
Thirdly, that "Juan had more brain than beard,
  And was not to be held in leading strings";
And fourthly, what need hardly be said twice,
"That good but rarely came from good advice."

4a Without [good] reason—of those sorts of things B
  b Without strong . . . B;   c sort . . . *In 1833 and in later*
                                                    editions.

66

67

And, therefore, doubtless to approve the truth
  Of the last axiom, he advised his spouse
To leave the parties to themselves, forsooth,
  At least as far as *bienséance** allows:
That time would temper Juan's faults of youth;
  That young men rarely made monastic vows;
That opposition only more attaches—
But here a messenger brought in dispatches:

2 Of the last maxim . . .
3 To [let] the parties . . .
4 [And not to encourage whispering in the house]

And being of the Council called "the Privy,"
  Lord Henry walk'd into his Cabinet,
To furnish matter for some future Livy
  To tell how he reduced the nation's debt;
And if their full contents I do not give ye,
  It is because I do not know them yet,
But I shall add them in a brief appendix,
To come between mine epic and its index.

8 between [this] Epic . . .

69

But ere he went, he added a slight hint,
  Another gentle common-place or two,
Such as are coined in conversation's mint,
  And pass, for want of better, though not new:
Then broke his packet, to see what was in't,
  And having casually glanced it through,
Retired; and, as he went out, calmly kissed her,
Less like a young wife than an aged sister.

1*a* he added a [few words]
  b   [few] hint[s]
3   mint[s]
7   Retired,—[but calm] *fragment*

70

He was a cold, good, honourable man,*
  Proud of his birth, and proud of every thing;
A goodly spirit for a state divan,
  A figure fit to walk before a king;
Tall, stately, form'd to lead the courtly van
  On birth-days, glorious with a star and string;*
The very model of a Chamberlain—
And such I mean to make him when I reign.

3 A Goodly [figure] for . . .
5a [The very Model of a Chamberlain]
 b Tall—stately—[well] formed . . .
6 On birth-days—[in a red or] *fragment*

71

But there was something wanting on the whole—
  I don't know what, and therefore cannot tell—
Which pretty women—the sweet souls!—call *Soul.*
  Certes it was not body; he was well
Proportion'd, as a poplar or a pole,
  A handsome man, that human miracle;
And in each circumstance of love or war
Had still preserved his perpendicular.

4 [It could not well be] Body—he was well
5 Proportioned—[indeff] [indefatigable] *fragment*
6a A handsome Man [like a poplar] *fragment*
 b A handsome Man [strait's like a poplar or a Pole]
7 And in [all] circumstance . . .
8 [Could] Had still [main] [sustained] his perpendicular

72

Still there was something wanting, as I've said—
  That undefinable "*Je ne sçais quoi,*"
Which, for what I know, may of yore have led
  To Homer's Iliad, since it drew to Troy
The Greek Eve, Helen, from the Spartan's bed;
  Though on the whole, no doubt, the Dardan boy*
Was much inferior to King Menelaus;—
But thus it is some women will betray us.

2 "Je ne sais quoi"
4 it [led] to Troy
5 The [Spartan] Greek Eve . . .

There is an awkward thing which much perplexes,
　　Unless like wise Tiresias* we had proved
By turns the difference of the several sexes:
　　Neither can show quite *how* they would be loved.
The sensual for a short time but connects us—
　　The sentimental boasts to be unmoved;
But both together form a kind of centaur,
Upon whose back 'tis better not to venture.

7 [And] both . . .

74

A something all-sufficient for the *heart*
　　Is that for which the Sex are always seeking;
But how to fill up that same vacant part?
　　There lies the rub—and this they are but weak in.
Frail mariners afloat without a chart,
　　They run before the wind through high seas breaking;
And when they have made the shore through ev'ry shock,
'Tis odd, or odds, it may turn out a rock.

2 are always [craving]
6 through [billows] breaking

75

There is a flower called "Love in Idleness,"*
　　For which see Shakspeare's ever blooming garden;—
I will not make his great description less,
　　And beg his British Godship's humble pardon,
If in my extremity of rhyme's distress,
　　I touch a single leaf where he is warden;—
But though the flower is different, with the French
Or Swiss Rousseau, cry *"Voilà la Pervenche!"**

2　For which see Shakespeare [that eternal] Garden
7a [Rather] [It is] *fragments*;　b [Or]—though . . .

[442]

Eureka! I have found it! What I mean
   To say is, not that Love is Idleness,
But that in Love such Idleness has been
   An accessary, as I have cause to guess.
Hard labour's an indifferent go-between;
   Your men of business are not apt to express
Much passion, since the merchant-ship, the Argo,*
Convey'd Medea as her Supercargo.

4*a* An [this] accessary ... B; *b* accessory ... *In 1833 and in later editions.*
7 [A violent] passion ...

77

"*Beatus ille procul!*" from "*negotiis,*"
   Saith Horace;* the great little poet's wrong;
His other maxim, "*Noscitur a sociis,*"
   Is much more to the purpose of his song;
Though even that were sometimes too ferocious,
   Unless good company he kept too long;
But, in his teeth, whate'er their state or station,
Thrice happy they who *have* an occupation!

4 purpose [even in] song
6 Unless [bad] company ...
7*a* But, [to return] *fragment*
 b But,—in his teeth—whateer [your] state ...

Adam exchanged his Paradise for ploughing,
   Eve made up millinery with fig leaves—
The earliest knowledge from the tree so knowing,
   As far as I know, that the Church receives:
And since that time it need not cost much showing,
   That many of the ills o'er which man grieves,
And still more women, spring from not employing
Some hours to make the remnant worth enjoying.

1 exhanged . . . *Misprint in 1823 edition.*

79

And hence high life is oft a dreary void,
   A rack of pleasures, where we must invent
A something wherewithal to be annoy'd.
   Bards may sing what they please about *Content;*
Contented, when translated, means but cloyed;
   And hence arise the woes of sentiment,
Blue devils,* and Blue-stockings, and Romances
Reduced to practice and perform'd like dances.

5*a* [When were they eer contented until cloy] *fragment*
  b   [even wh cloy] *fragment*

80

I do declare, upon an affidavit,
   Romances I ne'er read like those I have seen;
Nor, if unto the world I ever gave it,
   Would some believe that such a tale had been:
But such intent I never had, nor have it;
   Some truths are better kept behind a screen,
Especially when they would look like lies;*
I therefore deal in generalities.

2 [That I neer read Romance] like [what] I have seen
3 Nor if—[what] unto . . .

4 such [things could have] been
6 [Such things are better] *fragment*
8 deal in [generals, which is wise]

81

"An oyster may be cross'd in Love,"*—and why?
   Because he mopeth idly in his shell,
And heaves a lonely subterraqueous sigh,
   Much as a monk may do within his cell:
And à *propos* of monks, their piety
   With sloth hath found it difficult to dwell;
Those vegetables of the Catholic creed
Are apt exceedingly to run to seed.

3 heaves [the] lonely . . .
5 Monks—their [Surety]

82

Oh, Wilberforce!*'thou man of black renown,
   Whose merit none enough can sing or say,
Thou hast struck one immense Colossus down,
   Thou moral Washington of Africa!
But there's another little thing, I own,
   Which you should perpetrate some summer's day,
And set the other half of earth to rights:
You have freed the *blacks*—now pray shut up the whites.

No revisions.

[445]

Shut up the bald-coot bully Alexander;*
　　Ship off the Holy Three to Senegal;
Teach them that "sauce for goose is sauce for gander,"
　　And ask them how *they* like to be in thrall?
Shut up each high heroic Salamander,*
　　Who eats fire gratis (since the pay's but small);
Shut up—no, *not* the King, but the Pavilion,*
Or else 'twill cost us all another million.

No revisions.

84

Shut up the world at large, let Bedlam out;
　　And you will be perhaps surprised to find
All things pursue exactly the same route,
　　As now with those of *soi-disant* sound mind.
This I could prove beyond a single doubt,
　　Were there a jot of sense among mankind;
But till that point *d'appui** is found, alas!
Like Archimedes, I leave earth as 'twas.*

7a But till [you show] that point d'appui—Alas!
　b But till [I find] . . .

85

Our gentle Adeline had one defect—
　　Her heart was vacant, though a splendid mansion;
Her conduct had been perfectly correct,
　　As she had seen nought claiming its expansion.
A wavering spirit may be easier wreck'd,
　　Because 'tis frailer, doubtless, than a stanch one;
But when the latter works its own undoing,
Its inner crash is like an Earthquake's ruin.

5–6a [Your] wavering Spirit may be [oftener] wrecked
　　[Than your strong] *fragment*

6*b* staunch . . .
7   when [it] the . . .
8   [Tis worse than wreck tis] an Earthquake's ruin

86

She loved her lord, or thought so; but *that* love
    Cost her an effort, which is a sad toil,
The stone of Sysiphus,* if once we move
    Our feelings 'gainst the nature of the soil.
She had nothing to complain of, or reprove,
    No bickerings, no connubial turmoil:
Their union was a model to behold,
Serene, and noble,—conjugal, but cold.

4   'gainst the [grain] nature . . .
5*a* complain of [or] reprove;   *b* nor reprove

87

There was no great disparity of years,
    Though much in temper; but they never clash'd:
They moved like stars united in their spheres,
    Or like the Rhone by Leman's waters wash'd,*
Where mingled and yet separate appears
    The river from the lake, all bluely dash'd
Through the serene and placid glassy deep,
Which fain would lull its river-child to sleep.

4   Or like the Rhone [through] Leman's waters [dashed]
7*a* Through the [more deep and clear and] *fragment*
 b   [broad . . .] *fragment*

Now when she once had ta'en an interest
  In any thing, however she might flatter
Herself that her intentions were the best—
  Intense intentions are a dangerous matter:
Impressions were much stronger than she guess'd,
  And gather'd as they run like growing water
Upon her mind; the more so, as her breast
Was not at first too readily impress'd.

5 [Her] impression [was] much . . .
6 as [if] they run . . .
7 Upon her [Spirit—which] the more so that her breast
8 first [so] readily . . .

89

But when it was, she had that lurking demon
  Of double nature, and thus doubly named—
Firmness yclept in heroes, kings, and seamen,
  That is, when they succeed; but greatly blamed
As *obstinacy*, both in men and women,
  Whene'er their triumph pales, or star is tamed:—
And 'twill perplex the casuists in morality
To fix the due bounds of this dangerous quality.

2   and [of different] name
6a Wheneer [they fail] *fragment*
 b Wheneer their triumph fails . . .
7a And [I defy] the Casuists [of] Morality B
 b And twill perplex the Casuists in Morality B
 c   casuist . . . *In 1833 and in later editions.*

Had Bonaparte won at Waterloo,
　　It had been firmness; now 'tis pertinacity:
Must the event decide between the two?
　　I leave it to your people of sagacity
To draw the line between the false and true,
　　If such can e'er be drawn by man's capacity:
My business is with Lady Adeline,
Who in her way too was a heroine.

4 I leave [this] to . . .
7 My business [was] with . . .

91

She knew not her own heart; then how should I?
　　I think not she was *then* in love with Juan:
If so, she would have had the strength to fly
　　The wild sensation, unto her a new one:
She merely felt a common sympathy
　　(I will not say it was a false or true one)
In him, because she thought he was in danger—
Her husband's friend, her own, young, and a stranger.

2 I [do not] think she was [in] love with Juan
3 If so she would have [strength of mind] to fly
5 She merely [took] a . . .
8 [A] Her . . .

She was, or thought she was, his friend—and this
  Without the farce of friendship, or romance
Of Platonism,* which leads so oft amiss
  Ladies who have studied friendship but in France,
Or Germany, where people *purely* kiss.
  To thus much Adeline would not advance;
But of such friendship as man's may to man be,
She was as capable as woman can be.

4 [Young ladies who have learnt the word from] France
5 *In the following order of composition, the first two variants and the*
last one are fragments.
  [With it's seraphic German—ser]
  [Or with it's German]
  [Or with it's mist of German mysteries]
  [She was above a phantasy like this]
  [Or Germany: She knew nought of all this]
  [Mysterious]
6 To [this Impracticable novel-reading trance]
7 But of [a] friendship [such as Man's] to man be

No doubt the secret influence of the sex
　Will there, as also in the ties of blood,
An innocent predominance annex,
　And tune the concord to a finer mood.
If free from passion, which all friendship checks,
　And your true feelings fully understood,
No friend like to a woman earth discovers,
So that you have not been nor will be lovers.*

2　[Even] there—as [in relationship will hold]
4　And [make the feeling of] a finer mood
5–6　*Order of composition:*
　[I have searched the World and midst success or checks
　Of various kinds] *fragment*
　[Tis rarely found but would repay all checks
　If that a Mortal either could or would]
　If free from Passion['s] which . . .
7　[There's no] friend like a Woman [the World over]
8a　[But then] [she] [you must not be—neer have been—lovers]
　b　So that you [are not—have been—will be]—lovers

94

Love bears within its breast the very germ
　Of change; and how should this be otherwise?
That violent things more quickly find a term
　Is shown through nature's whole analogies;*
And how should the most fierce of all be firm?
　Would you have endless lightning in the skies?
Methinks Love's very title says enough:
How should "the *tender* Passion" e'er be *tough?*

This stanza was written crosswise and unnumbered in the margin on the manuscript.
1　it's breast . . .　*In 1823 edition.*
2　should it be . . .
3　[Since] Violent Things . . .
4　Is seen through Nature's [own] Analogies
7　[It's] Love's very title also speaks enough

Alas! by all experience, seldom yet
    (I merely quote what I have heard from many)
Had lovers not some reason to regret
    The passion which made Solomon a Zany.
I've also seen some wives* (not to forget
    The marriage state, the best or worst of any)
Who were the very paragons of wives,
Yet made the misery of at least two lives.

1a Alas! I [speak by] Experience—[never] yet
 b   quote . . .   seldom . . .
2 I had a paramour—and I've had many
3a [To whom I did not cause a deep] regret
 b   [some small] regret
 c Whom I had not some reason to regret
4 For whom—I did not feel myself a Zany
5 I [also had a wife]—not to forget
7 Who [was] the very paragon of wives
8a Yet made the misery of [both our] lives
 b   [many] . . .
 c   [several] . . .

96

I've also seen some female *friends* ('tis odd,
    But true—as, if expedient, I could prove)
That faithful were* through thick and thin, abroad,
    At home, far more than ever yet was Love—
Who did not quit me when Oppression trod
    Upon me; whom no scandal could remove;
Who fought, and fight, in absence too, my battles,
Despite the snake Society's loud rattles.

1–3 I'[de] also [had] some female <u>friends</u>,—by G—d!
    Or if the oath seem strong—I swear by Jove!
    They [stuck to me] through thick and thin—abroad
 4 yet [did] Love
 5a quit me when [each Circle] trod
  b   [the Tyrants] . . .

Whether Don Juan and chaste Adeline
   Grew friends in this or any other sense,
Will be discuss'd hereafter, I opine:
   At present I am glad of a pretence
To leave them hovering, as the effect is fine,
   And keeps the atrocious reader in *suspense;*
The surest way for ladies and for books
To bait their tender or their tenter hooks.

No revisions.

98

Whether they rode, or walk'd, or studied Spanish
   To read Don Quixote in the original,*
A pleasure before which all others vanish;
   Whether their talk was of the kind call'd "small,"
Or serious, are the topics I must banish
   To the next Canto; where perhaps I shall
Say something to'the purpose, and display
Considerable talent in my way.

5*a* Or [of that serious sort] *fragment*
 b Or serious, are [all] topics I must banish

Above all, I beg all men to forbear
   Anticipating aught about the matter:
They'll only make mistakes about the fair,
   And Juan too, especially the latter.
And I shall take a much more serious air
   Than I have yet done, in this Epic Satire.
It is not clear that Adeline and Juan
Will fall; but if they do, 'twill be their ruin.

1–2 Above all I beg [no one] to forbear
    Anticipating aught [that is to come]
  3 about the [pair]
  6 done in [my moral] Satire

100

But great things spring from little:—Would you think,
   That in our youth, as dangerous a passion
As e'er brought man and woman to the brink
   Of ruin, rose from such a slight occasion,
As few would ever dream could form the link
   Of such a sentimental situation?
You'll never guess, I'll bet you millions, milliards*—
It all sprung from a harmless game at billiards.*

  1 But [strange] things spring from little, [on a time]
  2 in my youth . . .
3–6 As eer brought [two people] to the brink
    Of ruin [from a little want of caution
    Arose from such a slight and slender] link
    [As none would dream of in the situation]

'Tis strange—but true; for Truth is always strange,
  Stranger than Fiction: if it could be told,
How much would novels gain by the exchange!
  How differently the world would men behold!
How oft would vice and virtue places change!
  The new world would be nothing to the old,
If some Columbus of the moral seas
Would show mankind their soul's Antipodes.

3   How [tame] would novels [seem] by the Exchange!
6a [Hav] [Twould seem] [Earth would n] *fragments*
 b [One] [A] new World . . .
7   [When once turned inside out] *fragment*

102

What "Antres vast and desarts idle,"* then
  Would be discover'd in the human soul!
What Icebergs in the hearts of mighty men,
  With Self-love in the centre as their Pole!
What Anthropophagi in nine of ten
  Of those who hold the kingdoms in controul!
Were things but only call'd by their right name,
Caesar himself would be ashamed of Fame.

On the last page of B below this stanza (numbered 100 on the manuscript) Byron wrote his usual signature-symbol and the date, "March 4th 1823."
1   [Here let us pause—we are not prest for time]
4   [What] With . . .
5a in nine of ten   B
 b is nine of ten   *In 1823 edition.*
 c are nine of ten   *In 1833 and in later editions.*
 d *The present text here follows Byron's manuscript.*
7   [If] Were . . .

Canto XV

1

Aʜ!—What should follow slips from my reflection:
  Whatever follows ne'ertheless may be
As àpropos of hope or retrospection,
  As though the lurking thought had follow'd free.
All present life is but an Interjection,
  An "Oh!" or "Ah!" of joy or misery,
Or a "Ha! ha!" or "Bah!"—a yawn, or "Pooh!"
Of which perhaps the latter is most true.

Cantos XV and XVI were published in one volume by John Hunt on March 26, 1824.

  All manuscript readings are taken from B (the Berg manuscript), Byron's first draft.

  On the first page of the manuscript above the first stanza is the date, "Mʰ 8ᵗʰ 1823."

2 follows [will] neertheless . . .
4 followed [fresh and] free
7 "Bah" or [Psha] or "Pooh!"

But, more or less, the whole's a syncopé*
    Or a singultus—emblems of Emotion,
The grand Antithesis to great Ennui,
    Wherewith we break our bubbles on the ocean,
That Watery Outline of Eternity,
    Or miniature at least, as is my notion,
Which ministers unto the soul's delight,
In seeing matters which are out of sight.

6 at least—[I have a] notion
8 [Of] seeing . . .

3

But all are better than the sigh supprest,
    Corroding in the cavern of the heart,
Making the countenance a masque of rest,
    And turning human nature to an art.
Few men dare show their thoughts of worst or best;
    Dissimulation always sets apart
A corner for herself; and therefore Fiction
Is that which passes with least contradiction.

3 [While all without's indicative] of rest
4 [Reducing] Human . . .

4

Ah! who can tell? Or rather, who can not
    Remember, without telling, passion's errors?
The drainer of oblivion, even the sot,
    Hath got blue devils* for his morning mirrors:
What though on Lethe's stream he seem to float,
    He cannot sink his tremors or his terrors;
The ruby glass that shakes within his hand,
Leaves a sad sediment of Time's worst sand.

7 The ruby [Goblet in] *fragment*

And as for Love—Oh, Love!—We will proceed.
   The Lady Adeline Amundeville,
A pretty name as one would wish to read,
   Must perch harmonious on my tuneful quill.
There's music in the sighing of a reed;
   There's music in the gushing of a rill;
There's music in all things, if men had ears:
   Their Earth is but an echo of the spheres.

4 Must [be our them] *fragment* *Intended to write* theme.
8 All Earth . . .

6

The Lady Adeline, right honourable,
   And honour'd, ran a risk of growing less so;
For few of the soft sex are very stable
   In their resolves—alas! that I should say so!
They differ as wine differs from its label,
   When once decanted;—I presume to guess so,
But will not swear: yet both upon occasion,
   Till old, may undergo adulteration.

5 [And] differ . . .
7 both [on some] occasion

7

But Adeline was of the purest vintage,
   The unmingled essence of the grape; and yet
Bright as a new Napoleon from its mintage,
   Or glorious as a diamond richly set;
A page where Time should hesitate to print age,*
   And for which Nature might forego her debt—
Sole creditor whose process doth involve in't
The luck of finding every body solvent.

2*a* Essence of the [Vineyard] yet
 b Essence of the [Vine and] yet
4   [And natural] as a Diamond [unset]
5*a* A [thing on which dull] Time should [never] print age
 b A [face . . .]
6   [For which stern] Nature should forego . . .
7   [That only] Creditor whose [long Claim] doth . . .

8

Oh, Death! thou dunnest of all duns! thou daily
    Knockest at doors, at first with modest tap, .
Like a meek tradesman when approaching palely
    Some splendid debtor he would take by sap:*
But oft denied, as patience 'gins to fail, he
    Advances with exasperated rap,
And (if let in) insists, in terms unhandsome,
On ready money or a draft on Ransom.*

1   [who] daily
5*a* But [gains no entrance;—then] *fragment*
 b But [entering not] *fragment*
 c But oft denied [and his] patience [be]gins to fail he
 d   [and when] . . .
7   And [entering] insists . . .

9

Whate'er thou takest, spare awhile poor Beauty!†
    She is so rare, and thou hast so much prey.
What though she now and then may slip from duty,
    The more's the reason why you ought to stay.
Gaunt Gourmand! with whole nations for your booty,
    You should be civil in a modest way:
Suppress then some slight feminine diseases,
And take as many heroes as Heaven pleases.

1   [Take Wealth—take all] [all—but] spare . . .
4   I [can't see how] *fragment*
5   [Old Skeleton! with Ages for your] Booty

Fair Adeline, the more ingenuous
    Where she was interested (as was said)
Because she was not apt, like some of us,
    To like too readily, or too high bred
To show it—(points we need not now discuss)—
    Would give up artlessly both heart and head
Unto such feelings as seem'd innocent,
For objects worthy of the sentiment.

1 Fair Adeline [ingenuous] the more ingenuous
2 Where she [liked]—was . . .
5 not [much] discuss
7 Unto [all] feelings [which] seemed innocent
8 [With] objects . . .

11

Some parts of Juan's history, which Rumour,
    That live Gazette, had scatter'd to disfigure,
She had heard; but women hear with more good humour
    Such aberrations than we men of rigour.
Besides, his conduct, since in England, grew more
    Strict, and his mind assumed a manlier vigour;
Because he had, like Alcibiades,*
The art of living in all climes with ease.

1   [Such] parts of Juan's History [as] Rumour
2   had scattered [here and there]
6a Strict, and his Mind [had taen] *fragment*
 b   assumed [the] a manlier vigour

His manner was perhaps the more seductive,
  Because he ne'er seem'd anxious to seduce;
Nothing affected, studied, or constructive
  Of coxcombry or conquest: no abuse
Of his attractions marr'd the fair perspective,
  To indicate a Cupidon broke loose,*
And seem to say, "resist us if you can"—
Which makes a dandy while it spoils a man.

3 Nothing affected—[artful—] or [destructive]
5 Of his [own] attractions . . .
7 "resist [me] us . . .

13

They are wrong—that's not the way to set about it;
  As, if they told the truth, could well be shown.
But right or wrong, Don Juan was without it;
  In fact, his manner was his own alone:
Sincere he was—at least you could not doubt it,
  In listening merely to his voice's tone.
The Devil hath not in all his quiver's choice
An arrow for the heart like a sweet voice.*

2 [But were] *fragment*
6 In listening [to his soft and silver] tone
7-8 [Perhaps] the Devil [of all his Armour's] choice
  [Has none more terrible than a] sweet voice

[461]

By Nature soft,* his whole address held off
    Suspicion: though not timid, his regard
Was such as rather seem'd to keep aloof,
    To shield himself, than put you on your guard:
Perhaps 'twas hardly quite assured enough,
    But Modesty's at times its own reward,
Like Virtue; and the absence of pretension
Will go much further than there's need to mention.

1*a* [Soft his Address by Nature, never put]
 b By Nature soft—his whole Address [neer put]
 c   [kept] off
8*a* than [I care] to mention
 b than [it suits] . . .

15

Serene, accomplish'd, cheerful but not loud;
    Insinuating without insinuation;
Observant of the foibles of the crowd,
    Yet ne'er betraying this in conversation;
Proud with the proud, yet courteously proud,
    So as to make them feel he knew his station
And theirs:—without a struggle for priority,
He neither brook'd nor claim'd superiority.

1 Serene—accomplish[ment]—cheerful but neer loud
5 but courteously proud
7 And theirs without [offence] *fragment*
8 brooked nor [showed] Superiority

That is, with men: with women he was what
  They pleased to make or take him for; and their
Imagination's quite enough for that:
  So that the outline's tolerably fair,
They fill the canvass up—and "verbum sat."*
  If once their phantasies be brought to bear
Upon an object, whether sad or playful,
They can transfigure brighter than a Raphael.*

6 their [Fancy can] be brought . . .

17

Adeline, no deep judge of character,
  Was apt to add a colouring from her own.
'Tis thus the good will amiably err,
  And eke the wise, as has been often shown.
Experience is the chief philosopher,
  But saddest when his science is well known:
And persecuted sages teach the schools
Their folly in forgetting there are fools.

1 no [great] Judge . . .
4 And [even] the Wise as [every] *fragment*
8 Their folly in [not deeming] there were fools

Was it not so, great Locke? and greater Bacon?
　　Great Socrates? And thou Diviner still,*
Whose lot it is by man to be mistaken,
　　And thy pure creed made sanction of all ill?
Redeeming worlds to be by bigots shaken,
　　How was thy toil rewarded? We might fill
Volumes with similar sad illustrations,
But leave them to the conscience of the nations.

2　Great Socrates? and [one Name Greater] still
3a　[And all] whose lot it [is] [was] to be [mis]　*Intended*
　　to write mistaken.
　b　Whose lot it is to be [the most] mistaken
　c　　　　　　　　　　　by Man . . .
5　[To leave the World by Bigot factions] shaken
6a　[And thyself] *fragment*
　b　[And thy life how] rewarded? . . .

19

I perch upon an humbler promontory,
　　Amidst life's infinite variety:*
With no great care for what is nicknamed glory,
　　But speculating as I cast mine eye
On what may suit or may not suit my story,
　　And never straining hard to versify,
I rattle on exactly as I'd talk*
With any body in a ride or walk.

1　upon a humbler . . .
3　what [the vain call] Glory
4　And speculating as I cast [my] eye

I don't know that there may be much ability
    Shown in this sort of desultory rhyme;
But there's a conversational facility,
    Which may round off an hour upon a time.
Of this I'm sure at least, there's no servility
    In mine irregularity of chime,
Which rings what's uppermost of new or hoary,
Just as I feel the "Improvvisatore."*

2 In this [same] sort . . .
7a [Which never flatters either whig or tory]
 b [Which rings no flattery or fav] *fragment* *Intended to write* favor
8 Improvisatore *B and 1824 edition.*

21

"Omnia vult *belle* Matho dicere*—dic aliquando
    Et *bene*, dic *neutrum*, dic aliquando *male*."
The first is rather more than mortal can do;
    The second may be sadly done or gaily;
The third is still more difficult to stand to;
    The fourth we hear, and see, and say too, daily:
The whole together is what I could wish
To serve in this conundrum of a dish.

4 may be [done] sadly done . . .

A modest hope—but modesty's my forte,
    And pride my feeble:*—let us ramble on.
I meant to make this poem very short,
    But now I can't tell where it may not run.
No doubt, if I had wish'd to pay my court
    To critics, or to hail the *setting* sun
Of tyranny of all kinds, my concision*
Were more;—but I was born for opposition.

4 tell when it will be done
8 Were more but [my] I . . .

23

But then 'tis mostly on the weaker side:
    So that I verily believe if they
Who now are basking in their full-blown pride,
    Were shaken down, and "dogs had had their day,"*
Though at the first I might perchance deride
    Their tumble, I should turn the other way,
And wax an Ultra-royalist in loyalty,
Because I hate even democratic royalty.

1 tis [always] on the weaker side
3 Who now are [weltering] in . . .
5–8 [I should not be the foremost to] deride
    Their [fall, but quickly take a] turn the other way
    And wax an Ultra-royalist [when Royalty]
    [Had nothing left it but a desperate Loyalty]

I think I should have made a decent spouse,
    If I had never proved the soft condition;
I think I should have made monastic vows,
    But for my own peculiar superstition:
'Gainst rhyme I never should have knock'd my brows,
    Nor broken my own head, nor that of Priscian,*
Nor worn the motley mantle of a poet,
If some one had not told me to forego it.*

2   If I had never [been a married man]
4a [Had Superstition lost her talisman]
 b [Had not the flesh made some small option]
5   [I think I never] *fragment*
6   [Broke my own head nor that] of Priscian
7   [And] [Or] worn . . .

25

But "laissez aller"—knights and dames I sing,*
    Such as the times may furnish. 'Tis a flight
Which seems at first to need no lofty wing,
    Plumed by Longinus or the Stagyrite:*
The difficulty lies in colouring
    (Keeping the due proportions still in sight)
With Nature manners which are artificial,
And rend'ring general that which is especial.

3   Which [by no means require a] lofty wing
4a Nor [needs] Longinus . . .;   b Nor asks Longinus . . .
5–6 [As] To marshall onwards to the Delphian Height
     The difficulty lies in colouring
     Byron made a mistake in his rhyme pattern here. Later he rejected
     his original line 5, substituted his original line 6 in its place, and then
     wrote the present line 6.
8   And render general . . .

The difference is, that in the days of old
    Men made the manners; manners now make men—
Pinned like a flock, and fleeced too in their fold,
    At least nine, and a ninth beside of ten.
Now this at all events must render cold
    Your writers, who must either draw again
Days better drawn before, or else assume
The present, with their common-place costume.

4   besides of ten
7a drawn before—[or seek the recent]
  b drawn before—[or take the present]

27

We'll do our best to make the best on't:—March!
    March, my Muse! If you cannot fly, yet flutter;
And when you may not be sublime, be arch,
    Or starch, as are the edicts statesmen utter.
We surely shall find something worth research:
    Columbus found a new world in a cutter,*
Or brigantine, or pink, of no great tonnage,
While yet America was in her non-age.

3a And [I will] *fragment*; b And when you cannot . . .
5a We surely shall find . . . B
  b We surely may . . . *In 1833 and in later editions.*

28

When Adeline, in all her growing sense
    Of Juan's merits and his situation,
Felt on the whole an interest intense—
    Partly perhaps because a fresh sensation,
Or that he had an air of innocence,
    Which is for innocence a sad temptation,—
As women hate half measures, on the whole,
She 'gan to ponder how to save his soul.

1 [Then] Adeline in all [new born] sense
4 Partly because [it was] a fresh sensation
5 [Perhaps] [Partly be] *fragments*
7 As Women [seldom think by halves] *fragment*
8 Began to ponder . . .

29

She had a good opinion of advice,
　　Like all who give and eke receive it gratis,
For which small thanks are still the market price,
　　Even where the article at highest rate is.
She thought upon the subject twice or thrice,
　　And morally decided, the best state is
For morals, marriage; and this question carried,
She seriously advised him to get married.

2 give [it] and . . .
5 She [deeply] thought upon . . .
7 and this [pos] question carried　*Intended to write* position.

30

Juan replied, with all becoming deference,
　　He had a predilection for that tie;
But that at present, with immediate reference
　　To his own circumstances, there might lie
Some difficulties, as in his own preference,
　　Or that of her to whom he might apply;
That still he'd wed with such or such a lady,
If that they were not married all already.

5*a* difficulties,—[first] in . . .
　b difficulties,—[or] . . .
7　That still [he would] wed . . .

Next to the making matches for herself,
  And daughters, brothers, sisters, kith or kin,
Arranging them like books on the same shelf,
  There's nothing women love to dabble in
More (like a stock-holder in growing pelf)
  Than match-making in general: 'tis no sin
Certes, but a preventative, and therefore
That is, no doubt, the only reason wherefore.

2 kith and kin
5 More [than] a [Merchant] Stockholder . . .
7 prevenatative . . .

But never yet (except of course a miss
  Unwed, or mistress never to be wed,
Or wed already, who object to this)
  Was there chaste dame who had not in her head
Some drama of the marriage unities,
  Observed as strictly both at board and bed,
As those of Aristotle, though sometimes
They turn out melodrames or pantomimes.*

2 [Unmarried]—or [a] Mistress . . .
3 Or Wed already—[much the same in] this
4 Was there [a] dame . . .
7 As those of Aristotle [on the Scene]

33

They generally have some only son,
  Some heir to a large property, some friend
Of an old family, some gay Sir John,
  Or grave Lord George, with whom perhaps might end
A line, and leave posterity undone,
  Unless a marriage was applied to mend

The prospect and their morals: and besides,
They have at hand a blooming glut of brides.

1 have some [yo] [good young man]
8 They have on hand [an enor *sic?*] a blooming . . . *Intended to write*
enormous?

34

From these they will be careful to select,
    For this an heiress, and for that a beauty;
For one a songstress who hath no defect,
    For t'other one who promises much duty;
For this a lady no one can reject,
    Whose sole accomplishments were quite a booty;
A second for her excellent connexions;
A third, because there can be no objections.

1 [For] these . . .
3 a Songstress [without one] defect
6 Accomplishments [are] quite . . .
7 [One damned] for . . .

35

When Rapp the Harmonist embargoed marriage*
    In his harmonious settlement—(which flourishes
Strangely enough as yet without miscarriage,
    Because it breeds no more mouths than it nourishes,
Without those sad expenses which disparage
    What Nature naturally most encourages)—
Why call'd he "Harmony" a state sans wedlock?
Now here I have got the preacher at a dead lock.*

5 Without [that] sad . . .

Because he either meant to sneer at harmony
    Or marriage, by divorcing them thus oddly.
But whether reverend Rapp learn'd this in Germany
    Or no, 'tis said his sect is rich and godly,
Pious and pure, beyond what I can term any
    Of ours, although they propagate more broadly.
My objection's to his title, not his ritual,
Although I wonder how it grew habitual.

1   either meaned . . .
4   Or No—[they say] *fragment*
8*a* [Which last I leave unto the Lords Spiritual]
 b [Which is but Continence] *fragment*

37

But Rapp is the reverse of zealous matrons,
    Who favour, malgré Malthus,* generation—
Professors of that genial art, and patrons
    Of all the modest part of propagation,
Which after all at such a desperate rate runs,
    That half its produce tends to emigration,
That sad result of passions and potatoes*—
Two weeds which pose our economic Catos.*

No revisions.

38

Had Adeline read Malthus? I can't tell;
    I wish she had: his book's the eleventh commandment,
Which says, "thou shalt not marry," unless *well:*
    This he (as far as I can understand) meant:
'Tis not my purpose on his views to dwell,
    Nor canvass what "so eminent a hand" meant;*
But certes it conducts to lives ascetic,
Or turning marriage into arithmetic.

1 [If] Adeline read Malthus—I [know not]
2 she had—[both it] his book's . . .
5a–6a [His talent I will not deny nor dwell
      On what as] *fragment*
  5b Tis not my purpose on [the] [such] views to dwell
  6b [On] what so [very] "eminent a hand" meant

39

But Adeline, who probably presumed
    That Juan had enough of maintenance,
Or *separate* maintenance, in case 'twas doom'd—
    As on the whole it is an even chance
That bridegrooms, after they are fairly *groom'd,*
    May retrograde a little in the dance
Of marriage—(which might form a painter's fame,
    Like Holbein's "Dance of Death"*—but 'tis the
        same);—

1 who probably [supposed]
2 enough of [worldly Goods]
3 in case twere doomed
7a Of Marriage which [like Holbein] *fragment*
7b–8 Of Marriage which might [furnish more variety
    Than Holb] *fragment*

40

But Adeline determined Juan's wedding
    In her own mind, and that's enough for woman.
But then, with whom? There was the sage Miss Reading,
    Miss Raw, Miss Flaw, Miss Showman, and Miss
        Knowman,
And the two fair co-heiresses Giltbedding.
    She deemed his merits something more than common:
All these were unobjectionable matches,
And might go on, if well wound up, like watches.

4 Miss Raw—Miss Flaw—Miss [Allman] and Miss [Noman]

There was Miss Millpond,* smooth as summer's sea,
    That usual paragon, an only daughter,
Who seem'd the cream of equanimity,
    Till skimm'd—and then there was some milk and
        water,
With a slight shade of Blue too it might be,
    Beneath the surface; but what did it matter?
Love's riotous, but marriage should have quiet,
And being consumptive, live on a milk diet.

1   There was Miss Millpond—[that smooth placid sea]
2a [Which did not show but yet concealed a storm]
 b That usual paragon, an only [child]
4a there was [a shade of blue]
 b there was some milk [of] water
7a [In Love there's something of Intoxication]
 b [That Marriage ought to] *fragment*
 c [That Marriage for his] [it's] [essence] should have quiet
8   And being Consumptive—[thrives most on Milk d]

42

And then there was the Miss Audacia Shoestring,
    A dashing demoiselle of good estate,
Whose heart was fix'd upon a star or bluestring;*
    But whether English Dukes grew rare of late,
Or that she had not harp'd upon the true string,
    By which such sirens can attract our great,
She took up with some foreign younger brother,
A Russ or Turk—the one's as good as t'other.

*Byron wrote "42" seven times and crossed it out before he started this
stanza.*

2a A dashing Demoiselle [of health and wealth]
 b   of [great poss] *Intended to write* possessions.
4   grew scarce of late
6   attract [th] great
7   with [a] some . . .
8   [Wh] [Whose] *fragment*

And then there was—but why should I go on,
    Unless the ladies should go off?—there was
Indeed a certain fair and fairy one,
    Of the best class, and better than her class,—
Aurora Raby, a young star who shone
    O'er life, too sweet an image for such glass,
A lovely being, scarcely form'd or moulded,
A Rose with all its sweetest leaves yet folded;

5 Aurora Raby—[who but then begun]
6 [The world] too [harsh] an image . . .

44

Rich, noble, but an orphan; left an only
    Child to the care of guardians good and kind;
But still her aspect had an air so lonely!
    Blood is not water; and where shall we find
Feelings of youth like those which overthrown lie
    By death, when we are left, alas! behind,
To feel, in friendless palaces, a home
Is wanting, and our best ties in the tomb?

5 [Those] *fragment*
6a By Death—when we [but look as lef] *fragment*
 b By Death—when we are left [as twere] *fragment*
7 [To earn experience—without those best] [ye] [ties] *Intended to write* years?

Early in years, and yet more infantine
  In figure, she had something of sublime
In eyes which sadly shone, as seraphs' shine.
  All youth—but with an aspect beyond time;
Radiant and grave—as pitying man's decline;
  Mournful—but mournful of another's crime,
She look'd as if she sat by Eden's door,
And grieved for those who could return no more.

1 [In figure and] *fragment*
2 In figure—[there was] something . . .
3 In [her sad] eyes . . .
6 Mournful [and] but [not as mournful of a] crime
7 sate by Eden's [gate]
8 And grieved for [those who were] *fragment*

46

She was a Catholic too, sincere, austere,
  As far as her own gentle heart allow'd,
And deem'd that fallen worship far more dear
  Perhaps because 'twas fallen: her sires were proud
Of deeds and days when they had fill'd the ear
  Of nations, and had never bent or bow'd
To novel power; and as she was the last,
She held their old faith and old feelings fast.

2 her own gentle [Nature] Heart allowed
3a And [loved] that . . .; b And [held] that . . .
4 twas fall'n her [race was] proud
8 She [kept] their . . .

47

She gazed upon a world she scarcely knew
  As seeking not to know it; silent, lone,
As grows a flower, thus quietly she grew,
  And kept her heart serene within its zone.

> There was awe in the homage which she drew;
>> Her spirit seem'd as seated on a throne
> Apart from the surrounding world, and strong
> In its own strength—most strange in one so young!

3 Flower [so] quietly . . .
8 In its strength [strange thing] in one so young!

48

> Now it so happen'd, in the catalogue
>> Of Adeline, Aurora was omitted,
> Although her birth and wealth had given her vogue
>> Beyond the charmers we have already cited;
> Her beauty also seem'd to form no clog
>> Against her being mention'd as well fitted,
> By many virtues, to be worth the trouble
> Of single gentlemen who would be double.

2 Of Adeline[s] . . .
6 as [one] fitted
7a By [qualities of every kind to double]
 b By many [qualities as] to be . . .
8 who [wish to] double

49

> And this omission, like that of the bust
>> Of Brutus* at the pageant of Tiberius,
> Made Juan wonder, as no doubt he must.
>> This he express'd half smiling and half serious;
> When Adeline replied with some disgust,
>> And with an air, to say the least, imperious,
> She marvell'd "what he saw in such a baby
> As that prim, silent, cold Aurora Raby?"

2 in the [triumph] of Tiberius

Juan rejoined—"She was a Catholic,
　　And therefore fittest, as of his persuasion;
Since he was sure his mother would fall sick,
　　And the Pope thunder excommunication,
If—" But here Adeline, who seem'd to pique
　　Herself extremely on the inoculation
Of others with her own opinions, stated—
As usual—the same reason which she late did.

4a　And the Pope [pass a strong] excommunication
　b　And the Pope thunder [his] . . .
6　Herself [upon] extremely . . .

51

And wherefore not? A reasonable reason,
　　If good, is none the worse for repetition;
If bad, the best way's certainly to teaze on
　　And amplify: you lose much by concision,
Whereas insisting in or out of season
　　Convinces all men, even a politician;
Or—what is just the same—it wearies out.
So the end's gain'd, what signifies the route?

No revisions.

52

Why Adeline had this slight prejudice—
　　For prejudice it was—against a creature
As pure as sanctity itself from vice,
　　With all the added charm of form and feature,
For me appears a question far too nice,
　　Since Adeline was liberal by Nature;
But Nature's Nature, and has more caprices
Than I have time, or will, to take to pieces.

2 against a [being]
4 charms . . .
5 to nice
6 Since [she] Adeline . . .

53

Perhaps she did not like the quiet way
    With which Aurora on those baubles look'd,
Which charm most people in their earlier day:
    For there are few things by mankind less brook'd,
And womankind too, if we so may say,
    Than finding thus their genius stand rebuked,
Like "Anthony's by Caesar,"* by the few
Who look upon them as they ought to do.

6 [As] finding thus their Genius rebuked

54

It was not envy—Adeline had none;
    Her place was far beyond it, and her mind.
It was not scorn—which could not light on one
    Whose greatest *fault* was leaving few to find.
It was not jealousy, I think: but shun
    Following the "Ignes Fatui" of mankind.
It was not—but 'tis easier far, alas!
To say what it was not, than what it was.

6 [A] Following these "Ignes fatui" of [Mankind]

Little Aurora deem'd she was the theme
    Of such discussion. She was there a guest,
A beauteous ripple of the brilliant stream
    Of rank and youth, though purer than the rest,
Which flow'd on for a moment in the beam
    Time sheds a moment o'er each sparkling crest.
Had she known this, she would have calmly smiled—
She had so much, or little, of the child.

2 discussion[s] . . .
3 A beauteous [billow of] the brilliant stream
4 youth—[and higher] than the rest

56

The dashing and proud air of Adeline
    Imposed not upon her: she saw her blaze
Much as she would have seen a glowworm shine,
    Then turn'd unto the stars for loftier rays.
Juan was something she could not divine,
    Being no Sibyl in the new world's ways;
Yet she was nothing dazzled by the meteor,
Because she did not pin her faith on feature.

2 she [was] her blaze
6 in the [Worldling's] ways
7 [He dazzled but astonished not her sense]

57

His fame too,—for he had that kind of fame
    Which sometimes plays the deuce with womankind,
A heterogeneous mass of glorious blame,
    Half virtues and whole vices being combined;
Faults which attract because they are not tame;
    Follies trick'd out so brightly that they blind:—
These seals upon her wax made no impression,
Such was her coldness or her self-possession.

3　A [sort] heterogeneous . . .
4a　vices [ill] combined
　b　vices [there] . . .
6　Follies [so shiningly] tricked . . .

58

Juan knew nought of such a character—
　　High, yet resembling not his lost Haidée;
Yet each was radiant in her proper sphere:
　　The Island girl, bred up by the lone sea,
More warm, as lovely, and not less sincere,
　　Was Nature's all: Aurora could not be
Nor would be thus;—the difference in them
Was such as lies between a flower and gem.

3a　[Yet] [Each were pure] *fragments*
　b　　　　[Each was a light but of a different] sphere
5　More [kind] warm as [lofty] and not . . .
7　difference [betwixt] them

59

Having wound up with this sublime comparison,
　　Methinks we may proceed upon our narrative,
And, as my friend Scott says, "I sound my Warison";*
　　Scott, the superlative of my comparative*—
Scott, who can paint your Christian knight or Saracen,
　　Serf, Lord, Man, with such skill as none would share
　　　　it, if
There had not been one Shakespeare and Voltaire,
Of one or both of whom he seems the heir.

2　[I thin] Methinks . . .
4　Superlative to . . .
6a　[Scott—of such talent—I could hardly have]
　b　Serf . . . skill that none . . .
8　[Who] [And adds a third to what was late a pair]

I say, in my slight way I may proceed
    To play upon the surface of Humanity.
I write the world, nor care if the world read,
    At least for this I cannot spare its vanity.
My Muse hath bred, and still perhaps may breed
    More foes by this same scroll: when I began it, I
Thought that it might turn out so—*now* I *know* it,*
But still I am, or was, a pretty poet.

No revisions.

61

The conference or congress (for it ended
    As congresses of late do) of the Lady
Adeline and Don Juan rather blended
    Some acids with the sweets—for she was heady;
But, ere the matter could be marr'd or mended,
    The silvery bell rung, not for "dinner ready,"
But for that hour, called *half-hour,* given to dress,
Though ladies' robes seem scant enough for less.*

4 Some acids with the sweets—[for both were] *fragment*

62

Great things were now to be achieved at table,
    With massy plate for armour, knives and forks
For weapons; but what Muse since Homer's able
    (His feasts are not the worst part of his works)
To draw up in array a single day-bill
    Of modern dinners? where more mystery lurks
In soups or sauces, or a sole ragoût,
Than witches, b—ches, or physicians brew.

1 atchieved . . .
2 [On] massy . . .
5 To draw [in tha] array . . . *Intended to write* that.

6 where [such] Mystery lurks
7 In soups and sauces . . .

63

There was a goodly "soupe à la *bonne femme*,"*
    Though God knows whence it came from; there was
        too
A turbot for relief of those who cram,
    Relieved with dindon à la Périgueux;
There also was—the sinner that I am!
    How shall I get this gourmand stanza through?—
Soupe à la Beauveau, whose relief was Dory,
Relieved itself by pork, for greater glory.

4a Relieved [itself by] with Dindon a la Perigueux   B
 b Parigeux   *Misprint in 1824 edition. Later editions vary in their spelling of this name.*
7 [much] whose Relief . . .

64

But I must crowd all into one grand mess
    Or mass; for should I stretch into detail,
My Muse would run much more into excess,
    Than when some squeamish people deem her frail.
But though a "bonne vivante," I must confess
    Her stomach's not her peccant part: this tale
However doth require some slight refection,
Just to relieve her spirits from dejection.

1–3 But I must [huddle] into one grand mess
        Or Mass for should I [run] into detail
        My [list] would run . . .
 5 [I like] *fragment*
 6 Her stomach [it is] not [the] *fragment*
 7 require [small] some . . .

Fowls à la Condé, slices eke of salmon,
  With sauces Genevoises, and haunch of venison;
Wines too which might again have slain young
      Ammon*—
  A man like whom I hope we shan't see many soon;
They also set a glazed Westphalian ham on,
  Whereon Apicius* would bestow his benison;
And then there was Champagne with foaming whirls,
As white as Cleopatra's melted pearls.*†

  4 A man—[whose like]—I hope . . .
  5 Also they set . . .
6–8 Whereon Apicius [had] bestow[ed] his benison
    And then there was Champagne with [creamy curls]
    [In which] Cleopatra [might have] melted pearls

                        66

Then there was God knows what "à l'Allemande,"
  "A l'Espagnole," "timballe," and "Salpicon"—
With things I can't withstand or understand,
    Though swallow'd with much zest upon the whole;
And "entremets" to piddle with at hand,
    Gently to lull down the subsiding soul;†
While great Lucullus' *Robe triumphal* muffles—
(*There's Fame*)—young Partridge fillets,* deck'd with
      truffles.

1 Then there was Heaven knows . . .
4 Though [eaten] with . . .
7a Lucullus [with] robe . . .
 b *The first edition prints* Lucullus' (Rôbe triumphal) muffles.
 c *Some modern editions print* Lucullus' Rome triumphal. . . . *The 1833
   and 1837 editions use the present text.*

What are the *fillets* on the victor's brow
  To these? They are rags or dust. Where is the arch
Which nodded to the nation's spoils below?
  Where the triumphal chariots' haughty march?
Gone to where victories must like dinners go.
  Further I shall not follow the research:
But oh! ye modern heroes with your cartridges,
When will your names lend lustre even to partridges?

1 What were the fillets . . .
2 To these?—they are [were *sic?*] or dust; [what] *fragment*
3*a* [Where all the Pontic spoils made such a show]
 b [Where the proud . . .]
 c [And] Which nodded [over] [Their *sic?*] *fragments*
4 Where the [long glittering] *fragment*
5 Gone—where [Conquests] must like dinners go
7–8 *Order of composition:*
But [think] ye modern Heroes . . .
But [when] Oh! ye . . .
[Will you provide] *fragment*
[Can't you contrive to dress us] *fragment*
[I wish to God you'de dress us some such partridges]
[Your names will] lend [no] lustre even to Partridges
When will your names lend lustre even . . .
        e'en . . . *In 1833 and in later editions.*

Those truffles too are no bad accessaries,
      Follow'd by "Petits puits d'Amour"—a dish
Of which perhaps the cookery rather varies,
      So every one may dress it to his wish,
According to the best of dictionaries,
      Which encyclopedize both flesh and fish;
But even sans "confitures," it no less true is,
      There's pretty picking in those "petits puits."*

4   [Although] [the] [to be prepared *sic?* to] *fragment*
5   According to the best vocabularies
6   Which [name the] *fragment*
7a [Even with] *fragment*;   b comfitures . . . *Misprint in 1824 edition.*
8   [I own a preference for] those "petits puits."

69

The mind is lost in mighty contemplation
      Of intellect expended on two courses;
And indigestion's grand multiplication
      Requires arithmetic beyond my forces.
Who would suppose, from Adam's simple ration,
      That cookery could have call'd forth such resources,
As form a science and a nomenclature
From out the commonest demands of nature?

2 expanded . . . *In 1833 and in later editions.*
6 have [culled *sic?*] such resources

The glasses jingled, and the palates tingled;
 The diners of celebrity dined well;
The ladies with more moderation mingled
 In the feast, pecking less than I can tell;
Also the younger men too; for a springald
 Can't like ripe age in gourmandise excel,
But thinks less of good eating than the whisper
(When seated next him) of some pretty lisper.

5 [for to a] Springald
6a Don't—like ripe . . . B
 b gormandize *In 1833 and in some later editions. Other editions also*
 print gormandise.
8 [Of] (When . . .

71

Alas! I must leave undescribed the gibier,
 The salmi, the consommé, the purée,
All which I use to make my rhymes run glibber
 Than could roast beef in our rough John Bull way:
I must not introduce even a spare rib here,
 "Bubble and squeak"* would spoil my liquid lay;
But I have dined, and must forego, alas!
The chaste description even of a "Bécasse,"*

3a [With which my rhyme would doubtless run much glibber]
 b [Which doubtless for my rhymes look much more glibber]
 c [Which doubtless make my . . .]
4–6 Than [with] Roast Beef in our rough John Bull [way]
  [A Griskin—chop—or even] a spare rib here
  [Would spoil all the delicacy of my] lay
 7 But I have dined—and [have not stre *sic?*] *fragment* *Intended*
  to write strength?

And fruits, and ice, and all that art refines
  From nature for the service of the goût,—
Taste or the *gout*,—pronounce it as inclines
  Your stomach! Ere you dine, the French will do;
But *after*, there are sometimes certain signs
  Which prove plain English truer of the two.
Hast ever *had* the *gout?* I have not had it—
But I may have, and you too, Reader, dread it.

3–4 [Pronounce that word exactly as] inclines
  Your [feelings;—Gout] *fragment*
 6 Which [show] plain . . .

73

The simple olives, best allies of wine,
  Must I pass over in my bill of fare?
I must, although a favourite "plat" of mine
  In Spain, and Lucca, Athens, every where:
On them and bread 'twas oft my luck to dine,
  The grass my table-cloth, in open air,
On Sunium or Hymettus, like Diogenes,*
Of whom half my philosophy the progeny is.

3*a* I must [though they are ancient friends] of mine
 b I must although a favourite [plate] . . .
 5 On them and bread [I've often deigned] to dine

74

Amidst this tumult of fish, flesh, and fowl,
  And vegetables, all in masquerade,
The guests were placed according to their roll,
  But various as the various meats display'd:
Don Juan sat next an "à l'Espagnole"—
  No damsel, but a dish, as hath been said;
But so far like a lady, that 'twas drest
Superbly, and contained a world of zest.

5 Don Juan [opposite] [an] [a l'Espagnole]
6 No Lady but a dish . . .

75

By some odd chance too he was placed between
   Aurora and the Lady Adeline—
A situation difficult, I ween,
   For man therein, with eyes and heart, to dine.
Also the conference which we have seen
   Was not such as to encourage him to shine;
For Adeline, addressing few words to him,
With two transcendant eyes seemed to look through him.

7 addressing [no] words . . .

76

I sometimes almost think that eyes have ears:
   This much is sure, that, out of earshot, things
Are somehow echoed to the pretty dears,
   Of which I can't tell whence their knowledge springs;
Like that same mystic music of the spheres,
   Which no one hears so loudly though it rings.
'Tis wonderful how oft the sex have heard
Long dialogues which pass'd without a word!

1 [Auro] [Aurora] *fragment*
3 [May be remitted] to the pretty dears
4 can't tell [how] their . . .
5 Like that [unheard high] Music . . .
6 [though] [as] it rings

Aurora sat with that indifference
    Which piques a preux Chevalier—as it ought:
Of all offences that's the worst offence,
    Which seems to hint you are not worth a thought.
Now Juan, though no coxcomb in pretence,
    Was not exactly pleased to be so caught:
Like a good ship entangled among ice,
And after so much excellent advice.

7 among an ice
8 After [too,] so much . . .

78

To his gay nothings, nothing was replied,
    Or something which was nothing, as urbanity
Required. Aurora scarcely look'd aside,
    Nor even smiled enough for any vanity.
The devil was in the girl! Could it be pride?
    Or modesty, or absence, or inanity?
Heaven knows! But Adeline's malicious eyes
Sparkled with her successful prophecies,

1 To his [small] nothings . . .
2 [the] Urbanity
5 The devil['s in] the girl . . .

And look'd as much as if to say, "I said it";—
    A kind of triumph I'll not recommend,
Because it sometimes, as I've seen or read it,
    Both in the case of lover and of friend,
Will pique a gentleman, for his own credit,
    To bring what was a jest to a serious end:
For all men prophesy what *is* or *was*,
And hate those who won't let them come to pass.

No revisions.

80

Juan was drawn thus into some attentions,
    Slight but select, and just enough to express,
To females of perspicuous comprehensions,
    That he would rather make them more than less.
Aurora at the last (so history mentions,
    Though probably much less a fact than guess)
So far relax'd her thoughts from their sweet prison,
As once or twice to smile, if not to listen.

2 and [quite] just . . .
3 of [perspective] comprehension
7 relaxed [from] her [smiles] from this sweet prison
8 As once or twice to smile—[if] [and seem] *fragment*

From answering, she began to question: this
    With her was rare; and Adeline, who as yet
Thought her predictions went not much amiss,
    Began to dread she'd thaw to a coquette—
So very difficult, they say, it is
    To keep extremes from meeting, when once set
In motion; but she here too much refined—
Aurora's spirit was not of that kind.

2 Adeline [whose] [began]
3 [Who hitherto had found things not amiss]
5 So very difficult ['twould seem] it is

82

But Juan had a sort of winning way,
    A proud humility, if such there be,
Which show'd such deference to what females say,
    As if each charming word were a decree.
His tact too temper'd him from grave to gay,
    And taught him when to be reserved or free:
He had the art of drawing people out,
Without their seeing what he was about.

1 had a [kind] of . . .
3 what [others] say
6 him [how] to be . . .
7 [According] *fragment*
8 Without perceiving what . . .

Aurora, who in her indifference
  Confounded him in common with the crowd
Of flutterers, though she deem'd he had more sense
  Than whispering foplings, or than witlings loud,—
Commenced* (from such slight things will great
    commence)
  To feel that flattery which attracts the proud
Rather by deference than compliment,
And wins even by a delicate dissent.

1a Aurora [in her cold indifference]
 b Aurora [in her first . . .]
5a–6 [She neither deemed his feelings were intense
     Nor thought he had pride enough—for She was proud]
5b [Be] Commenced . . .
7   than by Compliment
8a [Sweet Soul—she was so very innocent]
 b   [sagely . . .]

84

And then he had good looks;—that point was carried
  Nem. con. amongst the women, which I grieve
To say leads oft to *crim. con.** with the married—
  A case which to the Juries we may leave,
Since with digressions we too long have tarried.
  Now though we know of old that looks deceive,
And always have done, somehow these good looks
Make more impression than the best of books.

4 [Who] A Case . . .
5 we for long . . .
7 these same looks

Aurora, who look'd more on books than faces,
　Was very young, although so very sage,
Admiring more Minerva than the Graces,
　Especially upon a printed page.
But Virtue's self, with all her tightest laces,
　Has not the natural stays of strict old age;
And Socrates, that model of all duty,
Own'd to a penchant, though discreet, for beauty.

4 page[s]
6 of [good] old Age
8 Owned [that] to a . . .

86

And girls of sixteen are thus far Socratic,
　But innocently so, as Socrates:
And really, if the Sage sublime and Attic
　At seventy years had phantasies like these,
Which Plato in his dialogues dramatic
　Has shown, I know not why they should displease
In virgins—always in a modest way,
Observe; for that with me's a "sine quâ."*

6 why [it] should . . .

87

Also observe, that like the great Lord Coke,
　(See Littleton)* whene'er I have expressed
Opinions two, which at first sight may look
　Twin opposites, the second is the best.
Perhaps I have a third too in a nook,
　Or none at all—which seems a sorry jest;
But if a writer should be quite consistent,
How could he possibly show things existent?

2 [On] (See Littleton) [that when] I have exprest
4 [Quite] opposites . . .

88

If people contradict themselves, can I
   Help contradicting them, and every body,
Even my veracious self?—But that's a lie;
   I never did so, never will—how should I?
He who doubts all things, nothing can deny;
   Truth's fountains may be clear—her streams are
      muddy,
And cut through such canals of contradiction,
That she must often navigate o'er fiction.

No revisions.

89

Apologue, fable, poesy, and parable,
   Are false, but may be render'd also true
By those who sow them in a land that's arable.
   'Tis wonderful what fable will not do!
'Tis said it makes reality more bearable:
   But what's reality? Who has its clue?
Philosophy? No; she too much rejects.
Religion? *Yes;* but which of all her sects?

1   [A fable] *fragment*
2a [Are] [Int] *fragment*
 b Are false—but [are they] rendered also true
3   [But] those . . .
5   [They say] it makes . . .
6   But what's reality? [some say 'tis new]
7   [Some old—some past—some present—some to be]

Some millions must be wrong, that's pretty clear:
   Perhaps it may turn out that all were right.
God help us! Since we have need on our career
   To keep our holy beacons always bright,
'Tis time that some new Prophet should appear,
   Or old indulge man with a second sight.
Opinions wear out in some thousand years,
Without a small refreshment from the spheres.

3 have [much] need [on't here]
4 [And these dissentions *sic?* make a sorry sight]
7 [For Creeds could] wear out . . .
8 Without [some refreshment] from . . .

91

But here again, why will I thus entangle
   Myself with metaphysics? None can hate
So much as I do any kind of wrangle;
   And yet, such is my folly, or my fate,
I always knock my head against some angle
   About the present, past, or future state:
Yet I wish well to Trojan and to Tyrian,*
For I was bred a moderate Presbyterian.

1 But—here again—[I'm getting] *fragment*
2 [no one] hate[s]
3 So much as I do [their eternal] wrangle
7–8 *Order of composition:*
   [And what can be the reason? I was bred/A Presbyterian]
   [And what can be the reason I thus weary on
   Such things—Since] I was bred a Presbyterian?
   [Why should] [there is never *sic?*] *fragments*
   Yet I wish well [both] to Trojan and to Tyrian

But though I am a temperate Theologian,
   And also meek as a Metaphysician,
Impartial between Tyrian and Trojan,
   As Eldon on a lunatic commission,*—
In politics my duty is to show John
   Bull something of the lower world's condition.
It makes my blood boil like the springs of Hecla,*
To see men let these scoundrel Sovereigns break law.

This stanza was written crosswise in the margin on the manuscript.

5 duty 'tis to . . .
6 the [actual] world's condition

92a — correction: 93

But politics, and policy, and piety,
   Are topics which I sometimes introduce,
Not only for the sake of their variety,
   But as subservient to a moral use;
Because my business is to *dress* society,
   And stuff with *sage* that very verdant goose.
And now, that we may furnish with some matter all
Tastes, we are going to try the supernatural.

This stanza was written crosswise in the margin on B.

2 Are [matters] which I [merely] introduce
3 of [some] variety
4 [My] *fragment*

And now I will give up all argument;
　And positively henceforth no temptation
Shall "fool me to the top up of my bent";*—
　Yes, I'll begin a thorough reformation.
Indeed I never knew what people meant
　By deeming that my Muse's conversation
Was dangerous;—I think she is as harmless
As some who labour more and yet may charm less.

1　I know not—but give up the Argument

95

Grim reader! did you ever see a ghost?
　No; but you have heard—I understand—be dumb!
And don't regret the time you may have lost,
　For you have got that pleasure still to come:
And do not think I mean to sneer at most
　Of these things, or by ridicule benumb
That source of the sublime and the mysterious:—
For certain reasons, my belief is serious.

1　[Pray reader] did you . . .
7　[that] and the mysterious

Serious? You laugh:—you may; that will I not;
    My smiles must be sincere or not at all.
I say I do believe a haunted spot
    Exists*—and where? That shall I not recall,
Because I'd rather it should be forgot,
    "Shadows the soul of Richard"* may appal.
In short, upon that subject I've some qualms very
Like those of the Philosopher of Malmsbury.*

2   My smiles [are all] sincere—or [none] at all
3   believe [in] haunted Spot
4a [And in the] *fragment*
 b Exists . . . recall   *B, 1833, and later editions.*
 c   recal   *In 1824 edition.*
   The same variant spellings occur in Canto XVI, stanzas 6, 11, and 67.
5   [And I believe that Spirits with] *fragment*

97

The night (I sing by night—sometimes an owl,
    And now and then a nightingale)—is dim,
And the loud shriek of sage Minerva's fowl
    Rattles around me her discordant hymn:
Old portraits from old walls upon me scowl—
    I wish to heaven they would not look so grim;
The dying embers dwindle in the grate—
I think too that I have sate up too late:

1   (I [write] by Night . . .
3   of [wise] Minerva's fowl
5   from [high] walls . . .

And therefore, though 'tis by no means my way
   To rhyme at noon—when I have other things
To think of, if I ever think,—I say
   I feel some chilly midnight shudderings,
And prudently postpone, until mid-day,
   Treating a topic which alas but brings
Shadows;—but you must be in my condition
Before you learn to call this superstition.

1   though [it is] by no . . .
4   some [little] Midnight . . .
5a And [therefore I shall put off to] Mid-day
 b And prudently postpone unto Mid-day

99

Between two worlds life hovers like a star,
   'Twixt night and morn, upon the horizon's verge:
How little do we know that which we are!
   How less what we may be!* The eternal surge
Of time and tide rolls on, and bears afar
   Our bubbles; as the old burst, new emerge,
Lash'd from the foam of ages; while the graves
Of Empires heave but like some passing waves.

*On the last page of B below this stanza Byron wrote "End of Canto 15th,"
the date, "Mh 25th 1823," and his usual signature-symbol.*

1a Between two worlds [I] hover like . . .
 b Between two worlds [Man] hovers . . .
4   How less what [she shall] be! [though] the Eternal Surge
6a Our bubbles—as [they burst—] [and] [the] New emerge
 b Our bubbles—as the old burst [and] New emerge
7   Lashed [by] the foam of Ages—[while] the [Graves]
8   Of Empires [only heave so many] waves

Canto XVI

1

THE antique Persians taught three useful things,
    To draw the bow, to ride, and speak the truth.*
This was the mode of Cyrus, best of kings—
    A mode adopted since by modern youth.
Bows have they, generally with two strings;*
    Horses they ride without remorse or ruth;
At speaking truth perhaps they are less clever,
But draw the long bow* better now than ever.

For the date of publication see p. 456 of this volume.

All manuscript readings are taken from P (Pforzheimer manuscript), Byron's first draft, with the permission of The Carl H. Pforzheimer Library. On the first page of the manuscript above the first stanza is the date, "Mʰ 29ᵗʰ 1823."

No revisions.

The cause of this effect, or this defect,—
　　"For this effect defective comes by cause,"*—
Is what I have not leisure to inspect;
　　But this I must say in my own applause,
Of all the Muses that I recollect,
　　Whate'er may be her follies or her flaws
In some things, mine's beyond all contradiction
The most sincere that ever dealt in fiction.

No revisions.

3

And as she treats all things, and ne'er retreats
　　From any thing, this Epic will contain
A wilderness of the most rare conceits,
　　Which you might elsewhere hope to find in vain.
'Tis true there be some bitters with the sweets,
　　Yet mixed so slightly that you can't complain,
But wonder they so few are, since my tale is
"De rebus cunctis et quibûsdam aliis."*

6 [But] mixed . . .

4

But of all truths which she has told, the most
　　True is that which she is about to tell.
I said it was a story of a ghost—
　　What then? I only know it so befell.
Have you explored the limits of the coast,
　　Where all the dwellers of the earth must dwell?
'Tis time to strike such puny doubters dumb as
The sceptics who would not believe Columbus.

4 befel *In 1824 edition.*

Some people would impose now with authority,
    Turpin's or Monmouth Geoffry's Chronicle;*
Men whose historical superiority
    Is always greatest at a miracle.
But Saint Augustine has the great priority,
    Who bids all men believe the impossible,
Because 'tis so. Who nibble, scribble, quibble, he
Quiets at once with *"quia* impossibile."*

2 [Like] [As] Turpin's . . .
3 [Sages] whose . . .
5 has the grand priority
7–8 *Order of composition:*
  Because [it is so—"quia impossibile"]
  [That quia should keep quiet] *fragment*
  Because [it is so—unto all who nibble—he]
                [all those fools who nibble—he]
  Because tis so—who nibble—scribble—quibble he
  Quiets [with] at once with "quia impossibile"

6

And therefore, mortals, cavil not at all;
    Believe:—if 'tis improbable, you *must;*
And if it is impossible, you *shall:*
    'Tis always best to take things upon trust.
I do not speak profanely, to recall
    Those holier mysteries, which the wise and just
Receive as gospel, and which grow more rooted,
As all truths must, the more they are disputed.

1 And therefore—[cavil not at aught that's said]
5 recall. *See variants for Canto XV, 96, 4.*

I merely mean to say what Johnson said,
 That in the course of some six thousand years,
All nations have believed that from the dead
 A visitant at intervals appears;*
And what is strangest upon this strange head,
 Is, that whatever bar the reason rears
'Gainst such belief, there's something stronger still
In its behalf, let those deny who will.

7a [Against] such belief [the internal Sense is for it]
 b 'Gainst such belief—there something stronger still
8 behalf—[which] let those . . .

8

The dinner and the soirée too were done,
 The supper too discussed, the dames admired,
The banqueteers had dropped off one by one—
 The song was silent, and the dance expired:
The last thin petticoats were vanished, gone
 Like fleecy clouds into the sky retired,
And nothing brighter gleamed through the saloon
Than dying tapers—and the peeping moon.

2a The [feast digested, and] the dames admired
 b The Souper too . . .
5 petticoat [has] vanished, gone

9

The evaporation of a joyous day
 Is like the last glass of champagne, without
The foam which made its virgin bumper gay;
 Or like a system coupled with a doubt;
Or like a soda bottle when its spray
 Has sparkled and let half its spirit out;
Or like a billow left by storms behind,
Without the animation of the wind;

[Canto XVI]

2 Champaigne—[or like]
3 made its [first] [brighter] bumper gay
6 [Is] Has . . . let half the Spirit out
7 Or like a billow [when the Wind has] *fragment*

10

Or like an opiate which brings troubled rest,
 Or none; or like—like nothing that I know
Except itself;—such is the human breast;
 A thing, of which similitudes can show
No real likeness,—like the old Tyrian vest
 Dyed purple, none at present can tell how,
If from a shell-fish or from cochineal.*
So perish every tyrant's robe piece-meal!

2 Or none, [at all] or like . . .
4 A thing whereof Similitudes . . .
6 Dyed purple [no one] at present . . .

11

But next to dressing for a rout or ball,
 Undressing is a woe; our robe de chambre
May sit like that of Nessus* and recall
 Thoughts quite as yellow, but less clear than amber.
Titus exclaimed, "I've lost a day!"* Of all
 The nights and days most people can remember,
(I have had of both, some not to be disdained)
I wish they'd state how many they have gained.

 1 dressing for a [ball, or] rout[e] or ball
3*a*–5 [Sits like a Sedative while we] recall
    [Some] thoughts [it may be not so clear as] amber
    Titus [cried out] "Ive lost a day;"—of all
 3*b* recall *See variants for Canto XV, 96, 4.*
 7 [And] I have had [some] of . . .

And Juan, on retiring for the night,
  Felt restless, and perplexed, and compromised;
He thought Aurora Raby's eyes more bright
  Than Adeline (such is advice) advised;
If he had known exactly his own plight,
  He probably would have philosophised;
A great resource to all, and ne'er denied
Till wanted; therefore Juan only sighed.

6 philosophized

13

He sighed;—the next resource is the full moon,
  Where all sighs are deposited; and now
It happened luckily, the chaste orb shone
  As clear as such a climate will allow;
And Juan's mind was in the proper tone
  To hail her with the apostrophe—"Oh, Thou!"
Of amatory egotism the *Tuism,**
Which further to explain would be a truism.

2 and [then] now

14

But lover, poet, or astronomer,
  Shepherd, or swain, whoever may behold,
Feel some abstraction when they gaze on her:
  Great thoughts we catch from thence (besides a cold
Sometimes, unless my feelings rather err);
  Deep secrets to her rolling light are told;
The ocean's tides and mortal's brains she sways,
And also hearts, if there be truth in lays.

5 my [Mem] feelings . . .   *Intended to write* Memory.
7 and mortal brains . . .

Juan felt somewhat pensive, and disposed
　For contemplation rather than his pillow:
The Gothic chamber, where he was enclosed,
　Let in the rippling sound of the lake's billow,
With all the mystery by midnight caused;
　Below his window waved (of course) a willow;
And he stood gazing out on the cascade
That flashed and after darkened in the shade.

1　Juan felt somewhat [feverish and disposed]
5　With all the [mystic sound] by Midnight caused

16

Upon his table or his toilet,*—*which*
　Of these is not exactly ascertained—
(I state this, for I am cautious to a pitch
　Of nicety, where a fact is to be gained)
A lamp burned high, while he leant from a niche,
　Where many a gothic ornament remained,
In chiselled stone and painted glass, and all
That time has left our fathers of their Hall.

3–4　I state this (for I [pique myself] to a pitch
　　　Of nicety—where a fact [can be ob] *fragment Intended to write*
　　　obtained.
　5　burnt . . .
　7　In [stone carv] chiselled . . . glass [which] and all

Then, as the night was clear though cold, he threw
  His chamber door wide open—and went forth
Into a gallery, of a sombre hue,
  Long, furnished with old pictures of great worth,
Of knights and dames heroic and chaste too,
  As doubtless should be people of high birth.
But by dim lights the portraits of the dead
Have something ghastly, desolate, and dread.

1 [And] as . . .
7 [And in the Night] *fragment*
8 ghastly, [of dismay] and dread

18

The forms of the grim knight and pictured saint
  Look living in the moon; and as you turn
Backward and forward to the echoes faint
  Of your own footsteps—voices from the urn
Appear to wake, and shadows wild and quaint
  Start from the frames which fence their aspects stern,
As if to ask how you can dare to keep
A vigil there, where all but death should sleep.

1*a* The frowns of grim Knight[s] or [of] pictured Saint[s]
  b knights . . . saints *In 1824 edition. Since the "s" is clearly deleted*
     on the manuscript, Mary Shelley probably erred in copying. Byron
     did not read proof on this canto; he probably would have caught the
     rhyming error.
2*a* Look living in the Moon [and you expect]
  b   [till you might deem]
  3 [Some] [From your own footsteps' echo] *fragments*
6–7 *Order of composition:*
     [Steal from the walls till you almost discern
     Some portrait starting from his frame] *fragment*
     Start from the [walls] [in] [all] [stately steps and stern]
                         [with . . .]
     As if to ask [what] [then durst] [these] *fragment*

And the pale smile of Beauties in the grave,
    The charms of other days, in starlight gleams
Glimmer on high; their buried locks still wave
    Along the canvas; their eyes glance like dreams
On ours, or spars within some dusky cave,*
    But death is imaged in their shadowy beams.
A picture is the past; even ere its frame
Be gilt, who sate hath ceased to be the same.

8*a* Be [finished—they who sate—are not] the same
 b Be gilt; [the sitter] who sate hath . . .

20

As Juan mused on mutability,
    Or on his mistress—terms synonimous—
No sound except the echo of his sigh
    Or step ran sadly through that antique house,
When suddenly he heard, or thought so, nigh,
    A supernatural agent—or a mouse,
Whose little nibbling rustle will embarrass
Most people as it plays along the arras.

2*a* synonimous P; *b* synonymous *In 1833 and in later editions.*
6   A supernatural [rustle] or a Mouse
7   [He turned his eyes—perhaps with e] *fragment*

It was no mouse, but lo! a monk,* arrayed
  In cowl and beads and dusky garb, appeared,
Now in the moonlight, and now lapsed in shade,
  With steps that trod as heavy, yet unheard;
His garments only a slight murmur made;
  He moved as shadowy as the sisters weird,*
But slowly; and as he passed Juan by,
Glanced, without pausing, on him a bright eye.

2 In cowl and beads and [garb monastic] appeared
3 and now [los] lapsed in shade *Intended to write* lost?
4 steps that [seemed] as heavy . . .
8 [Turned] Glanced . . .

22

Juan was petrified; he had heard a hint
  Of such a spirit in these halls of old,
But thought, like most men, there was nothing in't
  Beyond the rumour which such spots unfold,
Coined from surviving superstition's mint,
  Which passes ghosts in currency like gold,
But rarely seen, like gold compared with paper.
And *did* he see this? or was it a vapour?

1a he had heard [some rumours]
 b he had heard [some] hint[s]
7 But [seldom] seen . . .

23

Once, twice, thrice passed, repassed—the thing of air,
  Or earth beneath, or heaven, or t'other place;
And Juan gazed upon it with a stare,
  Yet could not speak or move; but, on its base
As stands a statue, stood: he felt his hair
  Twine like a knot of snakes around his face;

He taxed his tongue for words, which were not granted,
To ask the reverend person what he wanted.

4 But could . . . on [his] base
5 [Stood like a Statue—and] he felt his hair
7–8 He taxed his tongue [to ask—but twas not] granted
[The reverend Gentlemen what twas] he wanted

24

The third time, after a still longer pause,
    The shadow passed away—but where? the hall
Was long, and thus far there was no great cause
    To think his vanishing unnatural:
Doors there were many, through which, by the laws
    Of physics, bodies whether short or tall
Might come or go; but Juan could not state
Through which the spectre seemed to evaporate.

3 thus [much] there . . .
4 vanishing [not] unnatural

25

He stood—how long he knew not, but it seemed
    An age,—expectant, powerless, with his eyes
Strained on the spot where first the figure gleamed;
    Then by degrees recalled his energies,
And would have passed the whole off as a dream,
    But could not wake; he was, he did surmise,
Waking already, and returned at length
Back to his chamber, shorn of half his strength.

3 Strained [to] on the spot whence first . . .

All there was as he left it: still his taper
    Burnt, and not *blue*, as modest tapers use,
Receiving sprites with sympathetic vapour;*
    He rubbed his eyes, and they did not refuse
Their office; he took up an old newspaper;
    The paper was right easy to peruse;
He read an article the king attacking,
And a long eulogy of "Patent Blacking."*

3 Receiving [Ghosts] with . . .
7 [He read] [The proof] *fragments*

27

This savoured of this world; but his hand shook—
    He shut his door, and after having read
A paragraph, I think about Horne Tooke,*
    Undrest, and rather slowly went to bed.
There couched all snugly on his pillow's nook,
    With what he had seen his phantasy he fed,
And though it was no opiate, slumber crept
Upon him by degrees, and so he slept.

4 slowly [and] went . . .

28

He woke betimes; and, as may be supposed,
    Pondered upon his visitant or vision,
And whether it ought not to be disclosed,
    At risk of being quizzed for superstition.
The more he thought, the more his mind was posed;
    In the mean time, his valet, whose precision
Was great, because his master brooked no less,
Knocked to inform him it was time to dress.

1 He woke [next morn]—and as . . .
7 Was [in proportion] *fragment*

He dressed; and like young people, he was wont
 To take some trouble with his toilet, but
This morning rather spent less time upon't;
 Aside his very mirror soon was put;
His curls fell negligently o'er his front,
 His clothes were not curbed to their usual cut,
His very neckcloth's Gordian knot was tied
Almost an hair's breadth too much on one side.

2 some [pains upon] his toilet . . .
4 soon [aside] was put
6 His cloathes [not settled] to . . .
8a [More rapidly] *fragment*; *b* Almost a hair's . . .

30

And when he walked down into the saloon,
 He sate him pensive o'er a dish of tea,
Which he perhaps had not discovered soon,
 Had it not happened scalding hot to be,
Which made him have recourse unto his spoon;
 So much distrait he was, that all could see
That something *was* the matter—Adeline
The first—but *what* she could not well divine.

2 He sate [down] pensive . . .

She looked, and saw him pale, and turned as pale
   Herself; then hastily looked down, and muttered
Something, but what's not stated in my tale.
   Lord Henry said, his muffin was ill buttered;
The Duchess of Fitz-Fulke played with her veil,
   And looked at Juan hard, but nothing uttered.
Aurora Raby, with her large dark eyes,
Surveyed him with a kind of calm surprise.

3 Something, [to Henry] but what [is] not [said] . . .

32

But seeing him all cold and silent still,
   And every body wondering more or less,
Fair Adeline enquired, "If he were ill?"
   He started, and said, "Yes—no—rather—yes."
The family physician had great skill,
   And being present, now began to express
His readiness to feel his pulse and tell
The cause, but Juan said, "He was quite well."

5 [Our] family . . .
7 His readiness to [practise] *fragment*

33

"Quite well; yes; no."—These answers were mysterious,
   And yet his looks appeared to sanction both,
However they might savour of delirious;
   Something like illness of a sudden growth
Weighed on his spirit, though by no means serious.
   But for the rest, as he himself seemed loth
To state the case, it might be ta'en for granted
It was not the physician that he wanted.

3a [His malady of Spirit seemed more serious]
 b However [contradictory or] delirious

[514]

6   rest [though] he [seemed very loth]
7   To state the [symptoms] it might . . .

34

Lord Henry, who had now discussed his chocolate,
   Also the muffin whereof he complained,
Said, Juan had not got his usual look elate,
   At which he marvelled, since it had not rained;
Then asked her Grace what news were of the Duke of
     late?
   Her Grace replied, *his* Grace was rather pained
With some slight, light, hereditary twinges
Of gout, which rusts aristocratic hinges.

3   [Remarked that] Juan had [a different look of late]
5   her Grace [if she] what news [came from] the Duke . . .
7   slight [twinges] light . . .

35

Then Henry turned to Juan and addressed
   A few words of condolence on his state:
"You look," quoth he, "as if you had had your rest
   Broke in upon by the Black Friar of late."
"What Friar?" said Juan; and he did his best
   To put the question with an air sedate,
Or careless; but the effort was not valid
To hinder him from growing still more pallid.

5   Juan; [as] he . . .
7   but [if] the . . .

"Oh! have you never heard of the Black Friar?
        The spirit of these walls?"—"In truth not I."
"Why Fame—but Fame you know's sometimes a liar—
        Tells an odd story, of which by the bye:
Whether with time the spectre has grown shyer,
        Or that our sires had a more gifted eye
For such sights, though the tale is half believed,
The Friar of late has not been oft perceived.

4*a* by the bye   P;   *b* by and by   *In 1833 and in later editions.*
5   Whether of late the Spectre . . .
6   Or that [we are] *fragment*
7–8   *Order of composition:*
    [To see] such sights—[has not been seen of late]
                        [has not been of late descried]
                                                [perceived]
    [So often—though the thing is half believed]

37

"The last time was—" "I pray," said Adeline,—
        (Who watched the changes of Don Juan's brow,
And from its context thought she could divine
        Connections stronger than he chose to avow
With this same legend)—"if you but design
        To jest, you'll choose some other theme just now,
Because the present tale has oft been told,
And is not much improved by growing old."

2 Don Juan's [face]
3 [You will not] *fragment*
6 To jest—to choose another theme . . .
7 Because the present['s rather old] *fragment*

"Jest!" quoth Milor, "Why, Adeline, you know
    That we ourselves—'twas in the Honey Moon—
Saw—" "Well, no matter, 'twas so long ago;
    But, come, I'll set your story to a tune."
Graceful as Dian when she draws her bow,
    She seized her harp, whose strings were kindled soon
As touched, and plaintively began to play
The air of " 'Twas a Friar of Orders Grey."

4   [Come Henry] [shall] [I must play to you] a tune
5–8 *Canceled first draft:*
    [With that she rose as graceful as a Roe
    Or Antelope]—or—[if you like] *fragment*
    [With that she rose and glided off as Snow
    Slips from the Mountain in the month of June
    And opening her Piano gan to play
        [standing] *fragment*
    Forthwith—"it was a Friar of orders Gray]
8*b* The [ballad—] "Twas a Friar . . .

39

"But add the words," cried Henry, "which you made;
    For Adeline is half a poetess,"
Turning round to the rest, he smiling said.
    Of course the others could not but express
In courtesy their wish to see displayed
    By one *three* talents, for there were no less—
The voice, the words, the harper's skill, at once
Could hardly be united by a dunce.

1   But add the words [said] Henry which [were]
4   [The] Of course . . .
6*a* [At once] *fragment*
 b Three talents [in a single she] no less
7   the words, the [Music] Harper's . . .

After some fascinating hesitation,—
   The charming of these charmers, who seem bound,
I can't tell why, to this dissimulation,—
   Fair Adeline, with eyes fixed on the ground
At first, then kindling into animation,
   Added her sweet voice to the lyric sound,
And sang with much simplicity,—a merit
Not the less precious, that we seldom hear it.

7 And sung . . .

1

Beware! beware! of the Black Friar,
   Who sitteth by Norman stone,
For he mutters his prayer in the midnight air,
   And his mass of the days that are gone.
When the Lord of the Hill, Amundeville,
   Made Norman Church his prey,
And expelled the friars, one friar still
   Would not be driven away.

1 the [Gr] Black Friar   *Intended to write* Gray?
4 Mass [for] of . . .

2

Though he came in his might, with King Henry's right,
   To turn church lands to lay,
With sword in hand, and torch to light
   Their walls, if they said nay,
A monk remained, unchased, unchained,
   And he did not seem formed of clay,
For he's seen in the porch, and he's seen in the church,
   Though he is not seen by day.

5a A Monk remained [and could not be] chained
 b   unchased and unchained

And whether for good, or whether for ill,
   It is not mine to say;
But still to the house of Amundeville
   He abideth night and day.
By the marriage bed of their lords, 'tis said,
   He flits on the bridal eve;
And 'tis held as faith, to their bed of death,
   He comes—but not to grieve.

3 still by the House . . .
7 [By their bed of death—he receives their] *fragment*
Byron probably intended to finish this line with the word breath.

4

When an heir is born, he is heard to mourn,
   And when aught is to befall
That ancient line, in the pale moonshine
   He walks from hall to hall.
His form you may trace, but not his face,
   'Tis shadowed by his cowl;
But his eyes may be seen from the folds between,
   And they seem of a parted soul.

1*a* he is heard . . . P; *b* he's heard . . . *In 1833 and in later editions.*
2 And when [is] aught is . . .
3 [Of] That . . .
5 [He] His . . .
7 seen [thro] from . . .

But beware! beware! of the Black Friar,
 He still retains his sway,
For he is yet the church's heir
 Who ever may be the lay.
Amundeville is lord by day,
 But the monk is lord by night.
Nor wine nor wassail could raise a vassal
 To question that friar's right.

3 is [still] the . . .
7 [And there is not a Vassal—whom Wine or Wassail]

6

Say nought to him as he walks the hall,
 And he'll say nought to you;
He sweeps along in his dusky pall,
 As o'er the grass the dew.
Then Grammercy! for the Black Friar;
 Heaven sain him! fair or foul,
And whatsoe'er may be his prayer,
 Let ours be for his soul.

This stanza is written in the margin of the manuscript.
6 Heaven sain him! [and us all]

The lady's voice ceased, and the thrilling wires
   Died from the touch that kindled them to sound;
And the pause followed, which when song expires,
   Pervades a moment those who listen round;
And then of course the circle much admires,
   Nor less applauds as in politeness bound,
The tones, the feeling, and the execution,
To the performer's diffident confusion.

2 kindled [it] to sound
6 [And] Nor . . .

42

Fair Adeline, though in a careless way,
   As if she rated such accomplishment
As the mere pastime of an idle day,
   Pursued an instant for her own content,
Would now and then as 'twere *without* display,
   Yet *with* display in fact, at times relent
To such performances with haughty smile,
To show she *could*, if it were worth her while.

3 mere pastime[s] . . .
5 and then [display] as twere . . .

Now this (but we will whisper it aside)
   Was—pardon the pedantic illustration—
Trampling on Plato's pride with greater pride,
   As did the Cynic on some like occasion;
Deeming the sage would be much mortified,
   Or thrown into a philosophic passion,
For a spoilt carpet—but the "Attic Bee"*
Was much consoled by his own repartee.

1a will [scribble] this aside
  b will [write down] this aside
2   Was—pardon the [pardon] . . .
4a Cynic on some [smart] occasion; b fit occasion
6   [To have his Carpet spoilt, but] *fragment*
7   [To have his Carpet spoilt] *fragment*

44

Thus Adeline would throw into the shade,
   (By doing easily whene'er she chose,
What dilettanti do with vast parade)
   Their sort of *half profession:* for it grows
To something like this when too oft displayed,
   And that it is so, every body knows,
Who have heard Miss That or This, or Lady T'other,
Show off—to please their company or mother.

2–4 [The pride of dilettanti—when] she chose
      [By doing what they made—if not a trade
      At least a] half-profession—for [when those]
  7a Miss That—[Sir] This, or . . .
    b Miss That—and This . . .

Oh! the long evenings of duets and trios!
    The admirations and the speculations;
The "Mamma Mia's!" and the "Amor Mio's!"
    The "Tanti palpiti's" on such occasions:
The "Lasciami's," and quavering "Addio's!"*
    Amongst our own most musical of nations;
With "Tu mi chamas's" from Portingale,*
To soothe our ears, lest Italy should fail.*

5 quavering [O Dios!"]
7 [The] "Tu mi chiamas's . . .

46

In Babylon's bravuras—as the home
    Heart-ballads of Green Erin or Grey Highlands,
That brings Lochaber back to eyes that roam*
    O'er far Atlantic continents or islands,
The calentures of music which o'ercome
    All mountaineers with dreams* that they are nigh
        lands,
No more to be beheld but in such visions,—
Was Adeline well versed, as compositions.

1a–2a [From] Babylon's Bravuras;—[to the simple/Home] ballads . . .
1b–2b In Babylon's Bravuras; [and] the home/Heart['s] ballads . . .
    4 continents [oer] Islands
    5 [Was Adeline] *fragment*
    6 are [near] nigh lands

She also had a twilight tinge of *"Blue,"*
  Could write rhymes, and compose more than she
    wrote;
Made epigrams occasionally too
  Upon her friends, as every body ought.
But still from that sublimer azure hue,
  So much the present dye,* she was remote,
Was weak enough to deem Pope a great poet,
And what was worse, was not ashamed to show it.

5 But still [was far] from . . .
8 And what was worse [cared little who might] *fragment*

Aurora—since we are touching upon taste,
  Which now-a-days is the thermometer
By whose degrees all characters are classed—
  Was more Shakespearian, if I do not err.
The worlds beyond this world's perplexing waste
  Had more of her existence, for in her
There was a depth of feeling to embrace
Thoughts, boundless, deep, but silent too as Space.

3   By [which] whose . . . are [placed]
8*a* [As deep as] *fragment*
  b Thoughts—[deep] boundless—deep . . .

Not so her gracious, graceful, graceless Grace,
  The full grown Hebe* of Fitz-Fulke, whose mind,
If she had any, was upon her face,
  And that was of a fascinating kind.
A little turn for mischief you might trace
  Also thereon,—but that's not much; we find
Few females without some such gentle leaven,
For fear we should suppose us quite in heaven.

6 but['s] that's . . .

50

I have not heard she was at all poetic,
  Though once she was seen reading the "Bath Guide,"
And "Hayley's Triumphs,"* which she deemed pathetic,
  Because, she said, *her temper* had been tried
So much, the bard had really been prophetic
  Of what she had gone through with,—since a bride.
But of all verse, what most insured her praise
Were sonnets to herself, or "Bouts rimés."*

1   heard [that] she . . .
5*a* [But of all Verse from Epic] *fragment*
  b So much, [that such a] bard [must] be prophetic
7   But of all [verse she most inclined] *fragment*

'Twere difficult to say what was the object
    Of Adeline, in bringing this same lay
To bear on what appeared to her the subject
    Of Juan's nervous feelings on that day.
Perhaps she merely had the simple project
    To laugh him out of his supposed dismay;
Perhaps she might wish to confirm him in it,
Though why I cannot say—at least this minute.

1 was the [Scope]
3 To bear on [th] what to her appeared the Subject
4 nervous [man] feelings . . . *Intended to write* manner.
5 Perhaps she [simply] had . . .
6 his [presumed] dismay

52

But so far the immediate effect
    Was to restore him to his self propriety,
A thing quite necessary to the elect,
    Who wish to take the tone of their society:
In which you cannot be too circumspect,
    Whether the mode be persiflage or piety,
But wear the newest mantle of hypocrisy,
On pain of much displeasing the Gynocrasy.*

4 tone of [good] Society

53

And therefore Juan now began to rally
    His spirits, and without more explanation,
To jest upon such themes in many a sally.
    Her Grace too also seized the same occasion,
With various similar remarks to tally,
    But wished for a still more detailed narration

> Of this same mystic Friar's curious doings,
> About the present family's deaths and wooings.

2 and [to] without . . .

54

> Of these few could say more than has been said;
>   They passed as such things do, for superstition
> With some, while others, who had more in dread
>   The theme, half credited the strange tradition;
> And much was talked on all sides on that head;
>   But Juan, when cross-questioned on the vision,
> Which some supposed (though he had not avowed it)
> Had stirred him, answered in a way to cloud it.

2 as Superstition
3 who held more in dread
4 The [dream]—half credited . . .
8 Had [caused his nerves—made answers rather clouded]

55

> And then, the mid-day having worn to one,
>   The company prepared to separate;
> Some to their several pastimes, or to none,
>   Some wondering 'twas so early, some so late.
> There was a goodly match too, to be run
>   Between some greyhounds on my Lord's estate,
> And a young race-horse of old pedigree,
> Matched for the spring,* whom several went to see.

2 The Company [began] to separate
7 And a [race] young . . .

[527]

There was a picture dealer who had brought
    A special Titian, warranted original,
So precious that it was not to be bought,
    Though princes the possessor were besieging all.
The king himself had cheapened it, but thought
    The Civil List (he deigns to accept,* obliging all
His subjects by his gracious acceptation)
Too scanty, in these times of low taxation.

6 The Civil list [too scanty] *fragment*
8 Too scanty, [to buy]—in times . . .

57

But as Lord Henry was a connoisseur,—
    The friend of artists, if not arts,—the owner,
With motives the most classical and pure,
    So that he would have been the very donor,
Rather than seller, had his wants been fewer,
    So much he deemed his patronage an honour,
Had brought the Capo d'opera,* not for sale,
But for his judgment,—never known to fail.

4 So [much] he would . . .
7 Had brought this Copo d'Opera . . .
8 But [merely as a Critical regale]

There was a modern Goth,* I mean a Gothic
  Bricklayer of Babel, called an architect,
Brought to survey these grey walls, which though so
    thick,
  Might have from time acquired some slight defect;
Who, after rummaging the Abbey through thick
  And thin, produced a plan whereby to erect
New buildings of correctest conformation,
And throw down old, which he called *restoration*.

2   [Thrower down of buildings]—called an Architect
3   these [old] walls . . .
6a a plan [whence] to erect
 b a plan [wherewith] . . .
7a New buildings—[wings—and with fitting] *fragment*
 b New buildings—[wings] [with] [in wondrous *sic?* conformation]
 c New buildings of the best delineation
8   [Which all] *fragment*

59

The cost would be a trifle—an "old song"*
  Set to some thousands ('tis the usual burthen
Of that same tune, when people hum it long)—
  The price would speedily repay its worth in
An edifice no less sublime than strong,
  By which Lord Henry's good taste would go forth in
Its glory, through all ages shining sunny,
For Gothic daring shown in English money.*

2 [Sung] to [some] thousands . . .
3 Of that same [Song] when people [sing] it long)
4 speedily [pay back] it's worth in
6 Through which Lord Henry's [Glory] would . . .
7 [In all it's] Glory *fragment*
8 For [Roman *sic?*] daring . . .

There were two lawyers busy on a mortgage
　　Lord Henry wished to raise for a new purchase;
Also a lawsuit upon tenures burgage,*
　　And one on tithes, which sure are Discord's torches,
Kindling Religion till she throws down *her* gage,
　　"Untying" squires "to fight against the churches";*
There was a prize ox, a prize pig, and ploughman,
For Henry was a sort of Sabine showman.*

1　There were two lawyers [wh] [call] *fragment*
5　[Firing the Counties till they impious war wage]

61

There were two poachers caught in a steel trap
　　Ready for jail, their place of convalescence;
There was a country girl in a close cap
　　And scarlet cloak (I hate the sight to see, since—
Since—since—in youth, I had the sad mishap*—
　　But luckily I have paid few parish fees since)
That scarlet cloak, alas! unclosed with Rigour,
Presents the problem of a double figure.

2　Ready [to be committed for their] *fragment*
3　Girl in a [mob] cap
7　That Scarlet Cloak—[God help us—when close wrapped]
　　　　　　　　　　Alas! [wrapped round]
8　[Displays] the problem . . .

Marginal jottings: "Mem: Steel traps Pith Poachers Woman Scarlet Cks Public Day Electioneering Interest." *Most of these jottings Byron utilized in the canto.*

A reel within a bottle is a mystery,
    One can't tell how it e'er got in or out,
Therefore the present piece of natural history,
    I leave to those who are fond of solving doubt,
And merely state, though not for the consistory,*
    Lord Henry was a justice, and that Scout
The constable, beneath a warrant's banner,
Had bagged this poacher upon Nature's manor.

6 [That] Henry was . . .

63

Now Justices of Peace must judge all pieces
    Of mischief of all kinds, and keep the game
And morals of the country from caprices
    Of those who have not a licence for the same;
And of all things, excepting tithes and leases,
    Perhaps these are most difficult to tame:
Preserving partridges and pretty wenches
Are puzzles to the most precautious benches.

1 judge[s] of pieces
2 keep [all] game
4 Of [people who] [all unqualified to take] the same
7 [Few thing] *fragment*

The present culprit was extremely pale,
    Pale as if painted so; her cheek being red
By nature, as in higher dames less hale
    'Tis white, at least when they just rise from bed.
Perhaps she was ashamed of seeming frail,
    Poor soul! for she was country born and bred,
And knew no better in her immorality
Than to wax white—for blushes are for quality.

1 Culprit—was [rather pale]
2a [Poor Soul] *fragment*
 b Pale—as . . . cheek [was] red
3 in [Dames] higher dames . . .
6 for she [has] was . . . .
7 And knew no better, [than to] *fragment*

65

Her black, bright, downcast, yet espiegle eye,*
    Had gathered a large tear into its corner,
Which the poor thing at times essayed to dry,
    For she was not a sentimental mourner,
Parading all her sensibility,
    Nor insolent enough to scorn the scorner,
But stood in trembling, patient tribulation,
To be called up for her examination.

1 bright—[and at times] espiegle eye
5 Parading [with] all . . .
7 But stood—[though patient] *fragment*

Of course these groups were scattered here and there,
   Not nigh the gay saloon of ladies gent.*
The lawyers in the study; and in air
   The prize pig, ploughman, poachers; the men sent
From town, viz. architect and dealer, were
   Both busy (as a general in his tent
Writing dispatches) in their several stations,
Exulting in their brilliant lucubrations.

1 groupes—were [not] scattered . . .
2 Not [in] the gay . . .
4 The prize Pigs—Plouchman . . .
5 From town—the Architect . . .
6 [Each] busy . . .
7 their separate stations
8 [Each busy with his] brilliant [avocations]

67

But this poor girl was left in the great hall,
   While Scout, the parish guardian of the frail,
Discussed (he hated beer yclept the "small")
   A mighty mug of *moral* double ale:
She waited until Justice could recall
   Its kind attentions to their proper pale,
To name a thing in nomenclature rather
Perplexing for most virgins—a child's father.

5 recall *See variants for Canto XV, 96, 4.*
7 To name—[what passes for a puzzle] rather
8 [Although there must be such a thing—a] father

You see here was enough of occupation
    For the Lord Henry, linked with dogs and horses.
There was much bustle too and preparation
    Below stairs on the score of second courses,
Because, as suits their rank and situation,
    Those who in counties have great land resources,
Have "public days," when all men may carouse,
Though not exactly what's called "open house."

2   Henry—[what] with . . .
5a Because [lik] as [in] [the] [a house of highest station]
 b Because as suits their [residence and station]
6a Those who [have Borough] Interest—[call] their forces
 b Those who in County Interest try their forces
7   Have [certain] days—[called public] *fragment*

69

But once a week or fortnight, *un*invited
    (Thus we translate a *general invitation*)
All country gentlemen, esquired or knighted,
    May drop in without cards, and take their station
At the full board, and sit alike delighted
    With fashionable wines and conversation;
And as the Isthmus of the grand connection,
Talk o'er themselves, the past and next election.

4 without Cards [or hesitation]
5 and [be] alike . . .

70

Lord Henry was a great electioneerer,
    Burrowing for boroughs like a rat or rabbit.
But county contests cost him rather dearer,
    Because the neighbouring Scotch Earl of Giftgabbit
Had English influence, in the self-same sphere here;
    His son, the Honourable Dick Dicedrabbit,

Was member for the "other Interest" (meaning
The same self-interest, with a different leaning).

2 [And had more] boroughs [than] a Rat or Rabbit
5 [Was very active] in the self . . .

71

Courteous and cautious therefore in his county,
    He was all things to all men, and dispensed
To some civility, to others bounty,
    And promises to all—which last commenced
To gather to a somewhat large amount, he
    Not calculating how much they condensed;
But what with keeping some, and breaking others,
His word had the same value as another's.

5 To gather somewhat to a large amount he
6 Not [having] calculat[ed] how much . . .

72

A friend to freedom and freeholders—yet
    No less a friend to government—he held,
That he exactly the just medium hit
    'Twixt place and patriotism—albeit compelled,
Such was his Sovereign's pleasure (though unfit,
    He added modestly, when rebels railed)
To hold some sinecures he wished abolished,
But that with them all law would be demolished.

1 to Freeholds—yet
2 a friend to [King and Court] he held
4 [Bet] 'Twixt place and patriotism—[although]·compelled   *Intended*
   to write Betwixt?
6 He [always] added modestly when voters railed

He was "free to confess"*—(whence comes this phrase?
    Is't English? No—'tis only parliamentary)
That innovation's spirit now-a-days
    Had made more progress than for the last century.
He would not tread a factious path to praise,
    Though for the public weal disposed to venture high;
As for his place, he could but say this of it,
That the fatigue was greater than the profit.

1 whence came this phrase?
2 Is [it] English? No—[but] only . . .
6 [Yet was as independent] *fragment*

74

Heaven, and his friends, knew that a private life
    Had ever been his sole and whole ambition;
But could he quit his king in times of strife
    Which threatened the whole country with perdition?
When demagogues would with a butcher's knife
    Cut through and through (oh! damnable incision!)
The Gordian or the Geordi-an knot, whose strings
Have tied together Commons, Lords, and Kings.

6*a* Cut [all] [the Gordian knots with one incision]
  b   [links with rash incision]
  c   [knot . . .]
7   [Which tied in one firm knot without confusion]
8*a* [The glorious—free—and happy Constitution]
  b [The three strings of our happy Constitution]

75

Sooner "come place into the civil list
    And champion him to the utmost"*—he would keep it,
Till duly disappointed or dismissed:
    Profit he cared not for, let others reap it;

But should the day come when place ceased to exist,
    The country would have far more cause to weep it;
For how could it go on? Explain who can!
He gloried in the name of Englishman.

1   Sooner [than that]—"Come Place into the list
5*a* But—[if the day should come]—when Place *fragment*
 b But—should the day come—[place] ceased to exist
6*a* The Country [not the] *fragment*
 b The Country would have the most cause to weep it
7   For how would it . . .

76

He was as independent—aye, much more—
    Than those who were not paid for independence,
As common soldiers, or a common—Shore,
    Have in their several arts or parts ascendence
O'er the irregulars in lust or gore,
    Who do not give professional attendance.
Thus on the mob all statesmen are as eager
To prove their pride, as footmen to a beggar.

2   Than [so] those . . .
3*a* [Just as a Bishop is] *fragment*
 b [Just as a regular common soldier or a w—re]
4*a* [Excuse both] [prostitutes] [words] *fragment* P
 b Have in their [two professions an] ascendance P
 c   [same asc] *fragment* P
 d ascendance   *In 1833 and in later editions.*
5*a* [Oer the Volunteers—on either score]
 b Over irregulars . . .
7*a* [And thus a hackney Statesman] *fragment*
 b [Say Constitution stead of prostitution]
 c [And] [St] [rogue for wh] *fragment* *Intended to write* Statesman,
    whore?
 d [And] Thus [oer] the Mob [or Statesman is as] eager
 e   [to] . . .
8*a* To prove [this] pride—as footmen [oer a] beggar
 b   [to] oer a beggar

[537]

All this (save the last stanza) Henry said,
    And thought. I say no more—I've said too much;
For all of us have either heard or read—
    Off—or *upon* the hustings—some slight such
Hints from the independent heart or head
    Of the official candidate. I'll touch
No more on this—the dinner bell hath rung,
And grace is said; the grace I *should* have *sung**—

4a Of—or upon—[some] Hustings . . .   P
 b Of—or upon . . .   *In 1824 edition.*
 c Off . . .   *In 1833 and in later editions.*
5a [Outline of an harangue—but I'll to bed]
 b Hints . . . heart and head

78

But I'm too late, and therefore must make play.
    'Twas a great banquet, such as Albion old
Was wont to boast—as if a glutton's tray
    Were something very glorious to behold.
But 'twas a public feast and public day,—
    Quite full, right dull, guests hot, and dishes cold,
Great plenty, much formality, small cheer,
And every body out of their own sphere.

3a Was won't to [vaunt—but why I cannot say]
 b Was won't to boast [in many a] as if a glutton's tray
6   [D—ned] full [d—ned] dull . . .
7   Great plenty—[sm] much . . .

79

The squires familiarly formal, and
    My lords and ladies proudly condescending;
The very servants puzzling how to hand
    Their plates—without it might be too much bending

From their high places by the sideboard's stand—
    Yet like their masters fearful of offending.
For any deviation from the graces
    Might cost both men and master too—their *places*.

6 [And] Yet . . .

80

There were some hunters bold, and coursers keen,
    Whose hounds ne'er erred, nor greyhounds deigned
        to lurch;
Some deadly shots too, Septembrizers,* seen
    Earliest to rise, and last to quit the search
Of the poor partridge through his stubble screen.
    There were some massy members of the church,
Takers of tithes, and makers of good matches,
And several who sung fewer psalms than catches.

3 Shots too, each September seen
6 some [jolly] Members . . .

81

There were some country wags too,—and, alas!
    Some exiles from the town, who had been driven
To gaze, instead of pavement, upon grass,
    And rise at nine in lieu of long eleven.
And lo! upon that day it came to pass,
    I sate next that o'erwhelming son of heaven,
The very powerful Parson, Peter Pith,*
The loudest wit I e'er was deafened with.

1 Country [wits] too . . .
3 To [look] instead . . .
4 And [to get up at eight—stead of] eleven
5 upon the day . . .

I knew him in his livelier London days,
    A brilliant diner out, though but a curate;
And not a joke he cut but earned its praise,
    Until preferment, coming at a sure rate,
(Oh, Providence! how wondrous are thy ways,
    Who would suppose thy gifts sometimes obdurate?)
Gave him, to lay the devil who looks o'er Lincoln,*†
A fat fen vicarage, and nought to think on.

1   I knew him in his [better days] *fragment*
2   [A diner out of the first] *fragment*
3   but [had] it's praise
7a [Transferred him to] *fragment*
 b Gave him [unto] the devil . . .
 c Gave him to [soothe] the devil . . .

83

His jokes were sermons, and his sermons jokes;
    But both were thrown away amongst the fens;
For wit hath no great friend in aguish folks.
    No longer ready ears and short-hand pens
Imbibed the gay bon mot, or happy hoax:
    The poor priest was reduced to common sense,
Or to coarse efforts very loud and long,
To hammer a hoarse laugh from the thick throng.

3 For [Laughter rarely shakes these] aguish folks
5 Took down the [happy] gay bon mot . . .
8 To hammer [half a] laugh . . .

There *is* a difference, says the song, "between
    A beggar and a queen,"* or *was* (of late
The latter worse used of the two we've seen—
    But we'll say nothing of affairs of state)
A difference " 'twixt a bishop and a dean,"
    A difference between crockery ware and plate,
As between English beef and Spartan broth—
And yet great heroes have been bred by both.

2 [Bet] A beggar . . .
3 we have seen
7 [Also] As . . .

85

But of all nature's discrepancies, none
    Upon the whole is greater than the difference
Beheld between the country and the town,
    Of which the latter merits every preference
From those who have few resources of their own,
    And only think, or act, or feel with reference
To some small plan of interest or ambition—
Both which are limited to no condition.

3 [Than that] between . . .
6 think or [speak] or feel . . .

But "en avant!" The light loves languish o'er
    Long banquets and too many guests, although
A slight repast makes people love much more,
    Bacchus and Ceres being, as we know,
Even from our grammar upwards, friends of yore
    With vivifying Venus,* who doth owe
To these the invention of champagne and truffles:
Temperance delights her, but long fasting ruffles.

6 who [must] doth owe
8 [Though] *fragment*

87

Dully past o'er the dinner of the day;
    And Juan took his place, he knew not where,
Confused, in the confusion, and distrait,
    And sitting as if nailed upon his chair;
Though knives and forks clanged round as in a fray,
    He seemed unconscious of all passing there,
Till some one, with a groan, exprest a wish
(Unheeded twice) to have a fin of fish.

3   [Confused among the] Confusion . . .
4   And [leaning] sitting as if [fixed] upon his chair
5   [Till] Though [knife] knives . . .
7   with a [bow]—groan . . .
8a (Unheeded twice) [to] [he'd help him to some] fish
 b   to have a [slice of] fish

88

On which, at the *third* asking of the banns,
    He started; and perceiving smiles around
Broadening to grins, he coloured more than once,
    And hastily—as nothing can confound
A wise man more than laughter from a dunce—
    Inflicted on the dish a deadly wound,

      And with such hurry, that ere he could curb it,
      He had paid his neighbour's prayer with half a turbot.

3 Broadening to grins he [hastened with] *fragment*
4 nothing [will] confound

89

      This was no bad mistake, as it occurred,
        The supplicator being an amateur;
      But others, who were left with scarce a third,
        Were angry—as they well might, to be sure.
      They wondered how a young man so absurd
        Lord Henry at his table should endure;
      And this, and his not knowing how much oats
      Had fallen last market, cost his host three votes.

2 The [Su] [Applicant] Supplicator . . .
5 They wondered how [Lord Henry could] *fragment*

90

      They little knew, or might have sympathised,
        That he the night before had seen a ghost;
      A prologue which but slightly harmonised
        With the substantial company engrossed
      By Matter, and so much materialised,
        That one scarce knew at what to marvel most
      Of two things—how (the question rather odd is)
      Such bodies could have souls, or souls such bodies.

1 sympathized
3 but [little] harmonized
5 By matter [very] much . . .
6a [So as to make one wonder] *fragment*
 b That one . . . at which to . . .
7a [How] [At] *fragments*
 b Of two things, [whereof] [both] [wherein there something odd is]
8 [How] *fragment*

[543]

But what confused him more than smile or stare
 From all the 'squires and 'squiresses around,
Who wondered at the abstraction of his air,
 Especially as he had been renowned
For some vivacity among the fair,
 Even in the country circle's narrow bound—
(For little things upon my Lord's estate
Were good small-talk for others still less great)—

1 than [frown] or stare
6 in the County . . .
8 Were [great] good . . .

92

Was, that he caught Aurora's eye on his,
 And something like a smile upon her cheek.
Now this he really rather took amiss:
 In those who rarely smile, their smiles bespeak
A strong external motive; and in this
 Smile of Aurora's there was nought to pique
Or hope, or love, with any of the wiles
Which some pretend to trace in ladies' smiles.

1 Was that he [saw] Aurora's . . .
2 upon her [lips]
4a [She smiled so rarely for] *fragment* P
 b In those who rarely smile their smiles bespeak P
 c   smile bespeaks *In 1824, 1833, and*
 d *The present text follows the manuscript.* *some later editions.*
5 A [something much mirth-moving]—and in this
7 Hope—Love—[or] any of the [gentle] wiles
8 [We are apt] *fragment*

'Twas a mere quiet smile of contemplation,
  Indicative of some surprise and pity;
And Juan grew carnation with vexation,
  Which was not very wise and still less witty,
Since he had gained at least her observation,
  A most important outwork of the city—
As Juan should have known, had not his senses
By last night's ghost been driven from their defences.

2   [With] *fragment*
3   And Juan—[who actually] grew . . .
5   Since he had [fixed] at least . . .
6a [And that's a great point] *fragment*
  b A most important [outpost] of the City
7   As [he] Juan . . .

94

But what was bad, she did not blush in turn,
  Nor seem embarrassed—quite the contrary;
Her aspect was as usual, still—*not* stern—
  And she withdrew, but cast not down, her eye,
Yet grew a little pale—with what? concern?
  I know not; but her colour ne'er was high—
Though sometimes faintly flushed—and always clear,
As deep seas in a Sunny Atmosphere

3   as usual [grave] not stern
8   in a [brighter] Atmosphere

But Adeline was occupied by fame
   This day; and watching, witching, condescending
To the consumers of fish, fowl and game,
   And dignity with courtesy so blending,
As all must blend whose part it is to aim
   (Especially as the sixth year is ending)*
At their lord's, son's, or similar connection's
Safe conduct through the rocks of re-elections.

1 [And] Adeline . . . with Fame
2 watching [with] witching . . .
3 of [the] Fish and Game
4 dignity and courtesy . . .
7 [That] their [Good] Lords'—[or] Sons—or [Friends—Famili]
                                        fragment

96

Though this was most expedient on the whole,
   And usual—Juan, when he cast a glance
On Adeline while playing her grand role,
   Which she went through as though it were a dance,
(Betraying only now and then her soul
   By a look scarce perceptibly askance
Of weariness or scorn) began to feel
Some doubt how much of Adeline was *real;*

1   Though this was [usual and] *fragment*
5a [Pondered] *fragment*
 b Betraying now and then her [secret] soul
6   [Merely] *fragment*
7   Of weariness or scorn;—[Juan] [felt a slight doubt steal]

So well she acted, all and every part
   By turns—with that vivacious versatility,
Which many people take for want of heart.
   They err—'tis merely what is called mobility,*
A thing of temperament and not of art,
   Though seeming so, from its supposed facility;
And false—though true; for surely they're sincerest,
Who are strongly acted on by what is nearest.

2 By turns—[and] [a] [even at once—with] versatility
5 not an Art

98

This makes your actors, artists, and romancers,
   Heroes sometimes, though seldom—sages never;
But speakers, bards, diplomatists, and dancers,
   Little that's great, but much of what is clever;
Most orators, but very few financiers,
   Though all Exchequer Chancellors endeavour,
Of late years, to dispense with Cocker's rigours,*
And grow quite figurative with their figures.

No revisions.

The poets of arithmetic are they
    Who, though they prove not two and two to be
Five, as they might do in a modest way,
    Have plainly made it out that four are three,
Judging by what they take, and what they pay.
    The Sinking Fund's unfathomable sea,*
That most unliquidating liquid, leaves
The debt unsunk, yet sinks all it receives.

3*a*   they would do . . .   *In 1824 edition.*
  b   they might do . . .   *P, 1833, and later editions.*
  4   four is three
  5   [If we may judge from each new year's display]
  6   [Of] Sinking . . .
7*a*–8   [Deserves its name—for all that it receives
       Is sunk—Except the unliquidat] *fragment*
  7*b*   [Deserves its name—all's sunk that it receives]
   c   That most unliquidating [of a] liquid leaves

100

While Adeline dispensed her airs and graces,
    The fair Fitz-Fulke seemed very much at ease;
Though too well bred to quiz men to their faces,
    Her laughing blue eyes with a glance could seize
The ridicules of people in all places—
    That honey of your fashionable bees—
And store it up for mischievous enjoyment;
And this at present was her kind employment.

2   seemed [no less] at [her] ease
5   [A ridicule] of people . . .

However, the day closed, as days must close;
　　The evening also waned—and coffee came.
Each carriage was announced, and ladies rose,
　　And curtseying off, as curtsies country dame,
Retired: with most unfashionable bows
　　Their docile esquires also did the same,
Delighted with the dinner and their host,
But with the Lady Adeline the most.

1*a* However the day closed [like every other]
　b   since days must close
3*a* [At last] *fragment*
　b [And Carriages] announced . . .
　c [And Coaches were] . . .
4*a* And [curtsied] off [the stage—their lords the same]
　b   [and Squires . . .]
　c And curtsying . . .
5*a* [With several most unfashionable bows]
　b [Retired—The Esquires] *fragment*
7*a* Delighted with the [fascinating] dinner . . .   P
　b   the dinner . . .   P
　c   their dinner   *In 1833 and in later editions.*

Some praised her beauty; others her great grace;
    The warmth of her politeness, whose sincerity
Was obvious in each feature of her face,
    Whose traits were radiant with the rays of verity.
Yes; *she* was truly worthy *her* high place!
    No one could envy her deserved prosperity;
And then her dress—what beautiful simplicity
Draperied her form with curious felicity!*

1   others—her [deportment]
4*a* [Whose every trait was like a ray] of Verity
 b   [beamed forth with rays] . . .
6   envy [such] her . . .
7   [such] beautiful Simplicity!
8   [Each flounce flared] with [a] curious felicity

103

Meanwhile sweet Adeline deserved their praises,
    By an impartial indemnification
For all her past exertion and soft phrases,
    In a most edifying conversation,
Which turned upon their late guests' miens and faces,
    And families, even to the last relation;
Their hideous wives, their horrid selves and dresses,
And truculent distortion of their tresses.

1   Meantime sweet . . .
2   By a [most social indemnification]
3   For her [subdued] *fragment*
5*a* Which turned upon [her] late Guests [minds] and faces
 b   the late Guests miens . . .
6*a* [Their Virtue—and their] *fragment*
 b [Their hideous wives—their horrid selves—and station]
8   And [Hottentot adjustment] of their tresses

101

First draft of stanzas 101 and 102 of Canto XVI (Courtesy of Carl H. Pforzheimer. Somewhat reduced)

True, *she* said little—'twas the rest that broke
    Forth into universal epigram;
But then 'twas to the purpose what she spoke:
    Like Addison's "faint praise,"* so wont to damn,
Her own but served to set off every joke,
    As music chimes in with a melodrame.
How sweet the task to shield an absent friend!
I ask but this of mine, to—*not* defend.

1   rest who broke
2   Forth into [one sarcastic melodrame]
3a [Of actual] [Bu] [Where] *fragments*
 b But then . . . [when] she spoke
4   Like Addison [with] "faint praise" . . .
5   served to [smoothe] off . . .
6   [As] Music [smoothing oer] a Melodrame
7   [How Sweet the task the] [Dear is the task] *fragments*

105

There were but two exceptions to this keen
    Skirmish of wits o'er the departed; one,
Aurora, with her pure and placid mien;
    And Juan too, in general behind none
In gay remark on what he had heard or seen,
    Sate silent now, his usual spirits gone:
In vain he heard the others rail or rally,
He would not join them in a single sally.

1   from this keen
2   on the departed . . .
4a [And] Juan [who] in general . . .; *b* [Next] Juan . . .
6   Sate silent [now with all] his usual spirits gone
8   [They could] not [raise him to] a single sally

'Tis true he saw Aurora look as though
  She approved his silence; she perhaps mistook
Its motive for that charity we owe
  But seldom pay the absent, nor would look
Further; it might or it might not be so.
  But Juan, sitting silent in his nook,
Observing little in his reverie,
Yet saw this much, which he was glad to see.

4–5*a* But seldom pay the absent, [who must brook
      This pleasing penalty] *fragment*
  5*b* Further; [but this I really do not know]   P
  c Further; it might or . . .   P
  d Farther . . .   *In 1833 and in later editions.*
  6   [Don] Juan . . .

107

The ghost at least had done him this much good,
  In making him as silent as a ghost,
If in the circumstances which ensued
  He gained esteem where it was worth the most.
And certainly Aurora had renewed
  In him some feelings he had lately lost
Or hardened; feelings which, perhaps ideal,
Are so divine, that I must deem them real:—

4*a* He gained [some ground] *fragment*
  b He gained [the] esteem where . . .
  7   Or [deadened] feelings . . .

The love of higher things and better days;
　　The unbounded hope, and heavenly ignorance
Of what is called the world, and the world's ways;
　　The moments when we gather from a glance
More joy than from all future pride or praise,
　　Which kindle manhood, but can ne'er entrance
The heart in an existence of its own,
Of which another's bosom is the zone.

2　The [yet] unbounded hope . . .
5a　from all [Glory and all] praise
　b　from all future pride and praise
6　Which kindle [often] but . . .
7　The heart [to that] in an . . .
8　is the [throne]

109

Who would not sigh Aι αι ταν Κυθερειαν !*
　　That *hath* a memory, or that *had* a heart?
Alas! *her* star must wane like that of Dian;*
　　Ray fades on ray, as years on years depart.
Anacreon only had the soul to tie an
　　Unwithering myrtle round the unblunted dart
Of Eros;* but though thou hast played us many tricks,
Still we respect thee, "Alma Venus Genetrix"!*

In the margin Byron wrote: "Mem. Alma Venus Genetrix."

3a　star must wane like . . .   P
　b　star must fade . . .　*In 1833 and in later editions.*
6　round the [undying] dart

And full of sentiments, sublime as billows
    Heaving between this world and worlds beyond,
Don Juan, when the midnight hour of pillows
    Arrived, retired to his; but to despond
Rather than rest. Instead of poppies, willows
    Waved o'er his couch;* he meditated, fond
Of those sweet bitter thoughts which banish sleep,
And make the worldling sneer, the youngling weep.

1   sentiments sublime [and serious]
2–3a [Of this world and the next—again the hour
    When people prop their pillows] *fragment*
3b [Found] *fragment*
4   [and] but to despond
5   Rather than [sleep;] instead . . .

111

The night was as before: he was undrest,
    Saving his night gown, which is an undress;
Completely "sans culotte,"* and without vest;
    In short, he hardly could be clothed with less;
But apprehensive of his spectral guest,
    He sate, with feelings awkward to express,
(By those who have not had such visitations)
Expectant of the ghost's fresh operations.

3   [A] Sans Culotte—and [also] without Vest
5   But [still] apprehensive of his [ghostly] guest
8   [The Ghost's renewal of his] Operations

And not in vain he listened—Hush! what's that?
  I see—I see—Ah, no!—'tis not—yet 'tis—
Ye powers! it is the—the—the—Pooh! the cat!
  The devil may take that stealthy pace of his!
So like a spiritual pit-a-pat,
  Or tiptoe of an amatory Miss,
Gliding the first time to a rendezvous,
And dreading the chaste echoes of her shoe.

1 in vain listened . . . *Misprint in 1824 edition.*
3 it is [his] the . . .
4 The Devil take that . . .
6 Or [light step] of an amatory Miss
7 [St] [Whose footstep beats less loudly than her] *fragment*

113

Again—what is't? The wind? No, no,—this time
  It is the sable Friar as before,
With awful footsteps regular as rhyme,
  Or (as rhymes may be in these days) much more.
Again, through shadows of the night sublime,
  When deep sleep fell on men,* † and the world wore
The starry darkness round her like a girdle
Spangled with gems—the monk made his blood curdle.

7 The [Stars around her like a Belt] *fragment*

114

A noise like to wet fingers drawn on glass,*
  Which sets the teeth on edge; and a slight clatter
Like showers which on the midnight gusts will pass,
  Sounding like very supernatural water,
Came over Juan's ear, which throbbed, alas!
  For immaterialism's a serious matter;
So that even those whose faith is the most great
In souls immortal, shun them tête-à-tête.

[CANTO XVI]

2 Which sets [one's] teeth . . .
5 Came [oer] Juan's ear—which [ached] alas!
6 [a] [most] serious Matter
8a In Souls immortal [shun a] tête a tête
 b   [dread a] . . .

115

Were his eyes open?—Yes! and his mouth too.
    Surprise has this effect—to make one dumb,
Yet leave the gate which Eloquence slips through
    As wide as if a long speech were to come.
Nigh and more nigh the awful echoes drew,
    Tremendous to a mortal tympanum:
His eyes were open, and (as was before
Stated) his mouth. What opened next?—the door.

3 Yet leave the [portal through which Men's] *fragment*
4 As wide as if [Brougham's speeches] *fragment*

116

It opened with a most infernal creak,
    Like that of Hell. "Lasciate ogni speranza
Voi che entrate!"* The hinge seemed to speak,
    Dreadful as Dante's rhima, or this stanza;
Or—but all words upon such themes are weak;
    A single shade's sufficient to entrance a
Hero—for what is substance to a Spirit?
Or how is't *matter* trembles to come near it?

4 Rima . . .
5 such [things] are weak
8a [You may deny it] [At] *fragments*
 b [When once divorced it don't like to come] near it

The door flew wide, not swiftly—but, as fly
   The sea-gulls, with a steady, sober flight—
And then swung back; nor close—but stood awry,
   Half letting in long shadows on the light,
Which still in Juan's candlesticks burned high,
   For he had two, both tolerably bright,
And in the door-way, darkening Darkness, stood
The sable Friar in his solemn hood.

1 but [it flew]
2 [As] Sea Gulls [fly] a steady . . .
4 Half letting in [the darkness] on . . .
6 two, [one] tolerably . . .
7 [One dimmer] *fragment*

118

Don Juan shook, as erst he had been shaken
   The night before; but being sick of shaking,
He first inclined to think he had been mistaken,
   And then to be ashamed of such mistaking;
His own internal ghost began to awaken
   Within him, and to quell his corporal quaking—
Hinting that soul and body on the whole
Were odds against a disembodied soul.

1 as he [before had] shaken
3 He first [began] to think he was mistaken
5 [And glared back on the Spectral] *fragment*
6 Within him [and] to quell his [further] *fragment*

And then his dread grew wrath, and his wrath fierce;
　　And he arose, advanced—the shade retreated;
But Juan, eager now the truth to pierce,
　　Followed, his veins no longer cold, but heated,
Resolved to thrust the mystery carte and tierce,*
　　At whatsoever risk of being defeated:
The ghost stopped, menaced, then retired, until
He reached the ancient wall, then stood stone still.

1　dread grew wroth [and] wrath grew [strength]
3　But Juan [now resolved to run all length]
5　[The Spectre stopped—dead short] *fragment*
6a　[Whatever] *fragment*
　b　At [some small] risk . . .
8　He [stood against] the wall . . .

120

Juan put forth one arm—Eternal Powers!
　　It touched no soul, nor body, but the wall,
On which the moonbeams fell in silvery showers
　　Checquered with all the tracery of the hall;
He shuddered, as no doubt the bravest cowers
　　When he can't tell what 'tis that doth appal.
How odd, a single hobgoblin's non-entity
Should cause more fear than a whole host's identity!*

7a　How odd—a [single shadow's disap] *fragment*
　b　　　　　　　　[Shade's] *fragment*

But still the shade remained; the blue eyes glared,
 And rather variably for stony death;
Yet one thing rather good the grave had spared,
 The ghost had a remarkably sweet breath.
A straggling curl showed he had been fair-haired;
 A red lip, with two rows of pearls beneath,
Gleamed forth, as through the casement's ivy shroud
The moon peeped, just escaped from a grey cloud.

1 [his] blue eyes . . .
2 [But with the Speculation of grim Death]
3 [But] one . . .
6 with [a] row of pearls . . .
7 [Flashed] forth as [the] through . . .

122

And Juan, puzzled, but still curious, thrust
 His other arm forth—Wonder upon wonder!
It pressed upon a hard but glowing bust,
 Which beat as if there was a warm heart under.
He found, as people on most trials must,
 That he had made at first a silly blunder,
And that in his confusion he had caught
Only the wall, instead of what he sought.

1 And Juan [now] puzzled . . .
5 people [upon] on most . . .
8 what he ought

The ghost, if ghost it were, seemed a sweet soul
   As ever lurked beneath a holy hood:
A dimpled chin, a neck of ivory, stole
   Forth into something much like flesh and blood;
Back fell the sable frock and dreary cowl,
   And they revealed—alas! that ere they should!
In full, voluptuous, but *not o'er*grown bulk,
The phantom of her frolic Grace—Fitz-Fulke!

On the last page of P below this stanza Byron wrote "End of Canto 16th,"
the date, "May 6th 1823," and a signature-symbol slightly different from
the usual one.

2 [The] [friar] [monkish] *fragments*
3 A [beardless] chin . . .
5 Back fell [by faint degrees the decen] *fragment*
6 And [it] revealed . . . ere [it] should
7 [A] [Relieved] [A] *fragments*
8 of [the] her frolic . . .

Canto XVII

1

THE world is full of orphans: firstly, those
    Who are so in the strict sense of the phrase;
But many a lonely tree the loftier grows
    Than others crowded in the Forest's maze—
The next are such as are not doomed to lose
    Their tender parents, in their budding days,
But, merely, their parental tenderness,
Which leaves them orphans of the heart no less.

Manuscript readings are taken from S fragment (Sterling manuscript fragment). The fourteen stanzas of this unfinished canto were first published by Coleridge in 1903. The present printing follows the capitalization and punctuation used by Coleridge, but adheres to the manuscript phrasing in several places where the Coleridge text departs from it.

On the first page of the manuscript above the first stanza is the date, "May 8ᵗʰ 1823."

4 Than [those more] crowded . . .

The next are *"only* Children,"* as they are styled,
　　Who grow up *Children* only, since the old saw
Pronounces that an "only" 's a spoilt child—
　　But not to go too far, I hold it law,
That where their education, harsh or mild,
　　Transgresses the great bounds of love or awe,
The sufferers—be't in heart or intellect—
Whate'er the *cause,* are orphans in *effect.*

2a [Tis well that they are only—for] *fragment*
 b Who grow . . . the old [saying]
3　Pronounces that [they invariably are]
4　But not to [multiply] *fragment*
5a That [wheresoever Excess—of] harsh or mild
 b That where[soeer] their Education . . .
7a [Children who] *fragment*
 b [Who suffers in his] heart or intellect
 c The Sufferers [or] in . . .

                              3

But to return unto the stricter rule—
　　As far as words make rules—our common notion
Of orphans paints at once a parish school,
　　A half-starved babe, a wreck upon Life's ocean,
A human (what the Italians nickname) "Mule!"*
　　A theme for Pity or some worse emotion;
Yet, if examined, it might be admitted
The wealthiest orphans are to be more pitied.

5a [A theme for Crabbe] *fragment*
 b A human [(what the Italians [call) a] "Mule"
7　Yet [on the whole it] *fragment*
8　The wealthiest Orphans are [most] to be pitied

Too soon they are parents to themselves: for what
    Are Tutors, Guardians, and so forth, compared
With Nature's genial Genitors? so that
    A child of Chancery, that Star-Chamber ward,
    (I'll take the likeness I can first come at),
        Is like—a duckling by Dame Partlett reared,
And frights—especially if 'tis a daughter,
The old Hen—by running headlong to the water.

2a Are Tutors—Guardians—[and so forth] compared
 b   [Chancery] . . .
4   [a] Star Chamber Ward
5a [Is like—I take] *fragment*
 b (I'll take the likeness I can't first come at)
7   And frights—[primari *sic?*] [more especially if daughter]   *Intended
    to write* primarily?
8   by running [straitway] to the water

5

There is a common-place book argument,
    Which glibly glides from every vulgar tongue;
When any dare a new light to present,
    "If you are right, then everybody's wrong!"
Suppose the converse of this precedent
    So often urged, so loudly and so long;
    "If you are wrong, then everybody's right!"
Was ever everybody yet so quite?

4 then every['s] body's wrong
8 Was every body [ever] yet so quite?

6

Therefore I would solicit free discussion
    Upon all points—no matter what, or whose—
Because as Ages upon Ages push on,
    The last is apt the former to accuse

Of pillowing its head on a pin-cushion,
Heedless of pricks because it was obtuse:
What was a paradox becomes a truth or
A something like it—as bear witness Luther!

6a [Through which the points] *fragment*
 b [Nor felt the] pricks because . . .

7

The Sacraments have been reduced to two,
And Witches unto none, though somewhat late
Since burning agéd women (save a few—
Not witches only b—ches—who create
Mischief in families,* as some know or knew,
Should still be singed, but slightly, let me state),
Has been declared an act of inurbanity,
Malgré Sir Matthew Hale's great humanity.*

6 but slightly—[I would] state
8 Hales's *S and 1903 edition.*

8

Great Galileo was debarred the Sun,
Because he fixed it;* and, to stop his talking,
How Earth could round the solar orbit run,
Found his own legs embargoed from mere walking:
The man was well-nigh dead, ere men begun
To think his skull had not some need of caulking;
But now, it seems, he's right—his notion just:
No doubt a consolation to his dust.

2 and to [cure] his talking
3 [That] Earth could . . .
4a [Was fettered from his] *fragment*
 b Found . . . from [all] walking

Pythagoras, Locke, Socrates*—but pages
    Might be filled up, as vainly as before,
With the sad usage of all sorts of sages,
    Who in his life-time, each, was deemed a Bore!
The loftiest minds outrun their tardy ages:
    This they must bear with and, perhaps, much more;
The wise man's sure when he no more can share it, he
Will have a firm Post Obit on posterity.

1   Pythagoras—[and] Socrates . . .
4   Who in [their] lifetime . . .
5   The loftiest Minds [anticipate] outrun . . .
7*a* [Secure *sic?* that when no more he can inherit he]
 b The wise man's sure when he [can] no more can . . .
8   Will [have] a firm . . .

10

If such doom waits each intellectual Giant,
    We little people in our lesser way,
To Life's small rubs should surely be more pliant,
    And so for one will I—as well I may—
Would that I were less bilious—but, oh, fie on't!
    Just as I make my mind up every day,
To be a "*totus, teres,*"* Stoic, Sage,
The wind shifts and I fly into a rage.

4 as well['s] I may
7 To be a [whole philosopher—and] Sage

Temperate I am—yet never had a temper;
　Modest I am—yet with some slight assurance;
Changeable too—yet somehow *"Idem semper"*:
　Patient—but not enamoured of endurance;
Cheerful—but, sometimes, rather apt to whimper:
　Mild—but at times a sort of *"Hercules furens"*:*
So that I almost think that the same skin
For one without—has two or three within.*

5 [Serious]—but [also very] apt to whimper
8 [Shows] one without—[and] two or three within

12

Our Hero was, in Canto the Sixteenth,
　Left in a tender moonlight situation,
Such as enables Man to show his strength
　Moral or physical: on this occasion
Whether his virtue triumphed—or, at length,
　His vice—for he was of a kindling nation—
Is more than I shall venture to describe;—
Unless some Beauty with a kiss should bribe.

No revisions.

I leave the thing a problem, like all things:—
    The morning came—and breakfast, tea and toast,
Of which most men partake, but no one sings.
    The company whose birth, wealth, worth, have cost
My trembling Lyre already several strings,
    Assembled with our hostess, and mine host;
The guests dropped in—the last but one, Her Grace,
The latest, Juan, with his virgin face.

2   breakfast—[and so forth]
3   Of which [we all partake] but no one sings
4a-5 The Company—whose birth—wealth—[name—and worth
    Have cost my] Lyre already . . .
4b The Company . . . worth [hath] have cost

14

Which best is to encounter—Ghost, or none,
    'Twere difficult to say—but Juan looked
As if he had combated with more than one,
    Being wan and worn, with eyes that hardly brooked
The light, that through the Gothic windows shone:
    Her Grace, too, had a sort of air rebuked—
Seemed pale and shivered, as if she had kept
A vigil, or dreamt rather more than slept.

1   Which [worst] is to encounter—Ghost or [body]—None
2   [Is] difficult to say . . .
7a   [Look] Seemed [grave]—and [looked] *fragment*
7b-8a Seemed pale—and shivered as if she [had slept
    But little] *fragment*
8b A vigil, or [dreamed] rather . . .

Beneath this stanza Byron wrote the number "15" but nothing more.

Rejected Stanza

[13]

[But Oh! that I were dead—for while alive—
    Would that I neer had loved—Oh Woman—
        Woman—
All that I write or wrote can neer revive
    To paint a sole sensation—though quite common—
Of those in which the Body seemed to drive
    My Soul from out me at thy single summon
Expiring in the hope of sensation—]

*This unfinished stanza (which follows stanza 12 on the manuscript) is
entirely canceled with wavy lines that make transcription rather uncertain.*
3 [All that I writ . . .]